In this book, Julia Ching offers a magisterial survey of over four thousand years of Chinese civilisation through an examination of the relationship between kingship and mysticism. She investigates the sage-king myth and ideal, and analyses the various skills that have been required as qualifications of leadership. She argues that institutions of kingship were bound up with cultivation of trance states and communication with spirits. Over time, these associations were retained, though sidelined, as the sage-king myth became a model for the actual ruler, with a messianic appeal for the ruled. As a paradigm, it also became appropriated by private individuals who strove for wisdom without becoming kings. As the Confucian tradition interacted with the Taoist and the Buddhist, the religious character of spiritual and mystical cultivation became more pronounced. But the sage-king idea continued, promoting expectation of benevolent despotism rather than democratisation in Chinese civilisation.

Lucidly written, the book will be of interest to anyone seeking to understand how today's China continues to draw on its past.

CAMBRIDGE STUDIES IN RELIGIOUS TRADITIONS 11

MYSTICISM AND KINGSHIP IN CHINA

CAMBRIDGE STUDIES IN RELIGIOUS TRADITIONS

Edited by John Clayton (University of Lancaster),
Steven Collins (University of Chicago)
and Nicholas de Lange (University of Cambridge)

MYSTICISM AND KINGSHIP IN CHINA

The heart of Chinese wisdom

JULIA CHING

University of Toronto

CAMBRIDGE
UNIVERSITY PRESS

PUBLISHED BY THE PPRESS SYNDICATE OF THE UNIVERSITY OF CAMBRIDGE
The Pitt Building, Trumpington Street, Cambridge CB2 1RP, United Kingdom

CAMBRIDGE UNIVERSITY PRESS
The Edinburgh Building, Cambridge CB2 2RU, United Kingdom
40 West 20th Street, New York, NY 10011–4211, USA
10 Stamford Road, Oakleigh, Melbourne 3166, Australia

First published 1997

Printed in the United Kingdom at the University Press, Cambridge

Typeset in Baskerville 11/12.5 pt. [CE]

A catalogue record for this book is available from the British Library

Library of Congress cataloging in publication data
Ching, Julia.
Mysticism and kingship in China:the heart of Chinese wisdom / by Julia Ching.
p.   cm. – (Cambridge studies in religious traditions; 11)
Includes bibliographical references and index.
ISBN 0 521 46828 0 hardback
1. China – Politics and government. 2. China – Kings and rulers.
3. Kings and rulers – Religious aspects. 4. Philosophy, Confucian.
I. Title. II. Series.
JQ1510.C493   1997
303.3'0951–dc21   96–51602 CIP

ISBN 0 521 46293 2 hardback
ISBN 0 521 46828 0 paperback

For Will Oxtoby,
without whom . . .

Contents

Preface

Wisdom. *Sapientia*. To know with insight and to act accordingly. When Europeans have been at a loss to describe Chinese civilisation, when they are not certain that it has either philosophy or religion, they fall back on the word 'wisdom'. There is something about the concept 'wisdom' that makes it the representation of an integrated whole, an all-encompassing unity that cannot be divided, a seamless web, if we wish to use the metaphor. And there is also something about wisdom that gives it as well a practical dimension, making it more than theory.

China appears to accept this designation. Throughout its history, Chinese civilisation has shown utmost veneration for the wise man, the sage (*sheng-jen / shengren*). Indeed, the one Chinese best known to the world is the figure of Confucius, to his own people the sage *par excellence*. And the Chinese mind has been characterised more by intuition than by analysis. There has always been the desire to know the *whole* of things, such as the meaning of life (Confucianism) and of the universe (Taoism), and to act accordingly. Even when Buddhism entered China, the Chinese reacted to its manifold variety of doctrines by harmonising the contradictions. They thereby created what has been called Chinese Buddhism, with its strength lying in its harmony of opposites, and its concern for praxis.

I plan to probe the origins of the Chinese tradition, to examine the matrix of its wisdom, and to see how the various parts have grown and become merged into a complex whole. And we shall do this with the help of certain hypotheses. Among other things, I know that Chinese civilisation had multiple origins rather than a single root. However, it grew and became what it was, *the wisdom that was China*, by the many parts with diverse origins blending together, adding to the layers of cultural heritage. Thus, the whole that this process produced was hardly a single tree, and more like a forest of trees, a huge bamboo grove, if we wish, but one where the roots are intertwined and the branches crossed. It has not necessarily become a maze, but it is a forest where one might easily lose one's way, if one enters there without charting a path after a careful study of the terrain.

By going back to the remote origins, I wish to find support for another hypothesis: that the many parts have become a whole because they have all remained faithful to a common inspiration – that the human being is open to the divine and the spiritual, attuned to the divine and the spiritual, and desirous of becoming one with the divine and the spiritual. I am here referring to the familiar adage that describes the harmony underlining Chinese thought and civilisation: that Heaven and humanity are one – *T'ien-jen ho-yi / Tianren heyi* (literally: Heaven and the human being join as one). It is an adage that has frequently been misunderstood by those who claim that the Chinese cannot distinguish between the two orders, the divine and the human. But it is an adage that I believe to have originated in that very mystic and ecstatic union between the human being and the possessing deity or spirit. This was the primeval experience, the experience of a shaman. It was never forgotten. It has been celebrated in songs, myths and rituals. It was formulated philosophically as an expression of the continuum between the human being as the microcosm of the universe as macrocosm. And this microcosm–macrocosm correspondence has been basic to most of philosophising in China. It was the expression of the profound experience of many mystics, whether Confucian, Taoist, or Buddhist. In later ages, with increasing Buddhist influence, it was also transformed into the philosophical adage – that All Things are One (*Wan-wu yi-t'i / wanwu yiti*) representing more pantheism than personal theism. And this articulation of human harmony with the cosmos is what I believe to lie at the very *heart of Chinese wisdom*.

In illo tempore ('Once long ago' or 'At that time'). Thus do the Gospels begin their chapters. Thus does Mircea Eliade describe the primeval, sacred time when humankind had its original experience of oneness with the deity. This was an experience recapitulated in myth and reenacted in ritual. Eliade speaks more of India, and of the Australian aborigines, than he does of Chinese civilisation. But his insight, *mutatis mutandis*, is reflected in the Chinese experience as well, as I have just described.[1]

THE SAGE-KING PARADIGM

It is my thesis that the charisma associated with shamanic ecstasy created the aura for the office of kingship, giving it a sacred, even a priestly character. But this charisma was eventually institutionalised and routinised, by a line of men who no longer possessed the gifts for summoning the spirits and deities. To support their power, however, they frequently resorted to the *suggestion* of charisma and of divine favour. They fabricated tales of divine or semi-divine origins; they consulted with the deities and spirits through divination, sacrifices and other rituals. Such examples abounded in the rest of Chinese history – following upon the end of the heroic period of the sage-kings.

I mentioned sage-kings. It is actually my belief that such never existed. There were shamanic kings, and their heirs fabricated the tales of divine ancestry. There were better and worse kings, as well as mediocre kings. But there were never sage-kings, if we are to take literally the exalted meaning of sagehood. However, later times, possibly those of Confucius and Mencius, looked back to the earlier ages and gilded them in retrospect; they created a myth of the sage-kings. Yes, the humanists and rationalists, with their vague memory of shamanic rulers of the past, created this myth, for the sake of having real rulers emulate such mythical figures as Yao and Shun and Yü who were made into paragons of human virtues: as humane rulers, filial sons, and self-sacrificing toilers. And so we have the sage-king paradigm, and it was to leave an indelible impact on Chinese civilisation as a whole.

The German philosopher G. W. F. Hegel has spoken of China in terms of the 'one man': the ruler. This was the term by which the ruler referred to himself (*ku / gu* or *kua-jen / guaren*, literally, the solitary man). If he was lonely in his responsibility, he was also solitary in his awesome power. Head and centre of the state and society, the ruler was the one to whom ecstatics and ethical spokesmen, as well as classical scholars and Taoist and Buddhist

---

[1] Consult Mircea Eliade, *Cosmos and History: The Myth of the Eternal Return* (New York: Pantheon, 1954).

clergy, turned for support and patronage. And he, in return, also depended on them for confirmation of his mandate and legitimacy, for advice in government and for implementation of his decisions. Besides, the Chinese ruler regarded himself as representing all human beings under Heaven, in his role as mediator between Heaven and Earth. He was advised, among other things, to practise yoga and meditation to clear his mind and heart, to be able to make wise decisions but also to achieve a certain mystical awareness of his own mediatorship by communing with the universe, and to offer important seasonal sacrifices associated with his office. And all under Heaven symbolically participated in his mediatorship when they in turn sought to commune with Heaven or the divine, by performing ritual sacrifices – but only to the gods or spirits appropriate to their own ranks, such as ancestral spirits – or even by meditating in private, and thus also seeking a higher consciousness of oneness with the universe.

And if I apply in part the insights of the phenomenologist of religion Mircea Eliade and of the sociologist of religion Max Weber to the case of China, I am not necessarily saying that Chinese civilisation is fundamentally similar to Western civilisation, or to Indian civilisation. As I shall show, and as our reference to Hegel suggests, I believe that Chinese wisdom is quite unique in itself, even when the inspiration behind it has universal affinities. Indeed, it is my assertion that Chinese wisdom represents a particular way of reflecting the insights gained from experience, that underscores harmony over conflict, and harmonisation over diversification.[2] And it is also my assertion that, strange as it may sound to those who have always focused on the apparently secular character of Chinese culture, the wisdom that was China was not only based on intuitive rationality, but also on mystical experience, even if, in the case of some early rulers, this was desired for the sake of governing better, and of keeping power, more than for the ecstasy of the experience itself.

I am therefore saying that in the Chinese experience, shamanic figures, the original, spontaneous, and charismatic religious individuals, were often, although not always, also the political leaders or kings, assisted by other, lesser, shamans. As such, they were also the

---

[2] For Max Weber, consult *The Religion of China: Confucianism and Taoism*, trans. and ed. by Hans H. Gerth (Glencoe, Ill.: The Free Press, 1951).

chief diviners of their realms, assisted by a bureaucracy of diviners. And they were the chief priests as well, assisted by an official clergy. As their charisma became routinised, the political leaders remained priests, eventually leaving their other functions to religious specialists. And even if a few of them sometimes permitted deputies to perform important sacrifices, they remained themselves the chief priests, whose prerogative it was to offer state sacrifices.

The Confucian scholars were sometimes powerful enough to gain the ear of a ruler, to participate in the office of kingship by serving as mediators on behalf of the people. But they were not, strictly speaking, priests. Other priests eventually emerged in China, belonging to the Taoist religion. While they occasionally assisted in the state rituals, they did not become the official clergy. They were never powerful enough as a church to oppose the state, as the Catholic church did in medieval Europe. Interestingly, they showed themselves heirs to the ancient shamans as a group, by incorporating shamanic rituals into their tradition. And if Taoist priests and Buddhist monks occasionally performed various forms of divination, the status of divination as such tumbled very early, to become the private exercise of those private individuals who knew how to use the Book of Changes, or the livelihood of lowly sooth-sayers in popular religion.

I speak of the *paradigm* because the institution of kingship goes back, in principle, to the sages of a mythical past, and became, for later generations, an ideal of striving, embodying all the virtues of humane government, as well as of a humanity open to the beyond. My argument is that the sage-king paradigm was able to persist so long, not only because of its intrinsic attractions of desirable good government, but also because of its functional transformations during history. The humanist philosophers who created it also transformed it – by appropriating it to themselves. They had witnessed that successful, actual rulers were usually despots rather than sages, while some of their own, especially Confucius, deserved far more the title of sage and the office of kingship. And so, the philosophers' fancy created a posthumous honour for Confucius: as uncrowned king (*su-wang*), judging the affairs of the world by his moral pronouncements in the classical texts which he supposedly wrote or edited, especially the Spring–Autumn Annals.

On the other hand, the philosophers also came to the conclusion that sagehood was not the preserve of an elect few, say those of royal blood, but was accessible to all. This was the doctrine of human perfectibility, articulated especially by Mencius. An implicit corollary was the natural equality of all human beings, and the potential for every man to become a king as well. This offered a solid basis for future political transformation, including the flowering of democracy, even if this never quite occurred. However, as we shall see, the sage-king ideal maintained such a strong hold over popular imagination that the country never expected more than a benevolent monarchy, or, perhaps we should say, a benevolent despotism.

Still, what was made explicit was a doctrine of rebellion, supported by the belief that Heaven gives the mandate to rule to the best person. And so we are to witness the rise and fall of many dynastic cycles, each of which claimed that heavenly mandate for itself, even if hardly any of the claimants would qualify as a Confucian sage. At the same time, a 'messianic' idea developed, within the bosoms of Confucianism, Taoism, and even Chinese Buddhism.

So the philosophers, especially the Confucians among them, emerged as the ethical and exemplary prophets of the tradition, ready from time to time to stand up to the kings when the latter abused their powers. They were not priests, except within the bosoms of their own families, where the *pater familias* celebrated the ancestral rituals. Occasionally, the officials among them also presided at minor, regional state cults and sacrifices, as the functions of a bureaucrat included also this cultic responsibility.

And the ancient texts that supported the sage-king paradigm were all enshrined in a canon of Confucian classics, becoming thereby also a repository of sagely authority, to be manipulated by the scribes and exegetes who interpreted them under the supervision of the state. This became its own saga, with its own twists and turns, and essentially made China the classical and literate civilisation it became. While philosophers also made use of exegesis for their own arguments, Chinese intellectual history fluctuated between periods dominated by philosophical thinking and periods when philology and exegesis flourished.

ONENESS OF HEAVEN AND HUMANITY

The sage-king paradigm was appropriated not only by Confucian humanists. It was similarly appropriated by Taoists and Chinese

Buddhists, even if each of them gave the paradigm a somewhat different meaning, and even when each fought the other as a rival for people's minds and hearts. As events unfolded, Taoism and Buddhism each inspired periodic revolts in the name of a messianic ruler, while they each gave their blessing and legitimation periodically to those actual rulers who favoured their respective religion, usually with no regard to particular merit. Quite separate from all this, and in private, Taoist and Buddhist mystics experienced the sagely bliss of mystical awareness, usually also articulated as that of oneness with the universe, or oneness with the Tao (*pinyin*: Dao). Such *personal* mysticism, benefitting the individuals only, was quite different from the more public shamanic ecstasy or the spirit–medium trances that certain Taoists also experienced, while in the service of others or of the religion itself.

In this way, I shall explain how the institutionalisation of the charisma associated with ecstasy could not terminate the ecstatic impulse in many individual persons. The shamanic character of Chinese wisdom persisted, even if shamans themselves did not retain the high social status granted them by antiquity. Indeed, this impulse survives in many practices of Chinese folk religion, if only in a fragmented fashion. And the union between the human and the so-called divine remained the goal of the mystics, both the theists, including polytheists – such as in religious Taoism – and the so-called pantheists, such as in philosophical Taoism, Ch'an Buddhism, and neo-Confucianism. Besides, I shall maintain that this union, as represented in the adage the Oneness of Heaven and humanity, or the Oneness of All Things, represented, in an analogical sense, both a philosophical belief and a mystical ideal. The two orders of the divine – or the natural – and the human, while always intertwined, were usually distinguished one from the other.

It is also part of my argument that the private appropriation of the sage-king paradigm reached a climax with the neo-Confucian movement, where the heirs to the ancient philosophers, influenced also by mystical strands coming from Buddhism and Taoism, seriously sought mystical experience for its own sake as well as for moral self-transformation. I am speaking of men like the twelfth-century Chu Hsi, and especially the late fifteenth-century Wang Yang-ming, and the late sixteenth-century Kao P'an-lung. Nevertheless, while sagehood and kingship went separate ways to a certain extent, the ideal of a sage-king refused to go away entirely. This is an important reason why China never abandoned a monarchical form of government until modern times, and why such a form often remains in force even behind the banner of republicanism.

I am not seeking to treat comprehensively and exhaustively the wisdom that was China. That would have included many other areas, especially literature and the arts. I am concentrating on the religious, philosophical, textual, and even political traditions, and I am discussing them selectively, with my focus on what wisdom means. Even in this case, I cannot cover everything. I acknowledge that I do not formally cover popular religion, that hybrid creature descended from archaic tradition, bearing influences from all the other traditions. I would mention also that while the Confucian classics teach a philosophy of life better known for its more rationalist emphases, Chinese rationalism is quite different from Greek or European rationalism. It remains inseparable from intuition, which is both the warp and the woof of that fabric we call Chinese wisdom.

Instead of regarding China's wisdom only as religion, or philosophy, or as a rich textual tradition, I am accepting it as all three and more. I shall follow an approach that involves methodologies borrowed from the history of religion and of philosophy, of philology and of hermeneutics, without limiting myself to only one of these. If anything, the closest is that of intellectual history, an approach that respects religion, accepts intuition, and regards practice as a test for the viability of tradition.

The sage-king paradigm arose out of the experience of ancient shamanic rulers, even if, in some ways, the gradual eclipse of ecstasy was accompanied by the growth of ethics and exegesis. An oral, shamanic tradition became supplanted in influence by a written and more rationalistic one. But the shamans never disappeared. Indeed, our thesis is that shamanism was absorbed into religious Taoism, where it received a textual, if secret, transmission. The great ethical spokesmen who emerged did so without always formally repudiating the ecstatics of the past. Instead, they exalted the shamanic kings as sages and moral exemplars. And their followers, the exegetes and those who studied and popularised their work, contributed to the moulding of a whole cultural tradition that may be represented as Chinese wisdom.

I seek to approach an integrated wisdom tradition, to look at a *whole* and to discover its heart. For Chinese thought has manifested a certain rhythm: a movement of activity, its *yang* side, in Confucian moral and social philosophy, usually dominant during the periods of political unity and social order; and a moment of passivity, its contemplative, *yin* side, in Taoist 'naturalism' and quietism, and Buddhist mysticism and religion. We shall contemplate it from these angles, while following the civilisation from its cradle, through its gradual growth and evolution. This took place not without conflicts and contradictions, to its present status in a modern world, where we believe it is undergoing dissolution, and perhaps, transformation.

The chapter divisions are thematic, and broadly chronological. Chapters 1 and 2 deal with the matrix of the wisdom in antiquity ('Whence'), namely, from the beginnings to roughly the third century BCE or a bit later, covering approximately the first three millennia. Chapter 3 continues from roughly the sixth century BCE on, with its focus on the classical period of the philosophers, considered the defining period of Chinese wisdom and 'Why' it became what it did – with the emergence of Confucius and his moral philosophy. Chapter Four covers the development of the sages' message in the next two millennia and more. Attention is given also to the place of religion in early philosophical thinking. Chapter 5 treats the legacy of the classical texts, which enshrined the wisdom attributed to the ancient sages, leaving it to later interpretations as well as manipulations.

With all their influence on the populace in general as well as the intellectuals and even occasionally on the political rulers, Taoism and Buddhism were 'other-worldly', each in its own way, often a refuge for the non-conformists. For this reason, the two traditions remained marginal in China. Isabelle Robinet even says: 'In a certain sense, it is the very vocation of Taoism to be marginal.'[3] Chapters 6 and 7 give more attention to Taoism and Buddhism, with special reference to their understanding and manipulation of the sage ideal. They also focus on the place of the shaman in Taoist philosophical texts, the shamanic character of both the Taoist and the early Chinese Buddhist religion, and Taoist and Buddhist messianism: topics that have not always received adequate scholarly attention. This treatment helps to give a comparative perspective to these two traditions, which together offer 'the other side' of Chinese

---

[3] Isabelle Robinet, *Taoist Meditation: The Mao-shan Tradition of Great Purity* (Albany: State University of New York Press, 1993), p. 2.

culture: the more reclusive and mystical as contrasted with the more public and rational system of Confucianism.

In saying this, I do not forget that my own thesis focuses on mysticism as being at the heart of Chinese wisdom, which, I maintain, remains a dynamic and action-related tradition. And then, on account of the emphasis on leadership in a context that is both sacred and secular, I can hardly bypass the question of authority, both religious and political. For this reason, the discussions of shamanic kingship, royal priesthood, ethical prophecy, and classical and scriptural exegesis usually presuppose the dimension of authority.

I concentrate much more on the formation of the wisdom tradition, rather than on those later developments leading to its decline and its near-dissolution in our own days. And then, in the final chapter, I deal more directly with political power and authority, which has been included briefly in the beginning chapters of the book. I examine this theme both in ancient Legalist thought and in the twentieth-century phenomenon of Mao Zedong's role. Limits prescribed for the size of this book prevent me from doing more, and I try to define my scope carefully. In my conclusion, I deal briefly with the limitations of Chinese wisdom and the problems that have confronted the Chinese tradition as it responds to the challenges of modernity, while seeking to offer a brief prognostication about the future direction – 'Whither'. In this way, I look at Chinese wisdom from various vantage-points, rather than breaking it up into different parts. And whenever I do discuss any parts, I shall hasten to put them together again, into a whole.

In carrying out this task, I attempt to maintain a comparative perspective, especially *vis-à-vis* other religious traditions. However, on account of space considerations, the comparisons are only occasional, to serve as a context, while permitting an in-depth look into China's own wisdom tradition. And while I speak principally of China, I do not neglect the many parallels and similarities – as well as important differences – between the Chinese wisdom tradition and those of her near neighbours like Korea, Japan, and Vietnam. My basic assumption is that, despite all the cultural and social differences between these countries and China, the civilisation of East Asia as a whole enjoys a unity that comes from shared cultural origins as well as historical exchanges. The sage-king paradigm is actually a shared legacy, but full discussion of this sharing is not possible.

In writing this book, I am helped by the work of many others, whether those who have gone before me, or others who are my contemporaries, writing in English, French and German, as well as in Asian languages. In the latter case, I refer especially to the original Chinese sources, as well as the secondary literature, in both Chinese and Japanese.

I also owe an intellectual debt to many persons. I have indicated several in my specific notes. Let me mention here as well the series of collaborative conferences between North America and Europe during the past decade, with such themes as scriptures and fundamentalism, and civil society, of which the most recent one, entitled 'State and Ritual in East Asia', took place in Paris, 28 June–1 July 1995. I learnt a lot from many of the participants. I should also acknowledge my local colleagues at Toronto, including James C. H. Hsü and R. W. L. Guisso; the former has helped to explain technical terms, and the latter has indicated useful bibliography. I should also thank my spouse, Willard G. Oxtoby, for his unfailing support, our former colleague John Berthrong, now at Boston, and Alex Wright and Ruth Parr, editors for Cambridge University Press, for their collaboration. Their insistence on the limitations of space actually obliged me to think things through more carefully, and perhaps, articulate ideas and evidence with less cumbersome verbiage. And I should thank Kwok-yiu Wong, for his help in preparing the glossary, the Chinese and Japanese portion of the bibliography, and the index.

In referring to translations from original sources, I have first consulted the original, and then usually adapted from one of the available translations, working with the one that appears the most suitable for the passage concerned. In citing bibliography, I follow the conventions of Sinology when giving references in Chinese, while usually making sure that the meaning of the titles given is understood. In the case of classical texts, and only of these, like the Book of Songs or the Book of Changes, the titles are not italicised. In the case of citations from the Analects, the chapter and verse sequence followed is that from D. C. Lau's translation, which varies sometimes from James Legge's. Quotations from *The Complete Works of Chuang Tzu* and from *Han Fei Tzu*, both translated by Burton Watson, copyright © 1968 by Columbia University Press, are reprinted with permission of the publisher. A glossary is supplied of special terms, with Chinese characters, and a select bibliography is provided.

Where transliterations from the Chinese are concerned, I usually follow the Wade-Giles system. In the case of special terms, I also give the *pinyin* along with the Wade-Giles whenever these terms first appear and there is a difference between the two. The authors and titles of publications that appeared in mainland China since 1949 are usually given in *pinyin*, unless the authors are long deceased. For the bibliography in Chinese, especially the primary sources, I follow the conventions of Sinology.

I hope that the readers will better understand this integrated tradition called Chinese 'wisdom', in which so many parts interrelate to form a whole, with the centre remaining that of the ideal of harmony between humankind and Heaven or nature, with its richness and contradictions, especially as manifest in the sage-king ideal. A critical note will not be missing, when we discuss certain abuses, whether these be ritual human sacrifice in the distant and not so distant past, or tyranny and dictatorship throughout history and even in our own days.

This book is being offered as a stimulus to further thinking, rather than as an effort to be scrupulously comprehensive about all that makes up Chinese wisdom. Attempts have been made to include what is possible, more to support my own hypotheses than to take in everything. When one looks at the whole from various perspectives, one cannot help missing some of its facets.

CHAPTER I

Son of Heaven: shamanic kingship

INTRODUCTION[1]

The earliest known religion is a belief in the divinity of kings
. . . [In] the earliest records known, man appears to us worshipping gods and their earthly representatives, namely kings.

. . .

Perhaps there never were any gods without kings, or kings without gods. When we have discovered the origin of divine kingship we shall know. But at present we only know that when history begins there are kings, the representatives of gods.[2]

In his well-known book, Arthur M. Hocart speaks of kingship as a gift of the gods, which is often inherited through a special lineage. Thus, the new king's accession to the throne, on the death of his predecessor, signifies continuity and stability, through a kind of religious logic that is tantamount to a deification of the deceased king, and, by extension, of his heir. This is also symbolised by the passing on of the royal regalia, whether these be the crown, sceptre, sword, seal or anything else. And then, frequently, sacrificial offerings accompany or follow the accession, serving as the sources of royal power.[3]

The sacred character of kingship in China is little studied, when compared to the subject of kingship, or the emperor system, in Japan or Egypt, where the divine character of the royal person – whatever that means – has been highlighted. Especially during World War II, the Japanese emperor was known to be considered by his subjects as

---

[1] A modified version of this chapter, under the title, 'Son of Heaven: Sacral Kingship in Ancient China', was presented at the State and Ritual conference organised by Prof. Pierre-Étienne Will of the Collège de France, 27 June–1 July 1995.
[2] A. M. Hocart, *Kingship* (London: Watts, 1941), p. 1.
[3] Consult also Robert S. Ellwood, *The Feast of Kingship: Accession Ceremonies in Ancient Japan*, a *Monumenta Nipponica* Monograph (Tokyo: Sophia University, 1973), pp. 34–5.

'divine', even a 'god' (*kami*), and much has since been written on the subject. The Chinese king or emperor has usually been regarded as a secular ruler, with no claim to divinity. But were things that simple?

In posing this question, and in seeking to give some answers, I am focusing in this chapter on ancient China – mainly the Shang (c. 1766–c. 1122 BCE) and the Chou (c. 1122–256 BCE) – within the context of its own religious history. But I also believe, first, that the study of antiquity is enhanced by some attention to later events; and second, that understanding of the Chinese religious tradition should not be in isolation from other traditions. Indeed, much can be gained when we regard religious phenomena across cultural barriers.

The discovery of antiquity

The mythical dragon is a flying reptile with feet and claws and a mouth that breathes fire. It was believed to be life-giving and rain-giving, and at the same time capable of bringing destruction. It became eventually the symbol of imperial majesty and power. During the past hundred years, the chase after the origins of certain fossil fragments called 'dragon bones' led to the discovery both of China's earliest writing system and of the human fossil called *Sinanthropus pekinensis*, the subsequently missing Peking Man. These were two separate incidents, the human fossil being unearthed some decades after the discovery of ancient writing now known as 'oracle bone writing'.

These discoveries, revealing a Pleistocene past earlier than Neanderthal Man, attracted world attention from specialists and the public alike. However, for a long time, scholars were not certain whether they belonged to the ancestors of the Chinese race. The opinion has since been voiced that the jaw bones and teeth indicate genetic relations to the Mongolian peoples in general, and the Chinese in particular.[4] Unfortunately, the remains of Peking Man disappeared mysteriously during China's war with Japan (1937–45).

We now know much more about prehistoric China, even the period before the Hsia (approximately 2205–1766 BCE). For the late

---

[4] Herrlee G. Creel, *The Birth of China* (New York: Frederick Ungar, 1937), pp. 40–2.

fifth and early fourth millennia BCE, we have evidence of potters'
marks, resembling an earlier form of writing, of divination by
scapulimancy (shoulder-bone divination), with the use of a variety of
animal bones, and of clay phallus objects apparently involved in
ancestral worship.[5] In any case, scholars now have expanded the
age of known Chinese history to about five thousand years. And one
can no longer speak of ancient civilisation as having arisen only in
the Yellow River Basin, since many very early finds have been
unearthed far away from that area, such as in present-day Szechuan
(Sichuan), in the country's west, or nearer the Yangtze basin, in the
southeast.[6] Most probably, Chinese civilisation had multiple origins
and is the composite of many regional cultures, each with its special
features.

I am speaking of China in two senses: as a civilisation, as I have
been doing, and as a state under historic and dynastic names. In the
latter sense, and for the period going back to four thousand years
ago and later, I am speaking about the area in today's northern
China, with a 'floating' boundary marked in the west by the Ordos
desert (called 'moving sand' or *liu-sha*), in the north by some
mountains north of the Yellow River, in the east by the sea, and in
the south by the Yangtze River. This is probably a generous
demarcation of Chou (1122–256 BCE) boundaries. Within this, the
heartland was the Yellow River Basin east of the Ordos, including
the present provinces of Shensi, Shansi and Honan, belonging to the
earlier Shang China (c. 1766–1122 BCE).

To know the past is important, not only for its own sake, but also
in order to appreciate the present better. For there is much of remote
antiquity, especially its religion, that still remains, albeit in altered
and fragmentary forms, in today's popular religion. And Chinese
civilisation in general – Chinese religion in particular – is better
understood when we see the *whole* picture, against five thousand
years of historical background, including both the so-called 'great
tradition' of the philosophers and the 'little traditions' of the
ordinary people. This kind of holistic panorama would permit us to

---

[5] Li Hsiao-ting, *Han-tzu te ch'i-yüan yü yen-pien lun-ts'ung* (On the origin and evolution of
Chinese writing) (Taipei: Linking, 1986), pp. 44–73; Kwang-chih Chang, *Art, Myth and Ritual*
(Cambridge, Mass.: Harvard University Press, 1983), pp. 112–14.

[6] See Jao Tsung-i, 'Foreword: Speaking of "Sages": The Bronze Figures of San-hsing-tui', in
Julia Ching and R. W. L. Guisso (eds), *Sages and Filial Sons* (Hong Kong: Chinese University
Press, 1991), pp. xiv–xx.

understand better as well the ethical humanism that developed so early – by putting it in the right perspective.

Unlike the ancient Greeks, the Chinese built in wood, and the structures, as well as their contents, have perished. They have also suffered catastrophic destructions of texts and other historical remains. Some knowledge of bronze inscriptions, studied especially since the eleventh century CE, has served as a beacon, especially for the period of the Chou. But for the period before the Chou, such as the Shang, extant texts only offer a royal genealogy with the barest mention of facts.

The Chinese people, as they are known today, are much less homogeneous than they appear. They descended from a multitude of ethnic groups, pushing into the heartland, from the west (as did the Chou), from the east (as did the Shang), and later, from the south (as attempted the Ch'u). The intermingling of these peoples made the ancient history and civilisation of the country we now know as China.[7]

Nevertheless, the ancient inhabitants of China's heartland thought of themselves – much as did the ancient Greeks – as the only civilised people on earth, inhabiting an *oikoumene*. And they were surrounded by barbaric tribes who lived on less hospitable terrains, called the Western *jung / rung*, the Northern *ti*[a] */ di*, the Eastern *hu* (derived from the word Tungu), and the Southern *man*. Many of these peoples were presumably covetous of the heartland, and often pushing to get there. Interestingly, the terms indicating these barbarians usually have components that refer to animals. The word for *ti*[a] has a 'dog' component, and the word for *man* has a 'reptile' component, thus indicating some kind of pejorative reference for the populations of the north and south, while the word for the Western *jung* has a 'spear' component, evoking war and battle.

We should also keep in mind the distinctions between nobility and commoner in ancient society. Here, we rely mainly on records left behind by the nobility, or at least on the orders of the kings and the high-born. There are exceptions, such as the folk songs in the Book of Songs, collected by the rulers' emissaries eager to find out the state of 'public opinion'. In the case of religion and ritual, what we know tends to be the religion and ritual of the kings and nobles, in which the commoners of antiquity had little part. With time, things

---

[7] Consult Hsü Cho-yün, *Hsi-Chou shih* (A History of Western Chou) (Taipei: Linking, 1984).

changed, especially on account of the disintegration of the feudal order by the third century BCE. But that is another story.

ORIGIN OF THE PARADIGM: SHAMANIC KINGSHIP

For some time, the ancient Chinese religion has been called a religion of the *wu*ᵃ, or *wu-chu* / *wu-zhu.* But who were these persons? Is it possible to draw a meaningful differentiation between the religious specialists of ancient China, between diviners (*pu* / *bu*), invocators (*chu* / *zhu*) and *wu*ᵃ, often called shamans? Was there an equivalent to the priestly class, as this was found in other ancient societies, especially in the Near East? Who were the men called *chu*, dedicated to the state cult in ancient China?[8]

The problem here is that, whereas we find a differentiation of sacrifices depending on the persons – gods, spirits and ancestors – to whom they were offered, we do not have a term which is exactly parallel to the English word 'priest'. The *Chou-li* or Institutes of Chou actually begins, not with religious, but with civil officials engaged in central administration. Interestingly, one term used to designate the Chou chief minister (*chung-tsai* / *zhongzai*) relates his office to grave mounds. And this office is also charged with ultimate supervision over the work of offering sacrifice, as well as over the ruler's meals. The division between the sacred and secular remains therefore blurred.

The wisdom of divination

The Chinese word for 'knowing' is *chih* / *zhi*. In its modern form, it has two components: a symbol representing an arrow on the left side, and another representing the mouth on the right. Possibly, a military etymology is suggested. Today, the usual explanation is that knowledge has a directionality like an arrow, and relies on the mouth for communication. The first-century-BCE Tung Chung-shu says, '[To know] is to predict accurately . . . The person who knows can see fortune and misfortune a long way off, and can anticipate benefit and harm.'[9]

---

[8] Consult Chang, *Art, Myth and Ritual*, ch. 3.
[9] *Ch'un-ch'iu fan-lu* (Luxuriant Gems of the Spring–Autumn Annals), Ssu-pu pei-yao (abbreviated as SPPY) ed., 8:10b. Consult David H. Hall and Roger T. Ames, *Thinking Through Confucius* (Albany: State University of New York Press, 1987), pp. 50–6.

To know is also to be wise. We usually think of wisdom in terms of holistic knowledge – understanding the world and life in the world in a profound sense, and in terms of practice – knowing how to live in the world, how to be a good human being, relating, helping, and even teaching others to be the same. But for many people in the past, wisdom meant especially knowing the future. The Book of Changes, a divination manual that became also a Confucian classic, speaks of the sage as the person who has foreknowledge of fortune and misfortune. To 'divine' is actually to seek the wisdom of foreknowledge of events, a wisdom belonging appropriately to the gods.

The Neolithic inhabitants of northern China – starting from the late fourth millennium BCE – appear to have been the first people anywhere to use animal shoulder blades for divination, by heating them and interpreting the cracks which ensue. The practice reached its height by Shang times, with the widespread use of tortoise shells in addition to shoulder blades. Tortoises were considered sacred animals, because of their long lives. They were supposed to have special power in contacting others in the spiritual world, especially ancestor figures, even after their deaths.[10] There is also evidence that divination manuals were followed, that are no longer extant. But did these also explain the logic of prognostication, or was that perhaps left to a higher form of reasoning?

In its earliest forms, the wisdom that divination brought might have come with the help of spirits or gods during the diviner's moments of trance. In the oracle records, a word is often placed between the name of the ancestor and the word for king, a word which means 'guest' (*pin / bin*) in modern Chinese. There is speculation that it refers to the king 'receiving as guest' a specific ancestor, or the Lord-on-High himself, to a kind of *séance* in which the two met. How it happened remains unclear. It has been suggested that the 'guest' might have been a shamanic figure, the prototype for the later (but ancient) institution of the spirit's impersonator or medium (*shih*[a] */ shi*, literally, 'corpse'), in whom the spirit descended, and to whom ritual offerings were made.[11] As the

[10] Kwang-chih Chang, *The Archaeology of Ancient China* (New Haven: Yale University Press, 1986), 4th ed., pp. 316, 364; and his *Shang Civilization* (New Haven: Yale University Press, 1980), pp. 32–3.

[11] Shima Kunio, *Inkyo bokuji kenkyū* (A study of the oracle letters rescued from the ruins of Yin's capital) (Tokyo: Kyuko shoin, 1958), p. 201; Chang, *Art, Myth and Ritual*, pp. 54–5; Ikeda Suetoshi, *Chūgoku kodai shūkyōshi kenkyū* (Ancient Chinese religion) (Tokyo: Tokai University Press, 1981), pp. 623–44.

ritual of divination became more and more systematised and rationalised, trance became less frequent and, in time, irrelevant.

The intimate relationship between divination and the ruling family may serve to explain why the Shang diviners were not heard of after the fall of the dynasty. Besides, the dynastic fall probably mitigated the enthusiasm for court divination, which was unable to prevent the catastrophe. After this, the Chou continued for a while ritual divination by shells and bones. But the practice itself remained important, and spread from the nobility to the commoners.[12]

The Book of Rites reports a somewhat amusing story of the results of a sixth-century-BCE divinatory ritual to decide the succession to a grand official in the state of Wei. The oracle had pronounced that the omen would come from the way the six sons bathed themselves and wore their jade pendants. Five of them hurried to bathe and put on the ornaments. The sixth refused, saying, 'Is there anyone who would bathe himself and wear jade on the occasion of a parent's death?' He was promptly singled out as heir, and the people of the state reportedly marvelled at the tortoise's wisdom.[13] Today, we might as well admire the diviners' psychological insight and personal wisdom.

Besides knowledge of the oracles, divination also relies on the knowledge of stars, and the knowledge of the symbolic meaning of human dreams. Indeed, the officials in charge of dream interpretation *chan-jen / zhanren*, apparently performed their duties with the help of their knowledge of stars. But there was another class of astrologers with the duty of interpreting celestial phenomena, including the eclipses of the sun and the moon.[14] These appeared to be usually experts at star-gazing, or proto-astronomers, and bureaucrats.

In divination, questions regarding eclipses of the sun and the moon were especially posed to the Lord-on-High, such natural events being then regarded as manifestations of heavenly displeasure with earthly conduct.[15]

---

[12] See Michael Loewe, *Chinese Ideas of Life and Death: Faith, Myth and Reason in the Han Period* (202 BCE–220 CE) (London: Allen & Unwin, 1982), pp. 92–103.

[13] *Li-chi Cheng-chu* (Book of Rites with Cheng Hsüan's commentary) SPPY ed., 3:10b–11a; James Legge, *Li Ki*, vol. 27 of F. Max Müller (ed.), *Sacred Books of the East* (Oxford: Clarendon, 1885), p. 181.

[14] *Chou-li Cheng-chu* (Institutes of Chou with Cheng Hsüan's commentary), SPPY ed., 25:1–3.

[15] Werner Eichhorn, *Die Religionen Chinas*, vol. 21 of C. M. Schröder (ed.), *Die Religionen der Menschheit* (Stuttgart: Kohlhammer, 1973), pp. 9–31; Chang Tsung-tung, *Der Kult der Shang-Dynastie im Spiegel der Orakelinschriften* (Wiesbaden: Otto Harrassowitz, 1970), 211–24; C. C. Shih, 'A Study of Ancestor Worship in Ancient China', in W. S. McCullough (ed.), *The Seed of Wisdom: Essays in Honour of T. J. Meek* (University of Toronto Press, 1964), pp. 186–8.

Possibly, the institution of divination began with a greater role for trance or ecstasy, but evolved into a mechanical exercise handled by a bureaucracy.[16] In divining with the help of the Book of Changes, today's diviners still have recourse to yarrow stalks, but acting somewhat as playing with a deck of cards. The fifty stalks are divided into two piles, in such a way that one would be of an even, the other uneven number. Then the diviner would set aside one pile, working only on the other, by removing four stalks at a time, until what remains offers a response: when the number left is even, a divided line is represented, when the number is odd, an undivided line is represented. This action is repeated three times, in order to arrive at each of the six lines, which means eighteen times.[17]

An idealised bureaucracy

We look into the Institutes of Chou for clues regarding the religious specialists of antiquity. Granted, of course, that the text presents an idealised bureaucracy more than a real one. We might yet presume that the ideal is based on some historical realities, supported as this is by other sources, and also that it gives expression to important cultural and social yearnings. In this case, the priority given by this text to religious functions is quite clear, in spite of the great historical divide we all know existed between the Shang times, when the rulers served the spirits and ghosts with utmost diligence, and the Chou times, when religious fervour had greatly diminished. Indeed, it appears that while the change in the cultural climate was real, resulting in the decline of divination and shamanism, the religious character of kingship remained indelible. It persisted during the centuries to come, bound up, as it was, with the question of a Mandate from a higher power and the legitimation this bestowed.

In ancient China, the official specifically charged with religious affairs was the Minister of Rites, the 'Great Senior Lineage Official', who was always under royal supervision. In the Institutes of Chou, the king's role is emphasised not only at the beginning of the book, but also just before the office of the Minister of Rites is introduced. Under royal supervision, this minister's office was in charge of 'the

[16] *Chou-li Cheng-chu*, 24:11–12.
[17] Consult *Chou-yi cheng-yi* (Correct meaning of the Book of Changes), SPPY ed., 7:17–18; see James Legge, *Yi King*, vol. 16 of F. Max Müller (ed.), *Sacred Books of the East* (Oxford: Clarendon, 1885), p. 365.

rituals toward heavenly deities, human ghosts, and earthly spirits, on which the state was founded, and for the sake of assisting the king in his task of building and protecting the country'.[18] Among other things, this man was in charge of sacrifices and sacrificial officials. He served the spirits and ghosts of the state with 'rituals of good fortune'. He offered burnt sacrifices with smoke, to the 'Supreme Heaven and Lord-on-High'; he offered bullocks on firewood to (the spirits of) the sun, moon and stars.[19] In the absence of the ruler, he presided over the great sacrifices. In this capacity, he was associated with the king in the royal priestly duties. Presumably, in ancient times, this man was a senior royal relative.

According to the same Institutes of Chou, the Ministry of Rites was a huge bureaucracy. It included specialists of banquet seating, of ritual apparel, of music, as well as of diviners, dream interpreters, *chu* and *wu*[a]. There was thus a place for each and all in the state bureaucracy.

The religion of antiquity

Divination always points to something else; it may be a helpful device, but it is not a substitute for more important rituals. It presupposes a belief in spirits and in their power to protect the living. Besides, as the abundant oracle records have shown, divination in antiquity was associated with sacrifice, and frequently served as a preparation for sacrifice. In other words, sacrifice was a much more important ritual.

In Western languages, the word 'priest', derived from the Greek *presbuteros*, refers primarily to an elder. It has come to denote a religious specialist devoted especially to cultic worship, and belonging to a profession as well as – in some cultures – a class. As such, the priest may occasionally appropriate the function of other specialists, whether medicine men, diviners, or magicians, but functions usually as someone with specialist knowledge of the deity and expert skills permitting the performance of cultic, especially sacrificial, duties. The priest's mediating powers depend upon his ability to influence the supernatural powers or the deity, whereas the magician's powers to manipulate nature rest upon *techniques* properly

---

[18] *Chou-li Cheng-chu*, 18:1a.   [19] Ibid, 18:1b.

applied, such as spells and incantations.[20] Moreover, the priest differs from the prophet, who is a messenger from on high, usually without cultic training or responsibilities.

Let us explore the meaning of *chu*, to decide whether the role is at all a functional equivalent of 'priest', and eventually, to distinguish between the *chu* and the *wu*[a], whom we also call a shaman.

According to the Han lexicon, *Shuo-wen chieh-tzu*, the word *chu* signifies a person who communicates through the mouth with the divine.[21] The Institutes of Chou gives various categories of *chu*, each a specialist class. First of all, there was the Great *chu*, a position parallel to that of the Great Diviner. He was in charge of six kinds of ritual formulas in the service of the deities, ghosts and spirits;[22] and six kinds of petitions.[23] He was also responsible for the composing of six kinds of ritual announcements;[24] the differentiation of six kinds of cultic titles and addresses;[25] nine kinds of sacrifices;[26] and of nine kinds of rubrics, including bows and prostrations. During the great suburban *chiao / jiao* sacrifices offered annually to the Lord-on-High, he was the chief supervisor and master of ceremonies, giving orders to junior ritualists, to the musicians, and to various subordinates.[27]

Thus the *chu* as a class were devoted to cultic services, that is, to sacrifices and prayer rituals – including ritual announcements, petitions, invocations and incantations. And I would assert, with Henri Maspéro, that the *chu* made up a class of official clergy. Their chiefs came from the upper nobility. We know, from a bronze inscription, that the eldest son of the Duke of Chou, Po-ch'in by name, served as a *Ta-chu / Dazhu* ('Great Shaman').[28] And if, as it

---

[20] Léopold Sabourin, *Priesthood: A Comparative Study*, Studies in the History of Religions, Supplements to *Numen*, vol. 25 (Leiden: E. J. Brill, 1973), 1–12.

[21] Consult the edition with Tuan Yü-ts'ai's commentary in *Shuo-wen chieh-tzu Tuan-chu*, SPPY ed., vol. 5, pt 1, 18a–b.

[22] In view of having good harvests, a good year, blessings and good fortune, avoidance of calamities and pestilences, and needed rains.

[23] Especially for use during calamities and pestilences.

[24] Including orders, announcements, eulogies of ancestors, oaths and various petitions and prayers to the deities and ancestral spirits.

[25] I.e., of gods, spirits, victims, grains and other sacrificial objects.

[26] I.e., whether offered to specific gods or without such specification, whether burnt sacrifices, or the sacrifice of the victim's internal organs, salted, spiced and cooked, whether including a meal of communion, and so on.

[27] For the above information, see *Chou-li Cheng-chu*, 25:3–8; French trans. in Édouard Biot, *Le Tcheou li ou rites de Tcheou* (Paris: Imprimérie Nationale, 1851), vol. 2, pp. 27–58.

[28] Consult Henri Maspéro, *China in Antiquity* (Amherst: University of Massachusetts Press, 1978), p. 112; Shirakawa Shizuka, *Chung-kuo ku-tai wen-hua* (Ancient Chinese civilisation), trans. into Chinese by Fan Yüeh-chiao et al. (Taipei: Wen-ching, 1983), pp. 142–3, 145.

has been suggested, the Duke of Chou himself had shamanic powers, then the line dividing the shaman and the *chu* would be a thin one indeed.

So far, we have spoken of both prayers and invocations. But are the two not different? Were the Chinese *chu* men of prayer, as well as of invocations? The answers to these questions depend in part upon our understanding of prayer and invocations. And in turn, they will decisively shape our understanding of the role of the *chu*.

I define prayer broadly, as human communication with the divine and spiritual. There are many kinds of prayer: formal and informal, collective or individual, depending often on whether it has a ritual origin and context, or whether it is personal prayer. Often, prayers with liturgical origin become later used as models for personal prayer. The biblical Psalms are a good example – so often an inspiration for personal prayer, and now considered to have been a hymn book of the Jerusalem Temple. Some psalms originated in liturgical context, while others were examples of spontaneous prayer, that became ritualised. Indeed, in the history of Western religions, liturgical prayer has usually been non-spontaneous, formalised, repeated by the priest or leader in a cultic situation. Within Christianity, various theological disputations took place, in the Middle Ages and later, regarding efficacy in such terms as *ex opere operato* (on account of the work itself) – referring to sacraments – and *ex opere operantis* (on account of the worker performing it) – referring to non-sacramental action. But there is generally no disagreement that such ritual formulae as exist in sacraments still represent prayer. Therefore the situation offers occasion for comparative study with what takes place in other liturgical and cultic traditions.

Some say prayer is more spontaneous and personal, perhaps even altruistic, that praise or prayer is thanksgiving rather than petition. They also say that invocations and incantations, as ritual formulas, have little, if any, meaning in themselves and are recited with the aim of acquiring certain favours from the spirits. In outlining the duties of the *chu*, we have already referred to ritual announcements, as well as to prayers of petition. So it would appear that the *chu* was not expected merely to recite quasi-magical formulas that have no intrinsic meaning.

The ritual texts offer much detail on the performance of sacrifice, but little information about the content of the prayers themselves. We have examples of announcements, such as made by the person

offering the sacrifice to an ancestral spirit, who presents himself and
his wife formally, and whose announcement is repeated by the *chu*.
In one place, the Book of Rites speaks of sacrificial offerings to the
inventors of dykes and water-channels. It gives a direct reference to
the prayer offered. This is an example of the prayer of petition,
which James Legge translates as follows:

> May the ground no sliding show,
> Water in the channels flow,
> Insects to keep quiet know;
> Only in the fens weeds grow![29]

Other sentiments, such as thanksgiving, are also expressed in the
prayers addressed by the ruler during the sacrifice to Heaven that he
performed, presumably in his capacity as High Priest. Many other
sources offer examples of prayers – including the Book of Songs,
with its occasional cries from the heart. We also have texts of prayers
by King T'ang and the Duke of Chou permeated by a spirit of self-
sacrifice. They do not come from ritual texts, but serve as good
examples of prayer offered in ritual contexts.

In the case of ancient Israel, the king probably performed
liturgical functions involving himself, but he did not offer sacrifices,
as did the much earlier patriarchs acting as heads of clans. Instead,
he left these duties to the priestly members of the tribe of Levi. But
in the case of ancient China, the person ultimately in charge of
offering sacrifices, and who presided at the principal sacrifices, was
the ruler or king himself. In this regard, he was the Great High
Priest, assisted by a Minister of Rites, his deputy, and by a team of
others, called *chu*, who participated in his priesthood. So long as we
remember that the king was the chief priest, we could call the others,
the *chu*, also priests or religious professionals who followed the ritual
manuals, and as officials of the state cult.

True, the word *chu* is related to the term for invocations, and even
incantations (*chou / zhou*) with its magical associations. And there
was actually an official *chu* who specialised in incantations. But
incantations presumably had their own beginnings, and could very
well be at the basis of many shamanic rituals. We know, from oracle
writing, that such incantations, or curses, to be exact, were made in
Shang times, by thousands of shamanesses, arrayed ahead of the

---

[29] *Li-chi Cheng-chu* 8:7a; Legge, *Li Ki, Sacred Books*, vol. 27, p. 432.

soldiers and playing drums while shouting out formulae at rituals called *wang*ᵃ (literally, 'looking afar'), to promote victory. The battle was also between shamanesses on both sides, since the victors killed the enemy shamanesses.[30]

We are speaking of incantations in the context of magic and shamanism. They are a different case from verbal formulas, uttered in religious contexts, that have no discernible meaning in themselves. Such formulas include 'speaking with tongues', a kind of ecstatic outburst in a religious or ritual context. Here perhaps, recent studies on Christian pentecostalism may be useful in casting light on certain rare phenomena. We know today that in their own ecstatic outbursts, Christians make verbal outpourings with inherent religious significance but no discernible semantic value.[31] And while here acknowledging the difference between magical incantations and speaking with tongues, I wonder whether ritual incantations in traditions like the Chinese originated in similar manifestations, namely, ecstatic circumstances. I offer a mere hypothesis here.

The shamans

To move now more specifically to shamanism. The word 'shaman' is a technical term borrowed from Siberian languages. The ecstatic shaman's role is most exemplified in the tribal societies of Siberia, the Arctic, and pre-contact North America. He or she serves the community by divination and healing, although in China, praying for rain has been a principal responsibility. Scholars agree that shamanism has to do with the claim of spirit possession and the ensuing ecstatic experience, but they do not find the word easy to define. For example, Raymond Firth scrupulously distinguishes between spirit possession, spirit mediumship and shamanism. According to him, spirit possession involves phenomena of abnormal behaviour which are interpreted by other members of society as evidence that a spirit is controlling the person's actions and probably inhabiting his body. In spirit mediumship the accent is rather on

---

[30] Consult Shirakawa Shizuka, *Chung-kuo*, pp. 51–2, 231–3. Later examples come from religious Taoism and from Buddhism. And here we have often an assemblage of words with little obvious meaning. Indeed, in the case of Tantric Buddhism, we have formulas called *dhāraṇis* believed to have inherent magic power.

[31] Consult William J. Samarin, *Tongues of Men and Angels: The Religious Language of Pentecostalism* (New York: Macmillan, 1972), especially pp. 88–93, 152–73.

communication. 'Shamanism', on the other hand, 'applies to those phenomena where a person, either a spirit medium or not, is regarded as controlling spirits, exercising his mastery over them in socially recognized ways.'[32]

All the same, there is a scholarly consensus that shamans are by definition ecstatics. They are described as *becoming* shamans through initiatory ecstatic experiences like pathological sicknesses, dreams and trances, followed by theoretical and practical instruction at the hands of the old masters. But it is always an ecstatic type of experience, including what resembles a *mystical* marriage with a god, that determines one's 'vocation'. They are alleged to have the ability of having visions, of *seeing* the spirits, whether of deceased humans or of animals, and of being able to communicate with these in a secret language (resembling animal language), such as during a *séance*. They are also described as being able to levitate, to make magical flights into the sky and magical descents into the underworld, to have mastery over fire and to cure sicknesses.

Is so-called spirit possession associated with shamanism a mystical experience? This depends on how the term mysticism itself is defined. If a transformed consciousness lies at the core of mystical experience, then shamanism, as represented by spirit possession, involves mysticism.

Shamanism dominates the religious life of North and Central Asia, but similar magico-religious phenomena have been observed among the natives of South and Southeast Asia, Oceania and even North America and beyond.[33] In seeking for its origin in China, the following passage from the fourth-century-BCE text *Kuo-yü* (Conversation between States) may be helpful:

Anciently, human beings and spirits did not mix. But certain persons were so perspicacious, single-minded, reverential and correct that their intelligence could understand what lies above and below, their sagely wisdom could illumine what is distant and profound, their vision was bright and clear and their hearing was penetrating. Therefore the spirits would descend upon them. The possessors of such powers were, if men, called

---

[32] Raymond Firth, *Tikopia Ritual and Belief* (London: Allen & Unwin, 1967), p. 26.

[33] Consult Mircea Eliade, *Shamanism: Archaic Techniques of Ecstasy* (Princeton University Press, 1964), pp. 5, 33–4, 71–2, 93–9; I. M. Lewis, *Ecstatic Religion: An Anthropological Study of Spirit Possession and Shamanism* (Harmondsworth: Penguin Books, 1971), pp. 18, 50–1; John A. Grim, *The Shaman: Patterns of Siberian and Ojibway Healing* (Norman: University of Oklahoma Press, 1983), pp. 25–32.

hsi / xi, and if women, *wu*[a]. They supervised the positions of the spirits at the ceremonies, took care of sacrificial victims and vessels as well as of seasonal robes.[34]

Interestingly, this description is of two worlds that were not just distinct, but also separate, with the *wu*[a] and *hsi* as mediators between them. In other words, these persons were able to move between the world of human beings and the world of spirits. They possessed certain unusual qualities that enabled them to do so, keeping communications between the two orders open. It is here that we find the positive attributes of ancient shamans, those who lived long before the fourth century BCE. Their principal characteristic is 'sagely wisdom' (*sheng*), given as the reason why the spirits would 'descend upon them'. Presumably, this is a reference to the trance experience. And we are also given the gender differentiation, without being told whether males and females performed different functions. Moreover, the duties stated appear to be little different from those of the priests or of the priests' assistants. What is not clear is the supervision 'of the spirits at the ceremonies'. Did this mean positioning in rank the names of spirits inscribed on tablets or images, or some duty involving trance?

We are, at this point, not able to answer precisely our own questions posed above. And we also note that the description given so far does not call them kings, or speak of them as holding political power. However, to the extent that the heavenly order was believed to be 'where the action is', that is, where decisions concerning human affairs are made, we may presume that shamans played an important role in human affairs, including the political realm, simply by performing their religious duties.

Some scholars assert that the Chinese *wu*[a] were not shamans in the strict, Siberian sense, but were mere 'spirit–mediums'. This is done when one draws a sharp distinction between shamans and spirit–mediums, as one might also between priests and invocators. But a broader definition in each case may be more helpful heuristically. Arthur Waley, for example, has described the *wu*[a] of ancient China as intermediaries in spirit–cults, experts in exorcism, prophecy, fortune-telling, rain-making and the interpretation of dreams, as well as magic healers. To use his words: 'Indeed the functions of

---

[34] *Kuo-yü*, Ch'u-yü (Dialogue between the states, Dialogue of Ch'u), pt 2, SPPY ed., 18:1a. The English translation is my own.

Chinese *wu*[a] were so like those of Siberian and Tungus shamans that it is convenient . . . to use shaman as a translation of *wu*[a].'[35]

We may define a shaman simply as a gifted, *charismatic*, religious figure, and an inspired healer, who has the power to control spirits, and even to call them down and have them speak through him or her. Such a person has usually undergone an initial, traumatic experience, called shamanic illness, which is interpreted as possession. Apparently, the involvement with spirits might begin with involuntary possession, but leads to the more voluntary kind, with the shaman taking more active control and even commanding the spirits to follow his or her commands.

K. C. Chang has pointed out evidence from oracle bone inscriptions linking the activities of kingship with those of shamanism. Examples include inscriptions stating that the king divined, or enquired in connection with wind- or rain-storms, rituals, or conquests. There are also statements that the king made prognostications pertaining to weather, the border regions, or misfortunes and diseases. In addition, there are inscriptions describing the king dancing in his prayers for rain, and prognosticating about a dream. As all of these were activities common to both king and shaman, we may take it to mean that the king was also a shaman.[36]

As those of an authority on ancient China, K. C. Chang's interpretations should have closed the case on the shamanic character of kingship. But the situation is not so clear, since the two fields, of China studies, and of the study of the historical phenomenology of religions, are quite big, and opinions may differ widely. Without being, technically, an ancient historian, I am trying to help the case by entering into the subject with some depth, offering textual, interpretive, historical, and cross-cultural clues.

This does not necessarily mean that the king was the only shaman. Rather, we have evidence that he was surrounded by assistants, some of whom were also shamans. We know some of the ancient shamans by name. They include persons with the surname Wu, presumably members of a shamanic clan. An important member was Wu Hsien, sometimes described as a grand ancestor of shamans, sometimes as a deity himself. There are also others.

---

[35] Arthur Waley, trans., *The Nine Songs* (London: Allen & Unwin, 1955), Introduction, p. 9. For shamanism in Korea, see Boudewijn Walraven, *Songs of the Shaman: The Ritual Chants of the Korean Mudang* (London: Kegan Paul International, 1994).
[36] Chang, *Art, Myth and Ritual*, pp. 46–7.

Perhaps the ten so-called 'immortal *wu*ᵃ' who assembled many disciples on Mount Wu were founders of different branches of 'sorcerers', each with different powers and functions. All this information comes from the *Shan-hai ching*, today regarded as having originated as a manual for shamans.[37]

We should point out that priests (*chu*) and shamans (*wu*ᵃ) performed different functions and were usually expected to have different qualities. The priests – and also the chosen victims – were expected to be perfect examples of humanity, without physical blemish or disability. The shamans, on the other hand, were often the opposite. The Japanese scholar Katō Jōken points out that the Duke of Chou was described as a dwarf and hunchback, and considered to possess shamanic powers.[38] He attempts even to prove philologically that both the duke's father King Wen, and his brother King Wu, were hunchbacks and shamans. Their spiritual qualification to the title of rulership or kingship was in the possession of superior intelligence and shamanic powers, while their physical appearance marked them out as such. Obviously, in their cases, physical imperfection was considered no obstacle to their performance of religious, even priestly duty, but even a sign of superior power.

In oracle inscriptions as well as historical texts, the *wu*ᵃ have been described as deformed and as hunchbacks. If a certain deformity was considered to be the sign of a possible religious talent, other disabilities have been regarded widely as the sign of possible compensatory gifts. The mythical K'uei, patron of musicians, is described as a one-legged monster who taught men how to play on stones to call down the gods and spirits. The ritual and historical texts also speak of the blind musicians who played an important part at sacrificial rituals, presumably including rain-dances. They included the Director of Music, and those who played flutes and bells and stone and skin instruments under his orders, in different melodies depending on which kinds of gods were being honoured, and indeed, were being asked to descend.

It would appear that in Chou times, the shamans in royal employ were only a small number of the actual shamans in the country. In

---

[37] See Yüan Ke, *Shan-hai-ching chiao-chu* (The Classic of Mountain and Sea, with annotations) (Taipei: Hung-shih, 1981), pp. 366, 411.

[38] *Hsün-tzu*, SPPY ed., 3:2a; *Lun-heng*, SPPY ed., 3:4b; Katō Jōken, *Chūgoku kodai bunka no kenkyū* (Tokyo: Meitoku, 1980), pp. 366–67.

contrast to the *chu*, who were priests, official 'prayer-men' of the state cult, the shamans were rather individuals chosen from out of all the social classes by their own gods and sometimes served only these gods. As subjects of the king, of course, they were supposed to be on call; in fact, most of them worked as individuals. Some belonged to a particular god, but most were able to enter into relations with several gods, or especially with the spirits of the deceased. To classify the *wu*[a] by their functions, we may speak of the simple spirit–mediums, the healers, the exorcists, the interpreters of dreams, the rain-makers, and others.[39]

Increasingly, scholars today are acknowledging similarities between religious traditions that have been regarded as widely divergent, without denying those differences that abound.[40] If we were to limit shamanism to its Siberian origins, we might find it difficult to relate the term to the Near East, where scholars have usually preferred to describe the Semitic religions as 'prophetic'. The prophetic movement in ancient Israel lasted several hundred years, throughout the entire span of the Hebrew kingdoms. Many associate it primarily with ethics, because of moral admonitions and condemnations in the Hebrew scriptures. Still, Hebrew society had long recognised so-called trance states and their associated unusual behaviour as possession by the spirit of Yahweh. We find Saul, Israel's first king, caught up in the activity of a band of ecstatic 'prophets' who danced to the flute, tambourine, and lyre. A thousand years later, another Saul, who took the name Paul, was still writing about 'prophesying' as one of the gifts of the holy spirit. And we have many instances of persons 'filled with the Holy Spirit' in the Acts of the Apostles.

Shamans as rain-makers

In ancient and historical China, the shaman was especially the 'rain-maker'. Here we find a duty which was very central to an agricultural society dependent on natural beneficence as it still is today. In oracle inscriptions, sacrifices to the nature deities and to the ancestors were recorded in much the same manner, sometimes with

---

[39] *Mo-tzu*, SPPY ed., 8:1–10; *Chou-li Cheng-chu*, 26:3–5.

[40] In an interesting recent book, Stevan L. Davies underscores the phenomenon of spirit possession surrounding the recorded miracles performed by Jesus in the Gospels. See *Jesus the Healer: Possession, Trance and the Origins of Christianity* (New York: Continuum, 1995).

a nature deity or a high ancestor associated with the Lord-on-High in worship. Occasionally, it is asked whether a ritual dance should be performed.

According to the Institutes of Chou, different genres of dances with drums and other instruments in stone and bronze, were performed in ancient China during different sacrificial rituals. A military dance took place at sacrifices to mountains and rivers, while 'feather' dances were performed at sacrifices to the spirits of the four directions. The dancers might have worn masks, and may be described as the earliest actors and entertainers. But the best-known dances are those devoted to rain-making, presumably to entertain the rain deity until he is amenable to human pleas for rain.[41] The rain deity was represented in earlier periods especially in the form of a dragon. Women dancers were preferred, as their sex was associated with rain, whereas men were associated with drought.[42]

In praying for rain, the oracle was usually consulted as well. The diviner asks counsel as to the need of making sacrificial victims, usually animals, to the Lord-on-High himself, or to the gods of rain or wind. The ritual was accompanied by crying and dancing, presumably working up to a trance. However, in those dire cases where neither dance nor animal sacrifice had been efficacious in bringing about rain, there was the custom sometimes of sacrificing the *wu*[a] himself or herself, by offering the individual(s) on the wood-pile, under the burning sun. It was a way of putting pressure on the gods, of 'extorting' rain from them. However, the classical texts cited many cases when this option was rejected as unreasonable.[43]

In the Analects (11:7), Confucius' disciple Tseng Tien makes reference to the rain altars of the River Yi as a place to go in late spring in proper seasonal robes and in the company of a group of young men and children – presumably trained in the music of rain dances. There, they would bathe in the river, follow the airs of the rain dance, and return home singing, after sharing in a sacrificial meal.[44]

This passage speaks lyrically of the music and dancing in late spring, but explains neither any religious setting, nor the need for praying for rain. And it raises as many questions as it may answer.

---

[41] *Chou-li Cheng-chu* 22:4–8.   [42] Tung, *Ch'un-ch'iu fan-lu* 16:2b–7a.
[43] *Li-chi Cheng-chu*, 3:21–22, Tung, *Ch'un-ch'iu fan-lu*, ch. 16. Wang, *Lun-heng*, 15:6b.
[44] Wang Ch'ung, *Lun-heng* 15:9b.

Traditionally, it has been understood as an indication of Confucius' approval of self-transcendence in nature and in music.

There were also other 'shamanic dances'. Such were used to expel evil or demonic influences, which could cause serious diseases. Shamans were medicine men and women, with knowledge of drugs and herbs.[45] They were called upon to summon the spirit back, in the case of some seriously ill person, and even in the case of the dead.

The Institutes of Chou describes the *wu*[a] after a description of the *chu*, and in fewer words. It speaks of the chief *wu*[a], as having special responsibility to supervise rain dances, and minor cultic functions, involving sacrificial tablets and other items, the summoning of spirits during funerals, and the healing of sicknesses. Thus the *wu*[a] played a role conjointly with the *chu* during funeral rituals, the males participating in the king's funeral rites, and the females participating in the queen's funeral rites. Besides, the female *wu*[a] had the special responsibility of performing rain-dances.[46] We shall be dwelling upon some of these recorded roles of the Chinese shaman.

According to the *Shuo-wen*, the *wu*[a] is a female person (indeed, a *chu*), who serves the invisible spirits and can call these down by dances. The term is related to its homophone, the word for dance, and points to the raising of one's sleeves in a dance-like gesture. It can refer both to a person who is skilled in dancing, and to someone holding in two hands the instruments of magic or divination. And it is often used in association with the word *chu*. When used particularly to refer to the *wu*[a], his or her special skills include praying in rain dances, communicating with the spiritual world, perhaps also predicting good or evil fortune, healing sicknesses and interpreting dreams. The Japanese scholar Kaizuka Shigeki has said that the word *wu*[a] refers to a mediator between the human world and the divine, while the word *chu* refers to the mouthpiece of God who transmits his messages to human beings, an expert in ritual incantations.[47]

Why is the shamanic character so important to kingship? I believe that is due to the perception of the shaman as someone who has

---

[45] Catherine Despeux, 'Gymnastics: The Ancient Tradition', in Livia Kohn (ed.), *Taoist Meditation and Longevity Techniques*, Michigan Monographs in Chinese Studies, vol. 61 (Ann Arbor: University of Michigan, 1989), p. 239.

[46] *Chou-li Cheng-chu*, 26:3–5; Biot, *Tcheou li*, vol. 2, pp. 69–84.

[47] Kaizuka Shigeki, *Chūgoku no shinwa: Kamigami no tanjō* (The mythology of China: the birth of the gods) (Tokyo: Iwanami, 1963), pp. 54–5.

privileged access to the gods or spirits through trances, who can therefore mediate between the human beings and the gods or spirits. In that sense, the shaman is a child of the gods, a son as well as a servant. We shall see how the early kings claimed themselves to be lineally descended from the gods, to have privileged access to them, to be their servant in sacrificial ritual, as well as in other functions.

The sacrifice of King T'ang

The information about King T'ang, the founder of the Shang dynasty, which we find in early texts, is much more rational than that about the sage Yü. According to several accounts, T'ang's conquest of Hsia was followed by many years of drought, during which he was presumably told by the diviners that Heaven could be placated only by a human sacrifice. Thereupon he went off to the official altar in the Mulberry Grove, purified himself by cutting his hair and his fingernails, placed himself on the firewood, and prepared to offer himself to the Lord-on-High. But no sooner was the fire lit, than rain came and quenched it.[48]

T'ang's prayer is cited in the terse language of the Analects and of *Lü-shih ch'un-ch'iu* as follows:

I, the child Li . . . do announce to thee, O most great and sovereign Lord,[49] If I, the one man, committed offences, they are not to be attributed to the myriad people. If the myriad people commit offences, these offences must rest on me alone, the one man. The lack of merit of one man should not make the Lord-on-High, the ghosts and spirits injure the lives of the people.[50]

And, Mo-tzu remarks, exalted as the Son of Heaven, T'ang was ready to offer himself as sacrifice to the Lord-on-High, the spirits and the ghosts, for the benefit of his people.[51] Since the offering of sacrifice is a specifically priestly act, I would describe T'ang's gesture of self-sacrifice as a supreme example of a king's acting as both priest

---

[48] The earliest extant version comes from *Mo-tzu*, ch. 4, p. 10a, in which the king is said to have first offered a young bull; later versions are found in *Hsün-tzu*, SPPY ed., 19:9b; *Lü-shih ch'un-ch'iu* (Spring–Autumn Annals of the Lü Family), SPPY ed., 9:3b–4a; *Huai-nan-tzu*, SPPY ed., 19:2b; *Kuo-yü* 'Chou-yü', part one, 1:13a; Wang Ch'ung, *Lun-heng* (Balanced Inquiries), SPPY ed., 5:11b–12b.

[49] Analects 20:1; English trans. adapted from James Legge, *The Chinese Classics* (Oxford: Clarendon, 1893–5), vol. 1, pp. 350–1.

[50] *Lü-shih ch'un-ch'iu* 9:3b–4a.

[51] *Mo-tzu*, ch. 4, p. 10 b. See Sarah Allan, *The Shape of the Turtle: Myth, Art and Cosmos in Early China* (Albany: State University of New York Press, 1991), pp. 43–6.

(*chu*) and victim while serving a shamanic (*wu*[a]) role for the sake of getting rain. And he did so after divination, as would have been expected. The sense of expiation for sins, committed either by himself or the people, should also be noted. This example also clearly affirms the presence of prayer – not just of incantations – in ancient China. And while it is yet impossible to guarantee the historicity of this event, I would point out (1) the existence of overlapping textual evidence; and (2) the assumption that the royal role was shamanic as well as priestly.

KINGSHIP AND SACRIFICE

The ancient Chinese had a three-tiered world view, of heaven above, the abode of the dead below, and earth, the abode of the living, in between. But the dead were not, so to speak, 'imprisoned' down under. The royal ancestors, perhaps considered as the most powerful among these, on account of a special relationship with the gods, continued to have power over the living, whether to protect or bless them or to punish and curse them. Although departed, they continued to expect for their nurture and enjoyment, sacrificial 'blood' offerings.

The Chinese word *chi / ji* (sacrifice) is said to derive from a graph representing the offering of meat, and possibly also wine, to some spirit. Originally, the practice began as a simple act of providing food for the dead.[52] Presumably, when the food appeared not to have been touched, the living maintained that the dead had partaken of it, without destroying its physical substance, thus allowing the living also to share in a spirit of 'communion'. According to the Shang oracle inscriptions, burnt offerings were made also to other than heavenly spirits. But later ritual texts describe an elaborate system of state sacrifices, each with its own name, offered to heavenly and earthly deities as well as to ancestral spirits. Records say that the sacrificial victims were burnt when offered to beings on high, buried when offered to earth spirits, drowned when offered to river deities (usually to appease them and avoid flooding), and cut into pieces when offered to the spirit of the wind (to stop a storm, or a pestilence). Only the food that remained of the burnt offering could

---

[52] Li Hsiao-ting (ed.), *Chia-ku wen-tzu chi-shih* (A compendium of oracle writings with explanations) (Hwakang, Taiwan: Institute for History and Philology, Academia Sinica, 1982), vol. 1, pp. 63–5.

be eaten by those who offered it. In any case, wine was probably poured out in libation in antiquity as it is still being done today.[53] Against this background, we can better understand the Book of Rites when it speaks of the importance of rituals and kingship, without neglecting certain secular responsibilities 'The ancient kings used [divination] stalks and tortoise-shells; arranged sacrifices; buried silk offerings; recited supplication and benediction; instituted statutes and measures. In this way the state has its rituals, the government departments their officials, the affairs their management, the rites their order of performance.'[54]

The offering of sacrifice was considered a privilege, belonging *par excellence* to the kings, and only by participation, to those under him: the royal kinsmen, the feudal lords, and their ministers. In this sense, sacrifice was both the duty and the privilege of the noble-born. According to their ranks and responsibilities, they were permitted to approach certain spirits and deities. The commoners were originally excluded from these rituals. They could not offer sacrifice even to their own ancestors, because they were said to have no ancestors. In fact, of course, it was a case of their ancestors not being important enough, not having the divine connections. And this is in itself revealing: that the ruling class considered itself to be an élite, set apart from those they governed by descent from divinity.[55]

Ritual performance offers a means of legitimation of royal authority, demonstrating to the king's subjects his position as mediator between Heaven, Earth and human beings:

The ancient kings feared that the rituals might not be understood by those below them. So they sacrificed to the Lord-on-High in the suburb, in order to determine the rank of Heaven. They offered sacrifices at the altar of earth inside the capital, in order to demonstrate the benefits derived from earth. They sacrifice to ancestors in the temples, in order to give fundamental place to human sentiments. They sacrifice to mountains and rivers, in order to honour the spirits and ghosts.[56]

53 Ch'en Meng-chia, *Yin-hsü pu-tz'u tsung-shu* (A comprehensive account of the oracle writings of the Yin site) (Beijing: Institute of Archaeology, Chinese Academy of Science, 1956), pp. 573–98.
54 *Li-chi Cheng-chu* 7:9a–b.
55 We may divide the sacrifices of antiquity into two classes: the 'interior' cult, taking place 'inside' the mausoleum of the deceased royal ancestors and the 'exterior' cult, taking place 'outside', honouring the Lord-on-High and a host of nature-deities. Ikeda, *Chūgoku kodai shūkyōshi*, pp. 407–44. We shall concentrate on the exterior cult.
56 *Li-chi Cheng-chu* 7:9b.

As mediator, the king stood at the centre of his bureaucracy, which had charge of sacred as well as of secular responsibilities.

So the royal kinsmen and the priests of the cult (*chu*) are at the [ancestral] temples; the three ducal ministers are at the court; the three classes of elders are at the college. The king is preceded by the shamans and followed by the chroniclers; the various diviners and blind musicians are at his left and right. The king is at the centre. His mind (*hsin* / *xin*) is detached from action (*wu-wei*), in order to be fully correct.[57]

Of course, in the early days, the secular bureaucracy also had its religious obligations. The ducal ministers presumably assisted the king in his sacrificial rituals; the elders presumably taught rituals to the young nobles at the colleges; the chroniclers were originally those who recorded ritual events; and the blind musicians made their own contributions at ritual performances.

The benefits of the royal observance of ritual are then listed, 'So when the rituals are performed in the suburb, the hundred spirits receive their offices; when the rituals are performed at the altar of the earth, the hundred products receive their fulfilments; when the rituals are performed at the ancestral temples; filial piety and affection are demonstrated.'[58] There is a difficult passage (Analects 3:10) in which Confucius declares that he had no desire to continue attending the great summer sacrifice (*ti*[b] / *di*) after the libation of wine has been poured out   with the intention of causing the descent of the deity – and just before the ruler went out to lead the animal victim inside. The word *ti*[b] refers here apparently to the 'great sacrifice' offered only by the ruler, in this case, by the ruler of the state of Lu as a descendant of the Duke of Chou whose house had been given the honour to perform such to the dynastic ancestor.[59]

One interpretation is that the *ti*[b] sacrifice was not being performed properly, hence his reluctance to be present. What I wish to point out here is the mention that the libation was poured out to invite the deity or spirit to descend: a shamanic move, even if, by Confucius' time, the rites relied on an impersonator of the dead, often chosen from among the younger kinsmen of the deceased whose spirit was being honoured.[60]

---

[57] Ibid.   [58] Ibid.

[59] See *Lun-yü cheng-i* (Correct meaning of the Analects) with Liu Pao-nan's commentary, SPPY ed., which contains a long explanation of the *ti*[b] and the circumstances in which the sacrifice was then being offered (3:9a–10b); see also Legge, *Chinese Classics*, vol. 1, p. 158.

[60] Consult also D. C. Lau (trans.), *Confucius: The Analects* (Harmondsworth: Penguin Books, 1979), pp. 68–9.

The worship of Heaven

It has been said that rites can alter the state of the world because they invoke power.[61] Sacrifices offered to the highest deity certainly invoke the highest power. There is some dispute as to whether sacrifices were offered to the Lord-on-High in Shang times. Some scholars, particularly Ch'en Meng-chia, have asserted that no clear record exists. This is due partly to the ambiguity of the term ti^c / di, a posthumous title given to deceased royal ancestors. The interpretation is related to that of regarding the Ti^c (same word) as a transcendent and supreme deity, lord of nature, but little interested in human affairs. And, while others might concede that Ti^c did receive sacrifice, they emphasise that the cult appeared to be mediated through the royal ancestor who was honoured alongside of him.[62]

The sacrificial cult to the Lord-on-High, if it was already performed in Shang times, appears to have been especially associated with individuals carrying a clan name Wu meaning shaman, as well as the simple name, Wu. The following example comes from an oracular context: 'On the day Chia-tzu, the oracle was asked whether the Wu should offer a victim to the Ti^c.' This word wu^a also appears in the context of sacrifices to nature deities, especially wind and rain, but not to ancestors. It is suggested that the Wu clan, perhaps natives of a place called Wu, served especially in the cult of the supreme deity, perhaps on account of their expertise in so-called shamanic activities, so that their name came to represent to later ages the shamanic profession itself.[63]

In any case, by Chou times, there is clear evidence that Heaven or the Lord-on-High received the sacrifices of young bulls offered to him. In all cases, special halls and yards in the royal ancestral temples were available for various kinds of sacrificial rituals, and bronze vessels of different sizes and shapes were at hand to hold the

---

[61] See also Edmund Leach, 'Ritual', *International Encyclopedia of the Social Sciences* (New York: Macmillan & Free Press, 1968), vol. 13, p. 524.

[62] See Ch'en Meng-chia, *Yin-hsü pu-tz'u*, 577, 580; Ikeda, *Chūgoku kodai shūkyōshi*, pp. 445–536; Léon Vandermeersch, *Wangdao ou la Voie Royale: Recherches sur l'esprit des institutions de la Chine archaïque* (Paris: École Française de l'Extrême-Orient, 1977), vol. 2, pp. 358–60.

[63] Akatsuka Kiyoshi, *Chūgoku kodai no shūkyō to bunka* (Religion and culture in ancient China) (Tokyo: Kadokawa, 1977), pp. 426–39.

raw and cooked offerings.[64] In Chou times, these were especially
called the Suburban Sacrifices (*chiao / jiao*).

The Suburban Sacrifices

The Rites of Chou speaks of a sacrifice to Heaven at a round altar at
the time of the winter solstice and a sacrifice to Earth at a square
altar at the time of the summer solstice. The Book of Rites notes that
this sacrifice to Heaven was made by burning the animal victim on a
blazing pile of wood, and that to Earth by burying the victim in an
earthen mound. It also associates both sacrifices with a ritual known
as the border or suburban sacrifice. This suburban sacrifice was
usually carried out in the southern suburb of the capital early in the
year according to the solar-lunar calendar. It was the religious act *par
excellence* of the reigning king.[65]

The suburban sacrifices offered in the open fields had grown in
importance especially during the early Han dynasty (206 BCE–220
CE), when altars were established in the northern and southern
suburbs of Ch'ang-an in the first century BCE.[66] The sacrifice to
Heaven was held in the southern suburb, while that to earth took
place in the northern suburb, thus allowing the ruler to harmonise
the principles of *yin* and *yang*.[67] But the sacrifices were performed
only intermittently, becoming established firmly as state ritual only
later, when the sacrifice to Heaven took on more solemnity as a
worship of the supreme deity, performed personally by the ruler as
Son of Heaven.[68] For a while, during the Han times and on account
of the Five Agents theory, five other heavenly deities were also
venerated, but that custom was later discontinued.[69] The Five
Agents are metal, wood, water, fire and earth.

---

[64] *Li-chi Cheng-chu*, ch. 8, sect. 11; see also 7:3–4, 14:1–27; English translation of ch. 14 is in
James Legge, *Li Ki, Sacred Books*, vol. 28, bk 20–2. See also Ikeda, *Chūgoku kodai shūkyōshi*,
pp. 299–404, 405–733, 785–806; Jung Ken *et al.*, *Yin Chou ch'ing-t'ung-ch'i t'ung-lun* (A
comprehensive discussion of the bronze vessels of Yin and Chou times) (Beijing: Institute of
Archaeology, Chinese Academy of Science, 1958), pp. 28–79. 'Yin' refers to the Shang
dynasty's last capital.

[65] For the sacrifice as it was performed in the Shang dynasty, see Akatsuka Kiyoshi, *Chūgoku
kodai*, pp. 537–96; for the Chou dynasty, see Henri Maspéro, *China in Antiquity*, pp. 135–40.

[66] *Li-chi Cheng-chu*, ch. 8, sect. 11. p. 1a; ch. 14 sect. 23, p. 1b.

[67] Pan Ku, *Han-shu* (Han Dynastic History), K'ai-ming ed., ch. 25.

[68] See the chapter on suburban sacrifices, 'Chiao-ssu', in *Han-shu* ch. 25A–B.

[69] Howard J. Wechsler, *Offerings of Jade and Silk* (New Haven: Yale University Press, 1985),
pp. 107–20.

If the suburban sacrifices were not always carried out, it was due to the rite's complicated regulations, elaborate details, and great expense. While the emperor alone was High Priest of the ritual, he was assisted and surrounded by many others, whether imperial relatives, court officials, military leaders, foreign dignitaries and others. Their rich apparel, the ritual vestments of all the others involved, including the beautiful gowns of musicians and dancers, and the exquisite sacrificial vessels and utensils, as well as all the other expenses involved in preparations of both the venue and the personnel, became at times forbidding to a struggling government. We know, however, that the rite was performed rather regularly during the T'ang dynasty (618–907).

The core symbolism of the sacrifice is the ruler's ritual offering made to the Lord-on-High, in a sacrifice in which his own dynastic ancestor has a share. At the round altar, the emperor moves into a sacred area and liminal zone which bridges the gap between the temporal world of human beings and the world of spirits and deities, into the presence of the supreme ruler of all. His ritual performances establish a bridge across space by means of which the power of the gods flows toward man. He also passes into sacred time, in which past, present and future coexist, to the extent that the ritual reenacts the bonding between Heaven and the Son of Heaven.

The animal victims are gifts to the gods in expectation of blessings and benefits. The victim's essence is transmitted to Heaven by means of the smoke produced by the fire, as is the case in sacrifices elsewhere, such as in ancient Israel. Thus sacrifice is a mode of communication between the human and the divine. The emperor's status and power are confirmed at the very moment he appears weak and powerless, subject of the Heaven. While he kneels and makes prostrations in front of the spirit throne, declaring himself a subject of the supreme sovereign, he is also acting out a role as the supreme human being, the 'one man' to whom alone is permitted this access to the divine. He will therefore emerge from the event with an invigorated kingship, and a greater legitimacy.[70]

A word should be said about the duality of the worship of both Heaven and Earth. Did this signify in any sense the duality of the supreme deity? The answer is No, as the cult to Earth was never equal in dignity and importance to the cult to Heaven. In any case,

---

[70] Wechsler, *Offerings*, pp. 121–2.

both have stopped, since the monarchy was toppled in 1911. Sacrifice – especially that to Heaven – as we have asserted, was the royal prerogative. With the elimination of kingship as an institution, the entire institution of civic religion has also fallen.

During the yearly cycle in the times of monarchy, there were other sacrifices to be performed. For example, the ploughing ceremony followed close upon the suburban sacrifice. This was when the King ritually turned the earth with a plough, tracing furrows on the ground of the sacred field in the southern suburb, to give an example to his subjects who depended on agriculture.

In this month [the first of spring], on the first day, the Son of Heaven prays to the Lord-on-High for a good harvest. And afterwards . . . with the handle and share of the plough in the carriage, at the head of the three dukes, the nine high ministers, the feudal lords and the great officials, he personally ploughed in the field dedicated to the Lord, . . . turning three furrows.[71]

This custom greatly impressed Jesuit missionaries writing back to Europe in the seventeenth and eighteenth centuries, and they, in turn, impressed European philosophers and their monarchs. Both the French (1768) and the Austrian (1769) courts carried out this ritual in conscious imitation of the Chinese.[72]

The Feng and Shan sacrifices

The suburban sacrifices took place outside, but not far from, the capital. The Feng and Shan sacrifices, dedicated to Heaven and Earth, took place much farther away, traditionally at or near Mount T'ai, in central Shantung, the single tallest peak in the region, rising nearly five thousand feet above sea level. The term *feng* refers to an earthen grave mound, and could be interpreted as an earthen altar. The term *shan* refers, in contrast, to the clearing of earth and debris in a specific area, possibly to prepare for sacrifice.[73] According to the *Po-hu-t'ung*, it might refer instead to 'sealing', for example, sealing a stone coffer containing jade tablets inscribed with an announce-

---

[71] *Li-chi Cheng-chu*, 5:3a; English translation adapted from James Legge, trans., *Li Ki, Sacred Books*, vol. 27, pp. 254–5.

[72] See Lewis A. Maverick, *China, A Model for Europe*, translation [with introduction] from the physiocrat François Quesnay's 1767 book *Le Despotisme de la Chine* (San Antonio: Paul Anderson, 1946), pp. 125–6.

[73] *Shuo-wen*, IA:9a.

ment to Heaven concerning dynastic successes, an activity that took place on an earthen altar.[74]

We remember that Shun allegedly offered a burnt offering to Heaven at Mount T'ai, from where he also made sacrifices to the spirits of mountains and rivers. Although this could not be considered historical, it points to an ancient tradition that associated Mount T'ai, a sacred mountain, with kingship and ritual, as well as with shamanism and the cult of immortals. In the Analects (3:6) Confucius expressed disapproval when told that the chief of the Chi family was about to sacrifice to Mount T'ai. Apparently, it was regarded as an act of usurpation on the chief's part. Perhaps, primitive rituals to the mountain's spirits, or to Heaven and Earth and all other spirits, evolved later into a sacrificial ritual offered to the supreme Heaven. But only six historical rulers are known to have performed there the Feng and the Shan. And these include the first Ch'in emperor, Emperor Wu of Han, Emperors Kao-tsung and Hsüan-tsung of T'ang, and Emperor Jen-tsung of Sung. In each case, these sacrifices performed political functions in announcing to the world the legitimacy of the rulers, who proclaimed that they had received the Mandate from Heaven, and also brought peace to the world.[75]

Human sacrifice

Was human sacrifice practised in early antiquity? Until the early part of the twentieth century, many experts tended to answer in the negative. But the consensus has shifted in the face of overwhelming evidence that cannot be otherwise explained. Besides, the practice was common in many ancient societies. The number of human victims varied from a few to as many as several hundred at one time, and archaeological discoveries of decapitated bodies support this probability. Both men and women were used as victims; the men were offered to male ancestors and the women to the female ancestors. Archaeologists claim that while male victims were found decapitated and even dismembered, the skeletons of female victims were found intact. Also, it appears that the skulls of certain human

---

[74] Pan Ku, *Po-hu t'ung shu-cheng* (Comprehensive discussions in the White Tiger Hall, with commentary), 1875 ed. (Taipei reprint, Rare Books Collection), 6:16a–17a.

[75] Consult Édouard Chavannes, *Le T'ai chan: essai de monographie d'un culte chinois* (1910 ed., Taipei, 1970 reprint), pp. 22–4.

victims, perhaps enemy chiefs, had also been used as a medium for divination, and still bear the inscribed records.[76]

Ritual human sacrifice was still practised at least until just before the time of Confucius. The *Historical Annals* tell us the story of the Ch'in capture of Duke Hui of Chin, who was nearly offered in a sacrifice to the Lord-on-High but was saved (645 BCE) after the intervention of the Chou king as well as the Ch'in duchess, his own sister.[77] Another account, in the Annals of Tso, describes the duchess's efforts on behalf of her half-brother:

She took her eldest son, the heir . . . her younger son . . . and her daughter . . . and together they ascended a terrace and stationed themselves on piles of brushwood . . . She addressed her children, saying, 'Heaven on high has sent down misfortune, making it impossible for our two rulers to meet in a friendly exchange of jades and silks, but instead to rush into battle. If the ruler of Chin [your father] arrives in the morning, we will die at evening; if he comes at evening, we die the next morning. It is up to [him] . . . to decide.'[78]

And so, by threatening to kill herself and her children, the duchess averted the terrible fate reserved for her half-brother as a war captive.

But human sacrifice as an abuse of power was also associated with the decline of shamanism, even if that could be attributed to the emergence of a more rationalist outlook, the rise of the many schools of philosophers, and the eventual dominance of Confucianism.[79]

An example relates to an ancient custom of annually offering a bride to the god of the Yellow River. It appeared that female shamans (*nü chu*) were consulted by local elders on the choice of the young girl, who was ritually dressed and drowned. The custom was much disliked by the populace for the loss of life, and the corruption out of which shamanesses and seniors enriched their own purses. An account in the *Historical Annals* tells the story (approximately late fifth century BCE) of a local official in Kaifeng, named Hsi-men Pao, who

[76] Jao Tsung-i, *Yin-tai chen-pu jen-wu t'ung-k'ao* (Oracle bone diviners of the Yin Dynasty) (Hong Kong University Press, 1959), vol. 1, p. 13; Akatsuka, *Chūgoku kodai*, 538; H. G. Creel, *The Birth of China*, pp. 204–14. According to Jao, these remains are preserved in the Institute for History and Philology, Academia Sinica, Nankang, Taiwan.

[77] *Shih-chi*, K'ai-ming ed., 5:19c.

[78] For the Chinese, see Legge's bilingual *Chinese Classics*, vol. 5, p. 165. For the English, see *The Tso Chuan: Selections from China's Oldest Narrative History*, trans. by Burton Watson (New York: Columbia University Press, 1989), pp. 33–4.

[79] *Kuan-tzu*, SPPY ed., 1:10b. Waley, *The Nine Songs*, pp. 11–12.

decided to do something about it. On the chosen date, he personally summoned the seniors and the shamanesses (*wu-chu*) who had selected the bride. He indicated that the chosen girl was not good enough, and that they should go and consult with the river god and report back to him. Then he threw them overboard. And, waiting in vain for their return, he turned to the other locals around and asked for volunteers to go and find out what was happening. Suitably intimidated, all agreed to abolish the barbaric custom of bride-offering.[80]

KINGSHIP AND KINSHIP IN PATRIARCHAL SOCIETY

The early Chinese kings, especially the Shang rulers, considered themselves as descendants of the demigods, and therefore also, as the kin of divinities. They looked upon themselves as leaders of a large, extended, kinship group, which had a 'clan name', but no 'family names'. Not surprisingly, many of them took wives from their own clans. Some say 'collective' marriage was practised, between groups of brothers and sisters. In such a presumably matrilocal society, children knew their mothers, not their fathers.[81] And while the rulers were males, the women, especially those of the aristocracy, enjoyed a fair degree of independence.

In the Book of Rites, there are references to exogamy as being preferable to endogamy, usually as a means to assure progeny, but also to make political alliances with strangers. It appears now that exogamy became established only in Chou times, together with the institutionalisation of the patriarchal system of lineages known as the *tsung-fa / zongfa* which served to maintain the ancestral cult, with its complex ritual regulations. Tradition has always attributed this work to the Duke of Chou, younger brother to King Wen, and regent for his son and heir, King Ch'eng.

The needs of the ancestral cult, as perceived by the Chou ruling class, led to the strengthening of patriarchal power, with the king serving as the ultimate patriarch, the *pater familias* of a large, growing state, where society was governed by ritual law, substituting patrilocal for matrilocal customs that had been prevalent earlier under Shang times, introducing the use of patronyms and subordinating

---

[80] *Shih-chi*, 126:271–72.
[81] On these and related subjects, I wish to acknowledge discussions with Chow Kai-wing of the University of Illinois, and also with Mark Edward Lewis of Cambridge University.

the ministers to their lords, the wives to their husbands, the sons to their fathers, and the younger siblings to their elders. This system rationalised the application of the ancestral cult to private and public life. It also effectively lowered the position of women, which had been much higher earlier, as it also rendered the kinship group and the patriarchal state all powerful *vis-à-vis* the individual.

Among other things, the patrilocal system assumed that wives remained 'outsiders', with different surnames than the families of their husbands, and possibly having dual loyalties. Witness the example of the Duchess of Ch'in, who asserted readiness to immolate herself and her children, in order to prevent the death of her half-brother, Duke Hui of Chin, also her husband's captive. Ritual law therefore decreed the women's subjugation to the members of the patriarchal family, be these their own fathers before marriage, their husbands after marriage, or their sons in widowhood.

The early Chou kings created institutions that made an impact on all of Chinese history and culture. Ostensibly to strengthen the ancestral cult, a feudal system called *feng-chien / fengjian* installed as feudal lords kinsmen whose territories encircled protectively that of the royal domain.[82] Even the Shang descendants were given a distant fief, that of Sung, where they could continue the veneration of their ancestors. The principle of hereditary succession to the royal throne was firmly established, and strengthened the institution of kingship, and with it, the patriarchal state.

As the Chou power continued to expand, the feudal system awarded various domains to the ruler's kin, whether these be his younger sons and brothers, of the same patronym, or those who were his chief allies, with whom his clan intermarried, who would therefore have different patronyms.

Such was the great age of feudalism. The political and administrative order was integrated with ritual order, as carefully recorded genealogies gave detailed instructions regarding sacrificial ranking as well as proper music. The lords had their vassals or retainers, and the peasants were tied to the land they worked, having to answer the calls of conscription and forced labour. Such was also the grand age of patriarchy, as aristocratic women lost the relatively higher status and greater freedom they had enjoyed in the Shang times. And even

---

[82] The term *feng* refers to enfeoffing, and the term *chien* to establishing. See Derk Bodde, 'Feudalism in China', in Charles Le Blanc and Dorothy Borei (eds), *Essays on Chinese Civilization* (Princeton University Press, 1981), pp. 85–108.

though the feudal order was not to last forever, many of the Chou
social institutions remained models for later times.

The ritual order remained the pivot of the patriarchal feudalism
which supported kingship and kinship during the eight centuries of
the Chou dynasty, and even long after. The term for ritual (li^a) came
to include all social, habitual practices, partaking even of the nature
of law, as a means of training in virtue and of avoiding evil. Ritual
governed the behaviour of the gentlemen, those of noble birth who
knew right from wrong, while penal laws governed the commoners,
those who were presumed ignorant of moral norms and could not
govern themselves. It is significant that the Confucian classical
corpus includes a group of ritual texts, which set forth the ancient
ritual system and its significance for life. These explain to us how an
ideal bureaucracy should function, as well as what a man or woman
of birth should do at every moment and during every crisis of life,
depending on his or her position in family and society. Interestingly,
many chapters deal with ritual regulations and rubrics regarding
mourning and funerals.

The emergence of Chinese humanism also took place during
those centuries. A procession of great minds of the sixth century BCE
and afterwards, making up the golden age of Chinese philosophy,
further contributed to the rationalist atmosphere of philosophical
reflection. They focused upon the place of the human in the
universe, the need of finding social order and harmony, as well as the
role of Heaven as the guardian of all. While these had different ideas
on many points regarding religion and morality, their common
impact was to strengthen the sense of human autonomy and
rationality, associating human destiny, fortunes and misfortunes with
the activities of human beings themselves rather than with the
authority of the ghosts and spirits. Consequently, the system of
religious orthodoxy, in belief as well as in ritual order, would not be
discarded, although its importance was relativised.[83] On the other
hand, the individual was subordinated to the extended kinship
system, and this, in turn, hampered the control of personal destiny.
With a few exceptions in pre-modern times, individuals have usually

---

[83] Ikeda, *Chūgoku kodai shūkyōshi*, pp. 929–44.

accepted their destiny within such a network of human relationships, which offered support when needed, but also restrained the individual's exercise of personal choice in many matters relating to his or her own life, and his and her own social role. In fact, the kinship system became a factor that restrained a ruler's arbitrary exercise of authority, and sometimes functioned as an ultimate control over state power itself. In that context, remarkable women living close to the centre of power were able sometimes to rule indirectly, with the connivance of their less competent male mates or juvenile sons, as empresses or empress dowagers.

Most probably, not all the historic kings had the special gift of communicating with the divine, but they presented themselves as descendants from ancestors with such shamanic and ecstatic powers: the ability to hear the voice of the gods and to act as their mouthpiece. In this charismatic role inherited with their office, the later kings continued to serve as the chief priest or Pontifex Maximus, jealously guarding their ritual roles, as kingship itself took on increasingly secular roles.

CHAPTER 2

Son of Heaven: kingship as cosmic paradigm

INTRODUCTION

Let us go back to the etymological origins of the word for 'king'. The Chinese character *wang*[b] (king, ruler, or prince) is found frequently on ancient oracle bones. The graph is sometimes supposed to represent a fire in the earth, other times an axe, but in any case designates without doubt the political ruler and his royal ancestors. The French scholar Léon Vandermeersch sees *wang* in relation to *shih*[b] / *shi* (officer, written with one vertical line going through a longer horizontal line to reach a shorter one), a term originally denoting 'male', and explains it as the *virile 'wang'*, father of the ethnic group, heir of the founder–ancestor's power. Thus kingship is placed in a familial and patriarchal context.[1]

The definitive character for this word is written with three horizontal lines, joined in the middle by a vertical line. The philosopher Tung Chung-shu (179–104 BCE) analysed this configuration by asserting that the three horizontal lines represent the heavenly order, the human order, and the earthly order, joined together by the vertical line representing the institution of kingship, which mediates among the three orders. This interpretation is reiterated in Hsü Shen's lexicon. Besides, the ancient rulers often referred to themselves as the 'one man' or the 'solitary one'. This highlights loneliness in the exercise of power and responsibility. It also serves to reinforce the notion of the king as collective man, as mediator between Heaven and Earth. So the king is the supreme mediator between Heaven and Earth. He is indeed the 'one man',

---

[1] See Léon Vandermeersch, *Wangdao*, vol. 2, pp. 13–18; Itō Michiharu, *Chūgoku kodai ōchō no keisei* (The structural characteristics of kingship in ancient China) (Tokyo: Sobunsha, 1975), especially pp. 128–33.

the 'cosmic man', who represents all human beings on earth in the presence of a superior Heaven.[2]

THE CENTRALITY OF KINGSHIP

The sacral character of kingship is better understood when we examine the various titles of kingship, of which the most basic has been *wang*. Traditionally, the ruler has also been called *T'ien-tzu / Tianzi* (literally, 'Child of Heaven', or 'Son of Heaven'), a title going back to Chou times.[3] Philosophically, this is justified by the doctrine of the Mandate of Heaven (*T'ien-ming / Tianming*), according to which the ruler possesses the mandate to rule, given to his dynastic founder, which is, however, maintained only by good government. And the title is more than just symbolic. It signifies a special relationship between the ruler and the supreme deity called Heaven, represented by the celestial firmament.

Recent Chinese scholarship has pointed out another interpretation for the word *t'ien* or heaven. It emphasises the closeness between this word, and the word *jen*[a] / *ren* for human being. It suggests that *t'ien* refers especially to the tip of the human head, which is pronounced *tien / dian*. But even in this case, the reference is to the highest, and, by extension, to the heavens, and even to the deity above who rules the heavens, the Shang people's Lord-on-High, which the Chou people called Heaven.[4]

In this connection, the term 'Son of Heaven' is said also to refer to the eldest son of the ruler, he who, by Chou times, was designated as royal successor. And, by association, the ruler's successor has also been regarded as standing in special relationship to Heaven, for a long time considered as a deified ancestor.

There is also another title, the combined term, *huang-ti / huangdi*, usually translated as emperor. Tradition has called those sage rulers who are legendary figures 'emperors' (either *huang* or *ti*[c]) and the

---

[2] Li Hsiao-ting (ed), *Chia-ku wen-tzu chi-shih*, vol. 1, pp. 113–27; Tung Chung-shu, *Ch'un-ch'iu fan-lu*, 11:5a; *Shuo-wen*, 1A:12b.

[2] This is attested to in the classical texts, such as *Shih-ching*, and the *Shu-ching*; see James Legge, *Chinese Classics*, vol. 4, pt 1, bk 1, ode 8; vol. 3, The Books of Shang, 'The Charge to Yüeh', bk 8, pt 1:1; p. 248; The Books of Chow, 'The Great Plan', bk 4:16; p. 333; and in many bronze inscriptions. Consult Hsü Chin-hsiung, *Ku-wen hsieh-sheng tzu-ken* (The philological origins of the phonetic components in Ancient Script (Taipei: Commercial, 1995).

[4] Liu Xiang (Hsiang), *Chung-kuo ch'uan-t'ung chia-chih kuan-nien ch'uan-shih hsüeh* (A philological inquiry into the traditional Chinese understanding of values) (Taipei: Kuikuan Publishing, 1993), pp. 18–19.

ancient rulers of historical times 'kings' (*wang*). However, in the third century BCE, the despotic Ch'in ruler, who unified the country by military might, called himself 'First Emperor' (*Shih-huang-ti / Shi-huangdi*). In so doing, he signified his wish that his dynasty would last forever, and he also appropriated to himself the two titles formerly given only to legendary sage rulers.[5]

To call oneself *huang-ti* is to call oneself 'king of kings and lord of lords', to use a Biblical expression that came from Persian usage. Historically, it usually happened when a ruler conquered more territories, and governed over a heterogeneous population. Examples from more recent history include Queen Victoria, who was crowned Queen of England and Empress of India. The appropriation of the title *huang-ti* by the First Emperor of China has been regarded as an act of *hubris*. And if later rulers continued to use it, their act was sometimes justified in the light of their extended rule over a much larger country, and with greater powers, in comparison with the Shang or Chou kings who were mere suzerains over a federation of feudal lords.

The title 'emperor' suggests exaltation as well as imperialism. The title 'king' (*wang*) has moral advantages. In political ethics, it was always preferred, as it kept the connotation of an ideal ruler, which the title 'emperor' (*huang-ti*) never acquired, or, more correctly, quickly lost. Even long after Confucius, philosophers spoke of the 'kingly way' (*wang-tao / wangdao*), that is, benevolent government, as the *ideal* way, in opposition to the 'despotic way' or *pa-tao / badao*, that is, rule by might.

Historically, there were instances of rulers who preferred the title 'king' to that of 'emperor'. During a period of political disunity, when, in the mid-sixth century, the ethnic Hsien-pei / Xianbei Yü-wen family assumed the throne in northern China, the new ruler called himself 'heavenly king' (*t'ien-wang / tianwang*). It was an admission of political weakness of his monarchical authority, the product of a tribal state. It was also a deliberate reminder of the golden age of the Chou dynasty, when the Son of Heaven was also styled King. In fact, the new dynasty used the name Chou in

---

[5] In the title *huang-ti*, both words, *huang* and *ti*[c], originally designated 'god', either as Lord-on-High (*Shang-ti / Shangdi*) or as Sovereign Heaven, *Huang-t'ien / Huangtian*. The word *huang* has also stood for an ancestral spirit of the ruling house. But even this secondary designation has been regarded as an act of usurpation on the part of the ruler, in an effort to divinise his forebears.

conscious imitation of the earlier royal house. Thus the new
sovereign announced that he preferred the older and idealised
political system, based on the joint sharing of authority by the Son of
Heaven and other princes. This was a short-lived measure, as the
monarch's title reverted, in 559, to the old *huang-ti*.[6] But the title was
also to be the one assumed by the nineteenth-century Hung Hsiu-
ch'üan, the Christian rebel against Manchu power, after his forces
took Nanking and made it the capital of their Peaceful Heavenly
Kingdom.

The meaning of another word, *sheng* (sage, sageliness), is often
used as an attribute of the sovereign. The ancient rulers of China
were known as sage-kings or sage emperors. Even much later, until
the last (Manchu) dynasty, the emperor was often addressed as His
Sagely Majesty (*Sheng-shang*; literally, the sage above). This is
evidence of the institutionalisation of the royal charisma, since no
historical sovereign has been considered a real sage. It calls to mind
the sage-kings of old, mythical figures like the Yellow Emperor, Yao
and Shun, venerated as sages by philosophers like Confucius, Mo-
tzu and Mencius, all of whom looked backward to a Golden Age of
the past when the people enjoyed peace and prosperity under the
government of ideal rulers assisted by wise ministers.

An increasingly extravagant ritual surrounding the person of the
ruler developed debasing all those who approached him with the
demand of numerous prostrations, more than made before an image
of a divinity in a temple. And indeed, the secular ruler regarded it as
his right *to declare as divine* those deceased subjects or ministers who
had served well the public or himself, while awaiting for his own
posthumous elevation to the status of an imperial ancestor by his
heir. Such was the pomp for the court on earth, which sought to
imitate what it considered to be heavenly splendour.

Kingship and divine descent

Oracle and bronze inscriptions as well as classical texts offer
abundant evidence that the ancient kings themselves officiated at
divination, and performed prayers, sacrifices and rain-dances,
dressed in appropriate robes according to the occasions. As the Book

---

[6] Li Yen-shou, *Pei-shih* (History of the Northern Dynasties), K'ai-ming ed., ch. 9, pp. 32–4.
Actually, the name Yü-wen apparently meant 'heavenly king' in their language.

of Rites states: 'The ancient kings made use of the yarrow stalks and the tortoise shell; arranged their sacrifices; buried their offerings of silk; recited their words of supplication and benediction; and made their statutes and measures.'[7]

In ancient China, the king was the 'One Man' of the classical texts, the ultimate mediator between the divine and the human. At all times, he was the paradigmatic priest and shaman as well as the political ruler and military leader. And he was responsible for all that happened in nature and society. True, the feudal lords officiated at many rituals each in his own realm, and the *pater familias* officiated at family rituals, each in his own household. But all did so to the extent that they exercised in their own domains, those that the king exercised for all under heaven.[8]

The ancient kings also claimed some kind of divine descent, whether we are to understand it totemically or otherwise. The Hsia dynasty goes back to the sage-hero Yü, the famed flood-controller, who appears in some accounts to have been born out of his father's body. Yü's wife, however, ran away, when her husband once allegedly turned himself into a bear (a shamanic, and even totemic suggestion). When he pursued her, she turned into a rock, which burst and gave birth to Ch'i, who later succeeded to the throne.[9]

The Shang dynasty had for its principal high ancestor the mythical Hsieh, whose mother, it is said, became pregnant after devouring a dark bird or swallow's egg. There is reference to such in the Book of Songs.[10] The Chou dynasty goes back to Chi, the 'Lord Millet', whose mother had allegedly trodden on the Lord *Ti*[c]'s footprint.[11] He himself would prove to be a good farmer and ruler, and even more importantly, the founder of sacrifices:

> The Lord Millet founded the sacrifices,
> And without flaw or blemish
> They have gone on till now.[12]

---

[7] *Li-chi Cheng-chu*, ch. 7, sect. 9:9a; Eng. trans. from Legge, *Li Ki, Sacred Books*, vol. 27, p. 385. Consult David N. Keightley, 'Shang divination and metaphysics', *Philosophy East and West* 38 (1988), 367–97.

[8] Consult Shima Kunio, *Inkyo bokuji kenkyū* (A study of the oracle letters rescued from the ruins of Yin's capital) (Tokyo: Kyūko shōin, 1958), p. 201; Chang, *Art, Myth and Ritual*, pp. 54–5.

[9] See David Hawkes, trans., *Ch'u Tz'u: The Songs of the South* (London: Oxford University Press, 1959), p. 48, n. 4; p. 50, n. 2.

[10] *Mao-shih cheng-yi* (The correct meaning of the Book of Songs with Mao Heng's commentary), SPPY ed., 20 / 3:9a; Eng. trans. adapted from Arthur Waley, *The Book of Songs* (New York: Grove Press, 1960), p. 275. See also David Hawkes, *Ch'u Tz'u*, p. 30, n. 1.

[11] Akatsuka, *Chūgoku kodai*, pp. 265–320; *Mao-shih cheng-yi* 17 / 1, 6a–b.   [12] Ibid.

Divine descent symbolises a direct access to the divine and the supernatural, and the kings of antiquity were already called Sons of Heaven, even if the rulers of historical China, unlike the emperors of Japan, never claimed for themselves any personal divinity. This is like the contrast between Mesopotamian and Egyptian concepts of kingship. According to Henri Frankfort, whereas in Egypt the king was a god descended among men, the Babylonian king was not a god but a human being charged with maintaining harmonious relations between society and the supernatural powers.[13]

Rituals as the legitimation of power

The English word 'power' is derived from the Latin *potere*, that is, to be able. Its French equivalent is *pouvoir*, also the verb 'to be able'. Power often comes from might. But might also wants to make itself *right*. And so the function of ritual is often to legitimise power, giving it an aura of *authority*, a word that is derived from the Latin *auctoritas*, pointing to the creator, maker, or producer, and by analogy, to the writer of a book.

The Chinese word for ritual (*li*[a]) is related etymologically to the words 'worship' and 'sacrificial vessel', with a definite religious overtone.[14] The ancestral cult was surrounded with ritual; so was the worship offered to Heaven as Supreme Lord. As a symbolic activity, ritual is a very important mode of communication everywhere. It reflects, expresses, and affirms the peculiar structural arrangements of a society. It confers legitimacy upon persons and institutions. It dramatises its content and the roles of participants, being 'staged' for the maximisation of the effects, to better capture the attention of the audience and intensify their commitments.[15]

The enthronement ceremony in East Asia (Chinese: *chi-wei* / *jiwei* or *teng-chi* / *dengji*) corresponds to the coronation of a king or queen in the West. The ritual of enthronement, like that of coronation, is always a renewal of the institution of kingship itself, as it is also a reenactment of the mythical first king's accession to the throne. It assures continuity with a declaration that resembles a confession of faith in reincarnation (whether or not the belief was formally articulated), in this case, of the spirit of the deceased ruler entering

---

[13] Henri Frankfort, *Kingship and the Gods* (University of Chicago Press, 1948), Introduction.
[14] Li Hsiao-ting, *Chia-ku-wen-tzu chi-shih*, vol. 1, p. 49.
[15] Howard J. Wechsler, *Offerings*, pp. 21–2.

into that of his successor. We recall here that in England, the announcement is usually made: 'The King is dead. Long live the King!' There is affirmation of order and continuity. And as Mircea Eliade observes, 'a new reign has been regarded as a regeneration of the history of the people or even of universal history. With each new sovereign, insignificant as he might be, a "new era" began.'[16]

THE RITUAL OF ENTHRONEMENT

Formerly in the time of the sage-kings of the three dynasties of Hsia, Shang and Chou, when they first founded their kingdoms and established their capitals, they had to select a site for the principal altar of the kingdom, where they erected the ancestral temple, and also choose luxuriant trees as a sacred grove for the earth altar.[17]

In the Chinese context, it is surprising that the ritual texts, which give so much detail for funerals and mournings, say nothing of the royal enthronement. The quotation from *Mo-tzu* speaks of making a sacred grove, the closest suggestion we have to an enthronement. The oracle and bronze inscriptions are all silent.[18]

Japan: enthronement and the Daijōsai

A recent example of the ritualisation of royal charisma took place in Japan, at Akihito's accession to the throne, and was widely reported in the Western press. On 12 November 1990, the world witnessed the event of the installation of a new emperor in Japan, as the son of Hirohito, known as Emperor Showa, started his reign, following upon the six decades which had been associated with his father's. The ceremony took place in the throne room of the main hall of the imperial palace, as 2,500 local and foreign dignitaries observed from their places in the courtyard. Hirohito had died in January 1989, and the heir had taken office immediately, but waited until formal mourning was over before celebrating his accession. When the time came, the fifty-six-year-old Akihito ascended the steps of an elaborate six-metre-high, eight-sided-canopied, lacquer throne, decorated with golden birds and filigree, to become the 125th emperor of Japan, in an institution traced back to 660 BCE. The ceremony was

---

[16] Eliade, *Cosmos and History*, p. 80.
[17] *Mo-tzu*, ch. 8; 'Explaining Ghosts,' Sect. 3, p. 5b.
[18] See D. H. Smith, 'Divine Kingship in Ancient China', *Numen* 4 (1957), 180.

accompanied by drums and gong, and courtiers bearing flags and swords.

In contradistinction to comparable Western ritual, the accession ceremony featured no crown for the new sovereign, and no anointing with oil. Instead, the world witnessed a simple proclamation, in which the new emperor pledged to observe the Constitution of Japan and discharge his duties as symbol of the state and of the unity of the people. The proclamation also stated that this was to be done in the same spirit as that of his father, Emperor Showa, who, throughout his long reign, 'shared the joys and sorrows of the people at all times'. This brief, secular ritual lasted about twenty minutes.

But the Japanese enthronement ceremony traditionally has two parts. The first part, as described above, is basically secular, resembling its Chinese counterpart, at which the heir also receives his regalia: in this case, the mirror, the sword, and the jewels. The problem comes with the second part of the ceremony, performed ten days later, called the *Daijōsai*. Traditionally a religious ritual, this ceremony became a subject of controversy in 1990 on account of the post-war constitutional separation of religion and the state, devised after the former emperor had announced himself to be a mere human, when Japan surrendered to the Allies in 1945.

The Daijōsai has been described as 'the Harvest Festival celebrated by the Emperor of Japan to seal his accession'.[19] It is also the occasion on which the new emperor, following his enthronement, performs for the first time the ceremonial offering of newly harvested grain to Amaterasu Ōmikami and the other gods. Literally, the terms mean 'Great Food Tasting', and can be traced back to the Chinese Book of Rites as an autumnal festival.[20] There is, however, no Chinese tradition linking this with the royal or imperial accession ceremony, as there is in Japan, where it goes back, with interruptions, to the seventh century. Performed in Kyoto, November, 1928, when Emperor Hirohito came to the throne, it was repeated in Tokyo, November, 1990, when his son was enthroned. Each time, a wooden palisade is put up, within which are constructed many buildings of rough timber and thatch, to be used only for that purpose, and then taken down again.

In ancient Japan the body of the emperor, the Son of Heaven, was

---

[19] Ellwood, *The Feast of Kingship*, p. 1.
[20] *Li-chi Cheng-chu*, ch. 9, sect. 14, 20a, where it is described as a 'sacrifice by the Son of Heaven'.

thought to be the 'receptacle of the spirit'. He was, so to speak, a 'lord who had a sacred body'. It is claimed that in the past, the Daijōsai was the occasion at which the heir to the throne covers himself with a futon and fasts, during which time the imperial spirit enters his body, and makes him the Son of Heaven. What takes place is like 'spirit possession', a fundamental condition for the person designated for the throne to become worthy of reigning.[21]

The enthronement ceremony in Chinese antiquity

The *locus classicus* for the enthronement ceremony is the Book of History. We find here an account of the transfer of power from the legendary emperor Yao to his successor, the equally legendary Shun. Allegedly, this took place on the first day of the year, before the tablet of Yao's first ancestor. After that, Shun assumed his royal duties. He checked the movements of the astral bodies; he performed the *lei* sacrifice to the Lord-on-High; he worshipped six other ancestral tablets in the shrine, together with the gods of mountains and rivers.[22] Then, in the second month of the same year, Shun made a tour of inspection of the realm, and paid a visit to Mount T'ai, where he also made a burnt offering to Heaven, and sacrificed from afar to the various mountains and rivers.[23]

We find here all the important duties connected to kingship, and assumed by the ruler usually right after accession: the attention to astronomy and / or astrology; the sacrifice to the Lord-on-High, to ancestral and other spirits; the tour of his realm or domain; and the burnt offering at Mount T'ai, presumably what would later develop into the *feng* and *shan* sacrifices. And these duties are all ritual, at least in orientation, and also, otherwise, in their own character.

In the same Book of History, there are two other relevant chapters, entitled 'Ku-ming' (Testamentary Charge) and 'K'ang-wang chih kao' (The Announcement of King K'ang), which together offer an account of the enthronement of an early Chou king. We find first the dying King Ch'eng, laying a testamentary charge on his brother, the grand protector, and other ministers, naming his son as successor and ordering them to assist him in coping with the challenges to come. His words are:

---

[21] Carmen Blacker, 'The *Shinza* in the *Daijōsai*: Throne, Bed or Incubation Couch?' *Japanese Journal of Religious Studies* 17 (1990), 179–90.
[22] Legge, *Chinese Classics*, vol. 3, pt 2, bk 1, pp. 32–5. [23] *Shih-chi*, K'ai-ming ed., 1:5b–c.

Coming after [Kings Wen and Wu], I, the foolish one, received with reverence the majestic decree of Heaven, and continued to keep the great instructions of Wen and Wu, without daring to go against these.
Now Heaven has laid affliction on me . . . Do you take clear note of my words, and use these to keep watch with reverence over my eldest son Chao and assist him in the difficulties of his position. Be kind to those who are distant and help those who are near. Encourage and keep peace between the states, great and small.[24]

Then, immediately following the king's death (1078 BCE), the heir was escorted to an apartment near the palace where the corpse was placed, so that he might serve as the principal mourner. Two days after the death, the grand protector ordered that a record be made of the deceased king's testamentary charge (*ts'e-tu* / *cedu*). Five kinds of jade and other important items were placed on display. The red knife, the great instructions, the great mace, the circular and pointed maces were placed toward the west. The large jade, those from the Eastern peoples, the heavenly sphere, and the River Chart were placed in a side chamber on the east. The dancing costumes from Yin, the large tortoise shell, and the large drum were placed in the western chamber. The great spear, the bow of Ho, and the bamboo arrows of Ts'ui, were in the eastern chamber.[25]

It is difficult to identify each and all of these objects on display. Presumably, the royal sceptres were included among the maces. The heavenly sphere had something to do with the movement of the stars; the river chart would continue to figure prominently in association with kingship. The tortoise shell could be prized for itself, and reminds one of divination ritual. The dancing costumes and the large drum could very well have shamanic associations.

And, seven days after the death, while the deceased lay in a coffin, the heir entered the hall, wearing a hempen cap and a skirt adorned with emblems of royal authority. There he found the high officials, all wearing hempen caps and red skirts, especially the grand protector bearing the great mace, and the grand supervisor of ritual bearing the cup and the mace cover. The feudal lords were also present. In the presence of the corpse, the grand historian (*t'ai-shih* / *taishi*) carried the testamentary charge and begged the heir to accept, saying:

[24] Legge, *Chinese Classics*, vol. 3, pt 5, bk 22, p. 548.
[25] Ibid, pp. 554–5. The River Chart is usually associated with the Book of Lo.

Our great deceased lord, leaning on the jade bench, announced his final charge, ordering you to continue to observe [the ancestors'] instructions, and rule over the Chou domain, complying with the great laws, and securing the harmony of all under heaven, in response to the bright instructions of [Kings] Wen and Wu.[26]

The heir, as a rule, first declared his unworthiness, then took over the cup and its cover from the supervisor of ritual. Advancing three times with a cup of wine, he offered sacrificial libations to the spirit of the deceased king, his father, signifying his acceptance of the charge. At that point the supervisor of ritual would announce: 'It has been accepted'.[27]

Thus he became a king (*wang*), the Son of Heaven, as the grand protector received from him the cup, descended the steps, and washed his hands, preparing to make a sacrificial offering in response, but only after having made obeisance to the new ruler. The new king responded ceremonially to this act. After this, the grand protector made his own sacrificial offering, before the ritual came to a close, and the feudal lords all left the temple gate.[28] Immediately afterwards, the new king conducted an audience for all his officials and the feudal lords, receiving their obeisance as well as gifts.[29]

In later ages, this classical model was usually followed, with small deviations. I am referring here to the two aspects of accession: the passing of the Mandate (*ts'e-ming* / *ceming*) through the announcement of the will of the deceased king (*chao* / *zhao*) and the acceptance of the regalia surrounding kingship. The situation was usually more complex when one dynasty succeeded another, whether after conquest or *coup d'état*. In that case, effort was often made to have the departing ruler of the previous dynasty issue announcements that praise the virtues and accomplishments of his usurper-successor. From the time of the latter Han dynasty on through the T'ang, the accession ceremony assumed two stages: that of the new ruler as Son of Heaven, and that of him as Emperor. The first stage entails reading from the 'Ku-ming' chapter of the Book of History; the second stage entails the reading of the deceased ruler's will, followed by the imparting of the imperial seal.[30]

---

[26] Ibid, pp. 558–9.
[27] The meaning of this is ambiguous, as it could refer to the spirits receiving the sacrifice, or to the young heir being told to partake of the wine himself. Consult Ibid, pp. 559–60.
[28] Ibid, pt 5, bk 22, p. 560.   [29] Ibid, bk 23, pp. 562–8.
[30] Fan Yeh, *Hou-Han shu* (History of the Latter Han Dynasty), K'ai-ming ed., 'On Rituals', pt 3, ch. 16, p. 44c–d; Wechsler, *Offerings*, pp. 84–6.

The title of Son of Heaven retains a strongly religious dimension even if the connotation became with time increasingly moral and ethical, bound up with the theory of the Mandate of Heaven and the importance of the worthiness of its bearer. It involves the religious responsibilities of offering sacrifices to spirits and deities, and the accession ceremony was not complete without the performance of certain sacrificial rituals on the part of the new king. And the ceremonial objects on display serving as royal regalia included items with presumably shamanic character. But the title Emperor refers more to secular duties and responsibilities.

Most enthronement ceremonies involve the transfer of regalia symbolising the mandate of government, and the continuity of political power. Still, these regalia, whatever they include, serve also in a magical way to protect their possessors and assure the safety of the state. And they legitimise political succession. In ancient China, during Shang and early Chou times, these were especially the mysterious Nine Cauldrons (*chiu-ting / jiuding*), huge bronze cast vessels representing not only the skills that went into their making, but also the power over both ritual and bronze-making. Legend says these were made by the sage King Yü and his son and heir Ch'i, founders of the Hsia dynasty, and became the symbol of royal legitimacy. They were supposed to have on them the maps of the Nine Provinces (*chiu-chou / jiuzhou*) that made up the country of that time. Allegedly, after conquering the Shang, King Wu of Chou carried away the Nine Cauldrons, which were later lost, perhaps while the capital was moved from the west to the east.

The ritual use of the Nine Cauldrons

An early reference to the Nine Cauldrons is in the Annals of Tso (Tso-chuan). In the year 606 BCE, the ruler of Ch'u advanced his troops to the border of the Chou royal domain, and asked about the cauldrons: whether they were large or small, light or heavy. He was obviously showing a political interest in them. He was told by a Chou royal prince that these had passed from the Hsia dynasty to the Shang and then to the Chou:

The bright virtue bestowed by Heaven has its limit and end. When King Ch'eng of the Chou dynasty fixed the cauldrons in place at his capital at Chia-ju [near Loyang], he divined by the tortoiseshell to determine the number of generations of the dynasty and was given the answer 'thirty', and he divined to determine the number of years and was told 'seven hundred'. This was mandated by Heaven . . . [T]he Mandate of Heaven is not yet ready to be transferred to another dynasty. It is too soon to ask if the cauldrons are heavy or light![31]

The Confucian moral tone is unmistakable in this text, with the royal prince urging the ruler of Ch'u to respect the Mandate of Heaven and forget about the material weight of the cauldrons, a question which might have implied a violent takeover. For us here, however, the interesting reference is to divination ritual, which was allegedly practised for a prediction of dynastic length. Obviously also, the cauldrons themselves were ritual objects conferring political legitimacy.

The Cauldrons (*ting*[a]) are also mentioned in *Mo-tzu*, who discussed them in a religious and sacrificial context:

In ancient times, King [Ch'i] of Hsia commissioned Fei Lien to dig minerals in mountains and rivers and cast *tings* at K'un-wu. He ordered . . . the tortoise of Mo-jo to be invoked. The tortoise said: 'let the *tings*, when completed, be four-legged squares. Let them be able to cook automatically, without fire, to hide themselves without being lifted, and to move themselves without being carried, so that they may be used for the sacrifice at the old site of K'un-wu. May our offering be accepted!' . . . Then the oracle was interpreted as saying: 'I have accepted the offering . . . When the nine *tings* have been completed, they shall be given over to three states. When the King of Hsia loses them the people of Yin will possess them; when the people of Yin lose them the people of Chou will possess them.'[32]

It is difficult to understand how the *ting*[a] might cook without fire, and move without being carried. However, the important points here are that (1) they were used for sacrificial ritual; (2) they were to be passed from one generation to another, and from one royal house to another during the Three Dynasties, serving thereby as symbols of authority. And K. C. Chang has this to say about these cauldrons:

---

[31] Legge, *Chinese Classics*, vol. 5, Bk 2, Duke Hwan, Year 2, p. 38. But the English translation here is from Watson, trans. *The Tso Chuan*, p. 82. Consult also Chang, *Art, Myth and Ritual*, pp. 95–6.

[32] *Mo-tzu*, ch. 11, Sect. 46, 'Ken-chu', 8b–9a. This text offers some explanations from various commentaries offering alternative wordings in some cases. The English translation is adapted from Y. P. Mei, *The Ethical and Political Works of Motse* (London: Probsthain, 1929), pp. 212–13.

The *chiu ting* stories are quite straightforward and suggest strongly that the possession of such sacred bronze vessels . . . served to legitimize the king's rule. These vessels were clear and powerful symbols: they were symbols of wealth because they *were* wealth and possessed the aura of wealth; they were symbols of the all-important ritual that gave their owners access to ancestors; and they were symbols of the control of metal, which meant control of exclusive access to ancestors and to political authority.[33]

In the Han and later ages, the regalia became six imperial seals of white jade, each little more than an inch square, topped by a handle with coiling dragons and tigers. Each had a different engraved text, beginning with the terms Son of Heaven or Emperor. By applying such to purple clay, the former were used in matters relating to foreign affairs, and the latter in matters relating to domestic affairs. There was also the great 'seal of the state' (*ch'uan-kuo hsi / chuanguo xi*), which served only as an emblem of power.[34]

KINGSHIP AS COSMIC PARADIGM

Heaven is so high and the stars are so distant. If we have investigated their phenomena, we may, while sitting at the same place, go back to the solstice of a thousand years ago. (Mencius 4B:26)[35]

We have spoken of the signification of the word *wang*, how it represents kingship as an institution that mediates between Heaven and Earth. In the Institutes of Chou, the king's role is emphasised in the following words: 'The king alone constitutes the kingdom. He determines the four corners and fixes the principal position. He plans the capital and the countryside. He creates the ministries and separates their functions, thus offering norms for the people.'[36]

To determine the four corners and fix the principal position was no simple task. The Chinese king was always concerned with the alignment of his realm with the stars and constellations. Thus the institution of kingship in China has always been bound up with what we may call sacral astronomy and sacral geography.

---

[33] Chang, *Art, Myth and Ritual*, pp. 97–101. Chang mentions that 'nine' means 'many'.

[34] Wechsler, *Offerings*, pp. 87–8. The T'ang records offer evidence of a very similar enthronement ritual for Emperor Chung-tsung (705), which became regularised with Emperor Su-tsung and afterwards. See Sung Shou, *et al.*, comp., *T'ang Ta-chao-ling chi* (The important decrees of T'ang), Ming edition (Taipei: Ting-wen, 1972), ch. 2, pp. 6–7.

[35] Eng. trans. adapted from Legge, *Chinese Classics*, vol. 2, pp. 331–2.

[36] *Chou-li Cheng-chu*, 1:1a; 18:1a, in Biot, *Tcheou li*, vol. 1, pp. 1–2, 396–7. English translation is my own.

The calendar and sacral astronomy

Indeed, as Son of Heaven, the ruler considers it one of his most important tasks to understand the intentions and feelings of Heaven above, in order to be able to act upon such an understanding. And 'Heaven', as we said, refers not merely to the supreme Lord-on-High, but also the firmament, which is his visible realm – to use Mircea Eliade's term, his 'hierophany'. The belief was that all heavenly phenomena had earthly effects, and served as signs of Heaven's pleasure or displeasure regarding the government of men. For this reason, eclipses had to be foretold, comets had to be understood. From the earliest times, astronomy became an officially supported science, protecting kingship and the monarchy. Among the oracle bone inscriptions, for example, we have the world's oldest record of the discovery of a new star (*nova*), around 1300 BCE.[37] The Chinese especially focused their interest on the circumpolar stars. Echoing an ancient belief that the celestial pole corresponded to the ruler on earth, around whom the court, and indeed, the world, revolved, the polar star – as the ancients observed it – was also called the Emperor star, and the star in the Little Dipper nearest the pole was named Crown Prince, the next in line there being the Son of the Imperial Concubine, and only after that the Empress.[38] Joseph Needham notes that according to Chinese observation, the pole star was not historically in the same position. Nor was the Little Dipper seen as a constellation similar to that for Western observers. Star maps or charts were also drafted, the favourite being that of the Big Dipper, with its tail pointing to the polar star. It is sometimes represented simply by dots joined by lines, that held a special interest for later followers of the Taoist religion.

Besides, a new calendar had to be calculated and promulgated, each time there was a dynastic change, as a sign of the legitimation.[39] 'A King must have his Mandate to be King. As king, he must change and rectify the first month of the year, change the colour of his apparel, institute rituals and music, so that these are uniform all under Heaven.'[40] The calendar offers a dynamic ordering of the seasons, a balance of fluctuating, complementary, and resonant forces. It was issued from the south gate of the palace at the new

---

[37] Joseph Needham, *Science and Civilisation in China* (Cambridge University Press, 1959), vol. 3, p. 424.
[38] Ibid, p. 261.   [39] Eliade, *Cosmos and History*, p. 54.   [40] *Ch'un-ch'iu fan-lu*, 7:2b–3a.

year, as the ruler's palace is in the north facing south.[41] An ancient system of day counting did not actually depend on astronomical observation. It combined a series of ten 'Heavenly Stems' (*t'ien-kan / tiangan*) with another series of twelve 'Earthly Branches' (*ti-chih / dizhi*), and by so doing, made up a sexagenary cycle.[42] It was used later for the marking of hours, months and years as well, serving not only simple calendrical calculations, but also astrological conclusions. For example, this sexagenary cycle was considered to have influence over human destiny. Thus, the 'eight words' making up the hour, day, month and year of our births are alleged to be a repository of our fortunes and misfortunes.[43]

The capital and sacral geography

And as Heaven is sacred, so is the Earth, considered as parallel to Heaven, in a relation like that of a spouse. The two were regarded almost as mirror opposites, and virtually inseparable one from the other. In the Institutes of Chou, the official in charge of the stars 'marks the movements of the sun, moon and stars; contemplates the changes all under Heaven, distinguishing fortunes and misfortunes. [He] distributes territories of the nine provinces according to the terrains of the stars.'[44]

There has been a popular belief that the early Han capital city of Ch'ang-an was built according to the constellation map of the two Dippers. Although current scholarly evidence does not support this, the belief is interesting in itself, as well as is the practice of situating the imperial palace always under the polar star, permitting the ruler to 'face south'.[45]

We cannot ignore the mathematical foundations that astronomical, calendrical, and even geographical correlations require. And the Chinese possessed as well a Pythagorean love both for mathe-

---

[41] See also Stephan Feuchtwang, *The Imperial Metaphor: Popular Religion in China* (London and New York: Routledge, 1992), pp. 27–8; Peter Weber-Schäfer, *Oikumene und Imperium: Studien zur Ziviltheologie des chinesischen Kaiserreichs* (München: Paul List Verlag, 1968).

[42] The simple names of these stems and branches are among the most often seen on oracle bone inscriptions, being used mostly as a day count, although they also provided royal names of kings.

[43] Consult Needham, *Science and Civilisation*, vol. 2, pp. 351–9, 383–5.

[44] *Chou-li Cheng-chu* 26:9a. Consult the French trans. in Biot, *Tcheou li*, vol. 2, pp. 113–14.

[45] Paul Wheatley, *The Pivot of the Four Quarters: A Preliminary Enquiry into the Origins and Character of the Ancient Chinese City* (University of Chicago Press, 1971), p. 443. Besides, the Chinese star maps appear to have been different from those in the West.

matics and for what mathematics may represent in terms of human destiny, in the so-called science of numerology. We have the Book of Changes, with its trigrams and hexagrams of broken and unbroken lines, interpreted as a text founded on binary arithmetic and applied to the use of divination. We know the legend of the River Chart (*Ho-t'u / Hetu*), which was – according to one version – allegedly carried out of water by dragon horses at the time of the mythical Fu-hsi, and the Book of Lo, which was supposed to have been presented to the sage King Yü, borne up by sacred turtles emerging out of the river Lo.[46] Each was interpeted as having mathematical reference. Needham calls them 'magic squares'. They represented the wisdom that assists a ruler in governing, which is why possession of such is associated with kingship.[47]

Until our own days, China has also called itself the Middle Kingdom. The name, indeed, tells us two things: that for a long time, in the popular consciousness of the Chinese people, their country was central to the world as they knew it; and that, for just as long a time span, there were Chinese scholars who believed in a sacred cosmography that has China in its very middle, perhaps as one of the nine continents, with the other eight spread out across the waters in the eight cardinal directions. Another interpretation, even more common, was that the Middle Kingdom *was* the then-known civilised world, the *oikoumene*, also called Shen-chou or the Divine Continent, and that it was made up of nine Provinces.

In the Analects of Confucius, we find a sentence about an ancient ruler 'As a ruler. . . Shun had nothing to do, but to hold himself in a respectful position, facing south.'[48] The reference here is to the legendary sage and king, Shun, the successor to King Yao. The puzzle has been that 'he had nothing to do' (*wu-wei*), a statement with Taoist implications. We might argue here that *wu-wei* could refer to the ruler's practising yoga or meditation and achieving mystical consciousness in a practice that seems like 'doing nothing'. Nevertheless, on this subject, we must await a later chapter for further development. Mainly, we get the picture here of a sovereign doing nothing except sitting idle on the throne, as it is, 'facing south'.[49]

---

[46] The story is an old one, as mention of it appears in Analects 9:8 as well as in the Book of History ('Ku-ming', or 'The Testamentary Charge').

[47] Needham, *Science and Civilisation*, vol. 3, pp. 56–62.   [48] Analects 15:5.

[49] Consult Herrlee G. Creel, 'On the origin of *Wu-wei*', in Creel (ed.), *What is Taoism? and*

But this is where the key to what he does lies: in facing south. Superficially, this may seem irrelevant, as it merely indicates the position of the throne. But in fact, it says much more than that. After all, as ruler, the Chinese king or emperor is a 'cosmic man'. He has to assure the harmony between Heaven, Earth, and human beings. His throne and his palace face south for that reason, since they are positioned like the Polar Star, 'which does not move, and yet commands the homage of all the stars around it'.[50] By harmonising his life with nature, he can undertake the task of regulating the cycle of months and seasons for the benefit of his subjects, and protect them from droughts and floods. And one symbol of his character as cosmic man is this 'Bright Hall' (*ming-t'ang / mingtang*), an institution going back to time immemorial, which disappeared mostly with the Chou dynasty, in spite of occasional later efforts to reinstall it.

The Bright Hall was allegedly patterned on a grid, as provided by the Book of Lo (*Lo-shu*), with the nine rooms as the nine cells of the magic square.[51] It represents the conviction that a cosmic law governs the universe, and that man's prime duty is to live in accord with this law. In the Bright Hall, the king, among other things, moved from room to room according to the seasons and the calendar, rotating according to the law of the universe in his role as Son of Heaven. Another structure, and what might have been at times the most important part of the Bright Hall, appears to be the sacred tower (*ling-t'ai / lingtai*), frequently mentioned in the classical texts. We hear of one built by King Wen of Chou near his capital at Hao, close to today's Xi'an. Mencius (IA:3) quotes from the *Shih-ching* in a conversation with King Hui of Liang:[52]

> When he built the Sacred Tower,
> When he planned it and founded it,
> All the people worked at it;
> In less than a day they finished it.

Other Studies in Chinese Cultural History (University of Chicago Press, 1970), pp. 48–78. Creel proposes that the ruler, by *wu-wei*, reigns, but does not rule, leaving the details of government to his ministers.

[50] *Analects* 2:1.

[51] Needham, *Science and Civilisation*, vol. 3, pp. 56–8. See also Marcel Granet, *The Religion of the Chinese People*, trans. by Maurice Freedman (Oxford: Blackwell, 1975), pp. 65–80; consult also Léon Vandermeersch, *Études sinologiques* (Paris: Presses Universitaires de France, 1994), pp. 191–204.

[52] Legge, *Chinese Classics*, vol. 2, p. 128.

When he built it, there was no goading;
Yet the people came in their throngs.
The king was in his Sacred Park,
Where doe and stag lay hid.

Doe and stag at his coming leapt and bounded;
The white herons gleamed so sleek.
The king was by his Sacred Pool,
Where the fish sprang so lithe.[53]

An Eden-like atmosphere is what the poem conveys. Presumably therefore, the sacred tower was situated in a beautiful park, what we might today call a nature reserve. Mencius mentioned it with nostalgia and with utopian yearnings. He did not specifically discuss the religious meaning of the place. But scholars presume that the tower was a high place, indeed, 'penetrating the heavens' (*t'ung-t'ien / tongtian*), where the ruler communed with the spirits, and it was this assumption that motivated later rulers to emulate the Chou kings. He was eager to point out to the King of Liang how King Wen shared with his people the pleasures of his sacred park.

And so, the role of the king becomes manifest in his *Sitz im Leben*, literally, sitting on a throne placed in a capital considered to be at the centre of the known civilised world,[54] or moving ritually according to the cosmic law from room to room in a Bright Hall, or communing with the spirits in a Sacred Tower.

KINGSHIP AND SAGEHOOD

As we go back to examine the identity of the ancient sage-kings, we shall discover the hidden riches of meaning in the word *sheng*, and understand thereby something about the sacred character of kingship in China.[55] This is not to say that only rulers were regarded as sages in antiquity. There were also others, be they ministers or other individuals. But while not all sages were kings, sageliness was definitely regarded as *qualification* for rulership. This brings us to the question: what was sageliness, and who were the ancient sages?

---

53 English translation adapted from Waley, *The Book of Songs*, p. 259; consult also Legge, *Chinese Classics*, vol. 4, pt 3, bk 1, ode 8. Waley calls it the Magic Tower; Legge calls it the 'marvellous tower'.
54 Consult Wheatley, *The Pivot of the Four Quarters*, pp. 449–50.
55 Consult Julia Ching, 'Who were the Ancient Sages?' in Ching and Guisso (eds), *Sages and Filial Sons*, pp. 1–21; Hans Küng and Julia Ching, *Christianity and Chinese Religions* (New York: Doubleday, 1988), ch. 1.

The 'sage'

The Chinese word *sheng* (sage) occurs frequently in the classical texts, where it refers to a wise and virtuous person, usually a ruler in remote antiquity. Etymologically, the oracle bone graph, made up of a big ear and a small mouth (or sometimes two mouths), is closely associated with acute hearing, perhaps hearing the voice of the spirits, and perhaps also communicating something of what has been heard. A variant form, from which the modern symbol is derived, adds the picture for the 'human' to the ear and the mouth.

It is easy to surmise that acute hearing was important in antiquity when human beings had to protect themselves from the elements, as well as from beasts and from marauding tribes. It is also interesting that the 'weathermen' of antiquity were also musicians. In the Taoist text *Chuang-tzu*, we read of the pipings of Heaven, Earth, and Man. The piping of Heaven refers to the wind blowing on ten thousand things; the pipings of Earth to the sound of the hollows roaring in the wind, and the pipings of Man refer to the sound of flutes and whistles. 'The Great Clod belches out breath and its name is wind. So long as it doesn't come forth, nothing happens. But when it does, then ten thousand hollows begin crying wildly . . . And when the fierce wind has passed on, then all the hollows are empty again.'[56] The Chou dynasty commissioned musicians, who were usually blind, to survey weather conditions on the basis of their knowledge of musical notation. It is said that at the time of the mythical Shun, a man called Mu, also regarded as a sage, was charged with listening to the harmonies of the wind. He was thought to possess such acute hearing that he could judge whether or not earth and wind were in harmony, according to the correctness of their airs and pitches. Should we doubt here the knowledge of the ancients with regard to musical pitch, it is good to point out that archaeological discoveries at Chia-hu, in Wuyang prefecture (Honan), unearthed a bone flute with seven holes, dating from the neolithic period, that is, about eight thousand years ago. The testing of this flute makes clear that there was a defined social structure even at that time. This also offers support for such passages as the following, 'When a great sage (*sheng*) rules the world, the energies (*ch'i*[a] / *qi*) of Heaven and Earth join

---

[56] See *Chuang-tzu*, SPPY ed., 1:10b–11a; Burton Watson, trans., *The Complete Works of Chuang Tzu* (New York: Columbia University Press, 1968), pp. 36–7.

together to produce the winds. When the sun appears, then the moon activates the winds to produce the twelve tones.'[57]

Besides acute hearing, powerful vision has also been a component of the meaning of the word *sheng*. The classical Book of History speaks of sageliness as making manifest 'perspicacity' (*jui* / *rui*), a word explained by the lexicon of Hsü Shen as 'profound and bright', and the character includes the component of an eye.

There is an expression, *tsung-mu* / *zongmu*, referring to 'vertical eyes', or eyes from which light radiates, which has also been applied to persons called sages. Fu-hsi, the great culture hero, allegedly had unusual eyes, as did the sage-king Shun. Presumably, they also had great vision, both physical and spiritual, able to distinguish the 'godly from the wicked'.[58]

A third attribute of the ancient sages was the magnitude of their accomplishments. We need merely examine the names of some of the former sage-kings. These reveal their legendary character as well as their contributions to culture. They include the three Sovereigns. According to one tradition, they were the Heavenly Sovereign, the Earthly Sovereign, and the Human Sovereign. They have also been identified with such figures as Fu-hsi ('Animal Tamer'), Sui-jen ('Fire-maker') and Shen-nung ('Divine Farmer'), who bear names that bespeak their merits. Fu-hsi, also called Pao-hsi (a name that indicates his culinary skills), and his spouse or sister Nü-wa (literally, 'Woman') are portrayed in murals and stone engravings found in Han graves as humans with intertwined serpentine bodies, with him holding either a square ruler or the sun, and her holding either a compass or the moon. Together, the two represent an ancestral pair, the primordial couple, who transmitted life as well as material culture to their many descendants. Nü-wa is also described as the repairer of the universe, after a cosmic battle of giants. She made use of multi-coloured stones to mend the heavens, and raised it over the earth with turtle legs. The historian Ssu-ma Ch'ien actually gives her as one of the Three Sovereigns, instead of Sui-jen.[59]

---

[57] *Lü-shih ch'un-ch'iu*, 6:3b. Consult Jao Tsung-i, 'Ssu-fang feng hsin-i' (The winds of the four quarters: A new interpretation) *Chung-shan ta-hsüeh hsüeh-pao*, 4 (1988) 68–9; see also Jao Tsung-i, 'Foreword: Speaking of "Sages" ', pp. xiv–xvi.

[58] Jao Tsung-i, 'foreword', p. xvi.

[59] For the Three Sovereigns, see Ssu-ma Ch'ien, *Shih-chi* (Historical Annals), K'ai-ming ed., 124:269–70; for the Five Emperors, see 1:3–7. This source names the Three Sovereigns as Pao-hsi, Nü-wa and Shen-nung. The later text *Po-hu-t'ung* omits Nü-wa, and lists instead Sui-jen.

Thus, these figures also represent the personifications of certain stages in the development of early culture. They are hailed as culture heroes in later texts, both Confucian and Legalist.[60] The Great Appendix to the Book of Changes speaks of Fu-hsi or Pao-hsi as the inventor of the Eight Trigrams, those straight and broken lines that together constitute the symbols of divination, as well as of nets for hunting and fishing, and of Shen-nung as the maker of ploughs.

The Three Sovereigns were followed in time by another series of wise rulers. The first of these was the Yellow Emperor, the reputed ancestor of the Chinese people. His successors in government included Yao and Shun, who, together with him, allegedly built canoes and oars, used oxen to draw carts and yoked horses to chariots, constructed double gates for defence and made bows and arrows.[61] These three are the best-known of the so-called Five Emperors, who also include two lesser-known ones. Emperor Yü, the Flood-controller and alleged successor to Shun, is not on this list, although he has always been venerated for his own contributions to humankind.

Going beyond myths: the sage-kings as human beings

There are two possibilities regarding the Three Sovereigns and the Five Emperors. First, that they were historical figures, as revered by tradition. Second, that they were products of the mythical imagination.

In the first case, should such a group have been historical figures, the stronger possibility is that the so-called later ones (Five Emperors) were historical. We have, besides, more information on them than on the earlier ones. I refer here to figures like Yao and Shun. In that case, it would be useful to examine more fully the details of the traditions that have come down regarding them.

In conventional records, whether history or philosophy, which have been sanctioned by the school of Confucius, legendary sage-kings like Yao and Shun are usually offered as role models of royal virtues. For example, Mencius and others have especially praised Emperors Yao and Shun. Yao has been represented as the embodiment of kingly virtue. In his time, the country needed much

---

[60] Consult *Han Fei Tzu*, SPPY ed., 19:1; English translation by Burton Watson, *Han Fei Tzu: Basic Writings* (New York: Columbia University Press, 1964), p. 96; *Chou-li Cheng-chu* (The Institutes of Chou with Cheng Hsüan's annotations), 'K'ao-kung chi', 39:3–5.
[61] *Chou-yi cheng-yi*, 8:3a–5a.

attention. Among other things, a flood was ravaging the empire, the memory of which would last for many centuries. 'The Flood still raged unchecked, inundating the empire; plants grew thickly; birds and beasts multiplied; the five grains did not ripen . . . The lot fell on Yao to worry about this situation'.[62]

Obviously, the ruler had to tame and control the natural environment for his people. To control the flood, Yao named Kun, who was himself a man with mythical features. But Kun met with no success even after nine years. In his old age, Yao also realised that his own son lacked the royal qualifications, and looked around for the best man available to succeed himself. He found a commoner, Shun, known as a filial son, whom he employed in government, married to his own two daughters, and passed the throne to him eventually. The Analects of Confucius quotes Yao as saying to Shun:

> Oh! Shun,
> The succession, ordained by Heaven, has fallen on thy person.
> Hold thou truly to the middle way.
> If the Empire should be reduced to dire straits
> The honours bestowed on thee by Heaven will be terminated for ever.[63]

In the Book of Mencius, following a long discussion that the Master had with his disciples, we have this conclusion: 'Yao recommended Shun to Heaven and Heaven accepted him; he presented him to the people and the people accepted him.'[64]

It is interesting that Shun should have been the paragon of Confucian virtues, especially that of filial piety. It is also interesting that once given the opportunity to govern, Shun also showed himself a wise and strong ruler. He named Yü to control the floods.

> In the time of Yao, the water reversed its natural course, flooding the central regions, and the reptiles made their homes there, depriving the people of a settled life . . . Yü was entrusted with the task of controlling it. He led the flood water into the seas by cutting channels for it in the ground, and drove the reptiles into grassy marshes.[65]

In carrying out his task, Yü demonstrated unusual devotion. He 'spent eight years abroad, passed the door of his own house three times without entering'.[66]

Shun eventually decided that Yü was more worthy of the kingly office than his own son. This time, the merit was hard work rather

---

[62] Mencius 3A:4.   [63] Analects 20:1; English trans. by Lau, *The Analects*, p. 158.
[64] Mencius 5A:5; Eng. trans. by D. C. Lau, *Mencius* (Harmondsworth: Penguin Books, 1970), p. 143.
[65] Mencius 3B:9.   [66] Mencius 3A:4

than family virtue. And so the passing of the throne from Yao to Shun, and from Shun to Yü, has been eulogised for the spirit of unselfishness it demonstrated. The time during which Yao, Shun and Yü lived and ruled, in spite of the known inconveniences of constant struggles against an inhospitable nature, has also been romanticised as a lost golden age.

But the pattern changed when Yü died, to be succeeded by his son Ch'i. It is said that Yü had initially chosen his minister Yi to succeed him, but that the people preferred Ch'i, his son. As Mencius puts it:

Yü recommended Yi to Heaven, and died seven years later. When the mourning period of three years was over, Yi withdrew to the southern slope of Mount Ch'i, leaving Yü's son in possession of the field. Those who came to pay homage . . . went to Ch'i instead of Yi, saying, 'This is the son of our prince.'[67]

The people appeared immensely grateful to Ch'i's father. Presumably, Ch'i himself had the basic qualifications as well. The line begun by Yü became the first known dynasty of China, the Hsia, a name that is sometimes used to designate the country itself.

And here too, we have the line of demarcation drawn between an earlier time, when rulers were unselfishly devoted to the people, and a later time, when they increasingly considered the empire to be their own possession. Every dynasty had a last ruler, frequently described as a wicked one, undeserving of the Mandate he inherited from his ancestors. Such a ruler, a tyrant, had to be forcibly overthrown, presumably by a wise and deserving person to whom the Mandate had been transferred.

So, in the case of later kings, the problem of succession was complicated by conquests. First, there was the conquest of King T'ang of Shang, who replaced the Hsia dynasty with his own. And then, there was the conquest of King Wu of Chou over the Shang dynasty. In T'ang's case, the conqueror acted also in the name of a greater power, to punish the 'bad last king' of Hsia, who had forfeited the mandate to rule.

There are other stories about virtuous first ministers who were regents for young rulers. Both Yi-yin, the chief minister to King T'ang, and the Duke of Chou, younger brother to King Wu of Chou, allegedly kept the throne ready for the sons and heirs to the

---

[67] Mencius 5A:6, trans. Lau, pp. 144–5.

deceased kings, and have been praised by Mencius and others for their devotion and selflessness.

The orthodox version is the one given by Confucian philosophers and official historians. But Sarah Allan's work has highlighted those extant accounts, from Taoist, Legalist, and other sources, that propose a different course of events, one that involved much more political manipulation on the part of the one who 'succeeded' to the throne. These make up the version of the school of 'political realism'. It is quite another question whether things really happened the way they claimed, to historical rather than mythical figures, or whether the Legalists propounded their version to make *their* point: that the ruler must be ever vigilant, to protect his own person and position.

For example, the Legalist text *Han Fei Tzu* had this to say about the passing of the throne from Yao to Shun 'Yao was the best of the six kings. Yet as soon as Shun became his follower, he gathered everyone about himself, and Yao no longer had the world.'[68]

Of the second event, the same text says simply: 'Shun forced Yao; Yü forced Shun.'[69] The problem with the second transfer of power is that Shun had first employed Yü's father Kun in the control of the floods, and then punished him with exile till death for a job badly done. Yet, according to official accounts, not only did he ask K'un's son to continue with the same job, but also was the son willing to comply, and was eventually asked to succeed to the throne.

On Yü's son Ch'i's succession, the *Bamboo Annals* says simply 'Yi interfered with the accession of Ch'i, and Ch'i killed him.'[70]

Ch'i's accession to the throne generally confirmed the hereditary principle. And the Hsia dynasty lasted until his descendant, Chieh, lost the throne to T'ang, the founder of the Shang dynasty (c. 1766 BCE). Then followed the conquest of Shang by Chou, after King Wu had killed the 'last bad king' of the Shang dynasty (1122 BCE). Shortly after that, King Wu died, and his younger brother, Duke of Chou, was regent for his young son, King Ch'eng. The conventional account describes the rebellion of the Duke's two brothers, who

---

[68] *Han Fei Tzu*, SPPY ed., ch. 16, sect. 38:3b; Sarah Allan, *The Heir and the Sage: Dynastic Legend in Early China* (San Francisco: Chinese Materials Center, 1981).

[69] *Han Fei Tzu* ch. 17, sect. 44:10a.

[70] For the *Bamboo Annals*, consult Legge, *Chinese Classics*, vol. 3, 118, note; Allan, *The Heir*, pp. 72–3. The problem with the *Bamboo Annals* is that the old version was lost after its initial discovery, and had to be restored from fragments many years later. First discovered in 279 CE, the text purports to go back to the third century BCE.

'suspected' the Duke's intentions and allied themselves with the son of the last Shang king. They were defeated and killed. But the Duke of Chou, the model of virtue for later ages, and Confucius' hero, was therefore on record as the killer of his siblings. Was he even someone who attempted to usurp the throne, one wonders?

There is sufficient moral and historical ambiguity surrounding the early legends and historical accounts, in which Confucian philosophers were to discover their models of virtue. Possibly, the Confucian school, especially Mencius, invented the myths of the virtuous sage-kings and their deference to the wise. In this endeavour, they could also have been helped by Mo-tzu, the fourth-century-BCE thinker, for whom the great Yü was a hero of the first magnitude. All these thinkers wanted the ears of the kings; they promoted the idea that the wise were fit to govern, if not as rulers, then at least as councillors.

Repossessing myths: the sage-kings as god symbols

Over fifty years ago, Ku Chieh-kang, Yang Hsiang-k'uei and others of the modern critical circle of Chinese historians, proposed the theory that the ancient sage-kings were god-figures. Their hypothesis was founded upon their critical examination of the fragmented materials in the early texts, be these classics, history or mythology. It associated the Three Sovereigns and the Five Emperors with the primeval Supreme One (*T'ai-yi / Taiyi*), which, in turn, represents the supreme being called God. According to them, the Three Sovereigns and the Five Emperors belong to the realm of mythology, but became regarded as human beings after a process of reverse euhemerisation during the Eastern Chou period. They pointed out that the word *huang* (sovereign), which may represent the rays of the sun, or a crown, or a king wearing a crown, has signified more often the adjective 'supreme' rather than the noun 'sovereign'.[71] Besides, the word *Ti*[c], usually reserved for the supreme God (*Shang-ti*, Lord-on-High), and used as a posthumous title to honour royal ancestors, was usurped as an imperial title (*huang-ti*, supreme emperor) to refer to the living ruler only in the third century BCE. Since the Chinese word for 'yellow' is also pronounced *huang*, the term *Huang-ti* (Yellow

---

[71] *Shuo-wen*, vol. 1, pt 1, 13a. Consult Ku Chieh-kang and Yang Hsiang-k'uei, *San-huang k'ao*, Introduction, in Lü Ssu-mien, *et al.*, *Ku-shih pien* (Arguments in ancient history) (1941 ed., Hong Kong reprint, T'ai-p'ing, 1963), vol. 7, pt 2, p. 51.

Emperor) may be interpreted also as referring to the 'Supreme God'.

According to these scholars, Yao and Shun were also deity figures, representing the highest god or the ancestral god of each of the two population groups within ancient China, the Western and the Eastern groups. Yao meant 'high', probably representing the God of the northwestern tribes. Shun was identical with Ti-Chün of the *Shan-hai ching* (Classic of Mountain and Ocean), and represents the God of the eastern Yin people.[72]

In the case of the Flood-controller Yü, many stories surrounding his birth and life, and the founding of the Hsia dynasty (3rd millennium BCE?), were mythological rather than historical. Mencius describes him as a 'Western barbarian', and critical scholarship has tended to look upon him as the god of the Western people, perhaps their earth-god (*she-shen*), in charge of mountains and rivers.[73]

So far, we have said nothing about creators or creator deities. While creation myths do exist in the Chinese tradition, they tend to come from later texts. Interestingly, the female figure, Nü-wa, has also been described as having created human beings. Supposedly, she first made the nobility by patting the earth together, and then strung mud together to make the commoners.[74] Here we have a mythological explanation for the distinction between classes.

Scholars who consider the ancient sages as deity symbols do not always agree on what it means to be a deity. Ku Chieh-kang and his circle tended to think that the Three Sovereigns, and perhaps also the Five Emperors, represented a supreme being, a personal God. But others prefer to regard the same sages as ancestral spirits, occupying a position lower than that of the supreme being. And it appears that the ancient Chinese worshipped a supreme deity who

---

[72] Yang K'uan, *Chung-kuo shang-ku shih tao-lun* (Introduction to ancient Chinese history), *Ku-shih pien*, vol. 7, pt 1, pp. 148–53. See also Wolfgang Munke, *Die klassische chinesische Mythologie* (Stuttgart: Ernst Klett Verlag, 1976), pp. 122–3, 161–74, 288–300, 336–43. This book is organised alphabetically; the author refers both to classical texts and to Western scholarship, especially to Bernhard Karlgren's works.

[73] Consult *Huai-nan-tzu* 19:7a, *Kuo-yü, Lu-yü* (Dialogue of Lu), pt 2, 5:11a; see also Yang K'uan, in *Ku-shih pien*, vol. 7, pt 1, pp. 359–64; Ku Chieh-kang and T'ung Shu-yeh, 'K'un Yü te ch'uan-shuo' (The legends of K'un and Yü), *Ku-shih pien*, vol. 7, pt 3, pp. 144–59.

[74] The account is given in quotations from a lost second- to third-century text, *Feng-su T'ung-yi* (Comprehensive meaning of customs). See Derk Bodde, 'Myths of Ancient China', In S. N. Kramer (ed.), *Mythologies of the Ancient World* (Garden City: Doubleday, 1961), pp. 369–408. See also N. J. Girardot, *Myth and Meaning in Early Taoism* (Berkeley: University of California Press, 1983), p. 204.

was also a great ancestral spirit. We might therefore more safely presume that the ancient sages represented ancestral spirits, or together pointed to the supreme deity who was also the great ancestral spirit.

KINGSHIP AS POLITICAL INSTITUTION

The sacral character of kingship can be traced back to antiquity, to a time when kings were regarded as semi-divine, or at least, the close confidants of the Lord-on-High. But the institution of kingship itself represents, in the language of Max Weber, the routinisation of charisma. The heirs to the ancient kings were no longer considered even semi-divine. But their office retained an aura of sacrality. And this aura was supported by philosophy, and passed down by ritual.

The 'Mandate' theory as philosophical foundation

The philosophical foundation for kingship is enunciated by the doctrine of the Mandate of Heaven, as presented especially in such classics as the Book of History and the Book of Songs. This doctrine has been regarded primarily as a theoretical justification for the Chou conquest of Shang. According to this theory, kings rule only by divine mandate, and the final Shang ruler's excesses led to the loss of this mandate for his house, just as the last Hsia ruler had been replaced by the first Shang king. In place of the last Shang king, Heaven installed as ruler the founder of the Chou dynasty, King Wu, the son of the deceased King Wen. The Book of Songs describes the father as having attained to the enjoyment of God's presence when the Mandate was given to his son. Much more than the ancestors of the Shang kings, King Wen appears to act as a kind of mediator, between the Lord on high and the people below. He is described, after his death, as being with the Lord-on-High, from whom his house has received a new mandate to govern over a country that used to be Shang China.

> The Mandate that Heaven gave
> Was solemn, was forever.
> And ah, most glorious
> King Wen in plenitude of power!
> With blessings he has whelmed us;
> We need but gather them in.

High favours has King Wen vouchsafed to us;
May his descendants hold them fast.[75]

In another classic, the Book of History, the Mandate theory is also mentioned:

We do not presume to know and to say that the lords of Yin (Shang) received Heaven's Mandate for so many years . . . But they did not reverently attend to their virtue and so prematurely threw away the Mandate . . . Now our king has succeeded and received the Mandate . . . Being king, his position will be that of a leader in virtue.[76]

The Mandate theory offered philosophical and religious rationalisation for a military conquest; it also sowed the seeds of future 'revolution', since the Mandate could be removed (*ko-ming / geming*) by Heaven from the undeserving ruler. The assumption here is that Heaven is not merely the protector of the ruling house, but the Lord and protector of all the people, whose well-being, indeed, takes precedence over that of the ruling house. The Mandate theory articulated in the classics associated with Confucius' name became prominent in the teachings of his fourth-century-BCE follower Mencius, who announced clearly: 'The people are of the utmost importance; the altars to the gods of earth and grain come next; the ruler comes last' (Mencius 7B:14).

The altars to the gods of the earth and grain were the symbols of the state and its sovereignty. Mencius also said that rulers who endanger these altars – that is, the independence or welfare of their state – ought to be replaced. Presumably, these rulers were also endangering their own people, who came first in the order of consideration.

Implicit in such political teachings is that government rests on popular consent. More explicitly, and coming after Mencius, the third-century-BCE Confucian thinker Hsün-tzu speaks of human beings coming together in society to achieve the strength and harmony without which they cannot conquer other beings, presumably the birds and beasts.[77] Before Mencius, the fifth-century-BCE thinker Mo-tzu already discussed the origin of social authority through a form of consent on the part of human beings who gather

---

[75] Eng. trans. adapted from Waley, *The Book of Songs*, p. 227.
[76] English translation adapted from Legge, *Chinese Classics*, vol. 3, p. 430.
[77] *Hsün-tzu*, sect.9, 5:8a; English in Burton Watson, trans., *Hsün Tzu: Basic Writings* (New York: Columbia University Press, 1963), p. 46.

together to prevent disorder and injury by the election of wise leaders.[78]

A fourth-century-BCE thinker, Han Fei Tzu, a staunch defender of the ruler's rights and an opponent to Confucian political philosophy, also says that the people are the ones who make a ruler:

In the most ancient times, when men were few and creatures numerous, human beings could not overcome the birds, beasts, insects, and reptiles. Then a sage appeared who fashioned nests of wood to protect men from harm. The people were delighted and made him ruler of the world, calling him the Nest Builder.[79]

The seventeenth-century English philosopher Thomas Hobbes' *Leviathan* came much later (1651), in which he described everyone as at war against everyone else in a state of nature. Hobbes discerned in this the basis of natural right in the human desire to live. Aided by reason, which he called the law of nature, human beings would agree to relinquish much of their sovereign right to all things in a contractual relationship to a state, while reserving certain individual liberties having regard to self-preservation. Thomas Hobbes cited intra-human conflict as what human beings wanted to avoid in joining together in political society, and so did Mo-tzu. Implicitly, they were saying that the human family is one, and that human beings in a state of nature had rights and liberties that they freely surrendered for the good of the whole.

Mencius was asked about regicide by the King of Ch'i, who cited the cases of Shang's replacing Hsia and Chou's replacing Shang. His answer was to 'rectify language'. A man who acts against humaneness or benevolence, he said, was an outcast not deserving of the title 'king'. There was then, no regicide, unless one was to call it tyrannicide (Mencius 1B:8).

Mencius' approval of tyrannicide had a decisive influence on Chinese history. Generations of rebels – and dynastic founders – appealed to this doctrine. In this regard, Confucian China experienced many dynastic changes, justifiable according to its own political ethics. But Japan had a different political evolution, and knew no dynastic changes.

There is a story of one dynastic founder who decided to defend his

---

[78] *Mo-tzu*, sect. 11, 3:1a–b; Eng. trans. in Burton Watson, trans., *Mo Tzu: Basic Writings* (New York: Columbia University Press, 1963), pp. 34–5.
[79] *Han Fei Tzu*, sect. 49, 19:1a; Eng. trans. in Watson, p. 96.

mandate to rule by expurgating the Book of Mencius. That was Chu Yüan-chang, founder of the Ming dynasty (1368–1644), a self-educated man from humble origins who realised that the revolutionary potential of that text could also be actualised by any of his rivals. But he was unable to overcome the protest of Confucian officials, one of whom, Ch'ien T'ang, announced that it would be an honour for him personally to suffer death for the sake of Mencius.[80]

A theory of tyrannicide developed much later in Christian Europe. In the twelfth century, John of Salisbury had written about the justifiability of tyrannicide in extreme circumstances. In the late sixteenth century, these ideas were more clearly enunciated by the anonymous Huguenot author of *Vindicae contra tyrannos* (1579) and by the Spanish Jesuit, Luis Mariana, author of *De rege et regis institutione* (1598–9). The former work was publicly burnt, and the latter was condemned by the Gallican parliament.[81]

CONCLUSION

The Mandate of Heaven theory might very well have been first proposed by the early Chou kings who overthrew the Shang to claim suzerainty over an entire country. It would serve as a double-edged sword: to legitimise the rule of some, while discrediting that of others, including the unworthy descendants of the dynastic founders themselves. Confucian philosophers have been eager to lend it support, emphasising moral responsibility for the rulers to govern wisely and humanely. To the extent that they did so, they were making themselves the teachers of kings and rulers, in the name of a higher authority, presumably that of Heaven, whose will they interpreted.

In conclusion, let me quote from some lines in the Book of Changes. They come from the commentary on the words of the text under the first Hexagram *Ch'ien* / *Qian* (Heaven), and speak best of the role of the ancient sage-king:

> The great man is one whose power is consonant with heaven and earth,
> Whose brilliance is one with the sun and moon,
> Whose order is one with the four seasons,

---

[80] See Ch'ien's biography in Chang T'ing-yü, et al., *Ming-shih* (Ming Dynastic History), K'ai-ming ed., 139:335c–d.
[81] Consult Julia Ching, *Confucianism and Christianity: A Comparative Study* (Tokyo: Kodansha International, 1977), p. 193.

Whose [prognostication] of good and evil fortunes is one with the
spirits and ghosts.
When he precedes Heaven, Heaven will not oppose him,
When he follows Heaven, he obeys the timing of its moments.
Since Heaven is not opposed to him,
How much less will be human beings or the ghosts and spirits![82]

The great man, the king, is the paradigmatic individual, reflecting
in himself so much of that which is greater than himself: the universe
as an organic whole, vibrant and alive. Harmony with the cosmos,
based on the microcosm–macrocosm correspondence between the
human and the cosmic, marks the great man's power, brilliance,
governance and good fortune. In the light of what we know about
sacral kingship, the rituals surrounding it, the life in harmony with
nature and following its cycles, such an exuberant statement is better
understood. In that same light, we may also understand better how
the very idea of a sage-king became exalted as an ideal type or a
paradigm, with an impact on Chinese civilisation and history that is
almost immeasurable.

[82] Richard J. Lynn, trans., *The Classic of Changes: A New Translation of the I Ching, as Interpreted by Wang Bi* (New York: Columbia University Press, 1994), p. 138.

CHAPTER 3

The moral teacher as sage: philosophy appropriates the paradigm

INTRODUCTION

The king is a sage, and the sage has semi-divine attributes, and the ability to maintain communication with the divine. This, in short, is what we have been talking about in the first two chapters: a sage-king paradigm from the remote past in Chinese history. In the time that followed, this paradigm continued to have relevance, while it was also being appropriated and transformed.

I shall discuss first the appropriation of the sage-king paradigm by scholars and in the name of philosophy. We start with Confucius and his early followers. But we shall not limit ourselves to a description of how this happened and what it meant. We shall also ask some other questions, regarding who Confucius was, and what his role has been in Chinese civilisation. Was he a traditionalist? A social reformer? A revolutionary? To these questions, what were the answers of history, and what are the answers today? These issues have relevance to our main inquiry concerning the sage-king and wisdom.

The classical age of the philosophers, followed by that of Confucian dominance, led to an age of classical exegesis with its own independent momentum and dynamism. Around the same time, the rise of Taoist religion and the introduction of Buddhism brought their own challenges, and their own responses to the sage-king paradigm. Between these events, there were many centuries of intellectual development. This chapter will deal principally with early Confucian thought, and the chapter following, with the neo-Confucian thought that arose very much later.

CONFUCIUS

First of all, there is the question of who and what Confucius was.

The name 'Confucius' is the Latinised form of 'Master K'ung', in Chinese, K'ung *fu-tzu* / *fuzi*. His proper name was K'ung Ch'iu (Kong Qiu), also styled K'ung Chung-ni (Kong Zhongni). The traditional dates for his life are approximately 552 to 479 BCE. For a man who lived so long ago, we can still find descendants today, in what has been called the world's oldest family. Over more than seventy-five generations the clan has kept careful genealogies, as the heirs were made state officials responsible for the cult offered in his honour. But the respect paid him did not make him a god.

Tradition says he was a rather tall man, and a direct descendant of the Shang royal house. K'ung described his own circumstances as humble, the occasion for his learning many menial things. Tradition gives his father as a fighting man of unusual strength, whose death left his young son nearly destitute.[1] We are not told how he became educated as an expert in rituals. The highest public office he occupied was for about a year at the age of fifty, as a kind of police commissioner in his home state. In over ten years of travel, K'ung visited many other feudal states of his time, seeking, but never finding, a ruler who would rely on his advice. In his old age, he devoted more time to teaching disciples, while also occupying himself with music and poetry, and with occasional conversations with rulers or ministers.[2]

This brief account leaves many questions unanswered. One such regards his parentage, for example: whether he was of illegitimate birth, the fruit of a romantic encounter between an old warrior and a much younger, probably impoverished, woman.[3] Another has to do with his political ambition. Given the fact that he articulated in his teachings a kingly or princely way (*wang-tao*) that would presumably bring peace and unity to the entire then-known world, and actively sought public office, did he also desire kingship for himself, and on his own terms? In other words, did Confucius hope to find a ruler like the Yao and Shun he praised, who would not merely use his advice or services, but also pass the throne on to himself as a worthy successor?

Reliable, surviving texts are scarce, not only because of the known

---

[1] *Shih-chi*, ch. 47.
[2] See Confucius' biography by Julia Ching, in *The Encyclopedia of Religion* (New York: Macmillan, 1987), vol. 4, pp. 38–42. See also Ching, *Confucianism and Christianity*, ch. 2; H. G. Creel, *Confucius: The Man and the Myth* (New York: J. Day, 1949).
[3] Consult *Shih-chi*, Biography of Confucius, ch. 47, p. 163.

historical catastrophes with their cultural casualties, but possibly also because Confucius became too important for later generations to tolerate any information in his biography that might be regarded as disrespectful.

Various hypothetical answers have been suggested. Historically, what we know is that Confucius became great as a teacher, and for his teachings. The first to accept students without regard to their family or class backgrounds, he spread the benefits of education to commoners, and became honoured by later generations as the teacher *par excellence.*

As a traditionalist

Confucius described himself as a traditionalist, and has usually been regarded as such by later generations. 'I have transmitted what was taught to me, without making up anything of my own. I have been faithful to the ancients and loved them' (Analects 7:1). And again: 'I love the past and am diligent in studying it' (7:19).

One mark of his traditionalism is his attitude to early religion. Confucius' attitude to religion in general has been characterised as ambivalent and somewhat self-contradictory. He was largely silent on what regards God and the after-life, and shows a certain scepticism toward ghosts and spirits (6:22). Yet he regards rituals (li^a) as cementing not only the familial order, but also the wider socio-political order, to the extent that a modern American philosopher, Herbert Fingarette, giving the Analects a fresh look, has called li^a 'holy rite' or 'sacred ceremonial'.[4]

In the Analects, we twice find mention of a priest (*chu*), T'uo by name, whom Confucius praised (6:16, 14:19) for his eloquence and smooth speech, and his conduct of rituals in a ducal ancestral temple. In fact, Confucius attributed to him, at least in part, the credit of having prevented the fall of Duke Ling of Wei, a person whom he described as totally lacking in moral principle.

The Analects mention (13:22) shamans (wu^a) as well, but only generically, and in some connection with divination. 'The Master said, "The southerners have a saying: A man devoid of constancy will not make a shaman or a healer. How well said!"'[5] And

---

[4] Herbert Fingarette, *Confucius: The Secular as Sacred* (New York: Harper & Row, 1972).
[5] Reference to the text of the third line of the hexagram *heng* (constancy) in the Book of Changes.

Confucius' high regard for constancy is disclosed elsewhere when he confesses: 'I have no hopes of meeting a good man. I would be content if I met someone who has constancy' (7:25).

Obviously, Confucius was aware of shamans. Clearly there were more shamans in the south. This, in itself, is an indication that if the ethos in the north had grown more rationalistic, diminishing the importance and need of shamans, the same was not true of the south. Taoism is said to have developed among recluses in the south, and could go back to the shamans of old. We have no real evidence to suggest the same of Confucius and his followers.

We find no particular mention in the Analects of any particular shaman, although Confucius did encounter a number of individuals who appeared to be hermits, and who thought him foolish for desiring to serve in government. The best known of these is the so-called madman of Ch'u (a southern state), who also figures in *Chuang-tzu*. He allegedly sang as he went past Confucius' chariot:

> O phoenix, phoenix,
> How dwindled is your power! . . .
> Desist, desist!
> Great in these days is the peril of those who fill office.[6]

The reference to the phoenix is most interesting. This large, red bird of the south, with its curved beak and long claws, sometimes identified with the real-life golden pheasant, was considered king of the birds. An emblem of beauty and warmth, and an omen of peace and prosperity, it is one of the 'Four Spiritual Creatures' (*ssu-ling / siling*), the other three being the dragon, the unicorn (*ch'i-lin / qilin*), and the tortoise. This mythical bird's first recorded appearance was in the reign of the mythical Yellow Emperor. After that, two phoenixes were said to have nested in Yao's palace. Most of the time, it is alleged to live in hiding, waiting for the moment when peace and reason will prevail in the world.[7] So this mention of the phoenix confirms Confucius' stature, even among hermits. But the note of warning is clear: in an age when the power of reason has waned greatly, it is wisdom to refrain from seeking active service.

Apparently, Confucius respected the religious specialists of his

---

[6] Analects 18:5; see Legge, *Chinese Classics*, vol. 1, pp. 332–3; the translation is from Waley, *The Analects of Confucius* (London: Allen & Unwin, 1938), p. 219. Consult *Chuang-tzu* 2:14–15; Watson (trans.), *Complete Works*, pp. 66–7.

[7] C. A. S. Williams, *Outlines of Chinese Symbolism and Art Motives*, 3rd revised edition. (Rutland and Tokyo: Tuttle, 1974), pp. 323–6.

time. In this, he contrasted with the great Hebrew ethical prophets, who conflicted with the priests of the temple cult.

The Analects also makes mention of several mythological sage-kings: Yao, Shun and Yü, but only briefly. Yao is praised with exuberance: 'Great indeed was Yao as a ruler. How majestic! Heaven alone is great, and Yao was equal to it' (8:19). Shun is lauded for giving order to the world with only five ministers helping him (8:20). And Yü is admired for his frugality, hard work, and 'filial devotion to the ghosts and spirits' (8:21). King T'ang, the founder of Shang, is not mentioned directly.

But Confucius was unstinting in his praise of the Chou institutions and of the Duke of Chou himself, as the great administrator (Analects 18:10) and as a sage he admired and saw in his dreams (7:5).

In the past, the Five (or Six) Classics have been attributed to Confucius, either as their editor or, especially in the case of the Spring-Autumn Annals, as a direct author. This attribution came especially from the second-century-BCE grand historian Ssu-ma Ch'ien, who says that Confucius organised the documents of the Book of History, edited the Book of Songs, deleting many that belonged to the earlier collection, revised the Rituals and Music, and wrote parts of the Book of Changes and the whole of the Spring–Autumn Annals for the state of Lu, distinguishing right from wrong in historical events for the whole world to see.[8]

Contemporary scholarship no longer takes this attribution of authorship seriously. But a question remains, on account of the importance of the relationship between Confucius and the Classics. Allegedly, the legacy of the classics represents Confucius as a traditionalist, eager to revive earlier Chou institutions at a time of social and political disorder. Actually, the link between himself and these works is less direct than assumed, and the selectivity with which the classics have been compiled and preserved is now usually taken for granted.

Confucius was a *skilful* traditionalist, who passed on to later generations those aspects of the culture of the past that he deemed valuable. Moreover, if he called himself a traditionalist, it was especially due to the fact that he was relying upon those whose

---

[8] *Shih-chi*, Preface by Ssu-ma Ch'ien, ch. 130, p. 279; see also his biography of Confucius, ch. 47, p. 163. The sixth classic was the lost work on music.

authority was greater than his own: the ancient sages, in particular the Duke of Chou.

As a reformer

In the traditional past, the wise man was the one who remembered antiquity with its rituals, which gave access to the divine while civilising the human order. Confucius once said with some pride that he had a better knowledge of the rites of both the Hsia and the Shang dynasties than what is reflected in those records of the rituals kept in the feudal states ruled by the Hsia and Shang royal descendants (Analects 3:9). And he made minute inquiries about every detail and rubric when he entered the grand temple dedicated to the Duke of Chou (3:15). He rebuked a disciple for wanting to do away with the offering of a sheep at the announcing of the new moon (3:17). It appears that the ritual itself had become obsolete, although the sheep was still being offered. But Confucius apparently thought that the ritual should not be forgotten.[9] Still, he was not for ritual extravagance, saying: 'With the rites, it is better to err on the side of frugality than on the side of extravagance' (3:4). And so, he shows flexibility about certain usages: 'A ceremonial cap of linen is what is prescribed by the rites. Today black silk is used instead. This is less expensive, and I follow the majority' (9:3).

We should give attention to Confucius' announced distaste for an item of ritual usage: human effigies or wooden burial figures (*yung*[a] / *yong*). These were made with moving limbs, the better to represent human beings capable of serving their lords and ladies in the world of the dead. Confucius is reported to have said that those who made such figures did not deserve to have posterity (Mencius 1A:4). And, as the fourth-century-BCE Mencius explained, it was an unequivocal condemnation of human sacrifice, even when performed symbolically. A sensitivity to the suffering of animals is also disclosed in Confucian texts: Mencius pointed out to the King of Ch'i that his humane feelings for the sacrificial bull awaiting slaughter (Mencius 1A:10) indicated an instinctively humane heart.

The Book of Rites, a Confucian text, records certain stories that indicate its disapproval of sacrificing the living for the dead. In one case, a disciple of Confucius heard that his brother's widow and

---

[9] See *Lun-yü cheng-yi* 4:1.

chief steward planned to bury some living persons with his dead brother in order to assure his service in the next world. He reacted by disapproving of this plan, saying that it was not proper, and adding ironically that should such a practice be followed, there were no candidates more appropriate than the widow and the chief steward themselves: 'If this cannot be omitted, my wish is that the two of you be selected for it.'

In another case, a son refused to follow his father's dying wish to have him buried in the same large coffin with two living concubines. His explanation was: 'To bury the living with the dead is contrary to propriety. How much more must it be to bury them in the same coffin.'[10]

Obviously, filial piety did not require blind obedience. In each case, the living were spared. Confucius was not uncritical in his appreciation of tradition, and has to be considered as a reformer of tradition.

Confucius genuinely loved rituals, and instructed others to observe them. For example, he related the practice of filial piety to ritual observance. 'Serve the parents during their lifetime with ritual propriety (li^a); bury the parents after their deaths with ritual propriety, and sacrifice to them according to ritual propriety.'[11] In the Analects, the word li^a does not refer just to rites, whether in general or in particular regard to sacrifices. By extension, it extends to the virtue that is related to the performance of rites, which has been called 'propriety', a sense of what is correct and proper. Confucius places much importance upon this virtue, in private life as well as in the government of the state. Propriety carries a risk of mere exterior conformity to social custom, just as a ritual might be performed only perfunctorily, without an inner attitude of reverence. As we know, Confucius emphasised the need of having the right inner dispositions, without which propriety becomes hypocrisy (15:18). In an illness, when a disciple requested that prayers be said for him, Confucius' answer shows that he considered a life well lived as preferable to intercessory petition (7:35). Yet he has also said: 'He who offends Heaven, has no one to whom he can pray' (3:13).

[10] The stories are from the 'T'an-kung'. See Legge (trans.), *Li Ki*, *Sacred Books*, vol. 27, pp. 182–4.
[11] Analects 2:5.

A REVOLUTIONARY PHILOSOPHY?

Confucius was a traditionalist in some ways, a reformer in others. Was he also a revolutionary? The question itself may sound shocking, granted our contemporary understanding of revolution as total and complete change of social and political institutions usually following the destruction of an *ancien régime*.

In Chinese, the word 'revolution' is rendered as *ko-ming / geming*, the changing of the Mandate to govern. In the case of Confucius, we might regard him as a revolutionary if he had the ambition to take over the governing Mandate, and bring about changes according to his own ideas. For all this to be deemed possible, he had to consider himself a sage, and therefore deserving of the Mandate.

From evidence we have, the revolution Confucius brought about was more moral than political. He sought to give new meaning to the word 'ritual'. And he sought to infuse with new life the human relationships on which society was built.

The moral transformation of ritual

For Confucius, the importance of the rites does not rest only in the external observance, such as in the offering of gifts and the accompaniment of musical performances, but even more in the disposition of the person making the offerings or attending the ceremony: 'The Master said: "Rites! Rites! Are jade and silk all that is meant by the rites? Music! Music! Are drums and bells all that is meant by music?"' (Analects 17:11). In even stronger language, he remarked: 'What can rites do for a person lacking in the virtue of humaneness (*jen*[b] / *ren*)? What can music do for a person lacking in humaneness?' (3:3). Among other things, he insisted that sacrifice is to be performed with the consciousness of the presence of the spirits (3:12).

Of course, *li*[a] (propriety) is related to *jen*[b]. The former refers more to social behaviour, and the latter, to the inner orientation of the person. *Jen*[b] is translated variously as goodness, benevolence, humaneness and human-heartedness. *Jen*[b] began as the virtue of kindness which distinguished the gentleman (*chün-tzu / junzi*) in his behaviour toward his inferiors. Confucius has transformed it into a universal virtue, that which *makes* the perfect human being, the sage. For this reason, Confucius shows a certain caution in speaking of *jen*[b]. He says:

Riches and honours are what men desire. If they cannot be acquired in the proper way, they should not be kept. Poverty and humiliation are what men dislike. If they cannot be avoided in the proper way, they should not be abandoned. If the gentleman abandons *jen*[b], how can he keep this name [of the gentleman]? (4:5).[12]

In many ways, Confucius resembled Socrates, gathering about himself a small group of disciples, many of whom shared his life, travels and tribulations. (Contemporary scholars dispute the traditional number of three thousand, and prefer a smaller figure, perhaps seventy-two.) In their midst, he was a fatherly figure, even if some of the disciples were only a few years younger than himself, and a few were even older. He practised what may be called the art of spiritual guidance, exhorting his followers to moderate the excesses of their temperaments by certain efforts of self-control aided by the practice of self-examination. He gives this general advice: 'When you meet someone better than yourself, think about emulating him. When you meet someone not as good as yourself, look inside and examine your own self' (Analects 4:17).

The Analects contains many passages in which Confucius gives personal advice to particular disciples: Tzu-lu, who was counselled to temper his impulsive and pugnacious nature, and Tsai-wo, who was rebuked for going to sleep in the daytime. We see also a touching witness to Confucius' special regard for Yen Hui, who was always happy, even in abject poverty. Yen's early death provoked his Master to cry out, with bitter tears, as did Job in the depths of his tribulations: 'Alas, Heaven is destroying me, Heaven is destroying me!' (11:9).[13]

It was also to Yen Hui that Confucius once asserted that the virtue of *jen*[b] means self-conquest for the sake of recovering propriety (*li*[a]). When asked further how this is to be achieved, he gave a teaching of abnegation or self-denial with these famous words on putting a guard over our senses: 'Look not at what is contrary to propriety; listen not to what is contrary to propriety; speak not what is contrary to propriety; make no movement which is contrary to propriety' (Analects 12:1).[14]

Such abnegation or self-control is encouraged for the sake of *jen*[b].

---

[12] English trans. adapted from James Legge, *Chinese Classics*, vol. 1, pp. 166–7.
[13] Consult Julia Ching, 'What is Confucian Spirituality?' in Irene Eber (ed.), *Confucianism: The Dynamics of Tradition* (New York: Macmillan, 1986), pp. 63–80.
[14] Legge, *Chinese Classics*, vol. 1, p. 250.

We do not find in Confucius' teaching the advocacy of asceticism for its own sake, or for the sake of whatever magical powers it may bring to the practitioner, as was the case in ancient India.

The morality of human relationships

There are those who call the Chinese spiritual universe one that knows no sense of transcendence. This is hard to accept when we think of the religious universe of antiquity, with the many sacrifices offered to deities and spirits. This is also hard to accept when we remember the reverence for Heaven, honoured as supreme deity. Nevertheless, it is quite true that in historical time, the Chinese focused more attention on interpersonal human relationships than on expressions of the fear of God. We might also describe the Chinese as having found transcendence in immanence. This is not necessarily a dialectical identification of two terms with apparently opposing meaning. Rather, it indicates that while the Chinese spiritual universe may be mostly immanental, it could still possess a dimension of transcendence.

The great merit of Confucius and the school named after him is the discovery of the ultimate in the relative – in the moral character of human relationships. The term for 'human' is *jen*[a], written like a human figure with two legs. And, as we have already mentioned, the term for 'Heaven' is *t'ien*, written like a human figure with two legs and a big head. It has been said that the supreme Heaven was the deification of the great ancestor. In any case, the human and Heaven are not very far apart, in the script as well as in human understanding and aspirations.

The Confucian respect for interpersonal relationships is demonstrated in the well-known 'Five Relationships'. These include ruler–minister, father–son, husband–wife, elder and younger brother, and friend and friend. Three of these are family relationships, while the other two are usually conceived in terms of the family models. For example, the ruler–minister relationship resembles the father–son, while friendship resembles brotherliness. For this reason, the Confucian society regards itself as a large family: 'Within the four seas all men are brothers' (Analects 12:5).

The Five Relationships are basically vertical in their orientation, delineating duties that the junior partners have to fulfil. Confucius, however, has articulated the need for mutual and reciprocal responsibilities. So a minister owes loyalty to his ruler, and a child filial respect to the parent. But the ruler must also care for his subjects, and the parent for the child. All the same, these relationships are undeniably tilted in favour of the senior partners: the father, the husband, the ruler, and the elder brother. And the relationship between friends is most often compared to that of older and younger brothers. For this reason, Confucian society has been authoritarian in orientation. And the duty of filial piety, the need of procuring progeny for the sake of assuring the continuance of the ancestral cult, has been for centuries the ethical justification for polygamy.

Let us note here Confucius' instructions regarding filial piety. His answers to various questions show his consideration of particular circumstances: the health of the sons, the need for travel, and the rest. In a difficult passage, he says: 'Today, filial piety means being able to support one's parents. But this can even be done for dogs and cats. If support is not accompanied with reverence, what difference is there?' (Analects 2:7).

Confucius' central doctrine is that of the virtue of *jen*[b]. In etymology as well as in interpretation, *jen*[b] is always concerned with human relationships, the graph being made up of the radical 'human' and the word 'two'. We shall usually refer to it as humaneness, but call it benevolence in citations where the word occurs. Its original meaning has been variously interpreted, as referring to the virtue of kindness proper to a man of noble birth, in his behaviour toward those below his station.[15] Confucius transformed its meaning, raising it to a universal virtue: that which makes one a gentleman. In a well-known passage, Confucius says that his way (*tao* / *dao*) is bound together by 'one thread', and his disciple, Tseng-tzu, goes on to explain that this one thread refers to the two virtues of *chung*[a] / *zhong* and *shu* (Analects 4:15).

With the word *chung*[a], later usage has been mainly in the political context, meaning loyalty to the ruler. Hsü Shen's lexicon, however, merely indicates that the ideogram composed of the graph *chung*[b] / *zhong* (middle) and the graph *hsin* (heart, resembling a flame) signifies having the heart in a middle position, and giving all that the heart can offer. I should explain it as loyalty (*chung*[a]) – loyalty to one's own heart and conscience, i.e., integrity.[16]

---

[15] Wing-tsit Chan, 'The Evolution of the Confucian Concept *Jen*', *Philosophy East and West* 4 (1955), 295–319; Katō, *Chūgoku kodai bunka*, p. 875.

[16] *Shuo-wen*, 10B:18a.

The word *shu* is usually defined in later usage as forgiveness. It, too, is written with a heart as a radical, underneath another word, *ju*[a] / *ru*, the phonetic, which means 'like'. In the Analects (15:24), it has been defined as reciprocity – respect of, and consideration for, others.[17]

On this interpretation, I depart somewhat from the position taken by Léon Vandermeersch in his book *Wangdao*. I agree with him that Confucius understands *jen*[b] as graded love, keeping always in mind the ramifications of social positions and relationships. But Vandermeersch has opposed *chung*[a] and *shu* to each other on the basis of social stratification, claiming that the former represents the inferior's ideal attitude toward the superior, and the latter its reverse. For myself, the equation of *chung*[a] with feudal loyalty or gratitude is simplistic.[18] I see in Confucius' teaching the germ of a doctrine of *natural equality*, to be further developed by the later Mencius.[19]

We should hear Confucius himself speak of reciprocity and neighbourliness, as he did in these simple words:

> To regard every one as a very important guest,
> to manage the people as one would assist at a sacrifice,
> *not to do to others what you would not have them do to you.*
>
> (Analects 15:24)

'Not to do unto others what you would not have them do to you.' This last line has been called the *negative* Golden Rule. But how it is to be applied in different circumstances continues to be a puzzle. What if the individual finds himself or herself in conflict between responsibility toward the kinship group and responsibility toward the state? How should one choose?

Once told by a public official about a young man who testified against his father, who had stolen a sheep, Confucius replied: 'In our village . . . fathers cover up for their sons, and sons cover up for their fathers' (Analects 13:18).

This answer has been perplexing to many Western scholars, who are astonished to see Confucius' encouragement of deviousness, and concerned about the protection of one's family as the source of many problems in how society relates itself to the state. Certainly, such a

---

[17] For this interpretation, I rely as well on Liu Pao-nan's commentary on the Analects. See *Lun-yü cheng-yi* 5:7–8.

[18] Vandermeersch, *Wangdao*, vol. 2, pp. 504–5.

[19] Consult Donald Munro, *The Concept of Man in Ancient China* (Stanford University Press, 1969), pp. 65–7.

statement appears naïve in the case of someone who wanted to serve government, can hardly endear the speaker to any ruler, and does not exemplify any kind of feudal loyalty on the part of Confucius.

That Confucius not only said it, but said so to a high official, is very relevant. It is indicative of the priority of natural relationships over artificial or contractual ones. In the course of time, as the country became unified, and as the state centralised all powers in its own hands, society could still resist the state's encroachments in the name of kinship duties, which the state, ironically, often had to support.

CONFUCIUS AS A SAGE

A historical person usually regarded as the greatest sage produced by East Asia, Confucius was no deity figure; he was a humanist and a scholar. But what was his self-understanding, and his understanding of sageliness? And how did Confucius perceive himself, his own accomplishments?

The following passage gives us insight into his self-consciousness, his sense of mission. It also discloses Confucius' high regard for rituals, and for the virtue of propriety which flows from them. It should help us appreciate the fundamentally religious character of his personality, with its profound sense of reverence for the Will of Heaven.

> At fifteen I set my heart on learning [to be a sage].
> At thirty I became firm.
> At forty I had no more doubts.
> At fifty I understood Heaven's Will (*T'ien-ming*).
> At sixty my ears were attuned [to this Will].
> At seventy I could follow my heart's desires, without
> overstepping the line. (Analects 2:4)[20]

To what were his ears attuned? Presumably, to Heaven's will. The same Chinese term can refer to the political mandate to rule. Here, it appears to have a more personal meaning, suggesting a special relationship with Heaven, and a special call to greatness. This means that Confucius was conscious of his own possession of wisdom or sageliness, which came to him from Heaven.

But what was Heaven for him? 'Heaven' was the name of the god

---

[20] English translation adapted from Lau, *Analects*, p. 63. *T'ien-ming* refers to Heaven's will in general, and sometimes to the Mandate of Heaven.

of the Chou people. By Confucius' time, the name was used interchangeably with that of Lord-on-High, the god of the Shang people. Scholars have tended to agree that Heaven remained a supreme, personal deity for Confucius, although he did not often invoke its name. After Confucius, the term came more and more to represent a superior moral force or nature.

By Confucius' time, with growing rationalisation, the ancient sages had gone through a process of euhemerisation. The term 'sage' had assumed a technical connotation in philosophical discussions, representing an ideal human being in a moral or even metaphysical sense, although the religious meaning was never forgotten. And while Confucius never openly called himself a sage, he was regarded as such by his immediate disciples and by later generations. He was never, of course, a ruler, and served as a minor minister for a brief period only. Yet later generations nearly made him a god, and actually called him a king – an uncrowned king. This itself had revolutionary implications. But the question as to whether Confucius himself was a revolutionary can be better answered later, in the light of the moral transformation of society which was a consequence of his influence.

Could Confucius be called a prophet, when we compare him to religious figures that emerged in the ancient Near East? Some have said no, maintaining that prophets are representatives of God, making known the word and will of God.[21] This position implies a *belief* in Christianity as a divinely revealed prophetical religion, and not just as a religion making such a *claim*. Others include Max Weber, who speaks of a prophet as messenger of a supramundane God of an ethical monotheism. But the same Max Weber has also said that a prophet is any man who 'by virtue of his purely personal charisma and by virtue of his mission, proclaims a religious doctrine or a Divine command'.[22]

Indeed, where the Chinese language is concerned, the meaning of a *chu*, which I render as 'priest', is actually closer to that of 'prophet', as a mouthpiece of a higher power. However, in the first chapter, I have explained the function of the *chu* in cultic terms, focusing on the pronouncement of ritual invocations, without particular reference to a revealed message or teaching.

---

[21] Küng and Ching, *Christianity and Chinese Religions*; see Hans Küng on p. 111.
[22] Quoted in Reinhard Bendix, *Max Weber: An Intellectual Portrait* (New York: Doubleday, 1962), p. 89.

As more understanding emerges of the Hebrew prophets, who were at an early stage ecstatics, and evolved into a role as 'ethical prophets' often opposed to the priests of the official cult only much later, we might also expand our definition of 'prophet' to help understand religious traditions in comparative light. Max Weber uses the term 'exemplary prophet' when speaking of Indian religious figures, and I would see no difficulty in applying this term to Confucius. Granted, of course, that there are differences, but there are parallels as well. Confucius was certainly an ethical teacher, with the consciousness of his mission as having come from on high. And he was an exemplary teacher, or prophet, in the sense that he himself lived what he preached, and became an example for many generations to come.

The differences have to do with the varying traditions: the Hebrew and the Chinese. The Hebrew religion developed an ethical monotheism after a long period of religious evolution, which had seen other forms of religious belief, including worship of nature deities. The Chinese tradition also evolved from an earlier belief in a supreme Lord and many subordinate ghosts and spirits, to a supreme Heaven, surrounded by the spirits of those who have done his bidding in life. One difference is Confucius' preferred reticence on the subject of Heaven or spirits, even when he apparently believed in such and participated in religious rituals. Another has to do with exemplariness. The Hebrew prophets appear to have been possessed, and driven, by their message. They preached ethical monotheism, but their role as prophets had little to do with whether they were themselves the highest models of ethical behaviour.

I therefore agree with H. H. Rowley, a Hebrew scholar and a China missionary, and author of *Prophecy and Religion in Ancient China and Israel*, in his portrayal of Confucius as a prophet. While my use of the term prophet is more Weberian than scriptural, I believe that recognition of certain parallels would eventually advance our study not only of the meaning of Confucius' mission, but also of the understanding of the Hebrew religion – as well as of Christianity – as religious traditions bearing similarities with many others, rather than being exclusivist religions of revelation.[23]

---

[23] Rowley's book was published by the University of London's Athlone Press, 1956. See pp. 125–6.

Benevolent government: the rectification of names

Confucius' political philosophy is founded upon the same norms for right and wrong, good and evil, as is the rest of his personal and social ethics. It is enunciated in the doctrine called the 'Rectification of Names' (*cheng-ming / zhengming*), a kind of language philosophy that he proposed when a disciple asked about what to do first in government:

'It would certainly be to correct language.'
'Can I have heard you right . . . ? Why has language to be corrected?'
'If language is incorrect, what is said does not agree with what is meant . . . and what is to be done cannot be effected.' (Analects 13:3)

In a terse formula, he said: 'Ruler, ruler; minister, minister; father, father; son, son' (12:11). And this has been translated as 'Let the ruler be a ruler, the minister a minister, the father a father, the son a son.'[24] These words are ambiguous, and have been interpreted in various ways. The preferred interpretation over the centuries has been that both ruler and minister, and father and son, have to strive to fulfil an ideal.

Mencius, too, was adamant about the reciprocity of respect inherent in the ruler–minister relationship. In his words:

If a ruler treats his ministers as his own hands and feet, the ministers will regard him as their belly and their heart. If the ruler treats his ministers as dogs and horses, the ministers will regard him as any other man. If the ruler regards the ministers as dirt and grass, the ministers will regard him as a bandit and an enemy.[25]

Confucius' words could be better understood with the help of Hsün-tzu, a third-century-BCE follower of the Confucian school, who explained:

Nowadays . . . the sages and true kings have all passed away. Men are careless in abiding by established names . . . names and realities become confused, and the distinction between right and wrong has become unclear . . . If a true king were to appear now, he would surely set about reviving the old names, and creating new ones.[26]

Confucianism as state orthodoxy

Before we can answer properly the question of whether Confucius was at all a revolutionary, we have to mention how the school

---

[24] Adapted from Lau, *Analects*, p. 114.   [25] Mencius 4B:3.
[26] *Hsün-tzu*, 16:2b; Watson (trans.), p. 141.

representing his teachings became recognized by the Han dynastic house as the orthodox system of thought – some would say, like a state religion – subsidised and supported by state power. This happened in the first century CE, under the dynamic Emperor Wu, who established an imperial college at the state capital and inaugurated examinations to assure a state-sponsored education in the Confucian classics.

We remember that Han China was an epoch when all under Heaven was unified under one ruler governing by Heaven's Mandate, and eventually with the help of Confucian orthodoxy. It was a development parallel to early Christendom under Constantine, who had a 'political theology' of one God, one Logos, one Emperor and one World – with philosophical monotheism applied to the monarchical order. No wonder the name Han became identified with the majority population of China, which has been so marked by the transformations that took place during those times.

The scholar who allegedly consolidated the gains of Confucianism was the second-century-BCE 'political theologian' Tung Chung-shu, who sought with metaphysical arguments to persuade the ruler to exercise benevolent government. Systematising traditional thought, he established Heaven, earth and man as a horizontal triad, with kingship as the vertical link between them.

Those who in ancient times invented writing drew three lines and connected them through the middle, calling the word 'king'. The three lines represent Heaven, earth and the human being, and that which passes through the middle joins the principles of all three . . .
Thus the king is but the executor of Heaven. He regulates its seasons and brings them to completion . . .
The great concern of the ruler is to watch over and guard his heart, that his loves and hates, angers and joys may be displayed in accordance with right.[27]

Sagehood as universally accessible

Confucius is known for accepting disciples without consideration of their class backgrounds. Mencius went a step further. He made it explicit that he regarded everyone as capable of becoming sages. ' "Is it true that all human beings are capable of becoming a Yao or

---

[27] *Ch'un-ch'iu fan-lu*, English trans. adapted from Wm. Theodore de Bary (ed.), *Sources of Chinese Tradition* (New York: Columbia University Press, 1960), pp. 179, 181.

a Shun?" he was once asked. "Yes," he answered.' The questioner pursued, making a point of comparing physical height (according to Chinese measure), ' "I heard that King Wen was ten feet tall, and King T'ang was nine. Now I am a little more than nine foot four inches, yet all I can do is eat rice! What should I do?" "What difficulty is there? All you have to do is make an effort." '

And he concluded, 'The Way is like a wide road. It is not at all difficult to find. The trouble with some people is simply that they do not look for it.'[28]

That Mencius was asked the question by someone else showed that the idea was not entirely new. But the fact that *he* confirmed it rendered it new, by giving it his own authority, which for later generations would be the authority of a sage, the one just next in rank to Confucius. This assertion was therefore revolutionary on two grounds: (1) that sagehood is no longer limited to rulers or high ministers, and therefore, that it is no longer a concept tied to politics, and (2) that everyone is therefore equal, in his or her access to this exalted state.

It is the philosophical appropriation of the sage-king paradigm, and it would eventually transform the paradigm, by 'privatising' the concept, and also by highlighting universal human perfectibility, which is another term for the natural equality of all human beings.

WHO WERE THE CONFUCIANS (Ju^b/RU)?

The Doctrine of the Mean (20:8), a Confucian text, names three cardinal virtues: wisdom (*chih* / *zhi*), humaneness (*jen*^{b}) and courage. After all, ancient Chinese society, like the Homeric society of ancient Greece, was an aristocratic, warrior society, for which courage (*yung*^{b}) was a paramount virtue. Even in Confucius' time, the majority of the fighting men were from noble families. Only the sons of the nobility had access to education, including a military as well as a civil education. If Master K'ung broke precedent with the past, it was in accepting disciples without regard to their class background.[29] Interestingly, the portraits we have of Confucius depict him usually in his flowing scholar's robes, but carrying a sword on his left hip.

[28] Mencius 6B:2; Eng. trans. adapted from Lau, p. 172.
[29] Consult Whalen Lai, '*Yung* and the Tradition of the *Shih*: The Confucian Restructuring of Heroic Courage', *Religious Studies* 21 (1985), 181–203.

The emerging scholars (Ju^b) and intellectuals (shih^b / shi)

While the name of Confucius became linked in Western languages to the tradition called Confucianism, the same did not happen in Chinese, where the tradition is called the tradition of scholars, or *ju^b*. Etymologically, the word *ju^b* is related to the word 'mild' (*jou / rou*),[30] and the modern scholar Hu Shih claims that it possessed the meaning of 'weaklings' or 'cowards' (*nuo*), referring originally to those dispossessed aristocrats of antiquity who were no longer warriors but lived off their knowledge of rituals or history, music, numbers or archery.[31]

That the Confucians were warriors turned into scholars certainly happened in Japan, where the *samurai* class got educated and turned to more peaceful pursuits during the Tokugawa period (1600–1868). The theory has been challenged in China's case. It has been pointed out that there had long been an 'intellectual class' since the Shang days, including religious and secular specialists who served with their brains rather than with the sword.[32] This does not necessarily mean that Confucians were the intellectual heirs of shamans. The Taoists have more reason to claim that legacy. It is clear that many minor aristocrats who responded positively to Confucius' teachings were from warrior families. Occasionally, during Confucius' travels, his disciples had to fight to defend him against attackers (Mencius 7B:18).

But it is interesting that a word like *ju^b*, referring to a 'mild' man who was not interested in fighting but engaged in the study of classical texts, came to represent the scholar, and particularly the follower of the Confucian school. The Japanese scholar Katō Jōken thinks that there were many such 'weaklings' in ancient China, some of whom were shamans. He even reasons that the term 'good man' (*shan-jen / shanren*) of the Analects also refers to such a mild and gentle person.[33]

In Analects 6:11, Confucius tells his disciple Tzu-hsia: 'Be a *chün-tzu ju^b / junziru* (gentleman scholar), not a *hsiao-jen ju / xiaorenru* (petty

---

[30] *Shuo-wen*, ch. 8A:2–3.

[31] See Hu Shih's article on Confucianism in the *Encyclopaedia of Social Sciences* (New York: Macmillan, 1930–5), vol. 4, pp. 198–201.

[32] Yü Ying-shih, *Chung-kuo chih-shih chieh-tseng shih-lun: Ku-tai p'ien* (The history of the intellectual class in ancient China) (Nankang, Taiwan: Academia Sinica, 1980), pp. 106–7.

[33] See Katō, *Chūgoku kodai bunka*, pp. 133–64.

scholar).' This is the only occasion in this text where the word *ju*[b] appears. It refers to a scholar, without specifying his lineage or partisanship. In the Book of Mencius, the same word appears twice, but each time signifies a particular group of scholars: the Confucians.

Hsün-tzu makes frequent reference to scholars (*ju*[b]), referring by the word to Confucians. In a conversation with King Chao of Ch'in, he describes the 'great Confucians' (*ta-ju / daru*) as ancient sages like the Duke of Chou, who always followed right even when he had to govern in his nephew's place and order the execution of his own rebellious elder brother. The Confucians (*ju*[b]) in general are men who model themselves upon the ancient sages, esteem the rituals as well as virtue, and bring honour to their rulers. When invited, they serve in government; when left alone, they remain obedient. They never compromise their moral principles, even at the risk of becoming poor and hungry.[34]

These are the words of a diplomat, of a man eager to please, to ingratiate himself and other *ju*[b] with the king.

The term *ju*[b] may be better understood in relation to the term *shih*[b], related to its homophone, to work or to serve (*shih*[c])[35] In antiquity, it had the primary meaning of an officer or a knight, a military man in the service of the king or of a feudal lord, and the secondary meaning of a man in official service. The *shih*[b] were minor aristocrats, men who originally fought for their kings and lords and, in later ages, served them in other capacities. But the word also had the extended and universal meaning of being a man, a husband. Still later, it came to refer to scholar officials, or just scholars, who represented the top of the social ladder, above the peasant farmers, the craftsmen, and the merchants.

In the classical and philosophical texts of our period, i.e., roughly from about the sixth century BCE to the first century CE, the word *shih*[b] usually represents a social class, an officer or an official, one who ranked after the grand official (*ta-fu / dafu*). Outside of emphasising that the *shih*[b] is a man who is resolute in the practice of virtues (Mencius 7A:9), the Book of Mencius mentions the term usually in the social context. The *shih*[b] is described (5B:2) in the Chou system of rank and income as serving under either a king or a feudal lord, and ranking after the chief minister and the grand official or counsellor. Among themselves, the *shih*[b] were divided into

---

[34] *Hsün-tzu*, 4:1–2.   [35] *Shuo-wen*, 1A:27b.

three grades. The senior *shih*[b] at a royal court received the same area of land as a viscount or a baron, and were the lowest officials with direct access to the king. In any feudal state, large or small, the *shih*[b] of the third grade was rewarded with an income in place of what he would get from cultivating land, that is, the same as a commoner in official service.[36]

With the distinctions blurring between the junior *shih*[b] and the commoner in public service, the term *shih*[b] eventually came to represent the scholar-gentry in general. We might say that while every *ju*[b] might be called a *shih*[b], not every *shih*[b] was necessarily a *ju*[b]. For example, magicians were called *fang-shih* / *fangshi*, 'men of special skills'. And eventually, Taoist priests would be called *tao-shih*[b] / *daoshi*.

The distinction between a *shih*[b] and a *ju*[b] emerges with more clarity when we examine the meaning of the Six Arts (*Liu-yi*) of antiquity, especially of the Chou times, which made up the educational curriculum of the time. These included archery, charioteering, music, writing (especially as found in oracle inscriptions), numbers (as used in divination by yarrow stalks), and of course, the rites.[37]

The Six Arts included both martial and literary skills. In both the Analects and Mencius, we find mention of such skills as involved in archery and charioteering, and we know that both Confucius and Mencius were trained in them. Archery is the subject for which we have the most evidence. It was taught in the Chou district and village schools as well as in a special 'archery school'.[38] An exercise in archery preceded the grand sacrifice of the Son of Heaven. But the training in archery appears to have been not merely one of skill, but also one of ritual comportment, and even more, of a disposition of respect and propriety. The Yi-li (Ritual Etiquette) quotes Confucius as saying: 'The gentleman is without a spirit of competition. Otherwise, should he not especially show it while doing archery? Yet each does not mount his bow . . . without greeting and effacing himself in the presence of the other . . . This is how the gentlemen practice competition!'[39]

---

[36] Legge, *Chinese Classics*, vol. 2, pp. 373–6; Lau, *Mencius*, pp. 151–2.
[37] *Chou-li Cheng-chu*, chs 5 and 7.
[38] Herrlee G. Creel, *The Origins of Statecraft in China* (University of Chicago Press, 1970), pp. 407–8.
[39] *Yi-li Cheng-chu* (The Ritual Etiquette with Cheng Hsüan's Commentary), SPPY ed., chs 5 and 7.

For true gentlemen, ritual comportment and the moral dispositions it nourishes carry over also to war. Mencius (4B:24) compares
the fate of the mythical Archer Yi (judged as lacking discernment in
the choice of friends), killed by his unprincipled and ambitious
disciple P'eng Meng, eager to eliminate a rival in the art, and the
story of a battle between the states of Cheng and Wei. Cheng's
commander-in-chief, a great archer, was ordered to invade Wei, but
developed a physical indisposition preventing him from handling the
bow. Normally, this would spell certain death at the hands of the
enemy, especially as his pursuer was the best archer in Wei. But he
knew also that his life would be spared, since this archer, his enemy,
had learnt his skills from his own disciple, a man who chose friends
and disciples with discernment. As the story unfolds, the pursuer
found the pursued and left him unharmed. Confronting a moral
conflict between a duty to the prince and a duty to a teacher's
teacher, the archer of Wei 'drew his arrows, knocked their tips off
against the wheel, and let fly a set of four arrows before he retired'.[40]

An education in the Six Arts was the privilege of the aristocrats,
including the *shih*[b], a group more numerous than the other members
of the nobility, from whom the Confucian as well as other schools
recruited many of their followers. Yü Ying-shih offers the hypothesis
that the intellectual transformation came from a 'philosophic breakthrough', the emergence of Confucianism which replaced the old
educational curriculum based on the Six Arts with a new one based
on the Six Classics.[41] We may add that since the Chinese military
tradition valued intelligence and strategy over brute strength, the
educational and social transformations were not difficult.[42]

In any case, the difference of opinion is not over whether the *shih*[b]
originated as a warrior class of minor aristocracy, but rather when
their transformation into intellectuals took place. And if the *shih*[b]
were trained in the Six Arts, so were the early *ju*[b], who came to be
known as 'masters' of the Six Arts.[43] By the time of Confucius, there
is question as to what had become of the Six Arts. The term came to
refer also to the Six Classics, namely, the Book of Changes (*Yi-ching*),
the Book of History (*Shu-ching*), the Book of Songs (*Shih-ching*), the

[40] English trans. in Lau, *Mencius*, pp. 132–3.
[41] Yü, *Chung-kuo chih-shih chieh-ch'en*, pp. 10–56.
[42] Consult Lisa Raphal, *Knowing Words: Wisdom and Cunning in the Classical Traditions of China and Greece* (Ithaca: Cornell university Press, 1992), p. 103.
[43] *Shih-chi*, Biography of Confucius, ch. 47, p. 163.

Book of Rites (*Li-chi*), the Spring–Autumn Annals (*Ch'un–ch'iu*), and the lost Book of Music.[44] This later list represents a much more literary selection of courses to study. The possibility is that most followers of the Confucian school preferred the pursuit of book learning, and became increasingly identified with such. Not that they were the only 'scholars' of books, but they were certainly scholars and experts of specific texts, the classics. And it is in this light that Confucians were represented by the scholarly followers of other schools, whether Mohism, Taoism, or Legalism.

Should we, however, regard both *shih*[b] and *ju*[b] as descriptive terms only, or had they each a moral or ideal character? The Analects speaks more of *shih*[b] than of *ju*[b], which became representative of the Confucian school only some time after the Master's death. The contexts include both social and moral ones. In a conversation with the disciple Tzu-kung, Confucius says that, on the highest level, the ideal *shih*[b] is a man with 'a sense of shame in the way he conducts himself [who] . . . when sent abroad, does not disgrace the commission of his lord'. At a grade below, the *shih*[b] 'is a good son in his clan' and 'a respectful young man in the village'. At still another grade below, such a man 'insists on keeping his word and seeing his actions through to the end'. When Tzu-kung then asked about the men who were then actually in public life, he got the answer: 'Oh, they are of such limited capacity that they hardly count!' (13:20).[45]

Even more, in the words of Tseng-tzu, the *shih*[b] is 'strong and resolute, for his burden is heaven and . . . [his] road is long. He takes benevolence (*jen*[b]) as his burden. Is that not heavy? Only with death does the road come to an end. Is that not long?' And this is echoed by another disciple, Tzu-chang, according to whom the *shih*[b] is 'ready to lay down his life in the face of danger', 'does not forget what is right at the sight of gain', nor 'reverence during a sacrifice nor sorrow while in mourning' (19:1). The reference both to readiness to die for the right cause and to ritual propriety reminds us of the martial character. The expectation of preferring right over gain is simply a moral one.[46]

By Hsün-tzu's time, in the third century BCE, the word *shih*[b] had lost much of its aristocratic connotations, and referred to men of

---

44 Pan Ku, *Han-shu* (Han Dynastic History), K'ai-ming ed., Treatise on Literature, ch. 30, p. 434; Preface to the *Ju-lin*, ch. 88, p. 582.
45 Legge, *Chinese Classics*, vol. 1, p. 271; see also Lau, *Analects*, pp. 122–3.
46 Consult Legge, *Chinese Classics*, vol. 1, p. 339; the English trans. is from Lau, *Analects*, p. 153.

talent in general, particularly to those many men who found service with a lord – any lord. The standards had generally lowered, and certain lords collected men of every description of talent, sometimes numbering in the thousands, and including petty thieves who, once recruited and eating from the lord's tables, were also called *shih*[b].[47]

Generally, the *shih*[b] became known as intellectuals. But given the social and moral qualifications, one can understand why the same English word, 'gentleman', is often used to translate both *shih*[b] and *chün-tzu / junzi* (literally: ruler's sons, princes). Sometimes, it is said that the *shih*[b] made up the lowest group of the *chün-tzu*. So we have here an even better example of a sociological term that Confucius transformed into a moral ideal type.

*The ideal gentleman (*chün-tzu*)*

Let us first discuss the opposition between the gentleman and the petty man. Speaking etymologically, it presupposes the distinction between the noblemen, literally, the ruler's sons (*chün-tzu*), and the small men (*hsiao-jen / xiaoren*), literally, the subject population. This is the meaning given to these terms in such classical texts as the Book of History and the Book of Songs.

Confucius made of the sociological term 'gentleman' a moral term and an ideal type. Let us take cognisance of the magnitude of scale of this transformation, which moved from defining the human being by birth to defining the person by moral character.

The independent references to the gentleman, as well as the references made to contrast it to *hsiao-jen*, are numerous in both the Analects and the Book of Mencius. Some of them are very well known. Confucius says, for example, that the gentleman 'is not a utensil', that is, not an instrument devoted to specific tasks, but a person whose dignity comes from a higher pursuit. He 'devotes his mind to attaining the Way and not to securing food' (Analects 15:31).[48] For Confucius, the ultimate goal of life is striving to become a sage. However, this goal is hard to reach, and the only sages known to him were the ancients. Accordingly he says, 'I have no hopes of meeting a sage. I would be content if I met someone who is a gentleman' (Analects 7:26).

---

[47] Yang Kuan (Yang K'uan), *Zhanguo shi* (History of the Warring States), 2nd ed. (Shanghai: Renmin, 1983), pp. 402–3.
[48] Legge, *Chinese Classics*, vol. 1, 303; Lau, *Analects*, p. 136.

In another famous statement that must sound irrational to a capitalist's ears, Confucius also says that the small man understands what is profitable, while the gentleman understands what is moral (Analects 4:16). It is a theme which was much discussed in classical and traditional China.

A disciple beset with anxiety was told that the gentleman is free from worries and fears, because, on examining himself, he should find nothing for which he must reproach himself (Analects 12:4). Mencius would add that on all occasions, he should reproach neither Heaven nor man (Mencius 2B:13). Mencius' description of the gentleman tends to be in affective terms, as someone 'kind to creatures, loving to the people, and affectionate to his family and relatives' (7A:45).

Indeed, it was Mencius who redefined courage in moral terms, not as the courage of raw emotions, not even only as the courage of will, coming from a singleness of purpose that controls passions, but even more as a courage grounded in humaneness and righteousness. Already, the Analects has Confucius saying: 'The determined scholar and the man of virtue will not seek to live at the expense of injuring their virtue (*jen*[b]). They will even sacrifice their lives to keep their virtue intact' (15:8). And Mencius says: 'I like life; I also like righteousness. If I cannot keep both, I will let life go and choose righteousness' (6A:10).[49]

In the philosopher Hsün-tzu, we find an entire chapter on the gentleman, and many references elsewhere. But the term takes on increasingly the tone of good breeding. In one context, the philosopher quotes from the Book of Songs, where the term *chün-tzu* obviously refers to the ruler himself:

> Gracious and splendid,
> Like a jade scepter, a jade baton,
> Of good fame, good aspect,
> The joyous gentleman
> Is regulator of the four quarters.[50]

Hsün-tzu continues:

[The gentleman] observes the proper degree of courtesy and obeys the rules of seniority. No improper words leave his lips; no evil sayings come

---

[49] Consult Ching, *Confucianism and Christianity*, p. 87.
[50] Consult Legge, *Chinese Classics*, vol. 4, p. 493; the translation is from Watson, *Hsün-tzu*, p. 148.

from his mouth. With a benevolent (*jen*[b]) mind he explains his ideas to others; with the mind of learning he listens to their words, and with a fair mind he makes his judgements.[51]

This tendency to characterise the gentleman in terms of good breeding reaffirms the aristocratic character of the Confucian school. While Confucius did accomplish a certain moral revolution, by transforming the mores of his times, there is no denying that he and his school represented a point of view that belonged to the scholar-aristocrats – the *shih*[b], and that his followers, called the *ju*[b], came mainly from the *shih*[b] class, representing a point of view coloured by the advantages and perhaps prejudices of this class. With the continuing decline of the *shih*[b] as a class and the cheapened connotation of the term itself, the term gentleman (*chün-tzu*) came more and more into its own. Many of these gentlemen were specialists on rituals. With the dissolution of the feudal order, some might have lived off their knowledge of ritual among commoners, as teachers, and as ceremonial directors or consultants, without serving at court.[52]

But the social sympathies of the followers of the Confucian school become even clearer when we examine the Confucians together with the fifth-century-BCE thinker Mo-tzu and his followers, the 'Mohists'. Mo-tzu was of humble origin; his very surname, Mo, may signify a tattoo mark, perhaps that given to a slave or a criminal, as he was called a 'lowly person', a man of humble origin.[53] Where Confucius and Mencius were satisfied with a modest way of living, and moved about in chariots, Mo-tzu subsisted on a frugal diet, clothed in a peasant's garb, and relied on his feet for transport. Even if he once studied under some Confucian masters, he departed from them to start his own school of thought that would give voice to the opinions of the commoners. The doctrine of universal love (*chien-ai* / *jian'ai*) which characterises Mohist thought is expressive of the philosopher-commoner's viewpoint in contrast to the doctrine of humaneness or benevolence (*jen*[b]), with its built-in special relationships, which gave it the name 'graded love'. By the time of Mencius, the Mohist school

---

[51] *Hsün-tzu*, 16:7a; Watson (trans.), p. 148.
[52] For a work that emphasises the role of ritual – including dance – in Confucian life, see Robert Eno, *The Confucian Creation of Heaven: Philosophy and the Defense of Ritual Mastery* (Albany: State University of New York Press, 1990).
[53] *Mo-tzu*, 12:1b.

had acquired much strength, and became, as did the Taoists and the Legalists, a rival to the Confucian *ju*^b. Its popularity continued into the third century BCE. And reflections can be found in the text *Hsün-tzu* about the Mohists, judged in a somewhat unfavourable light, among other things, as niggardly, lacking good breeding, and confusing names and realities.

Nevertheless, the physically weak scholars of the sixth century BCE strengthened themselves with moral authority and formulated a system of ethical humanism that retained some of the religious beliefs of the past while discarding and transforming others. Their power was that of words and ideas. They never succeeded in radically changing the political system; indeed, they sought merely to advise the rulers. After many trials and tribulations, they were entrusted by the Han emperors with the constructing of a state ideology. Unable to *make* real kings, they created an ideal king in the person of the deceased Confucius.

Finally, was Confucius a revolutionary? True, he served more as a selective and critical transmitter of ancient wisdom, preserving, in substance, the values of the patriarchal kinship society of the early Chou times. All the same, we cannot neglect the fact that in that role, he also transformed the wisdom of antiquity, handing down a legacy of humanistic wisdom, emphasising what is rational and contributing probably to the demythologisation of remote antiquity. We might say that Confucius' teachings have left behind some revolutionary results, to the extent that the feudal, aristocratic, military society eventually changed into a society where the highest values were ethical ones relating human beings to one another and to the society as such.

Besides, closely following Confucius' footsteps was Mencius, who became great in his own right. Where Confucius was respectful to feudal rulers, and modest about his own qualities, Mencius was straightforward and at times blunt, in manifesting his disapproval of the rulers' excesses. We have discussed many of Mencius' ideas already. We might add that these have a revolutionary potential, which was recognised in later ages. Where Confucius represented an appropriation of the sage-king paradigm because he himself became acknowledged afterwards as China's greatest sage, Mencius represented a further appropriation of the same ideal, which he would emphasise, belongs to everyone in the world.

THE LIMITATIONS OF CONFUCIANISM: THE SUBORDINATION OF WOMEN

Confucius might have been revolutionary in some respects, but in others, he was too much of a traditionalist, keeping the ways of Chou and rejecting those of earlier periods. An area in which Confucian humanism shows its limitations regards the role of women. The process for subjugating women to men began before Confucius, with the development of the patriarchal kinship system associated with the ancestral cult in the Chou period, together with confirmation of the hereditary male principle in successions to the throne. The ritual texts speak about the 'three obediences', subjecting women to their fathers, then to husbands, and then to sons during widowhood.[54] Doubtless, Confucius supported the patriarchal character of society in general. He has said: 'Women and people of low birth are very hard to deal with. If you are familiar with them, they get out of hand. If you keep your distance, they resent it' (Analects 17:25). We might note that women and people of low birth were both excluded from education. And while Confucius sought to be more inclusive in his teaching of disciples, he did not extend that privilege to women.

A story tells how Master K'ung once paid a visit to a lady infamous for her incestuous relationships, Nan-tzu, the wife of Duke Ling of Wei. This action makes us think he was not above some politicking with a ruler's inner court. That it happened shows that noble women in his times were still able to maintain their statuses while enjoying their notoriety, even receiving unrelated male guests on their own, as well as powerful enough over their spouses regarding the possible employment of these male guests. But this act greatly displeased the disciple Tzu-lu, and led the Master to swear (literally: with an arrow), 'If I have done anything improper, may Heaven's curse be on me, may Heaven's curse be on me!' (6:28).[55]

What did the oath mean? In my opinion, it was only a social visit, as the Master was above ingratiating himself sexually with a ruler's spouse, which, after all, would be a punishable crime. But the question was of propriety, and K'ung defended himself on that

---

[54] *Li-chi Cheng-chu*, 8: 9b.
[55] The translation is from Lau, *Analects*, p. 85. On the point of the oath-taking, consult Waley (trans.), *Analects*, pp. 240–1.

ground, which demonstrates a rather broad view of permissible social interaction between men and women.

Within the framework of Confucian thinking, the individual was regarded always as a member of a much more important, larger group, be that family or society. The gender question constituted therefore part and parcel of a larger complex of questions involving the Five Relationships.

If we examine Confucian texts, we actually find little treatment of the position of women and their obligations. But it is the little we do find that makes an important difference. For example, the Book of Changes was for ages past an important text for philosophical reflection. There, the Hexagrams Ch'ien (*Qian*, Heaven) and K'un (*Kun*, Earth) represent respectively the *yang* and the *yin* forces, and these in turn represent the male and the female. Thus woman is to man as earth is to Heaven, lowly and inferior, weak and receptive. To quote the words of the Great Appendix to the *Book of Changes*:

> The Way of Ch'ien brings about the male.
> The Way of K'un brings about the female.
> The Ch'ien knows the great beginnings.
> The K'un completes the finished things.[56]

The passage quoted cannot be said to have come directly from Confucius or Mencius, but from a later time when the Confucian school had become the established orthodoxy in the Han state. And in spite of the priority given to the husband–wife relationship there and in the ritual texts, not many great scholars and philosophers have devoted much attention to it in their writings. One of the best-known works governing women's behaviour was actually written by a woman: the second-century-BCE Pan Chao's *Nü-chieh* (Admonitions for Women), which instructed women to know and keep to their lace in a male-dominated society.[57]

Mencius emphasised that human nature is originally good, and therefore perfectible. He taught that every person could become a sage (Mencius 6B:2). Logically, the teaching has served to strengthen a basic belief in human equality, regardless of class or even gender distinctions. Mencius also emphasised that the taboo between the

---

[56] See *Chou-yi cheng-yi* 7:2a. Eng. trans. adapted by Cary F. Baynes from Richard Wilhelm (trans.), *The I Ching or Book of Changes* (Princeton University Press, 1967), p. 285; Lynn (trans.), *The Classic of Changes*, Introduction.

[57] Consult also Theresa Kelleher, 'Confucianism', in Arvind Sharma (ed.), *Women in World Religions* (Albany: State University of New York Press, 1987), pp. 135–60.

sexes should not prevent a man from helping to rescue a drowning woman, such as his sister-in-law. Let us quote the conversation (Mencius 4A:17):

'Is it the rule that males and females are not to touch each other in giving or receiving anything?'

'It is the rule.'

'If a man's sister-in-law is drowning, should he stretch his hand to rescue her?'

'He who would not rescue such a drowning woman is a beast. While it is the *general* rule that males and females not touch each other in giving or receiving, it is a *particular* exigency to stretch one's hand to rescue a drowning sister-in-law.'

In this way, human life and dignity – a *woman's* life and dignity – was placed before ritual law. On balance, however, the position of women continued to weaken as Confucianism gained ascendancy. And it would further deteriorate in later ages, with the emergence of the neo-Confucian philosophers. The Confucian tradition, for example, has always emphasised the importance of keeping the body in good form, as a filial response to the gift of one's parents and ancestors. But few Confucian philosophers before the twentieth century protested the custom of foot-binding which so deformed women, affecting not only their personal health, but also that of their children. While women were never formally excluded from the teachings of Confucian humanism, they were nonetheless excluded from many of its benefits, including those of a formal education.[58]

With the passage of time, and as the established school of thought, Confucianism took on more and more the rigidity of ideology. The position of women continued to decline, whenever this ideology was in force. The eleventh-century philosopher Ch'eng Yi is especially remembered for having said that it is better to starve than to remarry, which is what Chu Hsi reiterated in the twelfth century. After all, 'To starve to death is a very small matter, but to lose one's virtue is a very serious matter.'[59] And Chu took Ch'eng's ideas seriously enough to write to a disciple to urge him to counsel his widowed younger sister not to remarry. He continues, '. . . let her

---

[58] In this respect, we accept the fact that despite Confucius' personal efforts and those of many of his followers, education remained mainly élitist in traditional China, and appears still to be such in mainland China, on account of there being few schools and small enrolments.

[59] Consult *Erh-Ch'eng ch'üan-shu* (Complete Works of the Two Ch'engs), SPPY ed.; *Yi-shu* (Surviving works), 22B:3a.

understand that [just as when a dynasty falls,] the minister must remain loyal, so too . . . the widow must remain chaste . . . From the popular point of view, this is truly unrealistic, but in the eyes of a gentleman who knows the classics, and understands principles, this is something that cannot change.'[60]

Confucian society did offer a few protections for women, prescribing that a wife could not be divorced if she had no home to return to, if she had performed three years of mourning for a parent-in-law, or if the family had risen from poverty or a humble station to wealth and a high station after the marriage.[61]

In the order of nature, the husband–wife relationship precedes even that of the father–son, and certainly, that of the ruler–subject. In the order of social realities, however, the relationship of the wife to the husband was after all patterned on that of the minister to the sovereign. After Sung times, Chinese history witnessed an increasing centralisation of state power in the hands of the ruler, who regarded his ministers as servants rather than as partners, just as the women of his harem were all his concubines. Few intellectuals dared to criticise such a system, while real changes were only introduced in the twentieth century.

And the experience of women was in many ways shared by the men, who were themselves subject to fathers and rulers, in a patriarchal society which became increasingly 'collectivised' without offering protection to the individuals caught in the web. And Confucian humanism was likewise caught in the same web, serving the interests of the absolute state, which slowly drained it of its humanistic content.

CONCLUSION

The focus in this chapter has been the appropriation of the sage-king paradigm by the representatives of the Confucian tradition, especially the philosophers. But this development also witnessed the gradual diminution of the Confucian tradition itself, with its inherent

[60] Letter to Ch'en Shih-chung, in *Chu Wen-kung wen-chi* (Collected writings of Chu Hsi) (abbrev. as *CWWC*), SPPY ed., 26:26b–27a; Consult Wing-tsit Chan, *Chu Hsi: New Studies* (Honolulu: University of Hawaii Press, 1989), p. 540. Men were permitted to divorce their wives for any of seven reasons: disobeying the parents-in-law, not bearing a son, adultery, jealousy, incurable sickness, excessive talkativeness, or theft.

[61] Chan, *Chu Hsi: New Studies*, p. 539.

limitations, into a system of ideology serving the absolute monarchical state.

Against this perspective, we may understand why Confucius' reception by the twentieth century has been full of surprises. He was blamed at its beginning, especially during the May Fourth Students' Movement (1919), for all the ills of society. His teachings were criticised as shackles limiting personal freedom, and as promoting 'ritual cannibalism' that prevented individual fulfilment. He was vilified during the Cultural Revolution (1966–76), and especially in 1973–4 by the Anti-Confucius campaign in Communist China, which attacked his personal character. But then, in the 1980s and after, his reputation received rehabilitation as a new government denounced the political charade that lay behind the disastrous Cultural Revolution. His name even became identified with family values and the work ethic that presumably propelled East Asian societies to rapid economic development.

Will Confucius and his followers also have a few things to teach the future generations? We have to wait and see.

CHAPTER 4

The metaphysician as sage: philosophy again appropriates the paradigm

INTRODUCTION

We are speaking of the appropriation of the sage-king paradigm by the philosophers. This appropriation became further strengthened with the evolution of the theory of Oneness of Heaven and humanity (*T'ien-jen ho-yi*). This theory is usually interpreted within a metaphysical framework. I am doing so while keeping in mind the political Mandate of Heaven, as I understand by the term 'humanity' primarily the paradigmatic human person, the sage, who should also be king. The reasons for that will become clearer after the discussion.[1]

THE MYSTICAL CONSCIOUSNESS OF MENCIUS

'Oneness between Heaven and Humanity' usually refers to the correspondence and harmony between two realms: the human, and the natural or cosmic. We search in vain in the Analects and in the classics for an explicit articulation of these four Chinese words. However, the meaning is implicit as a philosophical presupposition for several of these texts, in particular the Appendix to the Book of Changes – actually a commentary added in the early Han dynasty. And we find in Mencius a philosophical development that we may well associate with these words. We do so if we remember that with Mencius, the term *t'ien* or Heaven has come to represent much more of a transcendent moral force, rather than the supreme personal deity that it appeared to have been with Confucius, 'For a man to give full realisation to his mind or heart is for him to understand his

---

[1] Heiner Roetz, *Mensch und Natur im alten China* (Frankfurt: Peter Lang, 1984), offers a very good analysis of this question.

own nature, and a man who knows his own nature will know Heaven. By retaining his mind or heart and nurturing his nature he is serving Heaven' (Mencius 7A:1).[2]

The Chinese word *hsin* may be translated as either mind or heart, or as both, since it is the seat of both intelligence and will. In the above passage, Mencius talks about 'realising' or 'fulfilling' the mind or heart, bringing out its full potential, and asserts that such will lead to 'knowing Heaven'. In other words, he is proposing a certain continuum between the mind or heart, which is within us, and Heaven, which we tend to think of as outside of us, as above us, and as transcending us. As he has also said, 'The myriad things are all within me. There is no greater joy for me than to find, on self-examination, that I am true to myself . . . This is the shortest way to humaneness [*jen*[b]]' (Mencius 7A:4).

'The myriad things' is another term for the exterior universe. But for Mencius, the universe is also interior to human beings. It is both inside and outside, both transcending our human limitations and yet immanent in us. The insight expressed has puzzled many Western scholars and philosophers, who have argued that what transcends cannot also be what is immanent. But it has also served as the principal foundation for much of Chinese thought, both for later followers of Mencius and for philosophical Taoism.

The 'oneness between Heaven and humanity' has been a troubling idea for Western philosophers. It seems to deny the separation between object and subject, the natural and human orders, the other and the self, transcendence and immanence. And that would indeed be so, if the statement were taken in its literal sense. Even Chinese philosophy has witnessed an entire spectrum of positions regarding this issue, with certain thinkers within Confucianism and Taoism (and, later, Ch'an Buddhism) favouring the 'oneness', to the point of almost denying 'otherness', and other thinkers preferring more distinction, or even complete separation between the natural and the human. And there are those others who understand the 'oneness' in an analogical manner, as maintaining a distinction between the two realms while pointing out a relationship of the human as microcosm to the natural as macrocosm. I shall be dwelling especially on this third interpretation.

That the transcendent is also immanent does not necessarily

---

[2] English translation adapted from D. C. Lau, *Mencius*, p. 182.

destroy the meaning of transcendence. What is being said is not perfect identity, but the discovery of the transcendent on one level, that of human consciousness, in the depth of the mind or heart. I am referring to an insight associated with mystical consciousness: what a fourteenth-century Western thinker, Nicolas of Cusa, has called the 'coincidence of opposites', holding that the divine may be discovered in the human heart. We are not necessarily also saying that the divine is present *only* in human consciousness. This is an insight also developed by the seventeenth-century German philosopher G. W. Leibniz, who sensed a personal affinity with Chinese thought, and whose own philosophy of the monads has affirmed a similar insight.[3]

At first sight, this may not seem to have anything to do with the political mandate to govern. But we remember that the Mandate comes from Heaven, and that, much earlier, Heaven was regarded as a personal deity. With philosophical evolution, as Heaven became a symbol for a transcendent moral force, the Mandate was still associated with it, and rulers were still responsible to this Heaven for their manner of governing. What has changed pertains especially to the extension of a particular relationship to Heaven from the ruler alone to the philosopher-sage, and through him, to everyone else.

After all, Mencius has also affirmed that everyone can be a Yao and a Shun. In so doing, he has extended the possibility of sagehood to everyone. In short, the exclusive connection between sagehood and kingship – including participating in kingship as a minister of state – is no longer accepted. Presumably, having seen that actual kings were usually not sages, Mencius and others have implicitly redefined sagehood, when they extend its accessibility to everyone.

By doing so, Mencius and others are also extending the meaning of *T'ien-ming*, Heaven's Mandate or decree, and applying it to everyone. Everyone has a call to greatness, to sagehood. Everyone has to respond to Heaven's will where it regards himself or herself, in the existential conditions in which each person finds herself or himself.

Mencius' assertion that sagehood is accessible to all did not remain unchallenged. This came especially in the third century, during the period of political disunity when society was highly stratified and class-conscious. Neo-Taoism, that school of so-called

---

[3] Consult Julia Ching and Willard G. Oxtoby (eds), *Moral Enlightenment: Leibniz and Wolff on China*, *Monumenta Serica* Monograph Series, no. 26 (Nettetal: Steyler Verlag, 1992).

'mysterious learning' (*hsüan-hsüeh* / *xuanxue*), with its commentaries on the Taoist philosophical texts, and with its accent on protest and romanticism, was prominent. Neo-Taoist philosophers were redefining sageliness as oneness with the indeterminate, metaphysical Tao. To them, this goal was difficult to achieve, and probably not for all.

The argument was that sagehood could hardly be universally accessible when sages were so few and far between. People were rather 'predestined to greatness' – in a sense reflecting the social order of the day – and sages too, were 'born', not made.

It took a young neo-Taoist philosopher, Wang Pi (226–49 CE), to refute this argument, which was formulated in terms of 'whether sages have emotions', with the assumption that having emotions would be a stumbling block for most mortals to achieve sagehood. To argue, however, that sages did not have emotions would not only restrict access to achieving sagehood, but would also render sages near-divine, or at least superhuman.[4]

Wang Pi asserted rather that sages had emotions, just like everyone else, but 'were not ensnared by them'. In other words, sages were human too, but they had spiritual intelligence (*shen-ming*), and were able to rise above the excesses of emotions in their responses to things and circumstances. His proposition would eventually win the day.[5]

The physical universe of Hsün-tzu

Not everyone agreed with Mencius either regarding the mystical presence of Heaven within, or associating it with sageliness. I have in mind Hsün-tzu, also a follower of the Confucian school. For over a millennium after the deaths of both Mencius and Hsün-tzu, it was the latter who was considered as the carrier of Confucius' mantle. His voice (and others like his) should be heard; it may also help us to understand Mencius better.

Mencius claimed that human nature was originally good, and gave that as a reason for human perfectibility. Hsün-tzu believed that human nature was originally wicked, but agreed with Mencius

---

[4] The question of human beings 'without emotions' comes from *Chuang-tzu*, 2:23b–24a.
[5] Consult Ch'en Shou, *San-kuo chih*, *Wei-chih*, K'ai-ming ed., ch. 28, p. 999c; Jung Chao-tsu, *Wei-Chin te tzu-jan chu-yi* (The naturalism of the Wei-Chin Times) (Taipei: Commercial Press, 1970), ch. 1.

regarding its perfectibility, provided it is straightened out by education and ritual discipline.

Mencius spoke in mystical terms about the oneness of Heaven and humanity. For him, human beings participate in the moral force that is Heaven. This is existentially so on account of the *ch'i*[a] (air, breath, energy) that is in the universe and in all living beings. And this *ch'i*[a] takes on a special moral character in the case of human beings, moral judgement being the distinguishing mark between humans and animals.

Many others of his time and even before and after were more seized by the meaning of natural phenomena, like eclipses of the sun and the appearance of comets, for human society. These were often interpreted as signs from on high, and as reflections on the moral quality of a ruler's government.

Hsün-tzu, however, regarded Heaven as physical nature. And he argued against the theory that natural phenomena have any relevance to human action. 'Heaven's ways are constant: they did not make [Emperor] Yao prevail, and they did not cause [Emperor] Chieh to perish. Respond to heaven with good government, and good fortune will result; respond to heaven with chaos, and misfortunes will result.'[6] Hsün-tzu goes on to define a perfect man as someone who can 'distinguish between Heaven and humanity'. 'Although the sage has deep understanding, he does not attempt to apply it to the work of Heaven . . . The sage does not seek to understand Heaven.'[7] A logical and systematic thinker, Hsün-tzu sought to separate human affairs from so-called supernatural signs and wonders. The fall of comets and other unusual phenomena occurs once in a while, he says, with the changes of Heaven and Earth and the mutations of the cosmic forces of *yin* and *yang*.

Among all such strange occurrences, the ones really to be feared are human portents. When the plowing is badly done and the crops suffer, when the weeding is poorly done and the harvest fails; when the government is evil and loses popular support . . . these are what I meant by human portents.[8]

He was followed, or even surpassed, in his rationalism by the Han thinker Wang Ch'ung (27–97?), who reasoned with a scientific mind

[6] *Hsün-tzu*, sect. 17, 11:9a. Eng. trans. adapted from Watson, p. 79.
[7] *Hsün-tzu*, Sect. 17, 11:9b–10a. Watson, p. 80.
[8] *Hsün-tzu*, sect. 17, 11:12b. Eng. trans. adapted from Watson, p. 84.

and disapproved of the superstitions of his times. Like Hsün-tzu, he sought to separate the realm of human affairs from that of natural occurrences. In his work, he reasons that Heaven did not punish wicked rulers like Chieh and Chou with droughts, floods and famines. The sage ruler Yao had a bad flood on his hands, and the good king T'ang had to deal with a severe drought.

> Good government is not due to the efforts of worthies or sages, nor is disorder the result of immorality . . . [when] there is scarcity of grain, the people cannot endure cold and hunger . . . This is not caused by the government but is the result of seasonal cycles . . . [Even] during the reigns of sage-kings, such calamities . . . occasionally occur.[9]

Actually, the Confucian school was at a crossroads. It could have gone a completely rationalist way, adhering to ritual, but only as an ornament for a gentleman's deportment, and forgetting the correspondence theory between humanity and nature. That it did not do so had a lot to do with another Han thinker, Tung Chung-shu.

TUNG CHUNG-SHU'S UNIVERSE OF CORRESPONDENCE

We should, however, go back a bit in time to the early Han, in order to understand the universe of thought that was introduced at the time when Confucianism became dominant. This takes us to Tung Chung-shu.

I am referring to ancient ideas regarding the two opposing and yet complementary forces, *yin* and *yang*, as well as a system of correlative or associative thinking focused on five primal elements viewed as active cosmic agents always engaged in a process of mutual interaction and change. These include water, fire, wood, metal and earth, each with a power over another, such as water over fire, fire over earth, earth over metal, metal over wood and wood over water. These five agents differ from the Greek or Hindu 'Four Elements' of earth, air, fire and water. They include an organic substance, wood, but neglect the all-pervasive air, presumably because Chinese philosophy regards air or *ch'i*[a] to be fundamental and thus prior even to the five agents. These five agents served a different purpose. Together with *yin* and *yang*, they formed a system of correspondence and correlation that integrated life and the universe in a powerful, if

---

[9] *Lun-heng* (Balanced Enquiries), SPPY ed., 17:12b–14a; Eng. trans. adapted from de Bary, *Sources*, p. 252.

somewhat mechanical, demonstration of the oneness between Heaven and humanity.[10]

For Tung, the kingship ideal offered the best expression of the continuity of the past and the present, of antiquity and of the realities of secular politics. In his words:

The ruler holds the position of life and death over men; together with Heaven he holds the power of change and transformation . . . Therefore the great concern of the ruler lies in diligently watching over and guarding his heart, that his loves and hates, his angers and joys may be displayed in accordance with right, as the mild and cool, the cold and hot weather come forth in proper season . . . Then may he form a trinity with Heaven and Earth . . . Then may he be called the equal of Heaven.[11]

A cycle of correlations matches seasons and colours and elements or agents to human emotions and even to dynastic changes. For example, the ruler's emotions are to be modelled on the seasons, showing joy and warmth in spring, encouraging the beginning of life and inflicting no severe punishments, and then duplicating heat by conferring rewards in summer, duplicating coolness in autumn, and cold in winter, the season for major punishments.[12] In all this, Tung is putting to work his beliefs in the 'oneness of Heaven and Man', especially as the man in question is the political ruler, as well as the mediator between nature and human society. And he does it in order to place certain limits on the ruler's absolute powers.

Regarding Heaven as a symbol of nature, as a moral force, and in some way still as a personal deity capable of rewarding the just and punishing the wicked, Tung articulated his own vision of the oneness between this Heaven and humanity, which he describes metaphorically:

In the human physical form, the head is large and round, like Heaven's countenance. The hair is like the stars and constellations. The ears and eyes, with their brilliance, are like the sun and moon. The nostrils and mouth, with their breathing, are like the wind. The penetrating intelligence that lies within the breast is like the spiritual intelligence [of Heaven]. The abdomen and womb, now full, and then empty, [make us think of] the myriad creatures.[13]

---

[10] Consult Julia Ching, *Chinese Religions* (London: Macmillan, New York: Orbis, 1993), pp. 153–6.

[11] *Ch'un-ch'iu fan-lu*, 11:7a–b; Eng. trans. in de Bary, *Sources*, p. 181.

[12] Fung, *History*, vol. 2, pp. 48–52.

[13] *Ch'un-ch'iu fan-lu*, Sect. 56, 13:1b–2a; English translation adapted from Fung Yu-lan, *A History of Chinese Philosophy* (Princeton University Press, 1953), vol. 1, p. 31.

It is interesting that the womb (*pao*[a] / *bao*) should be mentioned, as it makes Tung's paradigmatic human being, at least in this context, female.

In appropriating the sage-king paradigm, and making Confucius the uncrowned king, Han philosophers did not cease to expect of kings the conduct of sages. Countless moral exhortations were made by Confucian ministers to their sovereigns, and usually always by making reference to the legendary Yao and Shun as the ultimate royal role models. But the consequence of such appropriation is that (1) everyone can become a king, and (2) philosopher–sages have in some sense replaced kings as paradigmatic human beings, as mediators between the two orders, whether we call them human and natural (or cosmic), or human and divine. This second inference is especially borne out in the teachings of the later followers of Mencius: the neo-Confucian philosophers of the Sung (960–1277) and Ming (1368–1644) dynasties.

Indeed, the macrocosm–microcosm outlook in Chinese philosophy applies not only to a correlation between the natural universe and human nature, but also between both and human society, conceived frequently as an organism, in need of life and nourishment. The doctrine of sagehood is the foundation of such a political and social theory, since the sage gives life to the universe as well as to the society. For this reason, the sage is also the person most qualified for rulership. With the help of a chapter from the text *Chuang-tzu*, the expression that became current was 'sageliness inside and kingliness outside' (*nei-sheng wai-wang*), referring to the combination of interior wisdom and of exterior administrative skills that is required for a sage-king.[14] And although it came from a Taoist source, it became quickly appropriated by the Confucian tradition.

But, in the absence of sage-kings ruling from the throne, Confucian thinkers have evolved certain theories that permitted their own participation in the sage-king paradigm. They do so usually by focusing on the word 'sage', and the ideal of 'sageliness within', making it the goal of their own strivings. But the component of kingship was retained in an analogical and metaphorical sense. To the extent that they could participate in government, and also to the extent that they, like Confucius, could judge history through their own writings, they, too, sought to share in the kingship component of

---

[14] *Chuang-tzu*, sect. 33, 10:14a; 'All under Heaven', trans. by Watson, *Complete Works*, p. 364.

the paradigm. And for that reason, the sage-king paradigm never quite disintegrated into a simple sage paradigm.

CHOU TUN-YI'S AND CHU HSI'S GREAT ULTIMATE (*T'AI-CHI* / *TAIJI*)

Tung Chung-shu's time, and the centuries that followed, saw the flourishing of classical exegesis. Taoist thinkers also emerged, like the third-century Wang Pi and others. But the Confucian tradition had to wait until the eleventh century to witness the emergence of several great neo-Confucian thinkers with metaphysical inclinations. These persons exemplified the 'inner sageliness' ideal much more, even if they sometimes continued to offer uninvited counsel to the rulers. While they brought metaphysics to a great height, they had difficulties balancing the tension between the inner and the outer, until, we might say, helped by Ch'an Buddhist influences, the inner won out over the outer.

The great neo-Confucian philosopher Chu Hsi (1130–1200) was himself the son of a thinker and scholar, whose intellectual lineage goes back to Ch'eng Yi.[15] He also became enamoured of Ch'an Buddhist ideas. In fact, he himself indicated that the period of his engrossment in Ch'an was longer than a decade.[16]

Chu Hsi's philosophy is all the more representative of the Chinese humanist tradition as it is a conscious synthesis of previous philosophies. It comprises the naturalist and ontologist legacy of the Taoists and Buddhists, according to the interpretation of his predecessor, Chou Tun-yi (1017–73), as well as the psychist and culturalist legacy of the Confucians themselves, modified also by an undercurrent of Buddhist influences. The tradition was articulated by the brothers Ch'eng Hao (1032–85) and Ch'eng Yi (1033–1108), as well as their uncle Chang Tsai (1020–77).

For Chu Hsi, as for other representatives of the mainstream of Chinese philosophy, the world, the natural universe, is not only the 'environment' in which the human being finds himself or herself. It

---

[15] Ch'en Chien, *Hsüeh-pu t'ung-p'ien* (A general critique of obscure learning), in Chang Po-hsing (comp.), *Cheng Yi-t'ang ch'üan-shu* (Complete works) (1866-70), supplement, ch. 2; Huang Tsung-hsi *et al.*, *Sung-Yüan hsüeh-an* (Records of the Sung and Yüan philosophers) (abbrev. as *SYHA*), SPPY ed., ch. 34. Consult Satō Hitoshi, *Shūshi: oi yasuku gaku narigatashi* (Chu Hsi) (Tokyo: Shueisha, 1985), pp. 55–71.

[16] *CWWC*, 38:34b.

is also the archetype or the paradigm, of which the human being is an instance or manifestation. And it is above all the ontological model for human nature and existence. The world is knowable to us especially as an ontological model; it is important to us especially as such. The world and the human being are seen essentially as related, each to the other, incomprehensible except in terms of this relatedness. The world is macrocosm, the human being is microcosm. As Chang Tsai puts it:

Heaven is my father, earth is my mother,
And even a small creature as I finds an intimate place in their midst.
That which extends through the universe I regard as my body, and
    that which directs the universe I consider as my nature.
All people are my brothers and sisters, and all things are my companions.
The great ruler (emperor) is the eldest son of my parents, and the great
    ministers are his stewards.[17]

The cosmic ultimate

The philosophy of the Great Ultimate is a teaching influenced by Taoism. Textually based on the commentary on the Book of Changes, this philosophy offers a metaphysical interpretation of the cosmos, of its origin, its cyclical process of movement and of return to rest, in terms of the interaction of the cosmic force of *yin* and *yang* and the Five Agents – fire, water, wood, metal and earth – of change and transformation. The Great Ultimate is the *Tao* of the universe, less its cause than its source, its ontological exemplar. For that reason, the Great Ultimate is also called the 'Ultimateless' or 'Non-Ultimate'. It is the Infinite, the Limitless: that beyond which the mind can go no further. And it is at the same time time the Non-Ultimate, the Nameless: that of which the mind can form no determinate concept.

Let us quote here the words of Chou Tun-yi, and the interpretation given by Chu Hsi of these words:

> Non-Ultimate and yet Great Ultimate:
> Great Ultimate moving, produces *yang*;
> Moving to an ultimate, and becoming still,
> [Great Ultimate] in stillness produces *yin*. . . .

[17] From 'The Western Inscription', in *Chang-tzu ch'üan-shu*, SPPY ed., 1:1a–5b; Eng. trans. adapted from Wing-tsit Chan, *A Source Book in Chinese Philosophy* (Princeton University Press, 1964), p. 497.

Yang changing, *yin* uniting,
[Great Ultimate] produces Water, Fire, Wood, Metal, Earth; . . .
Five Agents are produced,
Each with its own nature. . . .
Essence of Two (*yin–yang*) and Five (Agents),
In wonderful union integrating . . .
[They] produce the Myriad Things.
The Myriad Things produce and reproduce,
In unending transformation.[18]

Chu Hsi interprets Chou Tun-yi's Great Ultimate with the help of Ch'eng Yi's concept of *li*[b], those 'principles' that constitute all things. *Li*[b] may be defined as forms or essences, as organizing and normative principles. *Li*[b] belongs to the realm 'above shapes', the realm of Tao. It is prior – although not in a temporal sense – to its coordinate, *ch'i*[a], translated sometimes as 'breath, ether', or 'matter–energy'. All things are constituted *both* of *li*[b] and of *ch'i*[a], somewhat as in the case of Aristotelian form and matter, with the difference that in Chu Hsi's system, *li*[b], the principle, is passive, and *ch'i*[a], the material, is dynamic. It is on account of *ch'i*[a] that we have becoming, individuation, and materiality. *Ch'i*[a] belongs to the realm of 'instruments' (*ch'i*[a] – a different Chinese word), the realm 'within shapes'.

The Great Ultimate is therefore the most perfect *li*[b], a kind of primal Archetype. It is also the *totality* of all the principles (*li*[b]) of the myriad things, as brought together into a single whole. Fung Yu-lan compares it to Plato's Form of the Good, and to Aristotle's God.[19] This is of course to be understood in the context of function, more than of substance. The Great Ultimate in Chinese philosophy *serves the function of* the Form of the Good in Platonism, or that of God in Aristotelianism.

The human ultimate

For both Chou Tun-yi and Chu Hsi, the Great Ultimate serves also as the paradigm and exemplar for the human being. For the Great Ultimate is the principle of highest excellence, comprehending within itself the plenitude of both being and becoming. And the

---

[18] For the Great Ultimate, see Chou Tun-yi, *T'ai-chi t'u-shuo* (Explanation of the diagram of the Great Ultimate), in *SYHA*, ch. 12. An English translation is given in Chan, *Source Book*, pp. 463–5.

[19] Fung, *History*, vol. 2, p. 537.

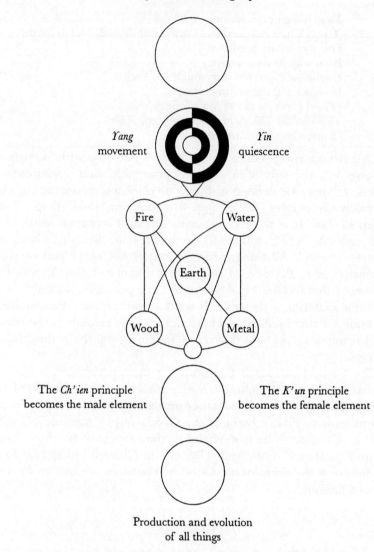

Production and evolution
of all things

Figure 1 Chou Tun-yi's diagram of the Great Ultimate

human being is the crown of the universe, receiving his own
excellence from the Great Ultimate and reflecting back upon it.

> Alone the human being receives the highest excellence and is
>   most spiritual;
> His shape is produced;
> His spirit develops knowledge;
> His five natures are moved, good and evil are separated;
> A myriad affairs emerge.[20]

The reference to 'five natures' is to be understood in terms of
man's innate ability to perform virtues, and correlates with the Five
Agents. We know that Mencius 2A:6 speaks of the four beginnings of
virtue. Mencius 6A:6 defends the original goodness of human nature
by appealing to the universal presence of commiseration, shame,
reverence and discernment between good and evil as the beginnings
of the virtues of humaneness or benevolence, righteousness, propriety and wisdom. But this accounts only for four virtues. Obviously, Chou names 'five natures' for the sake of correlating them to
the Five Agents.

In this case, which is the 'fifth' virtue? For Chou Tun-yi, a
Confucian much influenced by Taoism, this is 'stillness', quiescence
or tranquillity (*ching*ᵃ / *jing*), which he explains elsewhere as 'having
no desires' (*wu-yü*), or, we might say, being without selfish desires.
According to him, this stillness is the principal 'virtue' for the sage.

Indeed, the Great Ultimate holds the key to the explanation of
human greatness and excellence. The cosmic forces of *yin* and *yang*
prefigure the distinction between the 'shape' and 'spirit' of the
human being. The Five Cosmic Agents foreshadow the human
being's innate capacity for moral goodness, described by Mencius as
the 'Beginning of Virtue'. These are developed by the interaction
between the human body and the human spirit, which gives rise to
knowledge. And the emergence of a whole spectrum of human
affairs is itself a reflection of the production and transformation of
the Myriad Things from the Great Ultimate. The human being is
clearly *one* of the Myriad Things. He is also the greatest of these, the
only one which so well reflects the entire cosmos.

For Chu Hsi, as for the mainstream of Chinese philosophy, the
human being and the cosmos are each a paradigm, one of the other,
the microcosm of the macrocosm, so that evil loses its significance in

---

[20] *SYHA*, ch. 12.

the affirmation of human perfectibility, as expressed through the doctrine of sagehood. Of course, it is premature here to judge him for what may appear as *naïveté*, as insensitivity to the whole of human existence, or as inability to confront the entire human situation.[21]

Clearly, the sage establishes the Human Ultimate by the practice of virtues. And just as clearly, each of the virtues enumerated represents a universal virtue, under its one or another principal aspect. Thus, each of these virtues, and all of them together, define the nature of the sage himself as the Human Ultimate. And then, the macrocosm–microcosm parallels assure at the same time the endowment of the cosmos with a moral quality as well as the raising of moral goodness to the cosmic status. The sage takes on cosmic stature. His virtues have a creative and transforming influence, much like the forces of *yin* and *yang*. And so, in the cosmic drama of death and renewal, one may also learn to understand the hidden meanings of human existence.

Speaking therefore in symbolical language, Chou Tun-yi presents human greatness, in the sage, as the fulfilment of a Great Plan that goes beyond the human being, a plan involving the entire cosmic process. Evidently, however, the philosophy of Chou Tun-yi requires further elucidation. For example, what is the exact relation between the Great Ultimate and the Human Ultimate? Are they only parallels, or is there participation of one in the other? Is it only metaphor and hyperbole that he should speak of the sage as 'uniting his virtue with Heaven and Earth, his brilliance with the Sun and the Moon', and so on?

Chu Hsi has provided us with the needed elucidation in these matters. He has spoken in favour of a theory of participation. According to him, each of the myriad things, each human being, contains also the Great Ultimate in its entirety. But then, a different question arises: how can the Great Ultimate remain itself, and yet be present also in every individual person or thing? To this, Chu Hsi answers:

Originally there is only one Great Ultimate; yet each of the Myriad Things receives [and partakes of] it, each containing within itself the whole Great Ultimate. This is like the moon in the sky. There is only one moon; yet it

---

[21] Chung Tsai-chun, *The Development of the Concepts of Heaven and of Man in the Philosophy of Chu Hsi* (Nan-kang, Taiwan: Institute of Chinese Literature and Philosophy, Academia Sinica, 1993), especially ch. 6.

scatters its reflection upon the rivers and lakes, so that it is to be seen everywhere. One cannot say the moon has been divided.[22]

According to Fung Yu-lan's explanation, Chu Hsi means that every object, *in addition to* its own particular li^b (principle), which makes it what it is, also holds within itself the Great Ultimate – as the totality of all Principles.[23]

Universal participation in the Great Ultimate confirms the doctrine of the continuum of nature while also reinforcing the doctrine of universal access to sageliness. Speaking of the human realm, Chu Hsi obviously affirms that each individual person possesses all that is necessary to become a sage – to give actuality to the Human Ultimate within the self. After all, theoretically, any individual can become the ruler.

And Chou Tun-yi does not complete his explanation of the Great Ultimate with his eulogy of the paradigmatic human being. He goes on to speak of the perfect human, the Sage, as the Human Ultimate, the image *par excellence* of the Great Ultimate:

> The Sage settles all with the Mean, Rectitude, Humaneness,
>   Righteousness while centering on Stillness;
> He establishes the Human Ultimate.
> So the Sage unites his virtue with Heaven and Earth;
> He unites his brilliance with the Sun and Moon;
> He unites his order with the Four Seasons.[24]

But then, is this not an expression of the appropriation of the paradigm of the sage-king, of the teaching of universal Buddhahood and its understanding of Buddha-nature, to the extent of embracing everything, including trees and rocks and sand, everything in totality and in particularity. And how else indeed can we understand 'One in all and all in One', the Hua-yen Buddhist adage which was later adopted by neo-Confucian philosophers like Wang Yang-ming?

The wisdom of the Oneness of All Things integrates metaphysics with mystical insight. It demonstrates a genius for syncretism as well as the sophistication of symbolical representation and analogical participation, which, all together, brings into one system the philosophies of nature, of the human being, and of society, all of which,

---

[22] *Chu-tzu yü-lei* (Classified conversations of Chu Hsi) (1473 ed., reprinted Taipei: Cheng-chung, 1973), abbrev. as *CTYL*, 94:35b.
[23] Fung, *History*, vol. 2, pp. 534–7.   [24] *Sung-Yüan hsüeh-an*, ch. 12.

besides, are inseparable from ethics and politics. And of course, in
chapter 1 we have already talked about how sciences like astronomy
and geography helped the understanding of Heaven and Earth, as
well as supporting the belief in human mediatorship.

The Diagram and its brief Explanation of the Great Ultimate
cannot adequately explain themselves. We need also to turn to Chou
Tun-yi's treatise, *Penetrating the Book of Changes*,[25] a 'companion work'
to the Diagram. This is basically a treatise on the Human Ultimate,
the paradigmatic man, who has internalised the cosmic principles of
the Book of Changes. The movement has therefore been reversed: it
goes from microcosm to macrocosm.

Chou Tun-yi's obvious purpose here is to explain the Great
Appendix to the Book of Changes with the help of ideas taken from
the Doctrine of the Mean. In the Explanation of the Diagram, he
has given some emphasis to keeping Stillness, as the principal means
of establishing the Human Ultimate. Here, he presents Sincerity, the
universal virtue of the Doctrine of the Mean, as 'the root of the
Sage'. It is the root of the Five Constant Virtues, in itself quiescent,
'non-acting' (*wu-wei*), and yet the ground of discernment between
good and evil. According to him, the sage is the person who unites
action and non-action, while keeping always to the Mean in the
harmony of his emotions and penetrating all things through his
thought. The Way of the sage is modelled upon the Way of Heaven.
Thus the sagely man mirrors Heaven's creativity by his own teaching
of Humaneness and Righteousness. The Sage is man *par excellence*,
the Human Paradigm: 'And if the World has many people, its root is
in One Man.'[26]

The paradigmatic person governs the myriad affairs, judging
between good and evil. This is the old sage-king model, as appropriated by the philosopher, the conscious heir of Confucius, the
uncrowned king, who sees himself as the teacher of kings. We should
not be surprised to learn that Chu Hsi had the custom of writing
innumerable memorials to the throne, in which he repeatedly
instructed his ruler to rectify the imperial mind and make the royal
intention sincere. We need hardly elaborate on the superior attitude
such rhetoric represented. We might even infer that Chu was
exhorting the ruler to practise some form of meditation that would

---

[25] See *Chou Tzu T'ung-shu*, SPPY ed.   [26] *T'ung-shu*, ch. 11.

help him achieve moral and intellectual rectitude.[27] 'If the sovereign's mind is upright, all the affairs of the world will be correct. If the sovereign's mind is not upright, none of the affairs of the world can be correct.'[28]

And he once added this postscript to a memorial he submitted to Emperor Hsiao-tsung, 'People in the street falsely say that Your Majesty detests hearing about rectifying the mind and making the intention sincere . . . I, Your servant, know that this cannot be true.'[29]

Long tested by the absence of real sage rulers, the Confucian thinkers and scholars moved into the moral vacuum and appropriated for themselves the sage paradigm. They no longer claimed the throne for themselves; they claimed, rather, to be instructors and admonitors to the throne. But of course, the doctrine of the Great Ultimate may also be interpreted in favour of the established ruler, the Imperial Ultimate (*huang-chi* / *huangji*), regarded as centre of the human universe, which serves as a mirror image of the larger, natural universe. This has been done repeatedly, and it is possibly this political potential in Chou Tun-yi's and Chu Hsi's philosophy, which helped to make it eventually a state orthodoxy.[30] But Joseph Levenson has this to say:

On the level of causal mental association, to be sure, the Sung hierarchy of concepts – with room for just one at the top – might carry over to reinforce a hierarchy of men. Yet, psychology aside, if there is any systematic relation between *t'ai-chi* and the scope of imperial power, that relation is to the quietist strain in Confucian political thought, the immanentist, anti-power emphasis on the Son of heaven's necessary virtue.[31]

Levenson concludes that imperial sanction was offered to a 'neo-Confucian monopoly' not because 'the philosophy flattered the monarch', but because it was intellectually impressive. Besides, he reasons – and I agree – intellectual orthodoxy fosters intellectual docility, producing also political docility.

[27] Conrad M. Shirokauer, 'Chu Hsi's Political Career: A Study in Ambiguity', in Arthur F. Wright and Denis Twitchett (eds), *Confucian Personalities* (Stanford University Press, 1962), pp. 177–9, 183.
[28] *CWWC* 11:20b.   [29] *CWWC* 11:18B.
[30] This happened in 1313 under the Mongol Yüan dynasty, when the commentaries of Ch'eng Yi and Chu Hsi to the Confucian Four Books became the examination curriculum for the state. See the following chapter.
[31] Joseph R. Levenson, *Confucian China and Its Modern Fate: A Trilogy* (Berkeley: University of California Press, 1968), vol. 2, *The Problem of Monarchical Decay*, p. 66.

This was essentially what happened, as most scholars chose to enter government service as bureaucrats and functionaries. But it would be a mistake to say that the monarchy 'bought' the intellectuals. Many were those who chose to manifest their political loyalty by protesting injustice in the state's decisions, often at the risk of their own lives.

Moreover, as already pointed out, Chou Tun-yi and Chu Hsi had obviously hoped for an ideal king, a sage ruler – the kind that was never to appear. Fortunately, their political philosophy is only another side to their doctrine of sagehood, a doctrine that they appropriated for all, as did Mencius long before them.

CHU HSI'S REINTERPRETATION OF ANTIQUITY

In discussing the sage-king paradigm, which came down from ancient times, we might bring up the subject of Chu Hsi's appropriation of ancient myths and ancient ethos, especially those that were pertinent to kingship.

Myths reinterpreted by philosophy

A philosopher driven by a great intellectual curiosity, Chu also formulated the doctrine of investigating things and examining principles. He had, after all, an appreciation of things Taoist and a great desire to understand the origin and structure of the universe. His tendency was to use the theory of *yin* and *yang* and the Five Agents, as well as explanations deriving from the theory of numbers, to present his own philosophy of nature. In this light, we can understand his acceptance of such legendary materials as the River Chart and the Book of Lo, which had special associations with ancient kingship. As Chu himself puts it, 'Heaven and Earth cannot speak, and rely on the sage to write books for them. Should Heaven and Earth possess the gift of speech, they would then express themselves better. The River Chart and the Book of Lo are [examples of] what Heaven and Earth have themselves designed.'[32]

The River Chart and the Book of Lo have been represented as

---

[32] *CTYL* 65:9a. Consult *CWWC* 38:1a–2b.

diagrams. When both are compared with the numbers and emblems of the Book of Changes, it would be found that the emblems in the former are round, while those in the latter are square. According to the River Chart, 'The heavenly numbers are the odd ones of *yang*, the earthly numbers are the even ones of *yin*.'[33]

Chu prefers to interpret, whenever possible, in metaphysical terms, even where he acknowledges the possibility of other modes of understanding. We have seen this preference in his rendering of the meaning of *kuei-shen* / *guishen*, admitting the presence of 'ghosts and spirits' while seeking to understand them in terms of a philosophy of *li*[b] and *ch'i*[a], and even reinterpreting the terms to allow for a scientific understanding of natural phenomena. This he integrates into the cosmology of *li*[b] and *ch'i*[a], of the Non-Ultimate (*Wu-chi*), which is also the Great Ultimate. We might see in his efforts a final appropriation, in the name of philosophical wisdom, of ancient religious beliefs – beliefs that, with the help of Buddhist terms and ideas, became transformed into a philosophy of nature.

Spirit-Possession reinterpreted by philosophy

In many ways, Chu Hsi shows himself a rationalist thinker. When asked about understanding and serving ghosts (*kuei* / *gui*) and spirits (*shen*), he follows Confucius in assigning them a lower priority than that of understanding life and serving the living. Basically, he interprets them in terms of the extension and contraction of the *ch'i*[a] of *yin* and *yang*, correlating spirit with the upper soul (*hun*) and ghost with the lower (*p'o* / *po*). Life is present when *ch'i*[a] is gathered there. With death, *ch'i*[a] disperses, with the upper soul rising to Heaven and the lower soul returning to earth.[34]

Chu Hsi approves of divination as a manifestation of what is already present in the mind, therefore anticipating the modern psychoanalyst Carl Jung's explanations of how the oracles of the Book of Changes work.[35]

Ch'i[a] is everywhere between Heaven and Earth. The *ch'i*[a] of human beings is constantly and uninterruptedly connected to the *ch'i*[a] of Heaven and

---

[33] Chu Hsi, *Chou-yi pen-yi* (Original meaning of the Book of Changes), in *Chu-tzu yi-shu* (Surviving works of Chu Hsi) series (reprinted Taipei: Yi-wen, 1969), ch. 3, commentary on 'Appended Remarks', pt 1, ch. 9.

[34] *CTYL* 3:4A.

[35] Wilhelm and Baynes (trans.), *The I Ching or Book of Changes*, Introduction by Carl Jung.

Earth. Although we don't see it, whenever the mind moves, it always reaches *ch'i*ᵃ, and interacts with that which comes and goes, extends and contracts. For example, what happens in divination is all because of what exists in the mind.[36]

Interestingly, Chu also approves of shamans for the same reason: because they deal with a very real part of life. He thought it wise that shamans, including the females among them, held official posts in antiquity.[37] He discusses at some length the role of the impersonator of the dead (*shih*ᵃ) in ancient rituals, remarking that the grandson who was often chosen was expected to communicate with the spirit of the deceased through the same *ch'i*ᵃ that he received from his ancestors. Sincerity on the part of the impersonator during sacrificial rituals, he thinks, could effect the descent of the deceased's spirit. He says, 'Even today there are shamans who can cause spirits to descend. This is all due to the communication of *ch'i*ᵃ [between the living and the dead.] For this reason, the spirit comes to take possession of his [body.]'[38]

To support what he says about the impersonator, Chu even relates at length ethnological information from his own times regarding aboriginal behaviour. He has heard of an ethnic group who, on ritual occasions, chose a handsome man from among themselves as impersonator or spirit-medium, worshipped him, and treated him with food and drink to the point of intoxication. He also tells of another village of several dozen families where the heads of families rotated every year to serve in this role as a medium between the humans and the spirits, with the man chosen venerated as a kind of king (*chung-wang* / *zhongwang*, literally, 'middle king' or 'medium-king'), receiving prayers and sacrificial rituals. This man usually behaved with great reverence during his term of service, and would be blamed should floods and droughts occur.[39]

Sagely wisdom reinterpreted by philosophy

Chu Hsi was also the first Sung philosopher to make explicit use of the term *Tao-t'ung* / *daotong* (Transmission of the Way). He considered that the Way of the sages, initially passed by word of mouth from Yao to Shun to Yü, and then inherited by Confucius, was lost to posterity with the death of Mencius. For him it was rediscovered

---

[36] *CTYL* 3:1b–2a.   [37] *CTYL* 89:2b.   [38] *CTYL* 90:18b.   [39] *CTYL* 90:18a.

only in the Sung dynasty by his own intellectual forebears, the brothers Ch'eng Hao and Ch'eng Yi, their teacher Chou Tun-yi and their uncle Chang Tsai. He made certain that he meant by the transmission what passed from one mind and heart to another mind and heart: *Cor ad cor loquitur* (Heart speaks to heart).

And this is a way in which we may understand Chu's theory concerning this orthodox transmission of the Tao. He regarded it as being contained in sixteen Chinese characters, in a formula taken out of a chapter of the Book of History allegedly transmitted to posterity in 'The Counsels of Great Yü', Yü being the sage-king who was also the flood-controller.

> The human mind (*jen-hsin*) is prone to error,
> The moral mind (*Tao-hsin*) is subtle.
> Remain discerning and single-minded:
> Keep steadfastly to the Mean (*chung*[b]).[40]

The Confucian Tao, the message of its wisdom, is represented as a secret passed on from one sage-king to another by word of mouth. The words contain a warning and an exhortation, presented through the statement of a duality between a fallible human mind, and the subtle yet evasive moral mind or the Tao, encouraging the hearer to be discerning, and to keep to the Mean – a message of the Doctrine of the Mean.[41]

There are many interesting points observable here. A distinction is made between the human mind and the moral mind, and yet a direction is pointed out for those who should wish to recapture their oneness. This was at least Chu Hsi's interpretation. Wang Yang-ming (1472–1529) would emphasise that the human mind and moral mind are basically one and the same, and that it serves as the psychic centre of the universe. Partly influenced by Buddhism, Wang placed emphasis on *hsin* (mind-and-heart) as the seat of wisdom and goodness, the source, we may say, of human dignity and of potential sageliness.

We should give further attention to the term Mean, literally 'middle', sometimes translated as 'equilibrium'. It refers actually to the state of cosmic equilibrium, although it is also related to the Mean between the excesses of the emotions, or emotional harmony.

---

[40] Book of History, 'Counsel of Great Yü'. English trans. adapted from Legge, *Chinese Classics*, vol. 3, p. 61.
[41] Consult Wm. Theodore de Bary, *The Message of the Mind in Neo-Confucianism* (New York: Columbia University Press, 1989), pp. 9–13.

In the philosophers' language, it also refers to quiet-sitting, a Confucian, or more specifically, neo-Confucian, method of meditating, which seeks to have the person attain a mystical consciousness of oneness with the universe. Moreover, in the words of the Doctrine of the Mean, achievement of emotional harmony puts the person in touch with the harmony of the cosmos.

The Confucian Tao is usually represented as the moral law, or a moral Tao. But Chou Tun-yi's words point to the religious and the mystical. And such is also described as the 'heart of the message' passed on from sage-king to sage-king. The *difference* here is, that with Chu Hsi and the philosophers of his time and after, the mystical Tao is at the heart of the moral Tao, and this Tao has been passed on, after the age of sage-kings, by commoners like Mencius and presumably Chu Hsi himself. The sage-king paradigm has been appropriated by the philosophers, and it took the neo-Confucian thinkers of the Sung and Ming dynasties to pronounce this a fact.

We shall find similar expressions of a spiritual life from the writings of other followers of Confucianism and Taoism, whether philosophers or priests. Without pursuing kingship for themselves, and often as semi-recluses, they achieved in their transformed consciousness, the blissful awareness of their oneness with the universe, which presumably had inspired the ancient rulers, and given the king the status of mediator between humanity and the cosmos.

Courage reinterpreted by philosophy

Courage is usually understood as a military virtue, or military valour. Living at a time when the country was politically disunited, and favouring a strong government effort to recover the lost north from the Jurchen invaders, Chu Hsi also extols courage, a recurring theme in his conversations with his disciples.[42] In speaking about progress in study, he urges a disciple to have courage:

It's a waste of time. Go ahead bravely, with a single weapon on a lone horse. Why should one be afraid? The enemy is a human being; so am I. Why should I fear him? . . . When we see clearly the reasons, we would no longer fear the consequences . . . We would just see what is reasonable and act accordingly.[43]

---

[42] *CTYL* 120:3a.   [43] *CTYL* 120:7b.

Although the reference to the 'enemy' may be misleading, Chu is using a metaphor to encourage a faint-hearted student. He considers reason as an arbiter of emotions, capable of guiding a person in circumstances when a false fear may arise. His words might also be understood in the context of his own life, with the difficulties he encountered especially when accused of heterodoxy. The Confucian scholars might have been called 'mild' men, even 'cowards', but Chu sees their prophetical predicament in state and society as one that called for great personal courage.

For him, courage is supported by reason and caution, rather than being an impulsive response. Speaking of military role models, Chu wrote in a letter to a friend, 'Such a hero is trained in [constant] fear and trembling, as though facing a deep chasm or treading on thin ice. Should he permit his impulses to run away, he would not be able to get anywhere.'[44] It seems strange to associate courage with 'fear and trembling.' Chu Hsi is referring by that to a life of mental and spiritual alertness, with fear directed at making wrong moral moves. Such a fear is often associated with the word *ching*[b] / *jing*, reverence, an attitude directed at the sense of a transcending presence within one's inner self, which we may call the Great Ultimate. This sums up his doctrine of self-cultivation.[45] It also indicates to us how much Chu Hsi and other neo-Confucian philosophers have internalised a virtue that used to characterise an outstanding warrior in a feudal society, perhaps a king leading his army into battle. Instead, they made of courage a mark of inner sageliness.

There were Confucian scholars and thinkers who were also military figures. For example, Wang Yang-ming's philosophy led to dynamic action, as instanced by his own feats on the battlefield. His philosophy has been the principal inspiration behind contemporary Confucian thought, as represented by Tang Chün-i (d. 1978) and Mou Tsung-san (d. 1995), who were active in Hong Kong and Taiwan and were challenged and stimulated by ideas from the West. On the other hand, Fung Yu-lan (d. 1985), who remained in main-

---

[44] *CWWC* 36:29b–30a. The reference to fear and trembling is from the Book of Songs. Consult Legge, *Chinese Classics*, vol. 4, p. 333. It is cited in Analects 8:3; see Legge, *Chinese Classics*, vol. 1, p. 209.

[45] Consult Satō Hitoshi,'Kuan-yü Chu Hsi ching-shuo te yi-ke k'ao-ch'a' (An examination of Chu Hsi's Doctrine of Reverence), in Chung Tsai-chun *et al.* (eds), *Kuo-chi Chu-tzu hsüeh hui-yi lun-wen chi* (Proceedings of the International Conference on Chu Hsi) (Hwakang, Taiwan: Academia Sinica, 1993), pp. 12–13.

land China, has exhibited a greater influence from the more scholastic Chu Hsi.

It may be difficult for some people to reconcile Wang Yang-ming's military successes with his teachings on the universality of sagehood. Did he also concede to his enemies, for example, their access to sageliness? There appears no reason to think otherwise. In battle, Wang Yang-ming sought hard to decrease casualties, as the case of his pursuit in 1519 of a rebel prince, Ch'en-hao, demonstrates.

Another example was a later disciple of Wang's school. The thinker and intellectual historian Huang Tsung-hsi (1610–95) actively worked to promote the survival of the Ming dynasty, organising guerrilla resistance to Manchu invaders.

CHU HSI ON SPIRITUAL CULTIVATION

When we turn from Chu Hsi's cosmology and metaphysics of human nature to his practical moral philosophy, we shall find a certain continuity of both language and thought. In his ethics and theory of cultivation, Chu Hsi continues to speak of *T'ai-chi* (Great Ultimate), of *li*[b] and of *ch'i*[a]. He does not abandon one realm, that of speculative thought, in order to enter another, that of moral action and spiritual cultivation. He integrates the two in a philosophy that is, on every level, both theoretical and practical. As we examine Chu Hsi's practical doctrines at closer range, we shall discover further evidence against accepting a widespread, conventional image of him as a model of rigid moral propriety and a dispenser of prescriptions and proscriptions regarding the correctness of human relationships. True, Chu Hsi does speak of the Three Bonds and the Five Relationships – the warp and woof of Confucian social morality. He was himself a model of correct living, by his own account watchful over the least movements of his mind and heart. But he does not devote his principal attention to questions pertaining to duties and obligations, virtues and vices.

He appears rather to have set his mind on higher things. His doctrine of personal cultivation belongs to the realm of practical moral philosophy while also going beyond it, to embrace a spiritual and ascetic doctrine with mystical implications. It is also firmly grounded in the more speculative parts of his philosophy, namely, in his metaphysics of human nature, in his view of man as the microcosm of the universe, participating in the cosmic process and assisting in the perfection of the universe through his efforts of self-perfection. I do not deny that there can be problems with Chu's teachings – problems of consistency, either internally within his own philosophical system, or externally with the teachings handed down by Confucius and Mencius. Problems of internal consistency are minor, within a highly integrated and well-balanced thought structure, while problems of external consistency with the entire Confucian tradition deserve somewhat more attention and scrutiny, especially for those whose concern is doctrinal orthodoxy.

The doctrine of reverence[46]

The word *ching*[b] figures prominently in Chu Hsi's doctrine of cultivation. The fact that different scholars have translated the term differently (reverence, seriousness, composure) shows the difficulty of explaining its Chinese usage in general and Chu's intended meaning in particular. The usage of the word can be traced to various Confucian texts, including the Book of History, where the ancient sage-kings are described frequently as being 'reverentially obedient' to the Lord-on-High or Heaven, while their descendants are exhorted to imitate such reverence. With Confucius, the word is used more with regard to oneself than to a higher being: 'In retirement, to be sedately gracious, in doing things, to be reverently attentive, in contact with others, to be very sincere' (Analects 12:19). The Book of Changes continues in the same direction when it says: 'the gentleman practises reverence to maintain inner rectitude and righteousness to assure exterior correctness'.

For both Ch'eng Yi and Chu Hsi, 'reverence' points to the process by which the original unity of he mind is preserved and made manifest in one's activity. Chu speaks of abiding in reverence, defining it in terms of single-mindedness and freedom from distraction, and comparing it to the Buddhist practice of mindful alertness. He also associates it specifically to the teaching of 'vigilance in solitude' of the Doctrine of the Mean. And he is careful to guard his disciples against a 'dead' reverence that merely keeps the mind alert without also attending to moral practice. Following the way in Ch'eng Yi's footsteps, Chu Hsi continues to give the meaning of the word a dimension

---

[46] Consult Julia Ching, 'Chu Hsi on Personal Cultivation', in Wing-tsit Chan, *Chu Hsi and Neo-Confucianism* (Honolulu: University of Hawaii Press, 1986), pp. 273–91.

of depth which transforms it from the earlier, occasional usage in Confucian thought to a *doctrine* of personal and spiritual cultivation. In his words, 'Reverence does not mean one has to sit stiffly in solitude, the ears hearing nothing, the eyes seeing nothing, and the mind thinking of nothing . . . It means rather keeping a sense of caution and vigilance, and not daring to become permissive.'[47]

Elsewhere, he clearly says that reverence refers to keeping the principles of Heaven and getting rid of human passions. Reverence is obviously part and parcel of his philosophy of li^b and $ch'i^a$, pointing to the constant need of growing in virtue and keeping the passions under control.

The practice of reverence is very like that of 'recollection' in Western Christian spirituality. The English word 'recollection' is usually understood in terms of remembering. In spirituality, however, it is a technical term referring to the 'collecting' or 'gathering' of one's interior faculties, keeping them silent and 'recollected' in an atmosphere of peace and calm, in preparation for formal prayer or in an effort to prolong the effects of such prayer.

The Confucian term for meditation, quiet-sitting, suggests strong Taoist and Buddhist influences, calling to mind Chuang Tzu's 'sitting and forgetting' and the Buddhist practice of *dhyāna* (meditation), from which the name *Ch'an* or Zen is derived. Chu makes a special effort to show the distinctiveness of Confucian quiet-sitting and its difference from Taoist and Buddhist meditation. For the Buddhist, it is an exercise by which the mind concentrates upon itself to the exclusion of all distracting thoughts, for the sake of attaining unity and harmony with one's innermost self. For the Taoist, the same usually applies, frequently with an additional motive of preserving health and prolonging life. For the Confucian, unity and harmony are sought for, together with the knowledge of the *moral* self, of one's own strengths and weaknesses, in view of achieving self-improvement, of becoming more nearly perfect in the practice of virtues and the elimination of vices, and therefore in the fulfilment of one's responsibilities both in the family and in society at large.

Chu Hsi gives some importance to quiet-sitting also for making possible a fuller manifestation of the *t'ai-chi* or 'heavenly principle' within. What is implied is a cyclical movement: the return to one's

---

[47] *CTYL* 12:10b.

original nature, the recapture of the springs of one's being, and the enabling of this state of original equilibrium of nature and the emotions to permeate one's daily living. It is, however, different from the Buddhist practice of 'introspection', which has reference only to oneself and not to the larger world:

According to the Buddhist teaching, one is to seek the mind with the mind, deploy the mind with the mind. This is like the mouth gnawing the mouth or the eye looking into the eye. Such a course of action is precarious and oppressive, such a path is dangerous and obstructed, such a practice is empty of principles (*li*ᵇ) and frustrating. If they sound like us [Confucians], they are really quite different.[48]

Chu Hsi has been taken to task, especially by the seventeenth-century scholar Yen Yüan, for exaggerating the importance of quiet-sitting: for recommending the practice of spending half a day in quiet-sitting, and half a day reading books.[49] Actually, this reference comes up only once in his recorded conversations, in a specific context with a single disciple, even if it made a deep impression on some later thinkers.[50] Chu Hsi has guarded against excessive emphasis on quietude. He is reported to have said that 'the teaching of quietude is close to Buddhist and Taoist teachings. Our sages have not taught it. Today, scholars sometimes say that they should spend half a day daily in the practice of quiet-sitting. I find it a mistake.'[51] He corrects Chou Tun-yi by saying: 'Chou emphasises quietude and tranquillity (*ching*ᵃ). But the [other] word *ching*ᵇ should only be interpreted as reverence.'[52]

In answering questions about quiet-sitting, Chu Hsi is insistent that one need not sit like the Ch'an Buddhists, seeking to stop all thought. According to him, all one needs to do is to recollect the mind, to prevent it from dissipation, and thus to permit its natural brightness to radiate in a state of peace and concentration. Repeatedly, Chu associates tranquillity with moral behaviour, which is made easy by a disposition of reverence.[53]

Meditation, therefore, is a time when the person gathers himself or herself together inwardly, calms the emotions, examines the conscience, and fills the mind and heart with principles of right action in

---

[48] 'Kuan-hsin shuo' (On contemplating the mind), *CWWC*, 67:21b; Eng. trans. adapted from Chan, *Source Book*, p. 604.
[49] *Chu-tzu yü-lei p'ing* (A critique of Chu Hsi's *Classified Conversations*), p. 18b, in *Yen-Li ts'ung-shu* (Collected writings of Yen Yüan and Li Kung) (n.p.: Ssu-ts'un hsüeh-hui, 1923).
[50] *CTYL* 116:17b.   [51] Ibid, 62:25b.   [52] Ibid, 94:17a.   [53] *CWWC* 37:27a.

order that a disposition of reverence may permeate his or her entire life. And such is the kind of spiritual cultivation Chu wishes to see practised, not only by his own students but also by the rulers.

WANG YANG-MING: HUMANITY AS HEART OF THE UNIVERSE

According to the Book of Rites, 'the human being is the mind and heart (*hsin*) of Heaven and Earth.'[54] Coming over two centuries after Chu Hsi, Wang Yang-ming reveals the influence of Buddhist compassion on his philosophy, even while it is rooted in insights from Chinese antiquity. And he appears to be speaking of an ideal human being, not just of a sage-king. 'The great man', he says, 'is one with Heaven and Earth and all things'. Only the small man creates a separation between himself and others. The great man not only commiserates with suffering humanity, but extends his compassion to animals and plants, and even to broken rocks and bricks, because his 'humaneness [makes him] one with bricks and stones'.[55]

Humaneness (*jen*[b]) is no longer merely a universal virtue, but has been elevated to a cosmic status, uniting the human being with the universe. And humaneness comes from *hsin*, the source of all knowing and feeling.

Once, when Wang was taking a walk in the mountains, one of his friends pointed to the blossoming trees, and asked, 'If there is nothing in the world that is not outside of *hsin*, how is it that these trees hidden in the mountains can produce flowers that bloom and die without my *hsin* being in any way involved?' His reply was, 'Before you see this flower, the flower and your *hsin* are both dormant. When you see this flower, its color suddenly becomes clear. This shows that the flower is not outside of your *hsin*.'[56]

For Wang Yang-ming, reality is always dynamic, related to human consciousness. And only when flowers in the wilderness have become somehow activated by human knowing, do they become 'real'. And so, he presents the human *hsin* as the cause of the fundamental unity of all things: that which knows all things, and has the power to direct all things to their proper ends.[57]

---

[54] *Li-chi Cheng-chu*, 7:8a.
[55] 'Inquiry into the Great Learning', *Yang-ming ch'üan-shu* (Complete works of Wang Yang-ming), SPPY ed., 26:1b.
[56] Ibid, 3:14a.
[57] Julia Ching, *To Acquire Wisdom: The Way of Wang Yang-ming* (New York: Columbia University Press, 1976), pp. 144–5.

And indeed, Wang announced to the world that the 'streets are full of sages'. We cannot infer from this statement that the streets are full of people whispering to one another the famous 'sixteen characters' about sageliness that we quoted earlier. So he could not have meant that everyone in the bustling streets, male and female, old and young, educated and illiterate, scholar, peasant, merchant, soldier, or a simple pedlar, was already a sage as deserving of veneration as Confucius himself.[58]

But he did mean by it as well that everyone can become a sage, and is potentially already a sage. He can also be taken to mean that everyone can become a king, if he should also become actually a sage. This is basically the legacy of Mencius. Besides, during the intervening centuries, Mahāyāna Buddhism had developed in China the idea of universal Buddhahood: put simply, that all sentient beings have the potential to become Buddhas, or, to use a preferred term, *bodhisattvas* who voluntarily give up Nirvana and become reborn again in order to save more beings.

Wang was fond of repeating that 'One is All and All is One'. He is referring to the Buddhist teaching of the interconnectedness of all things. It reveals a unitary vision of the universe in which the phenomena that comprise conventional worldly experience and the noumenal truths that govern them penetrate and fuse with each other, and yet do so without losing their own identities. And so, everyone, every sentient being, and even every organic and inorganic thing in the universe, every experience of existence, is a microcosm, in which the entire universe of things and of experiences is reflected. Since the subject-object dichotomy is overcome, things as such and experience as such are not clearly differentiated. For that reason, T'ien-t'ai Buddhism, which also influenced Wang's philosophy, even speaks of *yi-nien san-ch'ien / yinian sanqian* (literally, one thought, three thousand): that the three thousand realms of existence – to use an exaggeration in differentiation – are all interwoven and immanent in one single instant of thought. This appears to be an exaggeration in synchronicity, but it actually points to the instant of mystical enlightenment, during which all becomes one in human consciousness.

And since the human being is the mind and heart of the universe, every human being could become the mediator between the world

[58] Ching, *To Acquire Wisdom*, ch. 5–6; Yamamoto Makoto, *Minjidai jugaku no rinrishisō* (The ethical thought of Ming Confucianism) (Tokyo: Rishosha, 1975), chs 3–4.

of humans and that beyond. Influenced by such teachings, Wang has merely dramatised the situation, and by so doing, completed the philosophical appropriation of the sage-king paradigm by making it universal property.

If the streets are full of sages, then all are perfectible, whether with or without education, and all can participate in rulership. We see here sprouting and growing the seeds of human equality, already implicit in Mencius' teachings. We see a ground being prepared ultimately for political democracy, even though it still took the introduction of Western ideas for the new seeds to be sown on this ground.

In emphasising the potential sageliness present in all, Wang also places less priority than did Chu Hsi on the cultivation of reverence and the practice of meditation. Not that he was against spiritual cultivation. Rather, he was for dynamic action, which is permeated by a spirit of contemplation. And he was opposed to excessive spiritual practices that kept the person passive and the mind idle.

More immediately, we see here the sage ideal, understood morally and mystically, commended to the attention of all.

In pre-modern China, critiques of political power were made obliquely or in secret. After the fall of the Ming, Huang Tsung-hsi wrote the *Ming-yi tai-fang-lu* ('Plan for the Prince'). It did not see print until the early twentieth century. A scholar and philosopher, he also reflected on the causes that led to the Ming downfall, and noted down his personal reflections, as well as proposals for the future. Offering the fruits of his scrutiny of the exercise of political power till his own times, he condemns rulers for regarding their domains as their private property, and their subjects as their servants and slaves. He proposes that law (*fa*) be established for the interest of all rather than of the few, and that government be by laws rather than men. And he denounces those laws that enslave the people as 'unlawful laws'.[59]

As a follower of the Yang-ming school, Huang combines the concerns of 'inner sageliness and outer kingliness'. Metaphysically and spiritually, he was for the cultivation of the inner man. And politically, he remained, in my view, a reformer, in the same sense as were Confucius and also Mencius, but not a revolutionary. He was

---

[59] See *Ming-yi tai-fang lu*, SPPY edition, chs 1–3; Eng. trans. by Wm. Theodore de Bary, *Waiting for the Dawn: A Plan for the Prince* (New York: Columbia University Press, 1993).

still awaiting the advent of an ideal prince who might make use of his ideas, putting into effect a benevolent despotism. He was not changing the structure of monarchy itself.

THE UTOPIAN UNIVERSALISM OF K'ANG YU-WEI (1858–1927) AND HIS SCHOOL

The seventeenth and eighteenth centuries witnessed a clear movement in Chinese scholarship away from philosophy to philology, producing a series of hard-nosed scholars who criticised the philosophical legacy of their recent past and returned to the more ancient classics with enquiring minds. Then the late nineteenth century actually saw the reverse happen in the person of K'ang Yu-wei. A patriot and reformer concerned about external threats against China's very survival, he wanted to transform traditional society and prepare it for the serious challenges being posed by Western powers. As a scholar trained in traditional scholarship, he wanted to ground these proposed reforms in classical precedents. In appearance, he was less the metaphysician, and more the daring political philosopher who had no hesitation about using the Classics only as footnotes to advance his own ideas. In fact, he and his disciples were inspired not only by Confucian ideals of serving state and society, but also by Wang Yang-ming's metaphysics, a Buddhist vision of the interrelatedness of all things, as well as a Buddhist impulse to save all sentient beings. In his metaphysical discussions, K'ang seeks to incorporate the findings of modern science, 'Great is the primal *ch'i*ª. It created heaven and earth. By Heaven is meant the spiritual substance of a thing (the universe). By earth is meant also the spiritual substance of a thing (the body) . . . Spirit is electricity with consciousness . . . Spirit is the power of consciousness, the consciousness of a soul.'[60] Regarding himself as a part of the universe represented by Heaven and Earth, K'ang expresses his affective belonging to a larger whole, 'Do all people have this mind that cannot bear to see the sufferings of others? Or do I alone have it? And why should I be so deeply affected by this?'[61] K'ang claimed that Confucius was a religious leader and a political reformer, who purposely attributed institutional reforms to antiquity in order to

---

[60] *Ta-t'ung shu* (On the Great Unity) (Shanghai: Chung-hua, 1936), pp. 3–4. Eng. trans. adapted from Chan, *Source Book*, p. 730.

[61] *Ta-t'ung-shu*, p.2; Eng. trans. adapted from Chan, *Source Book*, p. 729.

find precedents, even to the extent of fabricating the achievements of the legendary sages Yao and Shun. Thus he asserted that Confucius personally wrote all the Six Classics, and that his institutional ideas were meant not just for the Han dynasty, but for all ages.[62]

K'ang unabashedly made use of apocryphal texts to support his own points, building up a mysterious Confucius and an esoteric Confucian doctrine that he wanted to have established as religion. Discussing ideas from the Kung-yang commentary to the Spring–Autumn Annals, K'ang advocated the theory of the Three Ages: of Disorder, progressing to Approaching Peace, and finally to Universal Peace, looking forward to an ideal future rather than putting his faith in a golden past.

K'ang's controversial *Ta-t'ung shu* (On the Great Unity) elucidates his personal, utopian vision of the future. Regarded as a moderate reformer who promoted the cause of constitutional monarchy under the Manchu house, K'ang showed himself here a true universalist and an anarchist visionary. Voicing eclectic beliefs coming from Confucianism, Buddhism and Christianity, he called for the total abolition of all artificial boundaries between human beings, whether nations, governments, families, or social classes, in the name of a community of goods and spouses! However, he added that his own time was not ready for this ultimate fulfilment. It could be better served by a vision of 'Lesser Tranquillity'. The book was only published posthumously (1935), eight years after his death. Liang Ch'i-ch'ao, who was K'ang's best-known disciple and fellow re- former, described the effects of K'ang's important works on the scholarly community of the time as comparable to a cyclone, a volcanic eruption, and a huge earthquake.[63]

Even when he was wrong, K'ang was always interesting. And his utopian ideas, given that they were meant for the entire world, showed his universalist concerns. These concerns have always been an integral part of Confucian philosophy itself; he only made them more explicit. His disciple T'an Ssu-t'ung (1866–98) published a work, *Jen-hsüeh* (On *Jen*[b]), which advocated a revolution against Manchu rule in China, while expressing a Mahāyāna Buddhist desire to save not only his own country, but also the entire world,

---

[62] *K'ung-tzu kai-chih k'ao* (An enquiry into Confucius' institutional reforms), especially chs 7–12; Chan, *Source Book*, p. 728.

[63] See Liang Chi'i-ch'ao, *Intellectual Trends in the Ch'ing Period*, trans. Immanuel C. Y. Hsü (Cambridge, Mass.: Harvard University Press, 1959), especially p. 94.

and even all living species. He declared that one should not call oneself the national of a certain country, but should look equally upon all nations as one's own and all peoples as one's compatriots.[64]

The vaster their dreams, the more impractical these showed their authors to be. T'an would finally die with several other disciples of K'ang Yu-wei, after their failed efforts to introduce a constitutional monarchy. But their visions reveal the inspiration of the 'Oneness of Heaven and the Human' serving as an impetus, with strong influences from Confucian and even Buddhist sources, to save the entire living universe. K'ang and T'an, as well as Liang Ch'i-ch'ao, all believed in democracy as a better system of government than absolute monarchy. To that extent, they had learnt much from the West. And they perceived themselves as belonging to a larger unit than a country. This universalism is actually a legacy of the wisdom that was China, a country and a civilisation that for so long regarded itself as 'all under Heaven'.

In their political visions, K'ang Yu-wei and his disciples showed this universalism by transcending national boundaries. The earlier philologists, seventeenth-to-eighteenth century scholars like Yen Yüan and Li Kung, also did so by transcending the temporal boundaries – advocating a restoration of the allegedly ancient well-field system, a measure of land division that would benefit the peasants while also promoting the common good. These 'reformers' before K'ang's time looked back to a Golden Age of the past, as a prototype for the utopia they hoped to restore. This may be regarded as another dimension, part and parcel of the 'oneness of Heaven and man', that united past and present – including the deceased ancestors. And for a long time, when a person looked toward the future, he hoped to see in it a replica of the remote past, a past long gone but never forgotten. In spite of his preferences for a universal utopia, K'ang personally remained a monarchist, and sought, in vain, to restore the Manchu monarchy. Still, K'ang and his disciples were themselves much more forward-looking than earlier reformers, having been influenced also by Western ideas. As they recognised the limitations of Chinese national boundaries, they also sought to transcend these, not by military conquest, but intellectually by extending their own concerns and compassion literally to the entire universe.

---

[64] See T'an Ssu-t'ung (Tan Sitong), *Jen-hsüeh* (Shanghai: Zhonghua, 1962), especially pp. 76–81.

CHAPTER 5

The paradigm enshrined: the authority of classics

INTRODUCTION: LANGUAGE AND WRITING

Spoken words vanish at the moment of their utterance. For this reason alone, speaking and the principles governing oral transmission are difficult to document.[1]

In Christian New Testament studies, the scholar is engaged in discovering the living words of Jesus, whom Christians call the Lord. The English language does not necessarily specify a distinction between the spoken and the written 'word'. But the French have always spoken of scripture as 'la *parole* de Dieu'.[2]

The oral word usually preceded the written text, except in cases where the record came from a previously unarticulated memory. In practically all the world's religious and literary traditions, the oral tradition has preceded the written. This is especially observable in the case of India. In the Hindu tradition, brahmins memorised and recited the Vedas but for many centuries resisted reducing them to written form. In the Buddhist tradition, there was a significant lapse of time between the historical Buddha's death and the eventual recording of the scriptures.

In China's case, the written text has also been slow to follow the spoken word. The Confucian classics were transmitted orally for centuries before they were committed to writing – and long after the

---

[1] Werner H. Kelber, *The Oral and the Written Gospel* (Philadelphia: Fortress Press, 1983), p. 1. Consult also Walter J. Ong, *Orality and Literacy: The Technologizing of the Word* (London: Methuen, 1982).

[2] For a recent work on scripture, see Wilfred Cantwell Smith, *What Is Scripture? A Comparative Approach* (Minneapolis: Fortress Press, 1993). See also Frederick M. Denny and Rodney L. Taylor (eds), *The Holy Book in Comparative Perspective* (Columbia: University of South Carolina Press, 1985); and F. F. Bruce and E. G. Rupp, *Holy Book and Holy Tradition* (Manchester University Press, 1968). The last mentioned does not include the Indic or the Chinese religions.

invention of writing. Indeed, the character of the Chinese classics as oral tradition remains 'imprinted' on most of the written texts, whether as poetry which was meant to be sung, divinatory oracles intended for oral consultation, royal speeches and pronouncements, or dialogues between master and disciples. And only by keeping in mind the *oral* origin of the classical texts could one begin to make the discovery of the meaning of the written signs left behind – by going behind and beyond them, to that which gives them meaning: the *presence of the authors*, of the alleged sages, whose voices had *authority*.

The oral and written word are intertwined, to the extent that it has become difficult to discern one from the other. To find the author's voice, one must study the text. In fact, for classical and scriptural texts recorded long ago, the oral utterance can no longer be heard apart from the text. Even when impressed on the memory, it has been conditioned by the text. It would not have survived had it not been for the text. We come here to the marriage of language and writing.

True, the bond between Chinese language and writing appears at first less intimate than in the case of most Western languages. There is no single Chinese language, only a language family, comprising a multitude of dialects that are not always mutually comprehensible. Phonetic transliterations, including the kind we give in this book, are made from Mandarin or standard Chinese, to which a host of dialects (but not all) are related. And yet, they are all represented by the same script.[3]

And then, there is the distinctive character of the Chinese script, which is composed of ideographs: that the signs themselves – as well as the sounds – usually represent ideas. Theoretically, one could contemplate writing in Chinese and pronouncing the words in English or any other language. That is why the script has been a unifying factor in a country with so many different dialects. That is why the Chinese script could be, and was, taken over by Koreans and Japanese, whose spoken languages are very different from the Chinese. The script has remained relatively constant throughout two millennia of time, retaining today a three-dimensional character, covering phonology, philology, and what may be called semantics, to those familiar with etymology.

[3] Consult John Lagerwey, 'The Oral and the Written in Chinese and Western Religion', in Gert Naundorf *et al.* (eds), *Religion und Philosophie in Ostasien: Festschrift für Hans Steininger zum 65. Geburtstag* (Würzburg: Koenigshausen & Neumann, 1985), pp. 301–22.

In ancient China, the earliest deciphered *texts* were the oracle bone inscriptions. These were followed by the inscriptions on bronze vessels. Wooden, bamboo and silk manuscripts were also in use, especially with the rise of the discourse form in philosophical discussions, and of literary writing. Paper did not come into general use until the third or fourth century CE. It is thus common sense to suppose that the very scarcity of the copies enhanced the value of the texts that were known and circulated, among the few who were literate.[4]

Writing as magic

Writing, then, is magic: – one method of gaining power over the living word. The tradition of the living word was originally oral; it lives in being recited, and only later did oral tradition give place to graphic . . . Committing sacred texts to writing therefore was . . . intended . . . to attain power, since with the written word man can do just what he will.[5]

The myths have attributed the invention of writing to more than one person. According to some, Fu-hsi, the 'Animal Tamer', allegedly studied the marks of birds and beasts, from which he invented human writing to replace the primitive mnemonic device of making knots on cords.[6] According to others, he invented the Eight Trigrams used for divination, which became the forerunners of the script.[7] More particularly, the invention of writing has been attributed to the mythical Ts'ang Chieh, who is also said to have derived inspiration from the claw prints of birds.

The confusion of writing with divinatory trigrams is itself interesting, since the earliest deciphered written characters served the divination rituals. It also highlights the magico-religious character of the writing system, reflected even today in the practice of divination by word-analysis or glyphomancy. This happens, for example, when an expert splits a word into its various components and analyses their meaning in response to questions posed regarding future events.[8]

---

[4] Loewe, *Chinese Ideas of Life and Death*, p. 180.
[5] Gerardus van der Leeuw, *Religion in Essence and Manifestation*, trans. J. E. Turner (London: Allen & Unwin, 1938), pp. 435–6.
[6] See *Shang-shu K'ung-chuan* (The Book of History, with K'ung An-kuo's annotations), SPPY ed., Preface, p. 1.
[7] Consult Tuan Yü-ts'ai's preface to the *Shuo-wen*, 15A:1b–2a.
[8] Consult Wolfgang Bauer, 'Chinese Glyphomancy (*ch'ai-tzu*) and its uses in present-day

Writing has captured a power to rule men's minds: magical power in the case of charms and talismans, written in an esoteric script illegible except to the initiated; the power of the ancient sages in the case of the classics, which presumably recorded their words or deeds. This would eventually be acknowledged by political power as what also sanctioned its own authority to govern, and to govern well. With the dissemination of the texts, political power would permit and invite many others, the scholars, to participate in elucidating the classics, and therefore to assist in legitimating itself, while also sometimes giving it some guidance in the matter of governance.

The ancient Chinese called their ideographs 'names' (*ming*). To know how to write the name of something is to possess power over it. And the fact that Hsü Shen's Lexicon comprehends the words or names of ghosts and spirits as well as of mountains and rivers, animals and plants, rituals and institutions, means that it, too, has a certain 'mysterious power' of communication with the ghosts and spirits.[9]

Indeed, the decline of the shamans as a class favoured by the spirits and deities could be ascribed to the emergence of writing. *Their* charisma had not required literacy or textual knowledge. But increasingly, those with literary and textual skills took over the management of society. With all the new magic that writing brings, we might argue that its invention also marked a huge step toward secularisation. 'The power of the written word came from its association with knowledge – knowledge from the ancestors, with whom the living communicated through writing . . . knowledge from the past, whose wisdom was revealed through its medium.'[10]

The emergence of books has also been attributed to mythical events. The earliest to appear was the mythical Book of Lo, a gift from Heaven to Yü, the Flood-controller. It is usually discussed in connection with the River Chart, allegedly a gift to the mythical Fu-hsi, from which he is supposed to have derived the Eight Trigrams.[11] It became part of both the Confucian and Taoist legacies. Paper was invented in China around 105 CE or even earlier. Printing was

Taiwan', in Sarah Allan (ed.), *Legend, Lore and Religion in China* (Los Angeles: Chinese Materials Center, 1979), pp. 71–96.
[9] See Tuan Yü-ts'ai's epilogue, in *Shuo-wen*, 15B:1b–2a; 7b. See also William A. Graham, 'Scripture as Spoken Word', in Miriam Levering (ed.), *Rethinking Scripture: Essays from a Comparative Perspective* (Albany: State University of New York Press, 1989), p. 133.
[10] Chang, *Art, Myth and Ritual*, p. 88.
[11] A description of each in Taoist usage is given in Michael Saso, 'What is the *Ho-t'u?*' *History of Religions* 17 (1978), 399–403.

invented a few centuries later. Around the year 500, someone got the
idea of using carved seals as models for printing blocks. Taoists were
eager to use printing for their charms and talismans, and Buddhists
wanted to have printed scriptures for the spreading of their religion.
The world's oldest book, discovered in 1907, is the *Diamond Sutra* in
Chinese, printed in 868, and 'reverently made for universal free
distribution'.[12] The Confucian classics were printed for the first time
in the tenth century (932–53). The Buddhist canon followed in 983.
The first full Taoist canon was completed in 1019, although nothing
from it has survived.[13]

Writing as literary communication

It can be argued that writing was invented in China, less for
purposes of communication between human beings, and more for
communication between humans *and* the gods and ancestral spirits.
But writing was *utilised* also out of the practical need of aiding the
memory and of communicating with others, gods or humans. Such
needs were already felt when knots were tied on cords; such needs
were also filled when potters placed the markings on their handi-
work. These needs did not rule out initially the *religious* association of
writing itself. With time, however, writing took over an increasingly
secular function, and the Shang oracle bone writing was destined to
remain buried and unknown for a few millennia before its redis-
covery in the early twentieth century.

Léon Vandermeersch has pointed out the interesting effects of a
very long 'preliterary embryonic life' in ancient China, with about a
thousand years bridging the invention of writing and the emergence
of written discourse. The process was a complex one, with a
continual interaction between the spoken and the written word,
since, presumably, information was noted in one manner or another
before it was gathered together in discourse form. We may say that
the lapse of time has led to the independent and parallel growth of
speech and writing, formalising the latter, and keeping the act of
writing to remain quasi-sacramental as well as retaining its links to
calligraphy. Its slow emergence has also shaped the written discourse
itself, keeping it frequently in a poetic or quasi-poetic mode, as a

---

[12] Thomas F. Carter, *The Invention of Printing in China and Its Spread Westward*, revised by
L. Carrington Goodrich, second ed. (New York: Ronald Press, 1955), p. 13.
[13] Ibid, pp. 67–93.

record of songs and incantations (as with sections of the Book of Songs) or formal speeches (as with most of the Book of History) with ritual roots.[14] Besides, the role of writing as instrument has permitted the written records both of the religious rituals themselves (in the classical ritual texts) and of a didactic account of the events of history (in the Spring–Autumn Annals).

If we look into the Analects of Confucius (probably in existence before the third century BCE) we find a ubiquitous expression, *Tzu yüeh / Ziyue* (The Master said). It has been claimed that whereas the scribe recording the speeches in the Book of History had only written *for* the king, as his brush or stylus, and whereas the King himself had spoken only as a 'mouthpiece' for the ancestral spirits, the Master Confucius would go on record as someone who spoke *by his own authority*, 'not as the scribes'.[15]

In my opinion, the Analects bridges the gap between a magico–religious antiquity and a more rationalist and humanist mentality precisely because it is a record of oral transmission. This gives the words a sense of immediacy that is not found in topical, discursive treatises, bringing the readers a *presence* as well as a message.

It is therefore obvious why an intimate relationship should develop between Confucian scholars and their classics, those texts considered as the fount of all wisdom, that allegedly carry the words of their ancient teachers, that offer them a share in political authority through their own meticulous scholarship and insightful understanding of the words and sentences.

The classics are the custodians of the authority coming from the ancient sages. And their interpreters, the exegetes, have become the mediators of this authority. At a time when sages are no longer among ordinary human beings, their recorded words have taken their places and filled their presence. And the textual scholar, the exegete, has assumed a kind of priestly power, serving as a mouthpiece of the sages whose inspiration is recorded in the classics.

The sacred authority of the classics

The term *ching^c / jing* was generally used with reference to the books of the ancients – usually those attributed to the sages.[16] But the

---

[14] Consult Vandermeersch, *Wangdao*, vol. 1, p. 493. [15] Ibid, pp. 491–2.
[16] *Lun-heng*, 28:11b.

name of Confucius became associated, rather early, with those of the Six Classics. The corpus as such was only established in the Han dynasty, although several of the texts were mentioned in the Analects and in the Book of Mencius, and the whole group was called 'classics' (*ching^c*) in *Hsün-tzu* as well as in *Chuang-tzu*.[17]

The classics represent 'true learning', as distinct from false or perverse learning. They represent in retrospect a position of orthodoxy opposed to the deviations of falsehood or heterodoxy. Personally I consider this the result of two things: (1) an early sense of communication with the divine, and (2) a sense of the differentiation between true and false teachers or 'prophets' (be they shamans or shamanic kings), who claimed contact with deities and ancestral spirits, and of true and false sages, who took over even the authority of the sacred kings, to speak in the name of Heaven. And this is why the Confucian classics resemble religious scriptures – whether of the East or the West – more than Greek or Latin or Renaissance classics, which derive their authority from their own intrinsic value, as great literary and philosophical works, than from any divine or semi-divine authority.

The question of traditional attribution is in itself instructive, because of what it teaches about the authority of the ancient sages. The Book of Changes is a good example. Tradition has ascribed the core of the book, the Eight Trigrams, to the mythical culture-hero Fu-hsi. It has assigned the sixty-four Hexagrams, derived from the Trigrams, to King Wen of Chou, the beloved of Heaven (r. 1171–1122 BCE). The explanatory formulas of the Hexagrams are attributed to his son, the Duke of Chou (d. 1094 BCE), the architect of ritual and political institutions for the dynasty. Lastly, the longer Commentaries, called the Ten Wings, are attributed to Confucius. Now Fu-hsi, King Wen, the Duke of Chou and Confucius were all considered sages.

Religiously speaking, Confucius' alleged authorship or editorship has been decisive in certain texts being considered as classics, just as the Hebrew Pentateuch was credited with its authority from God through Moses, its alleged author. And yet, the *secular* character of the Confucian tradition, coming from its humanist emphases, so overpowered the religious past that the texts came down more as *classics* containing human wisdom than as *scriptures* revealing the

---

[17] See *Hsün-tzu* 1:4b–5b; Eng. trans. in Watson, pp. 20–1, where, however, the word 'classic' does not appear as in *Chuang-tzu*, sect. 14, 5:26a; Watson, *Complete Works*, p. 165.

wisdom of God. While the Confucian texts were not considered legal in inspiration, they have served the Chinese state much as the Jewish Torah had served the Jewish people, generating interpreters and exegetes who explained every line and every word. Indeed, the classical corpus could also be compared to an important secular document like the United States constitution, with its many accretions and amendments, and the generations of interpreters who both examine and manipulate its statements in the work of governance. As a set of texts that combine sacred and secular characteristics, the classics serve as well a political function, going back to the images of the sage-kings as supreme exemplars, and offering the actual rulers a blueprint for wise and benevolent government. No wonder the state intervened in the formation of the classical corpus and in the education of its scholars.

By one of its early measures, the Han government (191 BCE) lifted the Ch'in ban on certain types of literature, and sought hard to recover some of the texts lost by the Ch'in burning of books. This task was helped by those older scholars who had learned the texts by heart, and could recite them for the copyists. In this way, the authority of oral tradition continued to serve and supplement the authority of the written word.

But the burning of books and their later restoration served as a watershed in many ways. It signified the end of an age of creativity: when the voices of the ancient sages were heard and their words recorded. No wonder later generations debated the possibility of yet becoming sages, with the dawning of a new age – an age of classical exegesis, which served to preserve and to interpret the legacy of the past.

About the second century BCE, the classical texts became institutionalised by the establishment of Six Erudites with the responsibility of specialising each in one of the Six Classics. The institution was given a very focused mandate by the Han state, intent on cultivating Confucianism for its own political purposes. An imperial academy was also founded (124 BCE), where the Erudites would train and test students in the knowledge of the classics. In this way, the classics were established as orthodox, and became as well the means for the training and recruitment of the bureaucracy.

To prevent another 'burning of the books', and to assure the accuracy of the texts, the classics were literally engraved in stone, by imperial command (175–83 BCE). Over twenty such tablets were placed in front of the imperial academy for all to see. It was the first of six such efforts, also undertaken in the third century CE and later. One might say this was a moment of sweet victory for the Confucian school, but such action also established the authority of the state in the matter of textual accuracy.[18]

Intimately bound up with exegesis is the formation of a canon. And the history of exegesis becomes frequently a history of the power of ideas imposed by an intellectual or religious establishment over a society. The ideas themselves, coming from the classics or scriptures, may be independently powerful, even inspiring. But they are often made *oppressively* so by the power to be. I understand 'canonicity' to refer to the power considered inherent *in* the words of the text, from which the ideas are derived, and 'authority' to refer to the power *behind* the canonical text, associated with the alleged author as well as the force supporting the author, the force that has granted or confirmed legitimation to the classical canon, in the Chinese case, usually the force of law and government.

THE CANON ESTABLISHED

There is a dilemma inherent in hermeneutics: that understanding is always shaped by preconceptions, be these considerations of whether certain texts deserved to be called *classics*, and whether certain lines yield the meaning that the exegete has found there. To a large extent, the history of exegesis has been the history of disagreements between exegetes, and we cannot dismiss the attempts made over and again, to derive certain specific meanings from various classics.

Perhaps this is to be expected, on account of the normative value of the texts concerned. Exegetes and interpreters sought to partake of textual authority, by bending the words and sentences, as do our contemporary experts of the constitutions of a state, often with the intention of limiting the exercise of political power.

*The Apocryphal (*wei) *and prognostication (*ch'an / chan) *texts*

The Chinese word *wei* refers literally to the *woof* of the fabric. It has been translated as Apocrypha, highlighting the relationship between

---

[18] Hung Chin-shan, *Han-Wei Nan-pei-ch'ao pei-hsüeh chih yen-chiu* (A study of the stone tablets of Han, Wei and the Six Dynasties) (n.p., 1974).

itself and the Classics (*ching^c*, i.e., literally, the *warp*). Each of the two words has a 'silk' radical, signifying literally the warp and woof that are found in weaving, and that make – or break – the fabric.[19] The metaphor is all the more apt, since the ancients wrote on silk as well as wood and bamboo.

Of course, the *wei* were not considered 'apocryphal' by those who believed that they, too, had been composed or edited by sages, and that, together with the *ching^c*, they make up the fabric of wisdom left behind by Confucius. Not that the *wei* texts were classics; they claimed only to interpret correctly the classics – whether these be the Book of Songs, or the Analects of Confucius. And, to the extent that they refer to the hidden or esoteric meaning of the Classics, the Greek term *apocrypha* ('hidden') is etymologically appropriate to describe these Chinese texts as well.

Presumably, the apocryphal and prognostication texts emerged very early, before the decisive formation of the classical corpus, and were arbitrarily 'attached' to the classics. They never acquired normative status as classics, and survived only as fragments that found their way eventually into the Taoist textual corpus.

The *ch'an*, or prognostication texts, began as an independent genre, but became frequently confused with the Apocrypha. The *Historical Annals* record the presentation (251 BCE) to the First Ch'in Emperor by a magician-scholar Lu of the first such text, the *Lu-t'u* (*Lutu* or Diagram of Lu), which allegedly foretold the end of the Ch'in dynasty.[20]

Why did the apocryphal and prognostication texts make their appearance, early in the Han dynasty? Chou Yü-t'ung believes this to be the consequence of the influence of magicians, an influence attributed to the rulers' predilection for the esoteric arts, preceding the establishment of State Confucianism.[21] There is little reason to wonder. We only have to recall here that the Apocrypha and the prognostication texts had often provided rulers with supernatural means of legitimation for their authority.

Another event at the time concerned the discovery of texts in the old, pre-Ch'in script, which had been superseded. This gave rise to differing interpretations of the classics, and led to the emergence of the Ancient Script (pre-Ch'in) and Modern Script (second century BCE on) schools. The problem was not merely that of different

---

[19] *Shuo-wen* 13B, p. 2a.   [20] *Shih-chi*, ch. 6; p. 25.   [21] *Zhou Yutong jingxueshi*, pp. 52–6.

scripts, but also of different contents and meanings. It is made more complex by the fact that while certain ancient script texts were genuine, others would prove to be forgeries.

The Confucian classical canon was eventually established according to the rationalist consensus of the Confucian classical scholars, including to a certain measure, both ancient and modern scripts, but excluding apocryphal and prognostication texts. The establishment of Confucianism as state orthodoxy has been an ambivalent event, on account of state control and manipulation of the tradition. Confucian philosophy changed and evolved as it responded to political exigencies, becoming more and more subject to influences from Legalist positions strengthening the ruler's position. While the Erudites owed their status, and the preeminence of the classics they served, to political power, they did not always hesitate to criticise policies. But political power usually preferred those who could serve their own ambitions.

THE CONFUCIAN COMMENTARY (*CHUAN / ZHUAN*) TRADITION

Commentaries . . . dominated the intellectual history of most premodern civilizations . . . As Jose Faur has observed, 'The most peculiar aspect of the medieval thinker is that he developed his ideas around a text and expressed them as a commentary.'[22]

In Western scriptural exegesis, we hear of the painstaking work of reconstructing and establishing the texts from various manuscripts and variant texts. We also hear of the later efforts to discover and elaborate the various senses of the scriptures, such as the 'literal' sense sought after, even today, by both critical scholars and the less critical, and sometimes unschooled, pietists, and the 'hidden' or 'spiritual' sense, elucidated by those exegetes with a more philosophical and theological bent. We learn about the establishment of various early schools of biblical interpretation, such as the Antiochian school (in Syria and Palestine), practising a somewhat scientific 'exegetical' approach, and the Alexandrian school (in Egypt and North Africa), as represented by Origen, favoring an allegorical or 'spiritual' interpretation of the scriptures.

And then, canonical authority, if only in a secondary sense, also

---

[22] John B. Henderson, *Scripture, Canon and Commentary: A Comparison of Confucian and Western Exegesis* (Princeton University Press, 1991), Introduction, p. 3.

extended to later works known to have been written as commentaries on specific classics. This occurred usually when the commentaries became accepted as standard and were used for teaching in the Imperial Academy or as part of the official syllabus in the examination system.

We find in the Chinese case a development parallel to Western scriptural criticism. It begins with the difficult and controversial task of reconstructing the classical texts, accompanied and followed by the work of textual interpretation and the discussions and debates such reconstruction engendered. We find as well a tension between two directions: the critical and laborious task of determining the meaning of each word and each sentence, and the sophisticated, at times flamboyant, efforts of finding a larger meaning in the entire text, of transmitting the 'message' of the sages.

I can discern three periods in China's history of textual interpretation. During the Han period, the two directions were manifested in the literal or the allegorical interpretation of the classics. During the Sung period (960–1279), the two directions both became philosophical and hermeneutical, with adherence to the classical tradition as such, or impatience with its boundaries. During the Ch'ing period, the pendulum swung back from philosophical discourse to textual studies, most of the time favouring historical–critical exegesis, but toward the end manifesting a surprising attraction once more for allegorical interpretation.

Han exegesis: philology and moral allegory

The development of exegesis is best seen in the light of diachronic dialogue and dialectic. The exegetes of the earlier period of the Han dynasty (206 BCE–220 CE) were concerned with both the so-called 'literal' and the 'allegorical' meanings of the classics, even if the principles of interpretation were more implicit than explicit. But the methods of interpretation were not difficult to discern. They include 'lower' textual criticism, with detailed analysis of words and sentences within a classical text, based especially on philological interpretation, and the interpretation of one text with the help of cross references to other texts, usually from within the same classical corpus.[23]

---

[23] Kanō Naoki, *Ryōkan gakujutsu kō* (Scholarship in the Han Dynasty) (Tokyo: Iwanami, 1964.)

The differences between Ancient and Modern Script schools are not limited merely to the authentication of texts. There is also a question of differences of ideas and opinions. The Moderns were less rationalistic, and more open to 'correlative' thinking, including what comes close to what we may call superstition.

• *The Spring–Autumn Annals* The Spring–Autumn Annals has offered an interesting case for those who favoured the allegorical method. The short, laconic notices in these Annals covering the years 722–481 BCE in the small state of Lu require ingenuity on the part of any scholar seeking a broader interpretation or philosophical meanings. Besides, the main text had contributed early to variant interpretations, associated with the three subsidiary texts called commentaries, which themselves eventually acquired the status of classic.

The Annals of Tso played a special role in making Confucius an 'uncrowned king', but the Kung-yang commentary was the favourite of the allegorical school. Following upon Tung Chung-shu's suggestions, the scholar Ho Hsiu (129–82 BCE) elaborated on the 'Three Ages' theory, which divided the 242 years covered by the Spring–Autumn Annals into three groups. The latest years were those personally witnessed by Confucius, and then, going backward, came those that he heard of through oral testimony, and those he learnt of through transmitted records.[24] These 'Three Ages' were subsequently described in chronological order as those of Disorder, Approaching Peace, and Universal Peace.

Chinese utopian ideas have usually focused on time rather than place. The Chinese view of time has been usually described as cyclical and backward-looking, as shown in the preferred 'utopian' description of a Golden Past. This is found especially in the Section called *Li-yün* (Evolution of Rites) from the Book of Rites, which speaks of a remote past, when the 'world belonged to all', called the Great Unity (*ta-t'ung / datong*), and a time after that ruled by the early kings, called the Lesser Prosperity (*hsiao-k'ang / xiaokang*). Many reformers in history had wanted to restore the age of Lesser Prosperity, and a few visionaries even looked back to the Great Unity. But the 'Three Ages' theory has presented the possibility of projecting the past into the future in a different way: by claiming the possibility of progress through history, thus proclaiming a more linear view of time itself.

---

[24] *Ch'un-ch'iu fan-lu*, ch. 1; Fung, *History*, vol. 2, pp. 81–7.

Both Tung Chung-shu and Ho Hsiu belonged to the Modern Script school, which had much tolerance for apocryphal literature. They sought political influence in proclaiming their flamboyant reading of the classics. Their ideas were resurrected in the late Ch'ing period by the controversial scholar and reformer K'ang Yu-wei, who promoted their 'utopian' theories to advance his own socio-political agenda – an eclectic, Confucian, Buddhist, and even anarchist vision of a universal human community.

Practical application

Both the Modern Script school and the Ancient Script school wanted to make a practical impact on society. The latter concentrated on the Institutes of Chou, an idealised account of the early royal Chou institutions, considered a blueprint for social and political reform. Time and again, efforts were made to apply it in government, by Wang Mang and by Wang An-shih (1021–86), the Sung educator and reformer.

Practical application is something that follows textual interpretation, which it presupposes. In the case of the interpretation of the Institutes of Chou, what is at question is not the manner by which they *analyse* the words of the text itself, but their *acceptance* of the text as coming from the ancient sages, whose authority they carry. To restore certain institutions from a Classic was one of the means by which a ruler sought to cloak himself with the sage-king's mantle.

• *The Institutes of Chou* A regent for his son-in-law, the nominal emperor, and a lover of the classics, the first-century Wang Mang had scholarly credentials, and established a special Erudite's chair for the study of the Institutes of Chou. Taking his cues from the ancient script version of the Institutes of Chou and from the modern script version of the chapter on royal institutions in the Book of Rites, he promoted the so-called 'well-field' system. According to it, plots of land were divided into nine portions, like the Chinese word for 'well', with eight families each owning one portion and working together on the ninth portion in the middle which belonged to the state. He attempted (9 CE) to restore it by reclaiming all land for the Crown, and then redistributing it among the people, who were expected to repay a tenth of their produce as tax.[25]

---

[25] Consult Wang Mang's biography, in *Han-shu*, ch. 99a–c.

As a usurper of imperial power, Wang Mang assembled at court a large number of classicists, including actually both Moderns and Ancients. The best-known were such 'Ancients' as his National Preceptor, Liu Hsin (c. 46 BCE–23 CE), a Han imperial clansman and a specialist on the Institutes of Chou, and Mao Heng, the famous commentator on the Book of Songs. But his reign never achieved legitimacy – in spite of the omens and prognostications that proclaimed his mandate. He was eventually overthrown by another Han imperial clansman.[26]

Many hundred years later, the celebrated Sung dynasty scholar and statesman Wang An-shih also appealed to the Institutes of Chou for some of his reforms, which were undertaken with the active support of the Sung emperor. Wang personally composed a new commentary on the text: the *Chou-kuan hsin-yi* (New Meaning of the Institutes of Chou).[27] He instituted a new system of land registration in the name of the legendary well-field system, dividing all taxable land into units of one *li*[c] square, on which taxes were graduated according to land value. But both his commentary and his practical measures met with controversy by those who disapproved of the further centralisation of power, and his reforms did not have lasting results.

Obviously, textual interpretation carried with it political implications and consequences. But the authority of the classic was not always adequate in itself to guarantee the success of the measures implemented in its name. The failures of the two Wangs testified to a third force that played a role in the efficacy of reforms: the landlords' vested interests. And the appeal to a classic, whether genuine or not, was unable to change the outcome.

The merging of the two schools

In Chinese, 'philology' is *hsün-ku / xungu* (literally, 'explaining ancient words'). Since the Chinese script has 'dual', that is, audio-visual dimensions, Chinese philology searches for meaning from both the sound of the word and the appearance of the script.[28] Representing as a group the earlier and dominant opinion in exegesis, the Modern

---

[26] For Liu Hsin, see *Han-shu*, 36:165c–66a.

[27] See his preface to *Chou-kuan hsin-yi*, Four Libraries Rare Books ed., Special Collection, Preface, p. 1a. For the English trans., consult de Bary, *Sources*, p. 467.

[28] Consult Wang Nien-sun's preface to the *Shuo-wen*, p. 1.

Script scholars had their own specialisations in particular classics, forming tight-knit schools of transmission, with information passing from teacher to disciples. Emerging later, the Ancient Script scholars accepted as well the texts transmitted in the old style (allegedly what Confucius used), which they had transposed into the Han style.

• *The Book of History in Ancient Script* The scholarly disputes over the Book of History have focused on the question of the authenticity of certain chapters allegedly transmitted in the ancient script Generally speaking, the documents assembled in the Book of History fall into two main groups: speeches and addresses going back to the early Chou times, and *purported* speeches and addresses that are actually treatises on abstract principles of government, or idealised descriptions of the deeds of ancient sage-kings. The pieces belonging to the first group are more likely to be genuine, while those of the second group, coming from Ancient Script sources, have long been disputed.

We take as an example the 'Canon of Shun', which comes at the beginning of the book, and is cited in the Book of Mencius. The language of this piece cannot be earlier than the third century BCE, and the story is of the sage-king Yao ceding the throne to the sage-king Shun.

Two late Han exegetes deserve special mention for their enduring contributions: Hsü Shen and Cheng Hsüan. Hsü was an Ancient Script scholar, a man of broad learning and erudition, and reputedly peerless as a classical scholar. He expounded clearly upon the differences between the Ancients and Moderns in their interpretation of the Five Classics, and also left behind a famous lexicon (122 CE), presenting a range of meanings for each separate character, while showing also the interrelationships among the words.

The conflating of 'Modern' and 'Ancient' interpretations arose toward the end of the Han, with the emergence of the great exegete Cheng Hsüan (127–200 CE). Cheng studied from both the Ancients and Moderns, and synthesised their opinions in his own prolific works. His opponent was the younger Wang Su, who deliberately forged several texts, including the *K'ung-tzu chia-yü* (School Sayings of Confucius) and *K'ung Ts'ung-tzu* (Miscellaneous Confucians), as a basis to discredit Cheng.[29]

---

[29] Fan Yeh, *Hou Han-shu* 65:132c–33a. See also Kageyama Seiichi, *Chūgoku keigaku shi kō* (A study of the history of Chinese classical scholarship) (Tokyo: Daito Bunka University, 1970),

The Thirteen Classics

It was much later when the T'ang government embarked upon the ambitious project of first determining and promulgating the correct texts for the Five Classics (633 CE), and then compiling the series entitled _The Correct Meaning of the Five Classics._ This new edition was published together with what were regarded as the best available commentaries and subcommentaries, giving first the former, and then the latter, in smaller print following the main text. The series became in 653 CE the required syllabus for examination candidates, who were forbidden to deviate from the given interpretations.[30] Unfortunately, this led to a negative consequence, channelling all energy into memorising standard texts.[31]

The classical core remained the Five Classics, including Songs, History and Changes. But two of the other texts had very early commentaries which later acquired the status of classics. I am referring especially to the three texts surrounding the Spring–Autumn Annals: the lengthy narrative Annals of Tso (ascribed to Tso Ch'iu-ming, supposedly Confucius' contemporary), as well as the Kung-yang and Ku-liang texts, both extant in a 'catechetical' question–answer format. The ritual texts count also as three, including the more discursive Book of Rites, the idealised account called the Institutes of Chou, and the Ritual Etiquette of antiquity. Together with the ancient classical gloss called the _Erh-ya_, they made up an impressive group of Nine, which later expanded to include the Analects of Confucius, the Book of Mencius, and the Classic of Filial Piety, attributed to Confucius' disciple Tseng-tzu, thus making up the 'Thirteen Classics'.

The Sung classicists completed their compendium on the Thirteen Classics. But the mood in the country was already changing in favour of a smaller corpus of classical texts. This came with the persuasion among philosophers that the essential message of the sages had been lost in detailed textual exegesis, often irrelevant to life and to society. It was a reaction to the challenges posed by

53–6. P'i Hsi-jui, _Ching-hsüeh li-shih_ (A history of classical scholarship) (Taipei: Wen-hai, 1964), 24–9; Zhou Yütong, _Zhou Yutong jingxueshi_, pp. 9–14.

[30] Liu Hsü, _Chiu T'ang-shu_ (Old T'ang dynastic history), K'ai-ming edition, 73:270b–c.

[31] Morohashi Tetsuji, _Keigaku kenkyū josetsu_ (A preface to classical scholarship), rev. ed. (Tokyo: Meguro shoten, 1941), pp. 61–79.

Buddhist and Taoist metaphysics, with their claims of answering the big questions in human existence.

Exegesis was eventually eclipsed by this movement claiming to return to the original inspirations of Confucian thinking, accompanied by efforts to focus on a few texts rather than studying a huge collection. This development marked a turning inward, exalting the human spirit rather than external achievements. To use a Chinese expression, it disclosed the 'inner, sagely' concerns more than the 'outer, kingly' preoccupations. And it occurred after many centuries of Taoist and Buddhist dominance. 'The Sung scholars wrote books based on intuition and hypothesis, but they embodied what they said in personal experience, and read extensively, including in Taoism and Buddhism. That explains why their insights were sometimes better than those of the Han scholars, being based on a more profound thinking'.[32]

THE CLASSICS AND THE SCRIPTURES

Actually, the word *ching*[c] has the senses of both 'classic' and 'scripture.' But the norm-setting imperial library collections, made in the late eighteenth century, include only Confucian classics in the first category under the word *ching*[c], with a few Taoist scriptures and Buddhist texts entered under the word *tzu / zi*, that is as philosophical writings in a second category.[33] It is a sign that Confucian texts were supreme in an order of orthodoxy that merely tolerated other ideas and schools of thought.

Between Confucian, Taoist and Buddhist texts regarded as genres, there are, of course, similarities as well as differences. Confucius (or his disciples) could argue that the words of wisdom flowing from his lips were from Heaven, through his mediation of the wisdom of the ancients. But there remains an essential difference with the past oracles: in Confucius' case, there is no alleged *ecstatic* seizure by any deity or ancestral spirit. His special relationship with Heaven was grounded in an awareness of his own participation in an *ethical* wisdom that related human beings to Heaven.

[32] Liu Shih-p'ei, *Han Sung hsüeh-shu yi-t'ung lun* (Similarities and differences between Han and Sung scholarship) in *Liu Sheng-shu hsien-sheng yi-shu* (Surviving Writings of Liu Shih-p'ei) (n.p., 1936), vol. 15, 1b–2a.

[33] Chi Yün (ed.), *Ssu-ku ch'üan-shu tsung-mu t'i-yao* (Essentials of the catalogue of the four libraries collections) (Shanghai: Commercial Press, 1900).

A question of forgery

The story is that the scholar Fu-sheng of Jinan had hidden in the mountains twenty-eight sections of the Book of History, from which the incomplete version was reconstructed during the early Han dynasty. Still later, while Confucius' former lecture hall in Ch'ü-fu (Qufu) was being torn down to give way to the building of a noble's palace, more sections of the Book of History, as well as the Spring–Autumn Annals and the Annals of Tso, were found hidden between the walls, but in an old script that needed deciphering.[34]

We can visualise scholars acquainted with the old script who would produce texts for the classical corpus being restored. In some cases, they mingled the words they once memorised with others that they invented, claiming perhaps to have discovered such, and always with the hope of influencing a legacy that had come to be endowed with sagely power.

Forgery is a complex problem for a classical legacy with no clear authorship for its texts. Since authorship was presumed, rather than established, forgery was not considered a problem except for individual texts or sections of these, usually dating to a later period long after the classics have come into being.

In view of the interaction between the oral and the written traditions, it is interesting how certain forgeries claimed to record the spoken words of the ancient sages. Just as the *invented* Book of Deuteronomy purported to be a sermon of Moses, alleged author of the Hebrew Pentateuch, 'The Counsel of the Great Yü', a forged chapter in the old script in the Book of History, offers alleged words of wisdom passing from one sage-king to another, which became important for later, neo-Confucian, philosophers.

But even in these contexts, forgery remains a problem, especially if claims could continue to be made about the discovery of new texts. And it led eventually to an intellectual explosion – almost two thousand years later. During the last decades of the Ch'ing dynasty (1644–1911), K'ang Yu-wei (1858–1927) especially claimed that all of the ancient script versions of the classics were forged by Liu Hsin, to support his patron, the usurper Wang Mang (r. 9–23 CE), with ideological justification for the sweeping reforms he introduced.[35]

---

[34] Wang Ch'ung, *Lun-heng*, 28:1a–b; 29:1b.
[35] See Zhu Weizheng (ed), *Zhou Yutong jingxueshi lunzhu xuanji* (Select essays on classical exegesis) (Shanghai: Renmin, 1983), pp. 1–39.

Forgery as a Taoist and Buddhist problem

Imitation is the sincerest flattery, we have heard. And forgery is a common problem for traditions that revere the written word. The Confucian classical tradition was not alone in having this problem. Hebrew prophetic books, for instance, include textual interpolations added at a later time. The problem is especially prominent with Taoist and Buddhist texts. For comparative purposes, it is useful to discuss the common problem here.

Religious Taoism accumulated a huge body of scriptures called the *Tao-tsang / Daozang* or 'Taoist canon'. But the Chinese word *tsang / zang*, translated as 'canon', lacks the explicit meaning of 'measure' or 'norm', and refers more to a 'treasury'. This word is not used with regard to Confucian classics, which have always remained a smaller, more carefully defined, corpus. Hence not every text included in the Taoist canon is a *ching*^{c} or canonical scripture.

A key to resolving the mystery of authorship of many Taoist texts is the name of the person who supposedly 'discovered' the allegedly revealed text – in circumstances such as in a cave. Thus the neo-Confucian philosopher Chu Hsi proposes that the author of the *Yin-fu ching*, which gives the teaching of immortals as well as political and military advice, was no other than Li Ch'üan, the T'ang general who claimed to have discovered it in a cave and who ascribed it to the mythical Yellow Emperor.[36]

And here we find what is for persons of a historical bent the real problem of Taoist scriptures: the claim of revelation made for them. Why was this made in so many cases, especially when it could be so easily disproved?

There is, of course, the religious–psychological reason, where the author sincerely believed to have received his message from the gods in a trance. Here we touch upon ecstatic religion, claims of truth based on religious experience.

There is also the 'theological' reason – to support the text's teachings by claiming a higher authority, all the more so since the teachings often contain non-rational elements. After all, if Confucian classics claim to be the words of sages, and Buddhist sutras claim to have come from the Buddha, Taoist scriptures claim to be revela-

---

[36] See *Chu-tzu Yin-fu ching k'ao-yi* (Chu Hsi's study of the *Yin-fu ching*), in *Chu-tzu yi-shu* series, p. 1.

tions of the Tao. In the case of known forgeries, does this not spell intentional deceit?

Perhaps. I would not deny that some Taoists knowingly made false claims for some of their scriptures and, in many cases, had knowingly *fabricated* scriptures. But I wish to recall that in the past, authorship has always been reported by loose attribution. Even the Confucian Ancient Script school forged some of their classics. Perhaps the Taoists exercised less discretion, especially by appropriating to themselves texts coming from other traditions. At issue is the perennial question of appropriating scriptural authority for the proclamation of religious teaching. But it is interesting that the proponents of so many Taoist texts should have sought to do so in a coded language that can only be understood by the initiated. This indicates an important difference between Taoism and Buddhism: the former remained mainly an esoteric religion, whereas the latter was preached openly to the masses, and hastened to find a suitable language for the translation of its ideas into Chinese.

In fact, since few if any of the works included in any Buddhist canon can be said to have come directly from the Buddha himself, how can a text be regarded as genuine? We should, of course, take into consideration the consensus of the community. In the case of Theravāda, this means the Pali canon. And in the case of the Chinese Mahāyāna, this would also mean whatever the community has decided to include in their canon, no matter how long the distance of time might separate them from the historical Buddha.

But there were Chinese sutras that were locally produced, rather than translated, and yet acknowledged as, somehow, 'genuine'. These were compiled by unknown authors to make Buddhism more comprehensible to the people of the time, and include such important works as the *Fan-wang ching* (Sutra of Brahma's Net); *Kuan wu-liang shou ching* (Sutra of Meditation on the Buddha Amitābha), one of the three pillars of Pure Land Buddhism; the popular *Yüan-chüeh ching* (Sutra of Perfect Enlightenment); and the *Wu-liang yi-ching* (Sutra of Innumerable Meanings), considered to be the 'opening sutra' to the Threefold Lotus sutra.[37]

Other local products were considered 'spurious'. Some were plain forgeries, with little religious value. But others were allegedly composed by persons in ecstatic meditation, such as the fifth-century

---

[37] Mizuno, *Buddhist Sutras*, pp. 117–18.

nun Seng-fa, who recited innumerable works in her youth – between age nine and sixteen, and even in the presence of the devout Buddhist Emperor Wu of Liang (505 CE)![38] The important matter here is that ecstatic trance is not necessarily a seal of the revelatory character of the text. There is need for communal verification and support.

By the end of the T'ang dynasty (906 CE), the formation of the Buddhist canon was practically completed, even if a few scattered translations were made during later periods. In 983, the first Sung emperor ordered the cutting of blocks for the printing of the entire Chinese *Tripiṭaka*. This was the Shu (Szechuan) edition, with 1,076 entries in 5,048 chapters or *chüan / juan.* Some of the Buddhist scriptures were also inscribed in stone, often by private persons intent upon gaining merit for themselves and their ancestors.[39]

Pious sovereigns supported the printing of Buddhist texts and the spreading of their message for merit and devotion, or to please the believing multitudes. Besides, patronage was one way of controlling the religion. The Buddhist canon was useful to the state, serving as a constitution for the *sangha,* and the state exercised its prerogatives by making the final decision about which translations were fit for inclusion in the canon. The state, therefore, made the final decision as to what books would be included in the canon. It decided, of course, on the advice of experts. But it was the state's *imprimatur* that made a collection of books, the Buddhist canon. And the state used the canon as a sanction; it could and did punish members of the *sangha* for moral or ritual transgressions against the scriptures.

Confucian, Taoist and Buddhist texts each enjoyed state patronage, although not always in the same way. The fact that they did, shows us how the secular and the sacred are intermingled in the history of all the religious traditions in China.

THE CONFUCIAN UNIVERSE

The cosmos implicit in Confucian classics and preached by Sung Neo-Confucians was an interrelated and interdependent whole in which the moral and natural realms were merged. The Son of Heaven was the mediator between Heaven and the world ('all under Heaven'). The capital

[38] Ibid, p. 119.
[39] Kenneth Ch'en, *Buddhism in China: A Historical Survey* (Princeton University Press, 1964), 374–5.

from which he ruled was an *axis mundi*, a pivot about which the four quarters revolved.[40]

And just as that axis was symbolically recapitulated in every government office in the empire, so too was the hierarchical pattern of the emperor's dealings with his ministers universally repeated as officials dealt with subjects, fathers with sons, husbands with wives and the elderly with the young. Form and substance overlapped; since a harmonious order could be created only though ritual and etiquette, breaches in them rent its fabric. This view of a moral universe contributed to social stability. The most divergent oral traditions shared a Confucian ethical core, and even among the Buddhist clergy there was little inclination to mount a cultural or political challenge.

But how are we to understand and appreciate some two thousand or more years of the Chinese exegetical tradition? The subject itself may appear to belong more properly in a museum, with the stone classics. And yet, how can we understand modernity without regard to those forces behind it, in the past, with which it continues to be related, even if dialectically? Are there not other ideologies, the modern ones, each with its own scriptures and commentaries, that have replaced the traditional ideologies with their own exegetical traditions? We have only to think of Marxism–Leninism, and its scriptures on Dialectical Materialism, as well as its already impressive corpus of commentaries, still of some importance in Communist China.[41] Whether one likes it or not, exegesis has not gone out of fashion, even when the ideology has changed.

A moral hermeneutic

We speak of exegesis as the practice of interpretation, and hermeneutics as the theory of interpretation. In the Chinese case, we find an abundance of explicit and practical exegesis, but much less that is explicit on hermeneutical theory.

In the West, hermeneutics did not become a methodological approach to texts independent of biblical study until the nineteenth century, with the emergence of the philosopher and theologian

---

[40] John W. Chaffee, *The Thorny Gates of Learning in Sung China: A Social History of the Examinations* (Cambridge University Press, 1985), p. 19.
[41] J. M. Bochenski, *Soviet Russian Dialectical Materialism (DIAMAT)* (Dordrecht: Reidel, 1963).

Friedrich Schleiermacher in Germany. He saw his role as making intelligible what others have said in speech and text, and thus bringing hidden truth to light. He was eager to avoid misunderstandings, and focused on the authorial voice of the words and their meanings. And so was launched a universal approach to the understanding and interpretation of texts both biblical and secular, without concern for dogmatic interest.[42]

Already here we have the ambiguity of the theoretical or philosophical dimension touching on the principles of understanding, and the practical application of these principles to the written texts. Besides, depending on preference in emphasis upon one or the other, that is, the interpreter or the object of interpretation, we may have a difference of views regarding what hermeneutics is all about. For example, two basic positions are represented by Emilio Betti, who defends the autonomy of the so-called object of interpretation, and Hans-Georg Gadamer, who, while appreciating Schleiermacher, denies the possibility of having 'objectively valid interpretations'. To bridge the gap between subject and object, the work of understanding itself is seen as an experiential encounter with a historically transmitted work. This is the 'hermeneutical experience' involving a dialectical questioning allowing the text to 'talk back', and to call the interpreter's own horizon into question, while working toward an *Aufhebung* (elevation) in the Hegelian sense, a transformation of one's understanding of what one is seeking to interpret. This takes listening, with the 'inner ears', in order to hear, not only what the text says, but also what it does not.[43]

Where exegesis concerns itself with the *practical* task of explaining the written word in the classical texts, hermeneutics deals with the more theoretical *principles* of understanding underlying exegesis. And where the word 'exegesis' is usually employed with reference to scriptures or classics, the word 'hermeneutics' is used in a wider context, with reference to all texts, and by extension, even those not of print, such as works of art, science, and technology.

In the history of Chinese exegesis, with the similarities and differences among its practitioners, we can discuss its high and low points within a certain hermeneutical framework, drawing our principles of interpretation from from Chinese practice itself. We

---

[42] Hans-Georg Gadamer, *Truth and Method* (New York: Continuum, 1975), pp. 162–73.
[43] Richard E. Palmer, *Hermeneutics: Interpretation Theory in Schleiermacher, Dilthey, Heidegger, and Gadamer* (Evanston: Northwestern University Press, 1969), pp. 232–6.

identify a *moral* hermeneutics. In it, rationalisation continually accompanies an effort to draw moral principles from a corpus of texts belonging properly to different genres, whether oracles of divination, or lyrical poetry, or ritual prescriptions, and so on.

I speak of moralists and intellectualists in the context of hermeneutics. In applying these categories to pre-Sung events, I suggest that the term 'intellectualist' be applied to those more devoted to detailed analysis of words and sentences. The term 'moral' is then used for scholars concerned with discovering a moral dimension through a broadly allegorical method of interpretation. Keeping in mind the usually moral preoccupation (at least in declared intent, if not in fact) of these exegetes, we may add a third category of 'pragmatist' to include those scholars eager to put into practical application what they perceive to be classical institutional models.

This does not necessarily preclude a serious knowledge of the Classics or the help of teachers. But the work of teachers was less the transmission of exegetical skills, as in the case of the scholars of Han Learning, than that of provoking thought and inspiring insight. The question was not the passing on of a static truth, but the transmission of faith and dynamic understanding in the message of the ancient sages, to be discovered anew by every generation.[44]

The classics redefined: the Four Books

The philosopher Chu Hsi was chiefly responsible for the choice of the Four Books as the final, authoritative storehouse of Confucian wisdom, taking precedence over the Five Classics. We are speaking here of the Analects and the Book of Mencius, both records of conversations belonging already to the corpus of the Thirteen Classics, and the Great Learning and the Doctrine of the Mean, two chapters deriving from the Book of Rites. These were chosen for their philosophical and spiritual content, since they allegedly addressed metaphysical problems occupying men's minds. When taken as the main educational syllabus, they effectively *reduced* the scope of the Classics while permitting focus and concentration.

Interestingly, Chu Hsi was *the* Sung scholar remembered in later ages, both for his speculative genius and for his technical expertise in the classics. True, he is known more as a philosopher than as a

---

[44] Morohashi, *Keigaku*, pp. 136–48; Ching, *To Acquire Wisdom*, pp. 5–6.

classical scholar. But his philosophy is mainly articulated through his commentaries on the Four Books, which include the Analects and the Book of Mencius, and on the philosophical writings of his predecessors of the Sung dynasty. Chu punctuated, annotated and divided into chapters the texts of these Four Books. He divided the Great Learning into eleven chapters, and the Doctrine of the Mean into thirty-three. But he also did more than that.

He obviously wanted to counter the philosophical and spiritual onslaughts of Buddhism and Taoism, by focusing on those texts that most manifestly bring to light the essentials of Confucian philosophy and spirituality. Here, I am especially referring to a philosophy centred on the 'oneness of Heaven and man'. But by redefining the 'classical corpus', and even more, by offering his emendations to the texts of the Great Learning, Chu was doing more than interpreting a text deemed classical: he was also *editing* it, offering interpolations of his own.

I am referring especially to Chu's insertion of a paragraph of his own writing into the very brief fifth chapter of the Great Learning, on perfecting knowledge. Here he determined that the text was incomplete, that the original had suffered some loss. So he borrowed from Ch'eng Yi's commentary to add a paragraph, to explain that the 'extension of learning lies in the investigation of things' (*ko-wu / gewu*), which is accomplished by 'exhausting the principles (li^b) of all things'. And he added,

For there is no human spiritual intelligence that does not contain knowledge, while there is nothing in the universe that does not contain li^b. But when li^b has not been exhaustively investigated, knowledge cannot be complete. That is why the Great Learning begins its teaching by making scholars investigate everything in the universe, moving from what they already know to do so more exhaustively, in order to reach the ultimate. And after a long time of making such efforts, we shall one day achieve a sudden and penetrating understanding. We shall then apprehend [the qualities of] all things, inside and outside, subtle and coarse, and also make manifest the mind in its entire substance and all its functions. This is what is called investigating things; this is what is called reaching perfect knowledge.[45]

So Chu imposed his own philosophy, with its metaphysics of li^b or principle, and its belief in sudden mystical enlightenment which came to him from Ch'an Buddhism, on the *text* of the Great

---

[45] Eng. trans. adapted from Legge, *Chinese Classics*, vol. 1, pp. 365–6.

Learning, a work which was believed to have come down from the sages, and which he himself regarded to have come from Confucius' disciple Tseng-tzu. If he dared to do so, he must have considered himself a sage, even if later generations only venerated him as a great philosopher. And he referred to the names of the sages and worthies of the past, apparently to appeal to their authority for support for his own teachings, not necessarily derived from theirs.

Chu's tampering with the text of the *Great Learning* is unacceptable for a classical scholar. However, it pales next to the pronouncement of his contemporary and rival, Lu Chiu-yüan, who said that 'The Six Classics are all my footnotes'.[46] Lu was schooled in the Classics, but had no penchant for detailed scholarship. As a creative thinker, he was even unwilling to fetter himself with the traditional boundaries of classical references, and was ready to accept sages from everywhere. As he has also said:

> The universe is my mind;
> My mind is the universe.
> Sages appeared tens of thousands of generations ago.
> They shared the same mind, the same principle.
> Sages will appear tens of thousands of generations from now.
> They will share the same mind, the same principle.
> Sages appear over the four seas;
> They share the same mind, the same principle.[47]

Philosophically, Chu and Lu are said to represent the two extreme priorities found in the history of Chinese thought and scholarship: of intellectual inquiry and moral emphasis. But when compared with those scholars dedicated to words and sentences, Chu and Lu concurred in desiring to find the larger horizons of metaphysical and moral meaning and insight.

I refer here to two phrases taken from a classical text, the Doctrine of the Mean, which may illustrate this moral hermeneutic: *tao wen-hsüeh* / *dao wenxue* (intellectual inquiry) and *tsun te-hsing* / *zun dexing* (honouring virtuous nature). They were especially used by Chu and Lu to designate each other as 'moralists' or 'intellectualists', and the label 'intellectualist' always referred to him who prefers to ground his thinking in classical learning. The problem was the moralists' claim for their own private authority, that of their minds and hearts,

[46] Lu Chiu-yüan, *Hsiang-shan ch'üan-chi* (Complete writings) (abbrev. as *HSCC*), SPPY ed., 34:4a.
[47] *HSCC*, 22:5a.

which they regarded as one with the mind and heart of the sages. That was generally true of both Chu and Lu and also of the later Wang Yang-ming. After all, they were after the same goal of mystical enlightenment.

The work done by the Sung philosophers has been denounced by later scholars of the Ch'ing dynasty, as being uncritical and unobjective. However, when we take the broad view of the entire history of exegesis, we find that Sung scholars made noteworthy contributions, especially by their independent and critical spirit. In this, they were unlike the more credulous Han scholars, both Ancients and Moderns, who were generally unable to dissociate themselves from the fixed views and methods of their particular lineages.[48]

Yü Ying-shih has pointed out Chu's close resemblance to certain modern Western theorists, especially Emilio Betti, likewise concerned with the autonomy of the text as object of interpretation as well as with the possibility of objective knowledge to be derived from textual interpretation.[49]

The oral tradition revived

Chu Hsi's doctrine of *Tao-t'ung* describes the passing of the Tao initially from one sage-king to the next by word of mouth. It also acknowledges the loss of transmission during a period of centuries, only to be rediscovered by men much later. The implicit reference is to the priority of the oral over the written, and of personal discovery over the study of the texts.

In this light, an interesting phenomenon accompanying these developments was the emphasis on oral transmission. Probably following the examples of Ch'an monks who published recorded conversations of their great masters, and also going back to the Confucian models in the Analects and the Book of Mencius, students of famous philosophers began to note down for later publication the conversations with their masters. These *yü-lu* (recorded conversations) made up the largest repository of the new Confucian teaching. And as a genre, they expressed the attitude of the men who

---

[48] Liu Shih-p'ei, *Han Sung hsüeh-shu*, pp. 1–15.
[49] Reference is to Betti's article, 'Hermeneutics as the General Methodology of the *Geisteswissenschaften*', in Josef Bleicher (ed.), *Contemporary Hermeneutics* (London: Routledge and Kegan Paul, 1980), p. 85; consult Yü Ying-shih, 'Morality and Knowledge in Chu Hsi's Philosophical System', in Chan (ed.), *Chu Hsi and Neo-Confucianism*, pp. 238–9.

considered themselves to be primarily teachers of disciples, living with them in an intimate circle, and communicating to them the ineffable teachings of the sages, which could be easily distorted when given too ornate a form. We have today, therefore, the recorded conversations of Chu Hsi, classified according to subject matter, with discussions of nearly every chapter of the Four Books and of several of the Classics. We also have the recorded conversations of some of his predecessors, contemporaries, and others who came later, including Lu Chiu-yüan and Wang Yang-ming.

The revival of conversation as a literary genre illustrates once more the dynamic tension between the spoken word and the written text, with the philosophers preferring the fluidity of oral discourse to the exegete's preference for words and phrases. The problem, however, arises from the contradiction inherent in a lineal transmission of insights into a dynamic truth: a problem of criteria. How can it be decided that a certain man has attained any real insight at all, and what is the nature of such insight, and of truth itself? Chu Hsi's determination of the line of transmission did not provide any external criteria. It merely set up the authority of Chu himself, as the criterion of judgement regarding the orthodoxy of the insights of those whose names had been included among the transmitters of the Tao.[50]

THE FLOWERING OF CRITICISM: CH'ING PHILOLOGY

The Sung scholars tended to give voice to opinions without offering solid evidence; their main contribution lay in philosophical exposition. In this, they were followed by the Ming (1368–1644) thinkers, who had even less concern for grounding such in the classics. The Ch'ing (1644–1911) scholars called for more practical and objective studies, concentrating especially on the classics, and the seventeenth and eighteenth centuries proved to be a golden age of classical exegesis. Apparently, the Manchu emperors appeared to have been only too happy to patronise the intellectual pursuit of the meaning of words and sentences, while neglecting the Ming heritage of speculative thinking, which was more difficult to control and supervise.

[50] Ching, *To Acquire Wisdom*, p. 11.

From philosophy to philology

The Ch'ing classicists reacted to the dominance of the speculative neo-Confucian philosophy, by turning to a more practical and precise scholarship, focusing on what appeared to be objective truth as found in the Classics. For men like Ku Yen-wu (1613–82), as also for others, the task was the reconstruction of the specific and pristine meanings of the sages' words and utterances as these were found in the classical texts. They considered themselves to be pursuing 'Han learning', harking back to a time closer to the age of sages, and the time of the birth of the classics, at least as these have come to be known. And the method which they applied was called 'evidential research' (*k'ao-chü / kaoju*, literally, investigations and evidence), a developed and more scientific form of Han philology, which functioned with the support of ancillary disciplines including not only phonology, semantics, grammar, and redaction studies, but also epigraphy, bibliography, geography, and even mathematics and astronomy. Here they profited from the introduction of Western scientific knowledge by Jesuit missionaries. However, such scientific information served strictly an ancillary role. We have no evidence that the classical scholars learnt about methods of scriptural exegesis in vogue in the West.

Where neo-Confucian thinkers had first reduced theoretical issues to their fundamental principles before deducing conclusions, Ch'ing philologists reversed the habit by placing emphasis on concrete verifiable facts instead of abstract conceptual categories. For this reason Ku Yen-wu gave the rallying cry: 'The study of Classics *is* the study of principles (*li*[b]).' In other words, there is no Confucian philosophy without classical studies.

> The term *Li-hsüeh / lixue* ['study of principles'] was started in the Sung period. In antiquity the so-called study of principles was the study of Classics. Several decades of time were required before one could become an expert in it . . . Today, what is meant by the study of principles is Ch'an Buddhist philosophy. It is based, not on the Five Classics, but on the recorded conversations.[51]

By the inductive method is meant here the use of information and references from more than one classic to understand a specific word

---

[51] Ku Yen-wu, *T'ing-lin shih-wen chi: wen-chi* (Collected writings), Ssu-pu ts'ung-k'an first series edition, 3:102.

or passage in one classic. Ku and others criticised the Sung neo-Confucian philosophers' reinterpretation of the classics, and especially their introduction of Buddhist influence. Ch'ing scholars believed in giving proofs of evidence for their assertions, much as it is done in litigation. With his proofs of textual evidence, Yen Jo-ch'ü demonstrated that the ancient script chapters of the Book of History, suspected already by Chu Hsi, were indeed a later forgery. His aim had been to recapture the true intentions of the sages through the study of classical texts with their glosses, as well as phonological changes, a work akin to biblical textual criticism.[52] But if Hsien still showed respect for Chu Hsi, Yen Yüan (1635–1704) and his disciple Li Kung (1659–1746) did not. Both vehement critics of Sung and Ming thought as representing the culmination of Buddhism and Taoism, they preached a return to the days of Confucius and Mencius.[53]

Li Kung debates Chu Hsi's interpretation of the Great Learning. For him, *ko-wu* refers not to intellectual pursuit or the 'investigation of things', but to 'reaching into' or pursuing such tasks as 'making virtue manifest, loving the people, rendering the intention sincere, rectifying the mind, cultivating the self, ordering the family, governing the state, and bringing peace to the world'. These, in turn, require the learning of those 'things' or subjects recorded in the Institutes of Chou, such as ritual, music, archery, charioteering, writing, and mathematics, that is, the Six Arts of antiquity.[54]

But the greatest classical scholar of that time was Tai Chen (1724–77), who desired to discover philosophy from words and terms. His *Meng-tzu tzu-yi shu-cheng* (A Study of the Meanings of Words in the Book of Mencius) has been recognised as the best example of evidential research. Tai was a systematic and conscientious scholar, convinced that philology should be scientifically based, and made to serve the clarification of philosophical truth.

Thus Tai Chen gave himself to philological studies, moving from the *Shuo-wen* to the Sung compendium of commentaries and subcommentaries on the Thirteen Classics. But he was an exception in an age when classical scholars had become mere professional

---

[52] Benjamin A. Elman, *From Philosophy to Philology* (Cambridge, Mass.: Harvard University Press, 1984), pp. 29–31.
[53] Yen Yüan, *Ts'un-hsüeh p'ien* (On the preservation of learning), SPPY ed., 1:11–13. Yen wanted to restore the well-field system of the Institutes of Chou.
[54] Li Kung, *Ta-hsüeh pien-yeh* (Analysis of the *Great Learning*) in *Yen-Li ts'ung-shu* (n.p.: Ssu-ts'un hsüeh-hui, 1923), 2:8.

specialists, uninterested in broader questions of philosophical meaning. Rather, he himself was eager to find 'the mind of the sages'. As he put it 'When philology makes words clear, the ancient classics will be understood . . . and the meanings of the sages and worthies will be made manifest. Then also will be understood, [what Mencius calls] that which is common in our minds.'[55]

From philology to philosophy

We mentioned K'ang Yu-wei's efforts to offer a philosophy based on classical authority. In fact, with a few strokes of his brush, K'ang proclaimed as groundless most of the work done before him because it went back, not to Confucianism, but to the alleged first-century forgeries.

A word should be said about K'ang's assertions. First, were all the modern script texts forgeries by Liu Hsin? Here, a common-sense answer is that the very number of the texts virtually precludes the possibility of forgery by any single individual.[56] A much more logical hypothesis is that a series of individuals, becoming dissatisfied with the texts and doctrines of the Modern Script school, began to stress other texts and doctrines, which they maintained went back to Confucius himself. But the problem remains: where do the texts come from?

Presumably, they had various origins. Genuine ancient texts had been hidden and were discovered, as genuine modern texts were recorded from oral memory. But there were also many other texts to which it is more difficult to apply the adjective 'genuine'.

And how were their creations received? Eventually, forged parts of various classics were inserted into such texts as the Book of History and the other classics. Indeed, it is difficult for us to ascertain the integrity of any entire classical text, the Analects included, as having escaped additions and interpolations.

ANALYTICAL REFLECTIONS

There are important similarities and differences regarding Confucian classics and Taoist and Buddhist scriptures. In fact, Taoist and

---

[55] *Tai Chen wen-chi* (Collected writings of Tai Chen) (Beijing: Zhonghua, 1980), ch. 11, p. 168.
[56] Fung, *History*, vol. 2, p. 135.

Buddhist scriptures are quite different in their claims of revelation or inspiration as well as in their compositions, textual transmissions, and purported teachings.

The question of revelation

Scholars distinguish between revelation proper, where God or a superhuman power allegedly transmits both the form and the content of the message, and inspiration, where the divine or super-human guidance applies to content only. It may be said that in contrast to the Qur'an, which the Muslims claim to be the eternal word of God in both form and content, the Hebrew and Christian scriptures contain portions that are claimed to be revealed, and others that are only properly described as inspired.

Usually, when we use the word 'revelation' in a scriptural context, we limit it to the form-and-content claims of divine revelation made for religions like Judaism, Christianity and Islam. Both Taoist and Buddhist scriptures have been regarded rather as books of wisdom, incorporating the mystical insights of their alleged authors.

How is revelation transmitted? Whether there is a question of celestial voices, or of 'tablets' received, the metaphorical language points to a special kind of ecstatic experience.

Confucian classics have been traditionally attributed to sages, especially to Confucius himself as author or editor. But these claims do not usually include revelatory visions as the sources of inspiration. The apocryphal and prognostication texts were the exceptions, but only a few of them gained incorporation into the Confucian canon, and their presence therein appears as an exception to the rule. Confucian classics, especially the Book of History, may very well include statements made in a trance state, perhaps as messages received from on high. But the revelatory context has often been forgotten in later ages, and the texts are included because the words came from the sages, especially the ancient sage-kings, and contain an inherent wisdom.

I propose that some Taoist and Mahāyāna Buddhist scriptures may claim to be revealed documents, to the extent that they originate in ecstatic visions or trances of particular individuals. In this, they are quite different from Confucian classics.

One feature is common to all these textual traditions. This regards their form more than their contents. I refer to the interrelationship between the oral and the written traditions. It is a mark of the importance of oral tradition that the classical and scriptural texts often begin with the phrase: 'The King . . . said', 'The Master said', or 'Thus have I heard [from the Buddha]'.

This may be well and good, except for the problem of scriptural authority, which is much less reified in an oral, or 'semi-oral' tradition. But the written form gives room for manipulation, for imposing private interpretations – and these were abundant, especially in the case of Buddhist texts, which incorporate *upāya*, the principle of expedient teaching, of truth as skill-in-means.

The oral tradition tends to be fluid and dynamic, while the textual tradition can be more precise but static. If truth is intuition and experience, it is communicated from mind to mind, from heart to heart, and it is present as much in the process of communication itself as it is in the words – or the silence – which facilitate this communication. This is why generations of students continued to search for masters, not only to explain the truth that is already recorded, but also to help them *find* it for themselves. That is also why classical and scriptural texts are often recited aloud and committed to memory for recitation, including in a ritual or liturgical context. In a way, the reciter is seeking to identify with the text, and with the authorial voice behind the text. In another way, for religious Taoism and Buddhism, and within a liturgical context, the chanting becomes prayer, with the hope of touching the heart of the gods or spirits who may be regarded as real authors, or who understand best the coded language of the scriptures.

With Taoist and Chinese Mahāyāna Buddhist scriptures, the main criterion by which certain texts have been given the scriptural status is some kind of group consensus, usually on the part of a select group of monks or scholars serving as a kind of publication board under government support and supervision. This was also the case with Confucian classics. The difference is that the criterion for group consensus is not the same for Confucian scholars and Taoists or Mahāyāna Buddhists.

I should make a few distinctions between Taoist and Buddhist scriptures. In spite of all contrary evidence, the story was that the Buddhist scriptures were the Buddha's *ipsissima verba*, recorded by disciples around the time of his death and stored in caves and libraries before they were discovered and taken to China. The facts were quite different. But in spite of these facts, those scriptures regarded as the Buddha's sermons have been included in the Chinese corpus with the words _Fo-shuo_ ('The Buddha said') at the head of their titles, including numerous Mahāyāna texts. This is despite the contention sometimes made that, for the Mahāyāna case, the author is not the historical Buddha, but his _dharmakāya_ (literally, Body of Truth), or the eternal, cosmic, or divine Buddha. Strictly speaking, the inherent claim for Mahāyāna scriptures may be called 'inspiration' more than revelation, with the cosmic Buddha serving as a kind of Holy Spirit inspiring the authors of the texts, without determining the form and language.

In the Taoist case, the corpus includes many works regarded as 'heavenly books' that originated in trance, that could have been written in trance, by mystics or shamans claiming divine revelation. In the T'ang dynasty and later, many considered Lao-tzu – the divinised Lao-tzu – as having revealed all the principal texts in the Taoist canon.[57]

The classical legacy enshrined

Writing restructures consciousness. Once recorded as text, ideas become fixed, and require interpretation – both oral and written, while the text acquires the authority that belonged earlier to the author. This was what happened to the Confucian classics, as it did also to many other scriptures. And there were certain moments in time when the intellectual scene was _especially_ dominated by the study of the classics: during the Han and T'ang times, and during the Ch'ing or Manchu period (1644–1911).

In the recent past, two extreme opinions have been voiced regarding the authorship of the Confucian Classics. The textual scholar P'i Hsi-jui insists upon Confucius' authorship, saying that while the materials in the Classics have come mostly from earlier texts, Confucius was responsible for giving them a 'soul' by putting order into what was chaos. According to him, Confucius edited the ancient Songs, taking about three hundred poems out of a collection of three thousand, and selecting about a hundred documents out of over three thousand to create History. He also purportedly edited the rituals, and composed the words of explanation for the hexa-

[57] Ninji Ofuchi, 'The Formation of the Taoist Canon', in Holmes Welch and Anna Seidel (eds), _Facets of Taoism: Essays in Chinese Religion_ (New Haven: Yale University Press, 1979), pp. 261–7.

grams in the Changes, making it more than a divination manual. And he gave his moral judgement on historical events in the Spring– Autumn Annals. For P'i, while there were earlier texts, there could be no 'Classics' before Confucius.[58]

The modern critical historian Ch'ien Hsüan-t'ung, who also initiated the 'quest for the historical Confucius', denied any relationship between Confucius and the Classics. Insisting that the Five Classics are very different books, he claims that they were gathered in one corpus because of certain references in the Analects to Songs, History, Rituals, and Music and the reference in Mencius about Confucius composing the Spring–Autumn Annals. According to him, the corpus was established around the third century BCE, and, once this was done, other texts, such as *Hsün-tzu*, and the Han historians and philosophers, all refer to them as a group.[59]

True, the classical group of books is a heterogeneous lot, comprising diverse genres, and probably multiple authors even for the single works. This should not be surprising, when the Confucian canon is compared with the world's other classics or scriptures. The Christian Bible, for example, is really made up of two collections: the Hebrew scriptures, termed by Christians the Old Testament, and the Christian books in Greek, called the New Testament. Together, they make up a mosaic of literary genres, including oracles and folktales, proverbs and parables, documents, laws, letters, sermons, hymns and ritual records, many of these going back to a time of near and remote antiquity when oral tradition held sway.[60]

Ch'ien's judgements regarding the antiquity of the Book of Songs and the archival character of the Book of History have been well received. But the question remains: why should the Classics have been so closely associated with the memory of Confucius? Besides, what kind of books did Confucius use to teach his disciples, if not something like the Classics, as the Analects and other texts appear to indicate?[61]

Confucius need not be dissociated from all involvement with the

[58] P'i Hsi-jui (Pi Xirui), *Ching-hsüeh li-shih* (A history of classical exegesis) (1928 ed., Beijing: Zhonghua, 1959), pp. 19–20.
[59] See Ch'ien's letter to Ku Chieh-kang, in Ku Chieh-kang (ed.), *Ku-shih pien* (1926 ed., Taipei reprint, 1970), vol. 1, pp. 69–70; Ching, *Confucianism and Christianity*, ch. 1.
[60] Henderson, *Scripture*, p. 22.
[61] See especially Analects 7:17; *Shih-chi* ch. 126, p. 270. On this entire subject, consult Nemoto Makoto, *Chūgoku koten shisō no kenkyū* (A study of the thought of Chinese classics) (Tokyo: Ajia shuppansha, 1971).

classics, even if we do not know his specific role. The core of many of these classical texts goes back to the time of Confucius, and even to the time preceding him, which shows the ancient lineage of the school of *Ju*[b]. Each of them came from a different source and underwent a long period of evolution, acquiring some kind of moulding from Confucius and definitely receiving accretions postdating Confucius. All this agrees with his description of himself as 'a transmitter but not a composer, believing in and loving the ancients' (Analects 7:1).[62]

CONCLUDING REMARKS

Confucian classics differ from the classics of Western civilisation. The mainly Greek and Roman literature and philosophy produced during the West's 'classical period' (roughly seventh century BCE to fourth century CE) has no normative value except for the literary taste of the educated. Plato, Aristotle and the Stoics define philosophy as a genre, and offer models for clear thinking and good argumentation, but do not impose their authority on the minds of later generations. Homer for the Greeks and Virgil for the Romans recall classical mythology, but more for its poetic effect than for any intrinsic appeal to religious belief. Confucian classics straddle the areas of classic and religious scripture, functioning as both.

The reinterpretation of the classical legacy discloses the philosophers' distrust and suspicion of the written word, and sometimes even of the oral. Such a suspicion was well articulated early on in the Taoist text *Chuang-tzu*, although it is interesting that the heirs to the Confucian legacy should show the same attitude:

Duke Huan was in his hall reading a book. The wheelwright P'ien, who was in the yard below chiseling a wheel . . . said to him:
'This book that Your Grace is reading – may I venture to ask whose words are in it?'
'The words of the sages,' said the duke.
'Are the sages still alive?'
'Dead long ago,' said the duke.
'In that case, what you are reading is nothing but the chaff and dregs of men of old. . . . From the point of view of my own work . . . you can

[62] See Zhou Yutong (Chou Yü-t'ung), *'Liujing yu Kongzi de guanxi wenti'* (The question of the relationship between Confucius and the Six Classics) in Zhu, *Zhou Yutong jingxueshi*, pp. 795–806. This is basically taken from Chou's book, *Ching chin-ku-wen hsüeh* (Old and new script classical learning): (Shanghai: Commercial, 1929).

get it in your hand and feel it in your mind. You can't put it in words, and yet there's a knack to it somehow. I can't teach it to my son, and he can't learn it from me.'[63]

We may wonder: if a wheelwright's skills cannot be taught, what can? Every generation, it appears, has to reinvent its wheels. Still, many philosophers agreed with the wheelwright on the transmission of the sages' teachings.

The horizon of the present is continually being formed. In that we have continually to test all our prejudices. An important part of this testing is the encounter with the past and the understanding of the tradition from which we come. Hence the horizon of the present cannot be formed without the past . . . In a tradition this process of fusion is continually going on, for there old and new continually grow together to make something of living value.[64]

---

[63] *Chuang-tzu* sect. 13, 5:18a–b; Eng. trans. adapted from Watson, *Complete Works*, pp. 152–3.
[64] Gadamer, *Truth and Method*, p. 273.

CHAPTER 6

The mystic as sage: religion appropriates the paradigm

INTRODUCTION

Considering the Confucian classics from the past, the wisdom of China seems more secular than sacred. The humanistic legacy has made the greatest impact on Chinese civilisation itself and most impressed the outsider. To discover the spiritual and religious richness, one has to search and to dig into this very humanism, to the heart of its wisdom, where we find a surprising core of mysticism.

In the Book of Mencius (2A:2), we find mention of him 'nurturing the vast, flood-like *ch'i*ᵃ' as something that fills the body. The reference presumes that there is what is called *ch'i*ᵃ (breath, air, energy) that constitutes the universe, and that this *ch'i*ᵃ possesses a varied consistency. What is heavy in it tends to descend and makes up Earth, while what is light tends to ascend and make up the sky or heaven. The human being is regarded as possessing a mixture of two kinds of *ch'i*ᵃ, the denser kind in his body, and the other in his heart or spirit.[1]

Apparently, the belief was that yoga-like exercises could help to nurture one's *ch'i*ᵃ. The passage in Mencius has puzzled many who wonder whether the Chinese already practised some form of yoga in those early days. Today, we know of the tradition called *ch'i-kung* / *qigong* with its meditative as well as gymnastic aspects, a practice that is still vibrant and even spreading worldwide.

Is this a native tradition, or did it come from India, which has a known and strong yoga tradition? To the extent that there has been known cultural interaction between China and India, especially with the introduction of Buddhism, we can easily accept the idea of later

[1] Lau, *Mencius*, Introduction, p. 24.

borrowing, which must have taken place. But there was also more, and much earlier evidence in favour of its being a native tradition.[2]

Today, we know that these exercises go back a long time, maybe as early as the sixth century BCE.[3] In late 1973, archaeological discoveries at Mawangdui unearthed a silk manuscript with a picture of men and women practising *ch'i-kung* / *qigong* exercises in forty-four postures. This manuscript has been dated to the later part of the third century BCE, long before Taoism was considered an institutional religion.[4]

THE MYSTIC AS KING: RELIGION APPROPRIATES THE PARADIGM

Interestingly, the gradual secularisation of power did not entirely erase the perceived need to maintain a shamanic character for kingship. Surviving philosophical texts, written for the rulers in particular, offer teachings on spiritual concentration to help them maintain personal power and respond properly to events and situations.

Before proceeding further, we might make two points. First, the mystic king need not necessarily be a ruler who merely hides himself deep in a palace to nurture mystical consciousness; he might instead make use of his meditation mainly to help with decision-making in clarity of mind. Second, such practice does not necessarily make his decisions more ethical; a sharpened mind could also help to decide issues of war and peace, reward and punishment, without regard to ethical priorities.

It is interesting that the text to be examined is from the Legalist tradition, one that is concerned principally with political power. The fourth-century-BCE *Kuan-tzu*, attributed to a wise and manipulating minister who died about three centuries earlier, alludes to some form of Chinese yoga in maintaining stillness of the heart and keeping the vital energies within. It speaks of cultivating a very pure kind of

---

2 Consult Livia Kohn, *Early Chinese Mysticism: Philosophy and Soteriology in the Chinese Tradition* (Princeton University Press, 1992).
3 Joseph Needham, *Science and Civilisation in China* (Cambridge University Press, 1983), vol. 5, pt 5, p. 280.
4 Consult Robert G. Hendricks (trans.), *Lao-tzu Te-tao ching: A New Translation Based on the Recently Discovered Ma-wang-tui Texts* (New York: Ballantine Books, 1989), Introduction.

breath or *ch'i*[a], understood as the essence of stars, the life of grains below, which can make one a sage.[5]

> In all things the most spiritual
> Having it is living.
> Below, it generates the five grains,
> Above, it becomes the constellated stars.
> Flowing between heaven and earth,
> Call it ghost (*kuei / gui*) and spirit (*shen*)
> When stored within the breast
> Call that the sage.[6]

Indeed, the text speaks of a 'heart within a heart', a 'heart hidden in a heart', referring to an interior depth that enables spiritual stability, 'When my heart is ordered the senses are ordered, when my heart is stabilised my senses are stabilised. What orders it is the heart, what stabilises it is the heart. The heart is used to store a heart. Inside the heart there is another heart.'[7] With the heart in peace and the senses clear, one grasps everything in its unity. One is able to issue 'disciplined words' and impose 'disciplined tasks'.

I agree with A. C. Graham that there is a shamanic origin to such exercises, which aimed at a mental and spiritual discipline opening the practitioner to mystical consciousness.[8] To the extent that the question appears no longer to be the perceived descent of particular deities or spirits, in short, what we call 'spirit possession', the understanding has shifted from shamanic religion to spiritual exercise for the sake of the benefits this brings: unity within oneself, consciousness of unity with the cosmos, and inner clarity which enables wise decisions.

Another Legalist text, *Han Fei Tzu*, exhorts the ruler to 'know the origin of all things', to be 'empty and still', so that the course of nature may enforce itself, and all affairs may be settled by themselves, 'Empty, he knows the essence of fullness; still, he corrects all motion. Who utters a word creates himself a name; who undertakes an affair creates himself a form. When forms and names match, the

---

[5] Consult Kanaya Osamu, *Kanshi no kenkyū* (A study of Kuan Tzu) (Tokyo: Iwanami, 1987).

[6] *Kuan-tzu*, Sect. 49, ch. 16:1. Eng. trans. adapted from W. Allyn Rickett, *Kuan Tzu* (Hong Kong University Press, 1965), vol. 2, p. 99.

[7] *Kuan-tzu* 16:3b–4a; consult Rickett, vol. 2, p. 101. Interestingly, the Chinese word for senses is the same as the noun for officials, or the verb for managing, *kuan / guan*.

[8] A. C. Graham, *Disputers of the Tao: Philosophical Argument in Ancient China* (La Salle, Ill.: Open Court, 1989), pp. 101–5. See also Harold D. Roth, 'Psychology and Self-cultivation in Early Taoist Thought', *Harvard Journal of Asiatic Studies* 37 (1977), 612–22.

ruler will have nothing to worry about as everything reverts to its reality.'[9]

Other texts of roughly the same period, written from Confucian or Taoist perspectives, confirm the prevalence of ideas and techniques of meditation, and the importance for the sage's mind or heart to keep an inner purity and spontaneity by remaining detached from passionate desires. The fact that Mencius himself appears to have followed such practices shows that these have been appropriated by the intellectuals of the time for their own purposes, and not just as useful techniques for those who ruled.

Such evidence from a diversity of texts, as well as the mention in Mencius, argues for the various traditions that we call Confucianism, Taoism, or Legalism sharing a common matrix, from which developed certain spiritual practices and mysticism. By mystical experience, I refer to a transformation of consciousness, whether that is accomplished by meditative practice or in some other way. In itself, such mysticism as we have described is not always discovered in a religious context, and may be sometimes better described as secular. But I shall argue not only that it had religious, shamanic roots, but that it was to be appropriated by later religious traditions, including Taoism and Chinese Buddhism.

In speaking of trance states associated with shamanic kings, I am not always claiming for these a 'shamanic trance', especially when speaking in the context of later kings, successors to the ancient rulers, or to other individuals. I am referring mainly to a transformed consciousness in which the person experiences a sense of inner peace and stillness, sometimes even a sense of oneness or interconnectedness to the universe or all things. Such is my definition for 'nature mysticism'. And, if I use this term, I am not opposing it to any supernatural mysticism, but rather to devotional, theistic mysticism, where affective responses predominate in an experience of union between the subject and a higher deity. And I am not distinguishing it from so-called 'introvertive' mysticism (inward-turning, centring on the self) or 'extrovertive' mysticism (outward-turning, toward nature at large).[10]

Neither do I assert that all shamans were kings in antiquity. But I

---

[9] *Han Fei Tzu*, sect. 5, 1:10a.
[10] W. T. Stace, *Mysticism and Philosophy* (London: Macmillan, 1961), ch. 2.

do assert that the ancient kings were themselves the *chief* shamans, and in that sense derive their original mandate from their special claims of access to divinity. Moreover, it is my conviction that with the gradual secularisation of kingship as an institution, a certain trance state originally associated especially with the shamanic kings became the achievable goal for everyone. I am speaking of a state of transformed consciousness, sometimes manifested as shamanic trance and accompanied by paranormal behaviour, represented not only in archaic religious experience but also in the visions and revelations associated with religious Taoism and popular Chinese religion.

In China's case, it is my opinion that nature mysticism has predominated in the experience of many individuals, including Confucian and Taoist philosophers, as well as Ch'an Buddhists. Devotional, theistic mysticism may be found in religious Taoism, and in devotional, Pure Land, Buddhism.

Private individuals who are mystics may be presumed to sense an elation coming from that feeling of oneness with the divine, or the universe, that – in the case of nature mysticism – is somehow 'alive' and vibrating, whether in the self as subject, or as that larger, organic whole to which the self is related. There is, besides, a rapturous joy deep within the self as the centre of such consciousness. In some cultures, mystics have even been led to proclaim themselves divine and have suffered persecutions for such assertions. Witness the case of Meister Eckhart, who has said, 'If God should give my soul all he ever made or might make, apart from himself . . . my soul would not be satisfied, for I would not be blessed. If I am blessed, the whole world is mine, and God too, and where I am there is God, and where God is there I am.'[11]

The Taoist, Buddhist, and a few neo-Confucian mystics, who cultivated mysticism for personal fulfilment, without any political ambition, were usually not indicted for these pursuits. They were no mystic kings, even if, during those precious moments of 'peak experience' when they were in deep communion with nature or the thusness of things, they felt as though they were on top of the world.

---

[11] *Meister Eckhart: A Modern Translation*, trans. by Raymond B. Blakney (New York: Harper, 1941), p. 244.

Mysticism and nonduality

Before waiting too long, I should point out that the Taoist or Confucian view of nature is different from that of the West. It does not refer to what is *other* to the *self*, but to that which includes the human self. Nature is not a foe to be conquered, a resource to be harnessed. Nature is mother, and we are its children. Return to nature is in a sense, return to the eternal womb. In this 'nondualist' context, both Confucians and Taoists regard the human being as the microcosm of the universe, which is the macrocosm.[12]

The reference to nonduality suggests as well a certain experiential dimension of awareness, transcending the subject–object division. We read about the similarity of what I call nature mysticism to the discovery of the Tao. It is made in an apophatic (abstract or non-imaging) meditative processes, emptying the mind of all concepts, images, and affections. We understand this better when we reflect upon the effort of concentration in meditation, beginning with concentration on a certain object, be that, for example, the act of breathing, but concluding possibly with a state of consciousness where the inner faculties of mind and heart are all gathered at a point of stillness, beyond the subject–object division. This contrasts with kataphatic meditation, which fills the mind with concepts or images, such as in Christian discursive meditation or in visualisation exercises, such as of a Buddha-image, or of the inner viscera of the body and the 'Taoist' deities that rule them. In the latter case, that is, of visualisation, an experience transcending the subject–object division may also occur as the meditator identifies himself or herself increasingly with the object of meditation, for example, the Buddha-image.

However, there are subtle differences between the Confucian and Taoist perception of nonduality. Perhaps a story from the *Lü-shih ch'un-ch'iu* can give us a sense of the divergence between their understandings of the subject–object tension. In a section claiming that the justice of the ancient sage-kings is what brought peace to the world, we find this illustration:

A man from Ching lost his bow, but did not look hard for it, saying: 'A man from Ching lost it; a[nother] man from Ching will find it. Why should one look for it?'

---

[12] David Loy, *Nonduality* (New Haven: Yale University Press, 1988); R. P. Peerenboom, 'Nonduality and Daoism', *International Philosophical Quarterly* 32 (1992), 35–53.

Confucius heard it and said: 'Better remove the word "Ching."'
Lao Tan heard it and said: 'Better remove the word "man."'
So Lao Tan was the most just [of the three].[13]

In the first case, the individual who lost his bow rationalised that
there was no loss, since another of his countrymen was sure to find
it. He appears to have been a generous individual. In the second
case, Confucius intervened to remove a particular, regional designation, rendering the reflection a universalist and humanistic one. In
the final case, Lao Tzu intervened, to remove all opposition between
the subject and the object, until the meaning of the entire story was
dissolved.

The *Lü-shih ch'un-ch'iu* was an eclectic text favouring Taoism. But
the story also explains an essential philosophical difference between
Taoism and Confucianism, and the reason why the two traditions
flourished together, sharing certain presuppositions while diverging
on their interpretations of reality. In a way, it may also serve as a
Ch'an Buddhist riddle, revealing the Chinese transformation of an
originally alien tradition.

TAOISM AS MYSTICAL PHILOSOPHY

The word *Tao* ('the Way') is used by every school of thought,
including Confucianism and Buddhism. And 'Taoism' is an umbrella
term, covering philosophy, religion, magic, the healing and martial
arts and early science and technology. The very extent of its scope
may qualify it to be called 'wisdom', if by that word we also mean
some kind of encyclopedic knowledge. The heterogeneous character
of Taoism also creates problems, especially of coherence, while the
inherent secrecy of its often cryptic and even coded language makes
such problems even harder to resolve. Only in the twentieth century,
and with the help of non-Chinese scholarship – including Japanese
and Western – are we beginning to unlock secrets that have defied
generations of students.

The text *Lao-tzu* is usually considered to be no older than the
fourth or third century BCE, even if it incorporated older material.
We are not sure who was or were its authors.[14] The same mystery

---

[13] *Lü-shih ch'un-ch'iu*, 1:8b–9a.
[14] It has produced a wealth of commentaries. Consult Isabelle Robinet, *Les Commentaires du Tao
To King jusqu'au VIIe siècle* (Paris: Collège de France, Institut des Hautes Études Chinoises,
1981).

surrounds the author of *Chuang-tzu*. Allegedly, that came from a philosopher of the fourth and third centuries BCE, although only the seven 'inner chapters' appear to have come from one hand. The other fifteen 'outer chapters' and eleven 'miscellaneous chapters' expand the ideas in the inner chapters, but lack their power and vitality.[15]

Chuang-tzu shares with *Lao-tzu* the central concept of the Tao as the principle underlying and governing the universe, but shows a complete eremitical distaste for politics. The text resembles a collection of essays that make abundant use of parable and allegory, of paradox and fanciful imagery. It makes an ardent plea for spiritual freedom, not so much the freedom of the individual from social conventions and restraints, but rather a self-transcending liberation from the limitations of one's own mind – from one's self-interested tendencies and prejudices. And such freedom can only be discovered in nature itself, in the Tao. This involves a higher level of knowledge, the knowledge of wisdom, which goes beyond the distinctions of things, including that of life and death. Such mystical knowledge comes only with 'forgetting' the knowledge of all things and of the self.

Our usual impression of the Chinese is of a this-worldly people who see themselves as part of a larger kinship group. Taoists, however, were individualists when most of their intellectual contemporaries pursued social goals. Instead of seeking public office, the Taoist was satisfied with personal security, and the privilege of communing with nature. As a philosophy of recluses and for recluses, Taoism has preferred anonymity and articulates its teachings in riddles. As an esoteric religion, it discloses many of its secrets only to the initiated. Thus we have over a thousand texts in the Taoist canon, but few bear the names of their compilers or the date of their composition – or, we may say, of revelation.

In *Lao-tzu*, the Tao is described as existing before the universe came to be, an unchanging first principle, even as the ancestor of all things, that by which all things come to be. It is a philosophical attempt to conceptualise an earlier religious belief.

---

[15] Consult A. C. Graham, *Studies in Chinese Philosophy and Philosophical Literature* (Albany: State University of New York Press, 1990), pp. 283–321. Kuang-ming Wu, *Chuang Tzu: World Philosopher at Play* (New York: Crossroad, 1982); Kuang-ming Wu, *The Butterfly as Companion: Meditations on the First Three Chapters of the Chuang Tzu* (Albany: State University of New York Press, 1990).

Deep, it is like the ancestor of the myriad creatures.   (4:11)
It images the forefather of the Lord[-on-high].   (4:13)[16]

This serves also to show the dialectical method in Taoist thinking, and the effort to point to the nameless Tao as the first principle, indeterminate, and yet from which all things proceed to become determinate. In the Confucian classics, the 'Lord-on-High' refers to a supreme deity, while 'Heaven' has sometimes been given a creator's role, as that which gives birth to all things. The term 'Heaven' did not completely disappear from Taoist philosophical writings, appearing especially in *Chuang-tzu* alongside the term Tao, but *Tao* has obviously taken over 'Heaven' in *Lao-tzu*, as the natural Way as well as the human way, even the political way. If the Tao is no longer a personal deity, it remains a model for human behaviour.

There is mention in *Chuang-tzu* of 'sitting and forgetting' (*tso-wang / zuowang*), as well as of a 'fasting of the mind' (*hsin-chai / xinzhai*), which is different from fasting of the body. This requires the emptying of the senses, and of the mind itself, with a stated goal that resembles spirit possession. 'Let your ears and your eyes communicate with what is inside . . . Then even gods and spirits will come to dwell' (ch. 4).

I realise that *Chuang-tzu* is speaking here of private practice, and that these references eventually encouraged private mysticism, the kind that an individual may practise in a room or while contemplating nature, without concern for bringing about any public effects. But the text does not entirely neglect the mention of those whom society calls shamans, who have paranormal skills as well as the ability of inducing trance at will.

Other Taoist philosophical texts include the *Lieh-tzu* and *Huai-nan-tzu*. The latter is especially noteworthy as a *summa* of Taoist thought compiled in the second century BCE, which ranges from myth to philosophy, to proto-science, to mysticism, and of course, to governing according to rules discovered in nature itself.[17]

The shaman as a holy man

I wish to focus on such shamanic references in *Chuang-tzu*, which have often been overlooked. By 'holy man', I am referring to

---

[16] *Lao-tzu*, ch. 1. English translation adapted from D. C. Lau, *Lao Tzu: Tao Te Ching* (Harmondsworth: Penguin, 1963).
[17] Consult Charles Le Blanc and Rémi Mattieu (eds), *Mythe et philosophie à l'aube de la Chine impériale* (Les Presses de l'Université de Montréal; Paris: de Boccard, 1992).

someone who has appropriated privately to himself a paradigm of spiritual discipline recognized in the society. In the Chinese case, this paradigm had earlier functioned in the public domain, as the paradigm of the shamanic sage-ruler. The 'shamanic' passages in *Chuang-tzu* include the following lyrical descriptions of the perfect man:

There is a Holy Man living on the distant Ku-she Mountain, with skin like ice or snow, who is gentle as a virgin. He does not eat the five grains, but sucks the wind, drinks the dew, mounts the clouds and mist, rides a flying dragon, and wanders beyond the four seas. By concentrating his spirit, he can protect creatures from plagues and make the harvest plentiful.[18]

Chuang-tzu could very well have been actually referring to a shaman of traditional antiquity, his dietary habits, his shamanic 'flights', and his healing and other magical powers. From these lines, it would seem that the shamanic tradition has become by that time somewhat of a legend, peripheral to the society in which it was born, and yet, appropriating in the meantime a prestige coming from being a rarity. Yet the text glorifies him as a healer who prevents sicknesses and a protector of the harvest. And it attributes his successes to his ability to 'concentrate his spirit'.

There is also the description of a Perfect Man, who 'is godlike'.

Though the great swamps blaze, they cannot burn him; though the great rivers freeze, they cannot chill him; though swift lightning splits the hills, and howling gales shake the sea, they cannot frighten him. A man like this rides the clouds and mist, straddles the sun and moon, and wanders beyond the four seas.[19]

And besides, there is a 'True Man of old', who, like the Perfect Man, 'climbed heights without trembling, entered water without getting wet, entered fire without getting burnt . . . [He] slept without dreaming and woke without cares; he ate without savoring and breathed from deep inside.'[20] And all this has nothing to do with 'wisdom, skill, determination, or courage'. Rather, it is because such a person 'unifies his nature, nourishes his breath, unites his virtue, and thereby communicates with that which creates all things. [He] . . . guards what belongs to Heaven and keeps it whole. His spirit

---

[18] *Chuang-tzu*, ch. 1:6–7; English trans. adapted from Watson, *Complete Works*, p. 33. Consult also A. C. Graham (trans.), *Chuang Tzu: The Inner Chapters* (London: Allen & Unwin, 1981), p. 46.

[19] *Chuang Tzu* 1:21b; Watson, *Complete Works*, p. 46.

[20] *Chuang Tzu* 3:2a; Graham, *Inner Chapters*, pp. 84–5.

has no flaw, so how can things enter in and get at him?[21] Concentrating the spirit. Guarding the pure breath. We return once more to the language of yoga and meditation.

Arthur Waley has pointed out that certain other passages in *Chuang-tzu* referring to meditative practices actually speak about the 'mediums' (*shih*[a]) in a state of self-induced trance.[22] Waley makes a distinction between a shaman dancing and a medium in motionless trance. I agree that a distinction can be made, that is, between the charismatic shaman and the medium who was not always a professional. I also perceive a possible distinction in behaviour, such as between a private individual absorbed in meditation, reaching perhaps a transformed state of consciousness, rendering him or her somewhat 'motionless', which I shall consider as a kind of 'personal religion', and the professional shaman or spirit–medium engaged in a public or semi-public performance including so-called magical feats, which belongs more to 'shamanic religion'.

Indeed, frequent mention is made in *Chuang-tzu* of shamans, represented either by the word *wu*[a] or as persons with extraordinary powers. But the attitude is rather ambiguous. Shamans may serve as the mouthpiece for words of wisdom.[23] Yet the text can also be critical. For example, a 'divine shaman' (*shen-wu*) named Chi Hsien is ridiculed for his inability to practice proper physiognomy.[24]

While the 'Holy Man' described above seems to be a shamanic figure, it does not appear necessary that every person who concentrates his or her spirit, and guards his or her pure breath, be a shaman. With *Chuang-tzu* we find mention also of a remarkable woman, Crookback, who has a distinguished lineage for her wisdom.[25] Such a person may very well be like the Yen Hui who told Confucius how he 'sat and forgot' everything, metaphorically 'smashing up his limbs and body driving out his intellect and perception, casting off form and doing away with understanding'.[26] We are speaking here of a private mystic, pursuing apophatic meditation.

---

[21] *Chuang Tzu* 7:1b; Eng. trans. adapted from Watson, *Complete Works*, p. 198.
[22] See Waley, *The Way and Its Power* (New York: Grove Press, 1958), pp. 116–17. Reference is to *Chuang-tzu* 1:10a, 4:15b; 7:17b. See Watson, *Complete Works*, pp. 36, 116, 224.
[23] *Chuang-tzu*, 5:19a-b; Watson, Ibid, p. 154.
[24] *Chuang-tzu*, 3:17–18; Watson, Ibid, pp. 94–7.
[25] *Chuang-tzu*, 3:7a–8a; Watson, Ibid, p. 82.   [26] Watson, Ibid, p. 94.

TAOISM AS A SHAMANIC RELIGION

In its earliest form, institutional Taoist religion was a magico–ecstatic cult concerned with the healing of sicknesses, regarded as results of sin and offering a near political alternative to the collapsing central government of the Han dynasty. We are speaking of two highly organised religious movements that emerged in the late Han period, dividing their numerous following geographically across the country. The immortality cult, which had very early origins, became an integral part of institutional Taoism slightly later, but would eventually come to represent the entire movement of religious Taoism.[27]

Chang Ling, also called Chang Tao-ling, is said to have established his headquarters on Mount Ho-ming (Szechuan), where he received revelations from a host of spirits, offered sacrifices and cured the sick and organised a religious and even theocratic community. His son Chang Heng and grandson Chang Lu continued his work. The region under control was divided into twenty-four districts, each of which was placed under a 'grand libationer' with military as well as religious duties. Chang Lu allegedly gave his blessings in 215 CE to the rising Wei dynastic house, praising it as a 'pure Taoist government'.

Religious rituals were held in public assemblies, either regularly or occasionally. The Fast of Mud and Soot, for example, was designed to ward off maladies which were the consequence of sin. It might last several days to a week, in open air. As their foreheads were smeared with mud, the participants struck the earth with their heads, burning incense, asking for forgiveness from the gods, and praying for blessings and a long life, to the sound of the drum.[28]

Maspéro points out the shamanic aspects of this fast. For, excited by the noise, the vapours of the incense, and the emotions, some of the participants threw themselves on the ground in a trance, rolling about and lamenting, to be eventually called to order by those in charge of the ritual.[29] Some of these phenomena are similar to what

---

[27] Fukui Kōjun (ed.), *Dōkyō no kisoteki kenkyū* (Fundamental research in Taoism) (Tokyo: Shōseki bunbutsu ryūtsukai, 1965), 3rd edn., Sect. 1. Consult also Fukui Kōjun *et al.* (eds), *Dōkyō*, (Tokyo: Hirakawa, 1983), 3 vols.

[28] Henri Maspéro, *Taoism and Chinese Religion*, Eng. trans. by Frank A. Kierman, Jr (Amherst: University of Massachusetts Press, 1981), p. 385.

[29] Ibid, p. 385.

happens today in some of the Christian Pentecostal meetings, such as at the Toronto Vineyard, now called the Toronto Airport Christian Fellowship, where healings reportedly take place, often after rolling or shaking on the floor during trance.[30]

Mysticism and the Taoist scriptures

Religious Taoism accumulated a huge body of scriptures called the *Tao-tsang* ('Taoist Canon'), first issued in 1442, which includes over a thousand volumes compiled over fifteen centuries, a heterogeneous compendium of discursive and historical treatises as well as the more 'original' or 'revealed' scriptural texts. We find in this collection various records, commentaries, talismans and other miscellaneous materials. Many of the revered texts were destroyed in the thirteenth century. Some were later rediscovered, and together with other extant texts, make up the authoritative Ming edition (1607 CE) of the Taoist Canon, with 5,485 volumes or *ch'e*.[31]

In the Taoist case, the corpus includes many works regarded as 'heavenly books' that originated in trance, that could have been written in trance, by mystics or shamans claiming divine revelation. In the T'ang dynasty and later, many considered Lao-tzu – the divinised Lao-tzu – as having revealed all the principal texts in the Taoist canon.[32]

The Taoist Shang-ch'ing scriptures belong to the most honoured section of the scriptures. A certain Yang Hsi was reported to have received a nocturnal visit of a group of immortals some time between 367 and 370 CE. Among these was Lady Wei, who had died about thirty years earlier. To him, she revealed the Shang-ch'ing texts, which became the nucleus for the Mao-shan school of religious Taoism.

It is said that Yang asked her about the origin of scripture or *ching*[c]. Her answer echoes the Prologue of John's Gospel: 'In the beginning was the *ching*[c], and the *ching*[c] was with the Breath (*ch'i*[a]).'[33] And so, for the Taoists, the scriptures reveal the secrets of the

---

[30] Guy Chevreau, *Catch the Fire: The Toronto Blessing: An Experience of Renewal and Revival* (Toronto: HarperCollins, 1995), pp. 207–17.

[31] Consult Chen Guofu (Ch'en Kuo-fu), *Daozang yuanliu kao* (An Investigation into the Origin and Transmission of the Taoist Canon) (Beijing: Zhonghua, 1963), vol. 1.

[32] Ninji Ofuchi, 'The Formation of the Taoist Canon', in Welch and Seidel (eds), *Facets of Taoism*, pp. 261–7.

[33] *Su-ling ching*, in *Tao-tsang / Daozang* (abbrev. as *TT*), no. 1026.

universe, of which the most important concerns *ch'i*[a], whether understood as air, breath, or the mysterious energy associated with breathing. Their beliefs made sure that textual transmission was only made in the most solemn manner and only to the initiated.

Indeed, most of the Shang-ch'ing texts start by affirming their existence before cosmogenesis. They tell of their transcription in extravagant terms as having been done by deities in jade characters on golden tablets. They describe the celestial palaces and sacred mountains where they are preserved, even listing the deities who transmitted the scriptures to one another before revealing them to humans, much later.

The *ching*[c] can be better understood when compared to the *pao*[b] ('treasure') and the *fu* ('talisman'). The 'treasures' (e.g., the River Chart and Book of Lo) are alleged to have been sent miraculously by Heaven to signify approval and protection, especially to confirm the ruler's mandate. The *fu*, talismans, originally were contracts testifying to feudal bonds between lords and vassals, but served later as letters of credit and insignia of function, before they became for Taoists magic charms. Interestingly, the fifth-century Taoist Lu Hsiu-ching understood the reception of scriptural revelations as evidence for the legitimacy of the lineage of Taoist religious leaders, even evoking the Mandate of Heaven theory for support.[34]

The Taoist scripture is allegedly bestowed by Heaven in a manner similar to a treasure, and almost always contains some talismans. Originally, the scripture is a mere diagram or picture, and only later becomes a text; certain scriptures are essentially talismans around which an explanatory text has developed. It has the value of a contract in binding two parties: the divinities and the owner, who usually is head of a family – a natural family as well as a religious family. There are also *lu*[a] or registers listing the deities controlled by the owner of the document. These had been used to support the imperial mandate of individual rulers.[35]

The Chinese Taoist canon, like the Buddhist canon, received its approbation not only from a community of believers, but especially from the political authority. While we refer here to the *Tao-tsang* as the Taoist Canon, we must remember that it is actually more of a library of published books, a collection or series, rather than a

---

[34] Consult Catherine Bell, 'Ritualization of Texts and Textualization of Ritual in the Codification of Taoist Liturgy', *History of Religions* 27 (1988), 366–92.

[35] Robinet, *Taoist Meditation*, pp. 20–2.

corpus of books with canonical authority. Fortunately, sufficient coherence may be detected among certain textual groups to permit the scholar to find 'small islands of meaning'.[36]

Inducing trance: a wealth of techniques

By the word 'trance', I refer generally to a transformed state of consciousness. I do not here distinguish between a shamanic experience, which I regard as function-oriented, such as in healing or rain-making, and a mystical experience mainly with meaning for an individual person. In the Taoist mystical tradition, one could trace a line starting with a medium or an ecstatic figure and ending up with institutionalised religion. This line would pass through nature mysticism, but also through shamanism, already more organised and guided by a master and by the technique. For Taoist religion possesses a wealth of trance-inducing techniques, ranging from simple visualisation of the One, to interior visions within the human body of the viscera, to marching on the stars and communing with the astral symbols in the celestial universe.[37]

Such a tradition is based on the belief that the human body is a microcosm of the larger universe, of which it forms an integral part. This means as well that the human body is itself a small universe, the storehouse of *ch'i*[a], and the residence of the Tao. Such an understanding begins with the vision in traditional medicine of the body as a network of energy channels, pulses, moving fluids, and inner viscera. Indeed, the five viscera – liver, heart, spleen, lungs and kidneys – are correlated not only to the five senses, emotions, forms of body tissue, psychic centres and so on, but also to the Five Agents (wood, fire, earth, metal, water) in conjunction as well with the directions, the seasons, the grains and many other categories. In this context, the mind is not regarded as separate from the body, but as structurally related to it, flowing through it as a subtler form of *ch'i*[a] or energy. And since Taoists believe in the existence of deities, including astral deities, in the larger universe,

---

[36] Ibid, p. 2.
[37] For a general book covering many aspects of religious Taoism, including meditation, ecstasy, and scripture, consult Livia Kohn (ed.), *The Taoist Experience: An Anthology* (Albany: State University of New York Press, 1993). See also Sakade Yoshinobu, *'Ki' to yosei: Dōkyō no yoseijutsu to jujutsu* (*Qi* [Breathing, energy] and cultivation of life: the art of cultivating life and the art of talismans) (Kyoto: Jinbun shōin, 1993).

they also extend that belief to a parallel set of deities within the human body.[38]

Understandably, Taoist meditation techniques involve the body as well as the mind. In the first place, the body must be relaxed, its own *ch'i*[a] or energy in communion with the greater *ch'i*[a] or energy of the universe. For this reason, *ch'i-kung* exercises are based on breathing exercises, whether in a contemplative or active mode. For this reason as well, these exercises are coordinated with physical movements in *t'ai-chi* (literally, 'Great Ultimate') or so-called shadow-boxing. And one may therefore practise meditation while standing, walking, sitting, lying still, even sleeping, or doing formal exercises.[39]

Guarding the One[40]

Modelling their lives on nature, Taoists claim to have discovered their techniques by the observation of natural phenomena and processes, including animal and even foetal behaviour. Taoists speak of discovering a True Self within, and, by so doing, of achieving greater harmony with the rhythm of the cosmos outside as well. Such a 'True Self' is sometimes envisaged as a new birth within, of the gestation of new life coming to be.

Through meditative exercises usually involving some form of yoga or breathing technique, and the visualisation of an inner light representing the *ch'i*[a] or energy that inhaling brings us, the Taoist seeks an inner, ecstatic vision that enables him sometimes to see and visit inside his own body with the gods as honoured guests. Besides, such contact helps to drive away the toxin or evil spirits, and bring about physical as well as psychic healing.

In a fourth-century text, the Taoist Ko Hung speaks about such a form of concentration in meditation, entitled 'Guarding the One'. This term, the One, strikes one first as the Tao itself. It also refers to the T'ai-yi or Great One, worshipped in Han times as the highest God, presumed to reside in the Polar Star above, but capable of descending into the human hearts. This form of

---

[38] Kohn (ed.), *The Taoist Experience*, pp. 161–3.
[39] Sakade, *Dōkyō to yosei shisō* (Taoism and the thought of cultivating life) (Tokyo: Berikansha, 1992), pp. 223–6; Yasuo Yuasa, *The Body, Self-cultivation, and ki-energy*, trans. by Shinegori Nagatomo and Monte S. Hull (Albany: State University of New York Press, 1993).
[40] Consult Livia Kohn, 'Guarding the One: Concentrative Meditation in Taoism', in Kohn (ed.), *Taoist Meditation and Longevity Techniques*, pp. 125–58.

meditation is considered to be a relatively simple form of concentration.[41]

> Guard the One in the center of the Northern Culmen and in the
>   deepest abyss of yourself . . .
> Lessen desires, restrain your appetite – the One will remain at rest! . . .
> Guard the One and never lose it – the limitations of man will not be
>   for you!
> On land you will be free from beasts, in water from fierce dragons.
> No fear of evil spirits or phantoms,
> No demon will approach, nor blade attain.[42]

The symbolism of the T'ai-yi as the Great One is worth some discussion. This name of the deity has been associated with the concept of *T'ai-chi* (Great Ultimate), which also reveals an affiliation with the sage-king paradigm.[43] For the person practising Taoist meditation or concentration, the focus is usually on the deity symbol, as the practitioner takes the place of the deity's favourite son on earth, the king.

*Interior vision (*nei-kuan / neiguan*): viewing the viscera*

Of all the religious sects of Taoism, the Shang-ch'ing ('Great Purity') appears to possess the greatest wealth in techniques of meditation, which were assembled, codified, and further developed from a very ancient Chinese tradition. They succeeded in adhering to a perilous ridgeline situated between shamanism and mediumship and the processes of institutionalisation managed by the establishment of a church and the codification of its liturgy.[44]

There are techniques of meditation that focus on interior vision, that is, viewing the inner viscera of the human body, in order to assure their health, and their proper place as the abode of the gods there. After all, the viscera are reservoirs of spiritual power, and contain the spiritual elements of man. There is no separation between the inside and the outside. The body is the receptacle for the continued indwelling of the spirits, and the viscera must be in good health, if the spirits are to remain. Sickness was considered a

---

[41] See also Sakade, 'Ki' to yosei, pp. 73–94.

[42] *Pao-p'u-tzu*, SPPY ed., 18:2a–b; Eng. trans. in James Ware, *Alchemy, Medicine, Religion in the China of A.D. 320: The nei-p'ien of Ko Hung* (Cambridge, Mass.: M.I.T. Press, 1966), pp. 303–4.

[43] Consult Isabelle Robinet, 'The Place and Meaning of the Notion of Taiji in Taoist Sources Prior to the Ming Dynasty', *History of Religions* 29 (1990), pp. 373–411.

[44] Robinet, *Taoist Meditation*, p. 228.

consequence of spiritual disorder, and might lead to the gods' departure, which could prove fatal to human life.

The information for this comes especially from the *Huang-t'ing ching* (The Classic of the Yellow Court) which follows closely the *Huang-ti nei-ching* (Inner Classic of the Yellow Emperor), the oldest treatise on medicine.

Ch'i[a] is energy or vital breath, source of all things and foundation of cosmic unity. The original breath is equivalent to the Tao, but operates in two modes: *yin* and *yang*. This breath or energy should be conserved and nurtured, in practices like *ch'i-kung* or so-called embryonic breathing. And since health depends more on deep affinity between the human being and the cosmos, breathing techniques are regarded in high esteem.

Ching[d] is narrowly defined as sexual semen, but also considered to be cosmic essence, the humours of the viscera. It is recommended to make the *ching*[d] rise to the brain, either during sex, or other exercises. Saliva is regarded as precious nectar, and the swallowing of saliva takes place during meditation. In the *Huang-t'ing ching*, the circulation of the breath and the *ching*[d] seem as essential as the visualisation of the viscera. Such actions together bring about harmony within the body, as well as with nature at large.[45]

Isabelle Robinet speaks of this spiritual quest that takes place inside the body. And it is within the body that the Water of Life – the Primordial Breath and the nourishment of immortality – is found. However, this spiritual journey is long and difficult, and plagued by snares. 'The visualizations . . . and invocations of the visceral spirits may come at the beginning or end of meditation . . . or may be combined with more complex exercises.'[46]

The *Huang-t'ing ching* is devoted essentially to interior vision, not some form of intellectual or moral introspection, but visualising what is inside the body. To make the inner body luminous, one may consume magical herbs, frost or dew, or absorb luminous principles like the effluvia of stars, or use magical mirrors. Indeed, the Taoist must become himself a mirror to himself, to see himself as a divine form or a body inhabited by the gods. The viscera are living symbols, corresponding with the Five Agents, and by extension with the world, and so symbolic points connecting microcosm with macrocosm, man with nature. One must learn to see the form and

[45] Ibid, pp. 80–4, 90–6. [46] Ibid, p. 95.

function of the inner bodily organs, as well as the spirits that inhabit the body. It is necessary to have the 'mysterious light' shine and spontaneously spread itself throughout the five viscera so that they become luminous and the bodily spirits may return.[47]

As the *Huai-nan-tzu* also says: "The bladder is a cloud, the lungs are a breeze of air (*ch'i*[a]), and the liver, a wind; the kidneys are rain and the spleen, thunder. In this way, [the human being] becomes a trinity with heaven and earth.'[48]

The *Classic of the Yellow Court* seems esoteric on first reading. In our own days, with advances in alternative therapies of self-healing, we read in the West about various forms of biofeedback and visualisation, some of which involve also inner vision of the viscera, for purposes of pinpointing sickness, and assuring their cure. At issue appears to be a discovery of the deeper levels of the psyche and its powers, now studied by specialists interested in the confluence of psychiatry and mysticism.[49]

I remember finding at the White Cloud Monastery in Beijing an ink rubbing of a Taoist representation of the human body, called the Diagram of the Inner Scripture (*Nei-ching t'u* / *Neijing tu*). We may call it the symbolic map of the human body. It bears the outline of a foetus, or better still, of the left profile view of someone sitting in meditation, with the legs tucked in such a way that they have become invisible. Except that what you see is only obliquely human. It resembles a mountain with crags projecting from what is supposed to be the spinal column and the skull.

The diagram is definitely intended to help inner vision and even healing. Two circles in the head represent the eyes, which are the sun and the moon of the interior universe. And since in meditation, the light enters between the eyebrows toward the centre, this is identified with the North Pole. Within the picture, it is represented by steep mountains ringing a lake on which stands a terrace of lights. Somewhere above what seems to be the right eye sits an old man, bearing the likeness of Lao Tzu. Surprisingly, another human figure stands nearby with head and arms raised, a 'blue-eyed foreign monk', according to the description given. I understand the monk stands for the historical Gautama, or else Maitreya Buddha, or the

---

[47] Ibid, pp. 60–1.   [48] *Huai-nan-tzu*, 7:2a.
[49] Consult Stanley R. Dean (ed.), *Psychiatry and Mysticism* (Chicago: Nelson-Hall, 1975).

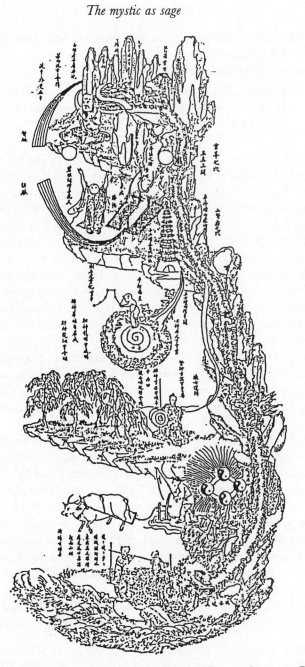

Figure 2 Diagram of the Inner Scripture (*Nei-ching t'u*). Nineteenth-century Baiyun Temple, Beijing.

legendary Bodhidharma, with his outstretched arms holding the weight of the heavens.

A verse on the rubbing gives these words:

> The white-headed old man's eyebrows hang down to earth;
> The blue-eyed foreign monk's arms support heaven.
> If you aspire to this mysticism,
> You will acquire its secret.[50]

The nose is in the valley, guarded by the ears, which are like towers. The water from the lake flows through a stream and a smaller lake into a fountain, representing the mouth and saliva. At its end, where the throat is positioned, is the tip of a pagoda with twelve grades, connecting as well as dividing the head from the torso. This middle region has its own pair of luminaries in the breasts, with clouds over the lungs, hiding the heart, surrounded by a ring of flames. The yellow court is there, the gathering for the body's sacred air. Somewhere above the circle stands the fabled Shepherd Boy playing with what resembles a constellation map. In Western terms, he represents the star Altair. Further from it is a granary representing the stomach, and beyond that is a forest marking the place for the liver and the intestines. Sitting at the inner edge of the forest is the divine Weaving Girl, busy at work, with a thick thread leading way up the back. She represents the star Vega. And every year, Altair and Vega appear to approach each other on the day that the Chinese celebrate as Lovers' Day.

We now enter the lower, aquatic, region. The two luminaries here are the kidneys. Their light is cast on four interconnected, circular diagrams of *t'ai-chi*, with *yin* and *yang* marked out by curved lines, presumably delineating the area under the navel, considered the seat of life and containing various vital organs. Toward the front of this region is a peasant working the field with his water buffalo, and underneath them, a mother and child sitting on huge wheels, with the woman apparently carrying some load. Presumably, we have the symbolic representation of human generation and of family, as well as of agriculture.

The front of the head region is marked by the two meridians along which the breath is circulated in *ch'i-kung / qigong*, with an

---

[50] The verse is adapted from David Teh Yu Wang, '*Nei Jing Tu*, a Daoist diagram of the internal circulation of man', *The Journal of the Walters Art Gallery* 49–50 (1991–2), p. 145. For the diagram, consult also Needham, *Science and Civilisation*, vol. 5, pt 5, p. 114; Kristofer Schipper, 'The Taoist Body', *History of Religions* 17 (1978), 355–88.

opening to permit the breath to enter. The back of the whole figure appears to be supported by the spine, which resembles a kind of road surrounded by mountains.

The diagram is not easy to interpret. We discern the three regions, called the Three Cinnabar Fields, of the head, the chest, and the area of the abdomen and under. These are very important in the practice of *ch'i-kung*, in which one conducts the breath from the Upper, through the Middle, to the Lower Cinnabar Field, going very slowly, and pausing frequently in meditation of the mysteries of our interior universe, until the breath or energy returns to the head through the spine, including its three 'strategic passes', marked by stone gates, the first and largest of which is at the tail bone, the second at the spine's middle and the third in the back of the head. The symbolic sustenance assists the practitioner to achieve mystical enlightenment or inner elixir.

I derive from such an image the tremendous reverence of the Taoists for the body. It is a small universe, the microcosm of the larger universe which is nature. It is a place where the myths and symbols of the larger universe find their meaning. As we learn from the title of this picture, the body is an Inner Scripture, summing up the whole of Taoist teaching, about the human and the superhuman, the natural and the supernatural.

Celestial flight: communing with the cosmos

The *Chuang-tzu* begins with a chapter called *Hsiao-yao yu* (*Xiaoyao-you*), that is, 'to idle about in distant excursions'. The text speaks of the flights of great birds or giant phoenixes, of human figures who 'mount the sun and moon', and 'walk beyond the four poles', referring to the mythical extremities of the then known world, to which Taoists ventured in their quest for secrets concerning life and immortality. The *Huai-nan-tzu* also talks about an excursion to the end of the world. And the text *Lieh-tzu* tells us of the historical King Mu of Chou, who allegedly was carried away by a magician's art, and transported beyond the sun and moon, up to the heavens.[51] Actually, some of the journeys were wholly internal, visionary excursions, even if Taoists are known historically to have travelled

---

[51] See *Lieh Tzu*, SPPY ed., ch. 3; *The Book of Lieh-tzu*, trans. A. C. Graham (London: John Murray, 1960), ch. 3.

from mountain to mountain to collect herbs as well as revealed scriptures. This is the way by which we may understand the *Li-sao* chapter in the *Ch'u-tz'u*, where the hero, Ch'ü Yüan supposedly travelled to the four corners of the earth, to touch those places where the sun bathes, to approach the mountain where the sun sleeps, thrashing it with a branch taken from the solar tree.[52]

The celestial flights are especially to the Three Luminaries – the sun, moon and stars – visible projection of the Three Breaths that animate the world. The adept accompanies the stars in their sidereal procession, taking nourishment from their exhalations, and frolics in paradisaical realms where he meets with deities.

There is a Taoist meditation known as the march to the Big Dipper, a constellation inhabited by deities. The model is the sage Yü, who as surveyor of the lands ravaged by the great flood, laid out, divided and measured the world, while opening up the mountain passes. As such, he regulates the universe with a sacred chart and the golden rule. And he has bequeathed to the Taoists his famous shamanic dance step. In this 'marching step', the adept drags one leg, and limps, as might the legendary Yü after his exhausting travails, in a kind of hopping movement evoking the rolling motion of mediums in trance, and following a line resembling that of the Big Dipper.[53]

We remember that on earth, the ruler represented the polar star, surrounded by his ministers and subjects, who represent the circumpolar stars.[54] The march to the Big Dipper has therefore an imperial reference, as the Taoist walks in the steps of a sage-king and seeks to be with the astral symbols of the imperial court below.

In practice, after setting up a sacred enclosure by summoning the planets, represented by the stars of Big Dipper drawn on a strip of silk, the adept dresses himself with star symbols, on the palm, the elbow, the breast, near the heart, the stomach, the knee and the foot, under the navel and on the head. Then he ascends, starting with the head of the constellation. Each time he passes over a star, he puts his right hand on his heart and points with his other hand in the direction of the star. Holding his breath and swallowing saliva, he closes his eyes to make the astral deity appear. He invokes the deity and advances his left foot on to the next star while holding his breath. He releases his breath as soon as he puts his right foot on the

---

[52] Consult Hawkes, *Ch'u Tz'u*.   [53] Ibid, p. 210.   [54] See chapter 2 above.

star. Rising up as a flying immortal, the mystic eventually arrives at the heavens by means of his march on the stars, which have become his vehicle.[55] Through such a meditation, the individual feels kinship with the cosmos:

> Heaven is my father,
> Earth is my mother,
> The sun is my brother,
> The moon is my sister.[56]

The above language calls to mind that of the sage ruler, whose power is consonant with heaven and earth, whose brightness is one with the sun and the moon. For who else is the 'sage', but the ancient shamanic ruler, the later moral philosopher, and the Taoist, and perhaps also the Buddhist mystic?

BUDDHISM: MYSTICISM IN PHILOSOPHY AND RELIGION

Buddhism, both as philosophy and religion, is grounded in the enlightenment experience of Siddhartha Gautama, the historical Buddha. We are speaking here of a mystical experience, followed by rational reflections articulated in the Buddha's sermons, outlining philosophical doctrines regarding suffering and its causes, selflessness and impermanence, and pointing to a higher level of truth. He also proposed a programme of action for spiritual liberation from the bondage of *saṃsāra*, that is, the ceaseless cycle of rebirth, which, together with the philosophical doctrines, became the basis of the Buddhist religion.

But we are dealing here with Chinese cultural symbols. Can we also include Buddhist mystics in our 'sage-king' context?

I believe we can, provided we speak about Buddhism after it was transformed by contact with Chinese culture. This transformation occurred as a foreign religion responded to an established culture, in this case, especially with the help of a kindred if rival system: Taoism. The interaction brought out certain shamanic features in early Chinese Buddhism itself, as well as philosophical discussions on questions like the two levels of truth, including the conventional

---

[55] Consult also *T'ai-shang chu-kuo chiu-min tsung-chen pi-yao* (The supreme secret essentials for assisting the state and saving the people), in *TT* 987, 8:1a–5a. Robinet, *Taoist Meditation*, p. 224.

[56] *TT* 987, 8:12a-b.

truth and a higher truth, with the preference given to the higher level, that of mystical wisdom.

Indeed, early Chinese Buddhism might be called 'Taoistic' Buddhism. It had two faces: an intellectual one, as a teaching based on the Perfection of Wisdom scriptures, interpreted in the light of neo-Taoist philosophy; and a practical one, as a magico-shamanistic religion, one that prayed for a long life free from illness. Generally speaking, the less educated among the commoners wanted a religion of healing and consolation, the rich and powerful sought immortality, and the intellectual aristocrats looked for philosophical insight.

As a magical religion, this Buddhism resembled, and occasionally merged with, the Taoism of the Celestial Masters sect – but with golden icons and many-tiered stupas that the latter did not have. It took root among the populace with rituals accompanied by the burning of incense, the chanting of scripture and the pronouncement of charms. But the alliance with Taoism would last only so long as it was useful to both parties, and relations eventually turned to rivalry.

The career of the early fourth-century foreign monk, Fo-t'u-ch'eng (d. 348), illustrates how Buddhism was responding to the demands of those from whom it sought to make recruits. He was known in Loyang as

good in making incantations to the deities, and able to manipulate ghosts [or spirits]. When he rubbed the palm of his hand with hemp oil mixed with rouge, he could see things happening a thousand leagues away clearly on his palm, as though [they were happening] in his presence . . . He divined affairs by listening to the sound of the bell, and his predictions never missed.[57]

This made him very useful to the rulers and warlords of his time. In the presence of one such, and allegedly to procure his faith, Fo-t'u-ch'eng 'took his begging bowl, filled it with water, burned incense, and uttered a spell. In a moment blue lotus flowers appeared with dazzling brightness and colour.'[58]

As Buddhism gradually evolved in China, it moved increasingly away from the early involvement in magic, and became more

---

[57] See Hui-chiao (497–554), *Kao-seng chuan* (Biographies of eminent monks), *Taishō Shinshū Daizōkyō*, (abbrev. as *T*), 45.2059, ch. 9, p. 383, where his life is given in the two chapters describing wonder-workers. See also Tsukamoto Zenryū, *A History of Early Chinese Buddhism: From Its Introduction to the Death of Hui-yüan*, Eng. trans. by Leon Hurvitz (Tokyo: Kodansha International, 1979), vol. 1.

[58] Ibid.

moralistic and rationalistic in its philosophical speculation, less exuberant in its ritual expressions, and more quietistic in its mysticism. Chinese Buddhism came of age with the development of the great Mahāyāna schools of T'ien-t'ai (*pinyin:* Tiantai), Hua-yen (*pinyin:* Huayan) and Ch'an, representing a substantial integration of Chinese philosophical genius with Buddhist religious inspiration. On account of our special interest in the 'Taoistic' aspects of ecstatic Buddhism, we shall single out Ch'an Buddhism for discussion.

Sutras as Buddha's sermons

The Sanskrit Buddhist term for scripture is *sūtra*, literally meaning a string or a thread, and basically referring originally to brief prose sayings that were 'strung' together, literally, on palm leaves. With time, however, the meaning expanded to include all the Buddha's sermons. And while Mahāyāna sutras were composed very much later, they too were called sutras, as they were composed in the same form as the Theravāda Āgamas, and were regarded as the Buddha's true teachings.[59]

In Christian liturgies, the Gospel passages recited aloud usually begin with the Latin phrase *in illo tempore*: 'At that time, Jesus said to his disciples', a phrase that is not always from the Gospel chapter itself, but used by the reader as an introduction to the chosen piece, to remind the congregation that they are hearing the words of Jesus. And in cases where miracles were reported, the Gospel narrative itself often ends with phrases like 'And the people, seeing this, rejoiced and praised God.'

As Buddha's sermons, sutras depend on him for their value as scriptures. They commonly begin with the phrase, 'Thus have I heard', attributing the accounts to follow to the great teacher, and they commonly end with some words like 'Hearing the Buddha's sermon, the entire audience rejoiced greatly and believed and accepted the teachings.'[60]

Not that sutras contain the Buddha's exact words, since they were not recorded at the time he spoke, but long afterwards, and were retained according to the mental capacities and dispositions of the hearers. Sutras, after all, are to be the teachers of future generations

---

[59] Kogen Mizuno, *Buddhist Sutras: Origin, Development, Transmission* (Tokyo: Kosei, 1982), p. 15.
[60] Ibid, p. 17.

in the same sense that Śākyamuni was the teacher of his contemporaries.[61] Sometime during the two centuries that separated the death of the historical Buddha and the birth of the first great Buddhist emperor, Ashoka (3rd cent. BCE), some sort of Buddhist canon, in the form of *oral* tradition, had appeared. Indeed, one difference between the Indian and the Chinese civilisations is that the change from the oral tradition to the written one was slower to take effect in the case of India.[62]

How the Theravāda canon was allegedly recorded deserves some attention, even if the account may not be entirely historical. And it helps to explain the phrase, 'Thus have I heard'. Legend says that, around 480 BCE, shortly after the founder's death, a First Buddhist Council was called by the great Mahā-Kaśyapa, summoning to the assembly all five hundred arhats or the Buddha's enlightened disciples, with the aim of collecting the Master's true teachings. And they had decided to include among the five hundred, the youngest disciple, Ānanda, who had not yet reached arhatship, but had been close to the Master during the last twenty-five years, and was known to possess a phenomenal memory. Tradition goes on to say that Ānanda became enlightened the night before the Council, and was therefore fully qualified to participate at the council.[63] The first-person pronoun in 'Thus have I heard' is often supposed to be Ānanda.

I mention this on account of the importance of personal enlightenment, which presumably offers insights into the teachings that only the ears can hear and the memory alone can store. The Council of the Arhats worked not only to assemble the words of the Buddha, but also to make sure that the inspiration behind these words was guaranteed by their own inspired understanding of their erstwhile Master. For similar reasons, those Buddhists who were more enlightened could usually teach others who were less, even if they happened to be lay rather than ordained, or women rather than men.

---

[61] Miriam Levering, 'Scripture and Its Reception: A Buddhist Case', in Levering (ed.), *Rethinking Scripture*, p. 63. Consult also Étienne Lamotte, 'La Critique d'authenticité dans le Bouddhisme', *India Antiqua* (Leiden: E. J. Brill, 1947), pp. 220–1; James P. McDermott, 'Scripture as the Word of the Buddha', *Numen* 31 (1984), 22–39.

[62] The Pali-language Buddhist Canon, called the *Tripiṭaka* because it was written on palm leaves and organised in three 'Baskets', was divided according to content, into *Vinaya* or discipline, *Sutras* or Discourses, and *Abhidharma* or Further Discourses. At least, this made the scriptural corpus finite for Theravāda Buddhists.

[63] Mizuno, *Buddhist Sutras*, p. 20.

The Mahāyāna branch developed quite differently. Many of the texts were composed in polemical debates against Theravāda claims, but ascribed to the historical Buddha himself, or sometimes, to the so-called 'cosmic Buddha', a personification of the Buddhist teaching or Dharma. And indeed, these multiplied over the years, until they made up a library.

For the Chinese Buddhists, there was in place a native model for understanding how the sutras were to be received. They compared the Buddha to their own sage Confucius, whose teaching was transmitted through the classics (*ching^c*), a term which was used to translate the Sanskrit word *sūtra*. Each school identified a sutra or a group of sutras as conveying the highest teachings, while claiming that others offered teachings suited to lower stages of understanding.[64] Also, they used the Chinese model of having disciples study a canonical text under the guidance of a master who used it to shape their character, as parallel to Confucius and Mencius.[65]

But there were also those who accepted the Indian view that the Buddha's words were to be used as 'skill-in-means' (*upāya*). Here, too, Chinese Buddhists like Seng-chao made use of insights from *Chuang-tzu* to say that the books of the sages contain only the tracks left by their mind. There is much that cannot be communicated directly, and much else that contact with the living presence of the sages might communicate. In fact, unless the meaning of the words is grasped in everyday experience, the words remain dead. This was especially true for Ch'an Buddhists.[66]

Certainly, in spite of attributions of authorship to the Buddha, historical or eternal, Buddhist scriptural interpretation has never been very rigid, in contrast to that in Western religions. There was never a central teaching authority to verify the exegetical work, while the very admission of *upāya* transforms truth itself into a kind of parable. The same breadth of tolerance applies to the Taoist scriptures, themselves written often as parables in an esoteric language inaccessible except to the initiated. We could also claim

---

[64] Consult J. W. De Jong, *Buddha's Word in China* (Canberra: Australian National University, 1968) regarding this process. Consult also Graeme MacQueen, 'Inspired Speech in Early Mahayana Buddhism I', *Religion* 11 (1981), 303–19.

[65] Holmes Welch, *The Practice of Chinese Buddhism, 1900–1950* (Cambridge, Mass.: Harvard University Press, 1967), pp. 310–14.

[66] Levering, *Rethinking Scripture*, pp. 65–6.

such breadth of tolerance for the Confucian classics, in spite of centuries of arguments over their meaning.

Inducing trance: Buddhist meditation

There are outward similarities between Buddhist and Taoist meditative exercises. One might even call 'Buddhist yoga' much of what the term *dhyāna* (meditation) covers. I refer to such practices as the preparatory technique of counting the breaths, leading to mental concentration (the contemplation of the body as perishable, composed of elements, impure and full of suffering); the visualisation of the internal and external images of various colours, and so on.[67]

Such similarities are due in part to the fact that the physical body, which is the given, is the same for the Buddhist as for the Taoist or anybody else. But doctrinal differences regarding human existence and the goal to be reached in meditation have led to differences in language as well in the categories that describe various dimensions of the exercise itself. Buddhists often use the term *ting*[b] / *ding* to refer to a stillness of mind to be achieved, which some have equated with *samādhi*. But the word remains vague, and can refer to both physical as well as mental experiences, including the states of consciousness achieved in meditation.

In this chapter, the Buddhist methods chosen for consideration tend to be apophatic in character, seeking to empty the mind rather than to fill it, in contrast to the kataphatic preferences of the Taoist techniques involving detailed visualisation discussed earlier. The choice is based on the evolution in Buddhist spirituality, culminating in the popularity of Ch'an Buddhist meditation.

The fifth-century Chinese monk Seng-chao, an early disciple of the great teacher Kumārajīva, is known for his famous treatise called *Chao Lun*, which contributed so much to the blending of Taoist and Buddhist philosophies. He uses the term 'sage' to refer to the Buddhist holy man, giving him many Taoist attributes. He also wrote four sentences about mystical experience, using a dialectical method and images from nature to describe the contrast between the interior silence and the exterior motions.

The raging storm uprooting mountains is always still,
The rivers run [into the ocean] without flowing;

---

[67] Erik Zürcher, *The Buddhist Conquest of China* (Leiden: E. J. Brill, 1959), vol. 1, p. 33.

The wild horses raise dust but remain motionless;
The sun and the moon revolve in their orbits, without going around.[68]

Like other Buddhists of his time, Seng-chao had long searched for
'a supreme religious experience' (*miao-wu / miaowu*, literally, a
'marvellous thing'). In his commentary on the *Vimalakīrti sutra*, he
makes mention of his own ecstatic experience. He also compares the
Theravāda experience of trance unfavourably with the Mahāyāna
experience.

The Hīnayāna [Buddhists] . . . become motionless like dry wood. [In the
case of] the Mahāyāna saint, the flicker of the mind has completely ceased,
his body fills the universe, and his reactions are always spontaneous and in
harmony with [nature]. In what he does, and in what he does not do, he
retains a majestic bearing.[69]

What exactly is the experiential difference between becoming
metaphorically like 'dry wood' or ceasing 'the mind's flicker', but
remaining spontaneous and in harmony with nature?[70] Presumably,
we are speaking here about a Taoist affirmation of humanity and
nature, which in Theravada Buddhism was regarded as something to
be surpassed and left behind entirely. Seng-chao was to have an
important influence on the development of Chinese Buddhism in
general, and of its Ch'an form in particular.

Ch'an Buddhism: the Chinese appropriation of Buddhist meditation

Ch'an (Japanese: Zen) is the Chinese transliteration of the Sanskrit
dhyāna, and refers to calming the mind and permitting the person to
penetrate into his or her own inner consciousness. Continual
practice can allegedly conduct to ecstatic trances or a blissful state of
equanimity and wisdom. As exercises of meditation, *dhyāna* had been
developed in India over the ages, but as a Buddhist sect or school,
Ch'an is a Chinese development. Its later spread to Korea and
Japan, and its recent popularity in both Europe and America, have
made Ch'an or Zen the best-known form of Buddhist religion.[71]

---

[68] See *T* 45.1858, *Chao Lun*, pt 1, p. 161a.
[69] *Chu Wei-mo-chi ching* (Commentary on the Vimalikīrti Sutra), *T* 38.1775, 2:344c. Eng. trans.
    adapted from Walter Liebenthal, *Chao Lun: The Treatises of Seng-Chao*, 2nd rev. ed. (Hong
    Kong University Press, 1968), p. 40.
[70] These words come from *Chuang-tzu*, sect. 2, 1:10a; Watson, *Complete Works*, p. 36.
[71] Consult Heinrich Dumoulin, *Zen Buddhism: A History*, trans. James W. Heisig and Paul
    Knitter (New York: Macmillan; London: Collier Macmillan, 1988–90), 2 vols. For the

In common with other Mahāyāna systems, Ch'an teaches that ultimate reality – *śūnyatā* (emptiness), sometimes called Buddha-nature – is inexpressible in words or concepts, and apprehended only by direct intuition, outside of conscious thought. Such direct intuition requires discipline and training, but is also characterised by freedom and spontaneity. This has led Ch'an to become something of an iconoclastic movement, relativising such other practices as studying or reciting the Buddhist sutras, worshipping the Buddha images, or performing rituals, which are regarded of no avail to the goal of spiritual enlightenment (in Chinese, *wu*[b]; in Japanese, *satori*). This is very much in the apophatic tradition that I have mentioned.[72]

Against a background of sectarian multiplication, *Ch'an* itself divided into many sub-sects or branches, depending on the varying emphasis on methods and techniques, involving also different beliefs regarding whether the goal of spiritual enlightenment is a sudden experience, or one that is achieved after a gradual process of cultivation. The subitist school is especially associated with the monk Hui-neng (638–713), allegedly illiterate, whose Southern school emphasises the sudden character of the enlightenment, and an iconoclastic attitude toward Buddhas and *bodhisattvas*, Buddhist scriptures and rituals. Rather than seeking the extraordinary, one is therefore to live an ordinary life and carry on the simple tasks. As Ch'an Buddhists said: 'In hewing wood and drawing water, there is the Tao.' And the famous monk Lin-chi has said:, 'To achieve Buddhahood there is no need for cultivation. Just carry on an ordinary task without any attachment. Release your bowels and water, wear your clothes, and eat your meals. When you are tired, lie down. The fool will laugh at you, but the wise man will understand.'[73]

Guarding the mind: a northern Ch'an meditation

The northern Ch'an school is usually associated with quiet meditation and gradual cultivation for the sake of achieving a state of

subtle relationship between Buddhism and Confucianism, consult Araki Kengo, *Shinpan Bukkyō to Jukyō* (Tokyo: Kenbun shuppan, 1993).

[72] Consult Peter D. Hershock, 'Person as Narration: The Dissolution of "Self" and "Other" in Ch'an Buddhism', *Philosophy East and West* 44 (1994), 685–710; Ueda Hizuteru, 'Silence and Words in Zen Buddhism', *Diogenes* 170 (1995), pp. 1–21.

[73] Chang Chung-yuan (ed. and trans.), *Original Teachings of Ch'an Buddhism: Selected from the Transmission of the Lamp* (New York: Grove Press, 1969), p. 100.

enlightenment. Its best-known representative is Shen-hsiu (c. 605–706), the presumed author of the treatise, *Kuan-hsin lun* (On Contemplating the Mind).

When asked what method to cultivate in the quest of the Buddha-way, Shen-hsiu once replied: 'Simply cultivate the single method of clear contemplation of mind. It includes all methods.'[74]

To control the mind, one must also control the cause of mental disturbance, which, for the Buddhist, is falsehood and evil. And here arises the need of controlling the six senses, and what the senses offer, called the Six Thieves. 'Simply be able to control the mind for inner illumination, and realize that insight is constantly shining. You will be forever free from the Three Poisons . . . The Six Thieves will not be allowed to cause disturbances, and innumerable merits will accumulate of themselves.'[75] The instruction seems simple, but that makes it harder to follow. Knowing Buddhist distinctions between the two levels of truth, is the practitioner to contemplate the illusory mind (*wang-hsin / wangxin*), or the true mind (*chen-hsin / zhenxin*)? Should one examine one's own mental activities, or go to a deeper level?

Usually, the answer is presumed to be for the true mind, sometimes described as 'no mind' or 'no thought' (*wu-hsin / wuxin*). And so, 'gazing at' or 'contemplating' the mind becomes visualisation of empty space, just as what one might do when sitting on a mountaintop and looking into the distance on all four sides – without limits.[76]

It appears that the beginner, usually a young monk, is instructed to sit cross-legged, and identify oneself with the 'mind of a son of the Buddha' in its undisturbed 'purity'. In its exercise, the metaphor for the pure mind is the 'empty sky':

If you behold the mind, and if it is pure, it is called the realm of the pure mind. You should not focus inwardly upon body-mind, and you should not focus outwardly your body-mind. There should be a relaxed, vast, and far-reaching inspecting (*k'an / kan*), an inspecting which everywhere encompasses the empty sky.[77]

[74] Robert B. Zeuschler, 'Awakening in Northern Ch'an', in David W. Chappell (ed.), *Buddhist and Taoist Practice in Medieval Chinese Society* (Honolulu: University of Hawaii Press, 1987), p. 97.

[75] The Three Poisons are worldly desire, anger, and stupidity. See *Kuan-hsin lun*, *T* 85.2833, 1273a–b. Eng. trans. adapted from Zeuschler, 'Awakening', p. 105.

[76] Bernard Faure, 'One-Practice Samadhi in Early Ch'an', in Peter N. Gregory (ed.), *Traditions of Meditation in Chinese Buddhism* (Honolulu: University of Hawaii Press, 1986), pp. 114–15.

[77] *Ta-ch'eng wu-sheng fang-pien men* (The Unborn *upāya* of the Mahāyāna), *T* 85.2834, 1273c. Eng. trans. by Zeuschler, 'Awakening', pp. 100–1.

And the reward is also promised as being quickly within reach: 'You
will transcend the ordinary and achieve the level of sagehood. It will
be right before your eyes and not far off in the distance. Enlightenment takes place in a moment.'[78]

Guarding the mind suggests a constant vigilance that is patient
and persevering in its efforts to attain enlightenment. Such an
attitude distinguishes the gradualist school from the subitist, with the
latter's recourse to certain techniques calculated to take the practitioner along a short-cut to the goal desired.

Southern Ch'an and the emptying of the mind

The mystical or ecstatic experience itself is seldom described in
Ch'an. Instead, Buddhist masters speak about the quest for Buddha-
nature, or Buddhahood, or ultimate reality, and they usually identify
such with the mind itself. The southern school especially developed
techniques for attaining such experience, including the shock technique of 'hitting and shouting', or of posing insoluble riddles (in
Chinese, *kung-an / gong'an*; in Japanese, *koan*) to press the mind to go
beyond any separation between itself and things. Such *kung-an* were
based on 'cases' of enlightenment experiences in the recorded
biographies of Ch'an masters, and any one of them was increasingly
regarded as containing everything necessary for serving as a catalyst
to awaken the Buddha-nature of the disciple.

Gradually, it was even felt that an entire *kung-an* story might lead
the mind to distraction, and that one should rather focus on the
essential point of the 'case', on its 'critical phrase' (*hua-t'ou / huatou*),
so to speak, as a meditative device. And thus a new school of Ch'an
Buddhism, the Lin-chi school, which was very much in favour of
sudden enlightenment, crystallised its teachings.[79]

An illustrative example is the case of the ninth-century monk
Chao-chou, who was once asked: 'Has a dog Buddha-nature or not?'
And he answered: 'No!' In this *kung-an*, the critical phrase, or word,
is the 'No!' Apparently, this answer contradicted the teaching of
Chinese Buddhism, regarding the universality of Buddha-nature in
all sentient beings. The Lin-chi patriarch, Ta-hui Tsung-kao, who

---

[78] Ibid.
[79] Robert E. Buswell, Jr, 'The "Short-cut" Approach of *K'an-hua* Meditation: The Evolution
of a Practical Subitism in Chinese Ch'an Buddhism', in Peter N. Gregory (ed.), *Sudden and
Gradual Approaches to Enlightenment in Chinese Thought* (Honolulu: University of Hawaii Press,
1987), pp. 343–7.

advocated *hua-t'ou*, cautioned disciples not even to try to resolve the *hua-t'ou*, but to give up the pride of believing that one has the conceptual tools to understand such. He made reference to several other *hua-t'ou* then in use, including the 'dry shit-stick' and the like.[80] After all, the point of the *hua-t'ou* is the shock technique, to jolt the disciple's mind and consciousness to a higher level of awareness.

But then, inference may also yield the answer. For what does the word 'No!' signify? Isn't 'No' itself the most meaningful word in the exchange, and in the entire Buddhist teaching? Does not this word signify emptiness, and with emptiness, the dialectical presence of Buddha-nature in everything?

We are speaking of a distinctively southern Ch'an style of meditation involving the stopping of mental processes in the so-called 'no thought' practice. The impression one receives is that the enlightenment experience is tranquil if rapturous, giving an assurance of insight into the 'thus-ness' of things. One sees things 'as they are', in their profundity, after having learnt to relativise them. The Ming dynasty monk Han-shan Te-ch'ing (1546–1623) has left behind a vivid record of his 'sudden awakening', which occurred while he was reading from the treatise *Chao-lun*, when the meaning of the passage came to him in a flash.

My joy surpassed all bounds. I jumped up and prostrated myself before the image of the Buddha, but, – oh wonder! – my body remained motionless. I lifted the curtain and went out to look round. A gust shook the trees in the courtyard and falling leaves whirled in the air. But in my vision not a single leaf moved, and I knew that the 'raging storm uprooting mountains' is eternally calm.[81]

The mystical breakthrough represents a total, human experience, body and mind, and Te-ch'ing reported going to the toilet during this experience, passing water but maintaining his inner stillness. 'How true', he said, 'The rushing streams do not flow'.[82]

The use of the dialectic, the reference to nature, both coming originally from Seng-chao, are evidences of the Taoist philosophical influence which had penetrated Ch'an Buddhism. In both the

[80] Buswell, 'The 'Short-cut', p. 350.
[81] Te-ch'ing, *Chao-lun lüeh-chu* (Comments on the treatise of Seng-chao), in *Hsü Tsang-ching* (Supplement to the Buddhist Canon), vol. 96, ch. 1, 294b; consult Liebenthal's translation, *Chao Lun*, pp. 40–1. Consult also Sung-peng Hsü, *A Buddhist Leader in Ming China: The Life and Thought of Han-shan Te-ch'ing* (University Park: Pennsylvania State University Press, 1978), pp. 70–2.
[82] Liebenthal, *Chao Lun*, Introduction, p. 41.

subitist and the gradualist forms, Ch'an Buddhism guides its followers toward a personal mysticism which is quietistic. And while Ch'an Buddhism prides itself on its nonrationalist stance, insisting upon the need to go beyond discursive thinking, it is actually a more 'rationalist' form of Buddhism with an iconoclastic attitude toward rituals, images and scriptures. As people who rely on their own innate powers (Japanese: *jiriki*), the Ch'an mystics may work toward a self-induced state of enlightenment, in a direct intuition of the mind, but they are theologically pantheistic rather than monotheistic or polytheistic. And if they seek enlightenment not just for its own sake, but also out of a disposition of compassion toward all creatures, they cultivate ecstasy in silence and privacy, without specific reference to other people, even if they happen to meditate in a group. Their behaviour is quite different from the shamans, who communicate with gods and spirits in public or semi-private trances, to the accompaniment of dances and music, and for the practical purpose of healing or divination.

Han-shan Te-ch'ing was a contemporary of a neo-Confucian scholar, Kao P'an-lung, who also left behind an account of his mystical experience, an experience he diligently prepared for and finally achieved, while visiting in the mountains.

Quite by chance I saw a saying by Ch'eng Hao, 'Amid a hundred officials, a myriad affairs and a hundred thousand weapons, with water as drink and a bent arm as pillow, I can still be joyful. The myriad changes are all man-made; in reality there is not a thing.' Suddenly I realized the sense of these words and said, 'That is it. In reality there is not a thing!' And as this one thought lingered, all entanglements were broken off. It was suddenly as though a load of one hundred pounds had instantly dropped off, as though a flash of lightning had penetrated the body and pierced the intelligence, and I merged in harmony with the Great Transformation until there was no differentiation between Heaven and humanity, the outer and the inner.[83]

We see here an obvious influence from Ch'an Buddhism, with the reference to the indeterminacy of absolute reality, and to the breaking of perceived entanglements. We also see the use of a Taoist term in the Great Transformation referring to nature and its cycle of

---

[83] Consult Huang Tsung-hsi, comp., *Ming-ju hsüeh-an*, SPPY ed., 58:17b; Eng. trans. by Rodney Taylor, in Julia Ching (ed.), *The Records of Ming Scholars* (Honolulu: University of Hawaii Press, 1987), pp. 237–8. The reference to Ch'eng Hao is from *Erh-Ch'eng ch'üan-shu*, SPPY ed., 6:3a; there is an interior quotation from *Analects* 7:15, about being joyful and content with few material comforts in life.

increase and decrease of *yin* and *yang* and the seasonal changes. The focus is on the merging of the self with nature in a transformed consciousness. But the occasion that led to this is a saying from another neo-Confucian, Ch'eng Hao, who spoke of contemplation while in action, and a rapturous joy in the midst of a busy life as a public official, which was so different from the life of a Buddhist monk or a Taoist recluse.

CONCLUDING REMARKS

So far, I have refrained from a discussion of the ethical value of mysticism. It is actually my opinion that a mystical experience does not necessarily have an ethical component, and, for this reason, has sometimes been described as 'beyond good and evil'. After all, so much of its character depends on the intention of the person: whether the quest is for an experience in itself, including the inner peace and calm, or for something more or beyond, which could be physical strength, mental concentration, ethical improvement, or spiritual fulfilment. Where the ancient kings looked for clarity of vision as help in decision-making, the modern Japanese *kamikaze* fighter sought unyielding strength to carry out a foregone conclusion: dying for his emperor. In the case of the Taoist or Buddhist mystic, looking for a foretaste of Heaven on earth, mystical experience might be desired for the sense of power or the ecstatic joy it brings.

This does not prevent a mystic, *any* mystic, from using his or her transformative experience to become more engaged in ethical concerns, if she or he happens to be so inclined. This was the case with Mencius. This was also the case with many others, monks and lay persons, and particularly the neo-Confucian scholars, for whom meditation and mysticism were not ends in themselves, but the means to self-improvement and the service of others.

CHAPTER 7

The sage-king as messiah: religion again appropriates the paradigm

INTRODUCTION

There are Western scholars who point out that movements with revolutionary ideology have often religious roots in millenarian, eschatological and messianic mass movements, usually associated with the Judeo-Christian tradition. They have said that the messiah idea is unique to the West, and that any manifestation of it in Chinese history and civilisation has to be the result of dissemination from the West. For example, Wilhelm Mühlmann argues that 'mystical religions', like Taoism and Buddhism, lack a linear concept of time, which is essential to messianic thinking, *new* ideas or revolutionary movements.[1] They have had the impression that East Asia has not known such movements as its own, except when ideas behind such have been exported from the West. After all, the so-called cyclical nature of time in the East supposedly prevents real change or expectation of such.

The Chinese concept of time

The fact is, the Chinese concept of time is not exclusively cyclical.[2] However, ideas of reincarnation or rebirth were not native to China, but came from China's West – India – and never quite replaced local Chinese concepts of time. These are constituted of both cyclical and linear elements. So time remains more spiral than cyclical, with a linear-like thrust.

---

[1] K. M. Schipper, 'Millénarismes et Messianismes dans la Chine Ancienne', in *Proceedings of the XXVIth Conference of Chinese Studies* (Rome: Istituto Italiano per il Medio e Estremo Oriente, 1979), pp.31–2.
[2] Joseph Needham, *Time and Eastern Man* ([London]: The Royal Anthropological Institute of Great Britain and Ireland, 1965), p. 29.

Starting over three thousand years ago, the Chinese measured time by using two interlocking sets of cyclical characters: the 'heavenly stems' and the 'earthly branches.' Such an invention made possible the counting of years, weeks, days, and hours.

On the one hand, they thought of time as compartmentalised, in terms of a cycle of successive seasons, emphasising alternation and interdependence. On the other hand, they also accepted continuous time and engaged in creating calendar systems covering many years or decades, as well as early and detailed historical chronicling. As Needham puts it, 'the cyclical does not necessarily imply either the repetitive or the serially discontinuous. The cycle of the seasons in the individual year (*annus*) was but one link (*annulus*) in an infinite chain of duration, past, present and future.'[3]

In chapter 5, I talked about the presence, in the classics, of utopian ideas relating to time that include both restoring a golden age of remote antiquity (the 'Ta-t'ung' or Great Unity) and progressing a present of 'Disorder' into a better future, through 'Approaching Peace', to the Great Peace or *T'ai-p'ing*. This was the theory of the 'Three Ages'. And the term *T'ai-p'ing* has been used historically as a stated goal by various groups claiming to be able to improve on the present, often through organised, even armed, opposition to the political establishment.

Messianic expectations

There is no doubt that the term 'messiah', meaning 'anointed one', has a Hebrew origin, referring either to the actual king of Israel, whether Saul, David, or Solomon, or the king in general, or, by Jesus' time, to a future king, who was to restore the kingdom and save the people from all evil.[4]

And then, as we know, the title was applied by Christians to Jesus, with the title *Christos*, a Greek translation of the Hebrew word. The doctrine also developed that Jesus would return to the world a second time, to bring to final fulfilment the messianic expectations. And similar ideas also emerged in Islam, where the expected ruler, to arrive at the end of the world, is called the *mahdī*, 'the rightly guided one'.

---

[3] Ibid, p. 9.
[4] Helmer Ringgren, 'Messianism', in *The Encyclopedia of Religion*, vol. 9, p. 469.

We are still talking about a political messiah in the Chinese case, with the expected saviour as someone who is somehow of divine or superhuman status. However, in using the term 'messiah', I am not suggesting any literal parallel. After all, anointing was never part of the Chinese or East Asian accession ritual. But I am suggesting that the idea of an expected political saviour has been very much a part of the Confucian as well as Taoist and even Buddhist traditions. A belief that the old order was near its end, and a new, better one, was approaching – a 'millenarian' belief – was often also associated with this expectation.

Taoists were prominent among these political activists, often rebels with a cause. Some of them regarded themselves as a chosen people (*chung-min / zhongmin*, literally, 'seed people'), wanting to bring about a new heaven and a new earth under the banners of a Prince of Peace. Indeed, during the Han period, long before the possible advent of Western influence, the Taoist movement has shown millenarian and apocalyptic characteristics within a linear concept of time.[5] History tells us what happened in 3 BCE, during a time of drought, when the cult of the mythical female figure, Hsi-wang-mu (the Western Queen Mother), enjoyed great vogue, inspiring processions and sacrifices, and circulating her promises of salvation and immortality to the believers. She was then visualised as an elderly person, a symbol of longevity. But any message from her was also a warning that the dynasty called the Western Han, with its capital in Chang'an, was near its end. Six years earlier, its power was taken over by the usurper Wang Mang.[6]

CONFUCIUS AS UNCROWNED KING

In this regard, the Confucian tradition has been underscrutinised by Western scholars. I would assert that during the same Han period, a dimension of Confucian thinking that came to the fore may be termed 'messianic'. That was pointed out by those who asserted that Master K'ung sought to promote the ideas of the ancients, including

---

[5] Needham, *Time and Eastern Man*, p. 29.
[6] *Han-shu*, ch. 27, pt 3. See also Michael Loewe, *Ways to Paradise: The Chinese Quest for Immortality* (London: Allen & Unwin, 1979), pp. 98–101; Alan K.-L. Chan, 'Goddesses in Chinese Religion', in Larry Hurtado (ed.), *Goddesses in Religion and Modern Debate* (Atlanta: Scholars Press, 1990), pp. 31–4.

those of the Shang times. It has been claimed that the Shang people always looked forward to a political saviour from their line, expected within five hundred years of the dynasty's fall, much as the fallen House of David did in Israel.

As a scion of a clan that traced its lineage back to Shang progenitors, K'ung was in a sense the fulfilment of these hopes. Such messianism was native to China, having emerged long before Christ's birth. It may be understood as a corollary of the kingship paradigm. Once the real king is expected to be an ideal ruler, people presumably would look forward to having such an ideal ruler over them.

It was suggested, during the Han dynasty, that K'ung did have the ambition of personally becoming king, which, of course, remained unfulfilled. This interpretation was circulating among scholars at least until the T'ang dynasty (618–906).[7] But by what right did K'ung perceive himself as deserving to be king? Was it lineage, or was it possession of wisdom?

Interestingly, the term *tzu*, to which *fu-tzu* ('Master') is related, had been first a term for royal princes and kinsmen. Then it became used as a polite term of address for persons in the position of grand counsellors. Toward the end of the Spring and Autumn period, it took on the meaning of 'teacher', and was applied to the great masters of disciples, and especially, to the philosophers among them. As for the term *fu-tzu*, it was first used for military officers of various ranks. Later it was applied to grand counsellors of feudal lords, and eventually, to expressing even higher esteem for a teacher and master than the simple term *tzu*.[8]

Let us reflect once more on the legends of Yao's and Shun's each leaving the throne to the best qualified, rather than to a son. We have mentioned that these legends were possibly popularised by Confucius and his school. Perhaps these were invented by them as myths, through selective reading of history accompanied by moral reflection.[9]

[7] Lo Meng-ch'e, *K'ung-tzu wei-wang erh wang lun* (Confucius as an uncrowned king) (Taipei: Hsüeh-sheng, 1982), pp. 69–87; Consult K'ang Yu-wei, *K'ung-tzu kai-chih k'ao* (Confucius as a political reformer), 1920 ed. (Taipei: Commercial Press, 1968 reprint), especially ch. 12.
[8] Yang Kuan, *Zhanguo shi* (The history of the Warring States) (Shanghai: Renmin, 1955 ed., 1980 printing), pp. 403–4.
[9] Wei Cheng-t'ung, *Ju-chia yü hsien-tai Chung-kuo* (Confucianism and modern China) (Taipei: Tung-ta, 1984), pp. 1–28.

In this light, we may appreciate better Confucius' statement: 'If [a king] is able to govern his state with the disposition of modesty and propriety (*li-jang / lirang*, i.e., 'yielding') [possibly including the idea of readiness to give it up], what trouble can he have? If he is unable to govern the state with modesty and propriety, what has he to do with the rites and propriety?' (Analects 4:13).

The ancients appear to have believed in the cyclical recurrence of sage-kings and good governments within a temporal framework that we may call spiral. At the very end of the Book of Mencius we have the following passage about the time periods that lapsed between sage-kings of old:

> Over five hundred years lapsed between [the time of] Yao and Shun and [that of King] T'ang . . . Over five hundred years [also] lapsed between [the time of] T'ang and that of [King] Wen . . . Over five hundred years lapsed between [the time of] Wen and that of Confucius . . . And over one hundred years have lapsed since the time of Confucius. We are so near in time to the sage, and so close in place to his home. And yet, is there no one [who is now a sage]? Is there no one [who is now a sage]?[10]

The final two sentences are the least explicit. But what Mencius seems to be suggesting is that, given the cyclical emergence of sages – most of whom were kings as well – Confucius was clearly an exception for not also having been a king. And, if that was a historical quirk, then what should be happening in his own day? One might even infer his saying: should not Mencius himself be also regarded as a sage? In that case, should he also not be given the responsibility that went with the role? And finally, the question is: why was he not accepted as such (as, of course, Confucius also was not)? What was Heaven intending to do with the world?[11]

True, there were presumably sage ministers as well as sage-kings: men like Yi-yin, who served King T'ang, and the Duke of Chou, who served his brother and nephew. That Confucius – and also Mencius – desired to serve in government is a well-known fact. They might very well have looked forward to serving a great sage-king. But even there, each would be bitterly disappointed.

---

[10] Mencius 7b:38. English translation is my own. Consult Lau, *Mencius*, p. 204; Legge, *Chinese Classics*, vol. 1, p. 502.

[11] The commentary tradition has interpreted these lines differently. Consult *Meng-tzu chu-shu*, SPPY ed., 14B, 6b–7b.

All the more, we might appreciate the lament of Confucius over the absence of portents for the coming of a great sage, destined to be king: 'The phoenix does not come; the river gives forth no chart. It is all over with me!' (9:9).[12]

The phoenix was the mythical winged messenger that announced the coming of the sage-king Shun. The river chart was among those treasures inherited by the Chou king on the occasion of his enthronement. It supposedly mapped out the trigrams from the Book of Changes in a magic arrangement of numbers and symbols that could have, among other things, served as the architectural blueprint for the royal Bright Hall. In this case, it would appear that he was expecting a new river chart, possibly to announce a new reign of peace and prosperity.

Was Confucius thinking of himself as the architect of peace and reason, or was he thinking only of an ideal ruler to whom he would be a wise minister? He could, of course, have thought of both. We have no doubt that he believed himself to be a wise man, even if he never called himself a sage.

The Han thinker Tung Chung-shu contends that Confucius received from Heaven shortly before his death the Mandate to establish new institutions to replace the decadent Chou dynasty. He built this theory on the recorded appearance of a mythical, unicorn-like animal called *lin*, as given in the Spring–Autumn Annals (481 BCE), and the story in the Annals of Tso of Confucius' having seen it.

There are things that cannot be brought to pass through [human] effort . . . Such was the hunt in the west which captured the *lin* – an omen of Confucius' receiving the Mandate. He then used the Spring–Autumn Annals to correct what was wrong and reveal the meaning of the changing of dynastic institutions.[13]

This became the starting-point for the veneration of Confucius as an 'uncrowned king' – governing history through his books, especially the didactic Spring–Autumn Annals. Such veneration was accompanied by his near-apotheosis in the apocryphal texts that abounded during the Han times. He is said to have been born of the union in a dream state of his mother with a semi-divine figure called

---

[12] For an explanation of the portents, see Waley, *Analects*, pp. 48–9.
[13] *Ch'un-ch'iu fan-lu* ch. 6, sect. 16, p. 2b. Consult Fung, *History*, vol. 2, pp. 71–2.

the Black Emperor. He was allegedly born in a hollow mulberry, which had sacred references. He carried on his breast a writing announcing a new dynasty. He was described as a huge man, in height and circumference, yet resembling a crouching dragon when seated. 'Sages are not born for nothing. They must surely institute something, to reveal the mind of Heaven. And Confucius, as a wooden-tongued bell, instituted laws for the world.'[14]

With the passage of time, the figure of Confucius re-emerged, not as a god, but as a philosopher, and an uncrowned king. The royal title would become part of the official title bestowed on him by the real emperors. In 1308, during the Mongol times, it became 'The Complete, Most Perfect Sage, King Wen-hsüan.'[15] This title is still on his tombstone in Qufu, the quiet town visited by many an emperor who had also personally offered him sacrifice here.[16]

In my opinion, Confucius did not merely gain a new status as uncrowned king. He too was made into a paradigm, elevated to an ideal type, that of a sage who was never a king. On the one hand, he became the model for the 'ten thousand generations', the model of a wise teacher, as well as an ideal for the ruler, the role model for both teachers and rulers, perhaps for everyone, much more than legendary figures like Yao and Shun ever could be.

But how were rulers to emulate him, if he himself was never one of them, and lacked the experience of rulership? Here, the Confucian response would be simple. For benevolent government, it was not experience of governing that counted, but the possession of the virtue of benevolence, or humaneness (*jen*[b]). For this, no one else could measure up to the sage from Qufu.

And so went the premise for a Confucian education, one that was to produce wise rulers as well as ministers. It would be a general education, indeed a moral education, shifting from the ancient system of education for a warrior nobility, to an education based on the alleged writings of Confucius himself, considered the fount of wisdom. 'The gentleman is not a utensil (*ch'i*[b] / *qi*)', Confucius had said. And so it would be.

[14] The reference is to Analects 3:24, which says: 'Heaven is going to use the Master as a wooden-tongued bell.' See Fung, *History*, vol. 1, pp. 128–9.
[15] '*Ta-ch'eng chih-sheng wen-hsüan wang.*' Wen-hsüan translates this as 'proclaiming culture'.
[16] See John K. Shryock, *The Origin and Development of the State Cult of Confucius: An Introductory Study* (New York: The Century Co., 1932), pp. 167–77.

How was an entire state to be administered by a few moral principles governing human relationships? The answer is: by a constant effort to keep to the model of late antiquity, and of the patriarchal kinship system of the early Chou times, even if political feudalism soon fell apart. And so, an entire state and society was made to serve the ancestral cult, as a huge extended family. New dynastic founders invented semi-divine ancestors, to whom they offered this cult and from whom they sought to derive more legitimacy. The cult itself provided the glue that kept clan and society together, keeping all individuals in their proper place, the men as fathers or sons, as superiors or subjects, and the women as the men's mates and helpers, as collaborators who provided sons to maintain the cult, 'to keep the incense burning' in front of the ancestral tablets, as the saying goes.

We are not certain that this was Confucius' own intention, he who played a role in the transformation of his own society, turning the descendants of warriors like himself into intellectuals concerned with pursuing the good. But it became the direction of an entire state and society during much of China's history. And so, the more time passed, the more Confucianism became the pillar of a patriarchal clan society – that looked more to the past for guidance than to the future for direction.

In appropriating the sage-king paradigm, and making Confucius the uncrowned king, Han philosophers did not cease to expect of kings the conduct of sages. Countless moral exhortations were made by Confucian ministers to their sovereigns, and usually always by making reference to the legendary Yao and Shun as the ultimate royal role models. But the consequence of such appropriation is that (1) everyone can become a king, and (2) philosopher-sages have in some sense replaced kings as paradigmatic human beings, as mediators between the two orders, whether we call them human and natural (or cosmic), or human and divine.

THE KINGSHIP PARADIGM IN TAOIST PHILOSOPHY

The Taoist text *Lao-tzu* demonstrates a certain ambivalence when it comes to the topic of the sage. It denigrates the Confucian concept, blaming social evils on the moral distinctions between benevolence and righteousness. Its aim seems to be that of purifying the mind, and returning the mind to its pristine state of indeterminacy:

Exterminate the sage, discard the wise,
And the people will benefit a hundredfold;
Exterminate benevolence, discard rectitude,
And people will again be filial;
Exterminate ingenuity, discard profit,
And there will be no more thieves and bandits.   (ch. 19)[17]

Certainly, the Taoists disagree with the assessment of the Confucians and Mohists concerning ancient sages. The names of Yao,
Shun and Yu come up frequently in *Chuang-tzu*, but are used
ironically to illustrate the unnatural preference for virtue over a long
life, or the unwholesome practice of governing with rewards and
punishments.[18] Taoists prefer to name other ancients as sages.
Prominent among these is the Yellow Emperor, mythical ancestor of
the Chinese people. By naming such, they are appealing to someone
even more ancient than Yao and Shun, whose institutions they
criticised.

Surprisingly however, Taoist writers from Chuang-tzu on usually
represent Confucius as a sage, while using him as a mouthpiece for
Taoist wisdom, sometimes in self-deprecatory irony, sometimes in
genuine Taoist reflection. We may therefore speak of them as
'reinventing' Confucius, making him into their own preferred image
and likeness. Eventually, with the emergence of Taoist religion, the
figure of Lao-tzu once more surfaced, not only as a sage, but also as
a deity figure, the incarnate Tao, and a transcendent symbol of this
Tao. And, with all this, he also served as a political messiah who
would bring peace to the world.

The Taoist sage: an ambiguous paradigm

'The sage keeps to the work that consists of doing nothing (*wu-wei*)
and practises the teaching that uses no words' (ch. 2).[19]

The term *wu-wei* literally means non-action. It does not signify the
absence of action, but rather, acting without artificiality, also without
over-action, without attachment to action itself. It may also signify
Taoist meditation or contemplation, that is, an exercise that resembles doing nothing, even if it involves total concentration of one's
being.

---

[17] Lau, *Lao Tzu*, 75.
[18] *Chuang-tzu*, 5:3–4; Watson (trans.), *Complete Works*, pp. 130–1.
[19] Adapted from Lau, *Lao Tzu*, p. 58.

By a superior wisdom, the sage is no longer affected emotionally by the changes of this world. He has not lost his sensibility, but he has risen above it. Such acceptance of the natural indicates an attitude of equanimity regarding life and death, rather than the desire solely to prolong one's life. This theme is much more prominent in *Chuang-tzu* than in *Lao-tzu*.

Perhaps we may use these words from *Chuang-tzu*, put into the mouth of Confucius, to describe this attitude among Taoist philosophers:

> Such men as they. . . wander beyond the [accepted] realm (*fang*); men like me wander within it. Beyond and within can never meet . . . They look upon life as a swelling tumor . . . , and upon death as the draining of a sore or the bursting of a boil. To men such as these, how could there be any question of putting life first or death last . . . ? Idly they roam beyond the dust and dirt; they wander free and easy in the service of inaction. Why should they fret and fuss about the ceremonies (*li*ᵃ) of the vulgar world and make a display for the ears and eyes of the common herd?[20]

Life is like a tumour, and death resembles the bursting of a boil. These are hardly beautiful metaphors. They are invoked to shock the reader, to communicate a sense of transcendence of both life and death. Indeed, *Lao-tzu* suggests a measure of asceticism, of withdrawal from the world – its pleasures, and even its cherished values. And while *Lao-tzu* also speaks of survival, it was religious Taoism that became so involved in seeking longevity and even immortality.

According to *Lao-tzu*, it is the person who can take care of his own life and body who should become ruler of the state. For,

> He who values his body more than dominion of the empire can be entrusted with the empire.
> He who loves his body more than dominion over the world can be given the custody of the world. (ch. 13)[21]

Is this Taoist sage ruler also a shaman? *Lao-tzu* is not clear about it. The emphasis on taking care of the body is accompanied by advice on governing. This appears initially devious and manipulative, disillusioning those who might regard the text as merely contemplative:

---

[20] *Chuang-tzu* 3:10–11; Watson (trans.), *Complete Works*, pp. 86–7.
[21] Adapted from Lau, *Lao Tzu*, p. 69.

In governing the people, the sage empties their minds but fills
their bellies, weakens their wills but strengthens their bones.
He always keeps them innocent of knowledge and free from
desire, so that the clever never dare to act.   (ch. 2)[22]

But *Lao-tzu* does not really differentiate between the mind of the
people and that of the sage. After all, 'The sage has no mind of his
own. He takes as his mind the mind of the people' (ch. 49).[23] This
one sentence has made Lao-tzu a favourite in times of popular
discontent.

Lao-tzu also offers political teachings, ostensibly to the ruler, and
these are the most controversial. Interestingly, the earliest extant text
of *Lao-tzu* that has been unearthed (1973) gives the chapters of
practical application under the heading of *te / de* before those more
general ones under the heading of *tao*; this fact is supposed to
highlight the practical and political use of the text during Han
times.[24]

We come now to the practical part of *Lao-tzu*, to the *way* of living
according to the Way. I refer here to its 'power' (*te*), that by which
the universal Tao becomes particular. It is the power of the natural,
of simplicity, even of weakness. Yet it teaches the lesson of survival,
of how to keep one's own integrity in a time of disorder. This is
possibly the most important practical lesson of Taoist philosophy,
and has had immense importance in the development of Taoist
religion.

Politically, Chuang-tzu is usually described as a hermit who values
life over the uncertainties of government service. But a closer
reading of the text, especially of the sections included in the 'inner
chapters', yields a different impression. Instead of a serene recluse,
remote from the affairs of human society, we can discern a man
passionately opposed to the laws of the time, both ritual and penal,
for causing so much senseless suffering and pain. This is my personal
interpretation of Chuang-tzu's preoccupation with those men
maimed and crippled by the law of the land for some one or another
offence. This is also apparent in a discussion of imperfect animals
and humans that cannot be offered in sacrifice.

In the Chieh sacrifice, oxen with white foreheads, pigs with turned-up
snouts, and men with piles cannot be offered to the river[-god]. This is

---

[22] Adapted from Lau, ibid., p. 58.   [23] Ibid., p. 110.
[24] Consult *Mawangdui Hanmu boshu: Laozi* (The Silk Manuscript of *Lao-tzu* unearthed at
Mawangdui), ed. by the Committee of Organisation of the Finds (Beijing: Wenwu, 1976).

something all the shamans (*wu-chu*) know, and hence they consider them inauspicious creatures. But the Holy Man for the same reason considers them highly auspicious.[25]

While it would be natural to associate the application of penal law with the Legalists, the text *Chuang-tzu* also blames the Confucians and Mohists for their insensitivity to human suffering.

In the world today, the victims of the death penalty lie heaped together, the bearers of cangues tread on each other's heels, the sufferers of punishment are never out of each other's sight. And now come the Confucians and the Mohists, waving their arms, striding into the very midst of the fettered and manacled men . . . Who can convince me that sagely wisdom is not in fact the wedge that fastens the cangue, that benevolence and righteousness are not in fact the lop and lock of these fetters and manacles?[26]

Chuang-tzu refers with respect to the ancient kings, whose knowledge 'encompassed Heaven and Earth', whose abilities 'outshone all within the four seas'. They did not act (*wu-wei*) and the world was governed.[27] But he does not appear to think only of rulers as sages. Also according to him, the sage is a contemplative, who keeps moving and yet remains still. Indeed, his mind in stillness is 'the mirror of heaven and earth'.[28]

With obvious amusement, he describes the sage's relationship with the cosmos, '[The sage] leans on the sun and moon, tucks the universe under his arm, merges himself with things, leaves the confusion and muddle as it is, and looks on slaves as exalted . . . He takes part in the ten thousand things and achieves simplicity in oneness.'[29]

There are passages in *Chuang-tzu* that purport to offer conversations between Confucius and Lao-tzu. In one case, Confucius found Lao-tzu perfectly motionless, just after he had finished washing his hair, which was spread over the shoulders to dry. On being asked what was happening to give him this solitary look, Lao-tzu explains that his mind was wandering 'in the Beginning of Things'. He goes on to explain that such wandering 'means to attain Perfect Beauty and Perfect Happiness. [And] he who attains Perfect Beauty and Perfect Happiness may be called a Perfect Man.'[30]

---

[25] *Chuang-tzu* 2:14a; Watson (trans.), *Complete Works*, pp. 65–6.
[26] *Chuang-tzu* 4:17a–b; Watson (trans.), *Complete Works*, p. 118.
[27] Watson (trans.), *Complete Works*, p. 145.   [28] Watson (trans.), *Complete Works*, p. 142.
[29] *Chuang-tzu*, sect. 2, 1:22b; Eng. trans. adapted from Watson, *Complete Works*, p. 47.
[30] *Chuang-tzu*, sect. 21, 7:18a; Eng. trans. adapted from Watson (trans.), *Complete Works*, p. 225.

As Confucius pursues the subject, Lao-tzu continues his exposition:

In this world, the ten thousand things come together in the One, and if you can find that One and become identical with it, then your four limbs and hundred joints will become dust and sweepings; life and death, beginning and end will be mere day and night, and nothing whatever can confound you – certainly not the trifles of gain or loss, good or bad fortune.[31]

The Tao, after all, is not a thing. It transcends all things, even if it is present in all things. It cannot be seen, heard, or described. To be one with the Tao, one has to go beyond distinctions and desires. Ontologically, this means that one has to become united with that non-being or nothingness (wu^c) which precedes all beings. Spiritually, one has to be without selfish desires, in one word, selfless.

Interestingly, the third-century neo-Taoist Wang Pi exalted Confucius above Lao-tzu as a *Taoist* sage, that is, as someone who achieved union with the eternal, indeterminate Tao. Other Taoists, however, would exalt Lao-tzu above the sage-figure; they would deify him.

Lao Tzu as messiah figure

The Taoist movements of the Han times have demonstrated certain millenarian and apocalyptic characteristics that resemble those that have been known in the West, even if the ideologies are different.[32]

We are discussing a religion that has maintained a belief in the supernatural, not only as *powers*, but also as *beings*. A trinity of deities evolved, which assumed different names in different periods. And while Confucius just missed deification, Lao-tzu early became a Taoist deity, and received animal sacrifices from Emperor Huan at court in Loyang (166 CE). Later we hear of the Primal Celestial (Yüan-shih T'ien-tsun), the supreme ruler Tao (T'ai-shang Tao-chün), a personification of the concept itself, and of the divine ruler Lao-tzu (T'ai-shang Lao-chün) presiding over a pantheon of lesser deities including mythical figures and deified human beings. Indeed, it appears that long after the fading of the Western Queen Mother as the expected one, the divinised Lao-tzu projected a messianic thrust, as an awaited political saviour.[33]

---

[31] Ibid, p. 226.   [32] Schipper, 'Millénarismes', pp. 31–2.

[33] A manuscript of the *Lao-tzu pien-hua ching* (The Classic of the transformations of Lao-tzu), discovered at Tun-huang, possibly dates to the early seventh century, although parts of it might have been much earlier; see Anna Seidel, *La Divinisation de Lao-tseu dans le Taoïsme de Han* (Paris: École Française d'Extrême-Orient, 1969), pp. 59–128.

The *Classic of the Transformations of Lao-tzu* elevates Lao-tzu to the status of a personified supreme principle, as the origin of all things, and the law of their mutation.

> He is the sublime essence of spontaneity, the root of the Tao.
> He is the father and mother of the doctrine,
> The root of heaven and Earth . . .
> The sovereign of all deities.[34]

Time and again, Lao-tzu is said to have appeared in the guise of counsellor to the sage-kings of old. Indeed, many historical sages were but reappearances of Lao-tzu himself. And the text ends with allusions to the misery of the common people and the general atmosphere of revolt against the Han dynasty.

With the beginning of the Celestial Masters sect, Lao-tzu no longer appeared as a worthy sage, but only in the glory of a supreme deity, the personification of the Tao, with his throne on Mount K'un-lun, and with the earthly Celestial Master as his representative. Although the millenarian movements did not disappear, we have evidence pointing to the successive Heavenly Masters as believing that they had the authority from on high of legitimating each dynasty, by promising the support of the Lord Lao.

The regionally diverse origins of the Taoist religion reveal a common shamanic character, manifest in claims of revelations through trance, and of powers of magical or faith-healing, which were much more important than any quest for immortality. First, an obscure figure Yü Chi, sometimes called Kan Chi (early 2nd cent. CE), probably of Shantung, claimed to have received from the spirits a book called the *T'ai-p'ing ch'ing-ling shu* (The Book of Pure Commands of the Great Peace), with teachings influenced by Yin–Yang and Five Agents theories, and a new method for commanding spirits to bring blessings and heal sickness. It also has a soteriological thrust, with warnings of impending disasters in the loss of cosmic and sociopolitical harmony.[35]

Yü's sect, called the Great Peace sect (*T'ai-p'ing Tao*), active in what is today the provinces of Kiangsu and Chekiang, concentrated on the healing of the sick with charms and water, and prayer assemblies where incense was used. His popularity drew ire from the

---

[34] Anna K. Seidel, 'The Image of the Perfect Ruler in Early Taoist Messianism: Lao Tzu and Li Hung', *History of Religions* 9 (1969–70), p. 223.

[35] This text is no longer extant; we have today the *T'ai-p'ing ching* (Classic of the Great Peace), which is considered to be a later version of that earlier text.

warlord of the Kiangsu area, and he was killed around 200 CE. However, his followers continued to pray to him, claiming that he had not died, but had become an Immortal. The text he left behind influenced a younger contemporary (although the two might never have met), called Chang Ling or Chang Tao-ling – founder of the Celestial Masters sect – as well as the later founders of the Ling-pao and Mao-shan sects.[36]

In the late second century, the T'ai-p'ing rebellion, also named the 'Yellow Turbans' revolt after the headgear worn by its followers, broke out in the name of a messianic king called Huang-Lao Chün (Yellow Emperor and Lao-tzu rolled into one as Ruler). This was at the time while Lao-tzu was allegedly appearing to the sect founder Chang Tao-ling. Possibly, the *T'ai-p'ing-ching* originated in the circle of those individuals who attempted to influence the ruler in the direction of reform during the Han dynasty. Their lack of success led then to the revolt (184–215), involving hundreds of thousands of Taoists in eastern China and spreading to a large part of the country.[37]

The year 184 was *chia-tzu* in the Chinese sexagenarian calendar, marking the beginning of a new sixty-year cycle. But Han time-keepers who watched out for special events based their calculations more on the *yin* and *yang* system of the Book of Changes, which predicts a total destruction after certain long periods, when the *yang* is exhausted. What was to follow is a kind of 'end of the world' scenario, accompanied by a new era of justice and peace, with the arrival of a Messiah, a new Lao-tzu, sometimes called Li Hung.[38]

Together with these ideas, talismanic writings also advanced the belief that Taoists constituted an elect group (*t'ien-jen / tianren*), literally, heavenly men), also called the Pure, the Very Pure, the Great Pure. Stories abounded as to how this faithful group would be transported to a special heaven, before the apocalypse and for their own protection, to await the rebirth of the new universe, as the seeds of a new people, sometimes said to be 360,000 strong.[39]

While the Yellow Turbans revolt failed, Taoist messianism became the inspiration for successive movements of political protest, orga-nised by secret societies throughout history, and the reason why the

---

[36] Consult *San-kuo chih*, K'ai-ming ed., 1:117c; *Hou-Han shu*, K'ai-ming ed., 6:123b; Fukui Kōjun, *Dōkyō*, sect. 1, ch. 2–3; sect. 2, ch. 2.
[37] Seidel, 'The Image', 228–30.   [38] Schipper, 'Millénarismes', p. 40.   [39] Ibid, p. 45.

religion has always been regarded until today with suspicion by the various governments.

Taoist messianism is evident in the *T'ai-p'ing ching* (Scripture of Great Peace), dated to the first century BCE. Even if only extant in an incomplete and partially restored version (7th cent. CE), it is sometimes regarded as the most important text in religious Taoism after the *Lao-tzu*. It looks forward to a future epoch of Great Peace, and teaches a doctrine of salvation. Its saviour is a 'divine man' in possession of a 'celestial book' that teaches the return to ideal government, while awaiting the arrival of the fullness of time, the Great Peace. The divine man has the mandate of passing the revealed words on to the 'true man' (*chen-jen / chenren*), a prophet figure who is to transmit the texts to a ruler of high virtue. This prince is to rule by the Tao and its power. He is to be a benevolent ruler, governing with the help of his ministers and the people at large, careful to maintain harmony within the realm but slow to punish.

Actually, Taoist philosophy received a new impetus soon after the end of the Han. As rulers were being replaced by their erstwhile ministers usurping the throne, intellectuals were not only reflecting on the meaning of the ruler–minister bond, but also wondering whether the sage Shun had also usurped the throne from the sage Yao. 'We now know how these things happen,' some of them were saying.

Commentaries were written on the Book of Changes, *Lao-tzu*, and *Chuang-tzu* – the former two by Wang Pi, who regarded the Tao to be the absolute, and the ruler to govern by non-action, allowing all things to manage themselves, the latter by Hsiang Hsiu and Kuo Hsiang, whose Tao meant absolutely nothing at all, and whose political views were similar to Wang's.[40]

Some questioned the need for any ruler. Hsi K'ang, for example, criticised the pomp and wealth surrounding rulership, and asserted that a sage would rule the world with reluctance, taking 'the ten thousand things as his own mind'. Juan Chi went one step further, advocating the abolition of rulers and governments.[41]

---

[40] Consult Mou Tsung-san, *Ts'ai-hsing yü hsüan-li* (Natural ability and philosophical meaning) (Taipei: Student Bookstore, 1983), chs 3–6.

[41] Consult Donald Holzman, *Poetry and Politics: The Life And Works of Juan Chi*, A.D. 210–263 (Cambridge University Press, 1976), especially ch. 10; Mou Tsung-san, *Ts'ai-hsing*, ch. 8–9; Jung Chao-tsu, *Wei-Chin te tzu-jan chu-yi* (The naturalism of the Wei-Chin times) (Taipei: Commercial Press, 1970), ch. 2.

After all, *Chuang-tzu* says: 'Cudgel and cane the sages and let the thieves and bandits go their way; then the world will be at last well ordered!'[42] And, for these latter-day followers of the Taoist philosophers, the way of 'sageliness within and kingliness without' can be reinterpreted to mean the dissolution of individual self-consciousness and collective self-consciousness, in order to reach harmony on a higher level.[43]

Religious Taoism and political legitimation

In offering services to the state in power, an institutional religion is no longer promoting an alternative to the established order, as when it is inspiring messianic faith in a saviour yet to arrive. Rather, it is helping to establish itself, which often happens when the society is in relative good order. Institutional Taoism helped occasionally to legitimise the state, and, in turn, enjoyed its protection. The best-known occasion was in 442, when K'ou Ch'ien-chih, made the celestial master by Emperor T'ai-wu of the T'o-pa Wei (311–535), initiated the emperor as a Taoist, presenting him as well with a talismanic script (*lu*b) that confirmed his Mandate.[44] Although the investiture was theoretically that of a Taoist priest, it had in this case the significance of political legitimation, since the *lu*b has been described in Confucian apocryphal writing as a magic script, like the River Chart and the Book of Lo, which confirms the Royal Mandate, and since the initiated was the actual ruler. Following this, the emperor also declared Taoism to be the state religion. And although this declaration was later rescinded by his immediate successors, two of these continued to receive the Taoist investiture.

Under the T'ang dynasty, Taoism served once more to legitimise the new state, when the imperial house, in 620 CE, claimed descent from Lao-tzu and established a temple in his honour as divine ancestor at the place where he allegedly revealed the text *Lao-tzu*. Taoism was placed before Confucianism, and Buddhism was degraded as a foreign religion. Not that Confucianism, with the great state sacrifices it supported, was forgotten. Emperor Kao-tsung offered the *feng* and the *shan* sacrifices early in his reign and

---

[42] Eng. trans. adapted from Watson (trans.), *Complete Works*, p. 109.

[43] Yü Ying-shih, *Chung-kuo chih-shih chieh-ts'eng shih-lun*, pp. 316–19.

[44] Wei Shou, comp., *Wei-shu*, K'ai-ming ed., ch. 114, chapter on Buddhism and Taoism, p. 299c.

permitted his wife, the Empress Wu, to participate in these offerings, thus setting a precedent for her role as full partner to him as Son of Heaven and chief priest. She would later seek more, becoming the only female ruler, '*T'ien-tzu*', in her own right, after his death. But she preferred Buddhism during her own reign (690–704). After the T'ang restoration, Emperor Hsüan-tsung (r. 713–55) became the first ruler to write a commentary on the *Lao-tzu*. He also created a system of Taoist education and became a priest himself in 748. Under Emperor Wu-tsung (r. 840–6), Lao-tzu's birthday became a public holiday celebrated for three days, while Buddhism suffered the worst persecution in history.

The Sung imperial house also sought Taoist legitimation. Emperor Chen-tsung (r. 997–1023) claimed to have received miraculously certain celestial texts in his palace, which had previously been announced to him in a dream by a divine person. Reportedly found in the palace, these heavenly texts praised the ruler for his virtues and confirmed the legitimacy of his dynasty. In return, the emperor ordered the celebration of Taoist rituals and wrote a commentary on the *Lao-tzu*. Following Emperor Hsüan-tsung's footsteps, he also offered the *feng* and *shan* sacrifices at Mount T'ai, and built temples throughout the country, dedicated to the Three Pure Ones of the Taoist religion, who were to remain the objects of worship until our own days. Apparently, he also received certain golden tablets that gave witness to the perfect accord between the ruler on earth and the Lord-on-High.[45] Emperor Hui-tsung (r. 1101–26), another great devotee, wrote one more commentary on the *Lao-tzu*, and claimed to have received some new revelations from a Taoist deity in whose honour he built temples throughout the country.

A new Taoist sect influenced by Buddhist ideas of monasticism and celibacy, the Perfect Truth, contributed to peace in the country when its leader, Ch'iu Ch'u-chi (1148–1227), visited Genghis Khan in Central Asia to advise him to spare the lives of his conquered subjects. In return, he was put in charge of all the religions of the realm (1222). But Taoist–Buddhist rivalry led to the burning of the Taoist canon in 1281, although the Mongol Emperor Cheng-tsung (r. 1295–1307) would invite a priest to celebrate for him the Taoist

[45] Consult also W. Eichhorn, *Beitrag zur rechtlichen Stellung des Buddhismus und Taoismus im Sung-Staat* (Leiden: E. J. Brill, 1968), pp. 17–18, 119–20; M. Kaltenmark, '*Ling-pao*: Note sur un terme du taoïsme religieux', *Mélanges publiés par l'Institut des Hautes Études Chinoises*, vol. 2 (Paris: Presses Universitaires de France, 1960), pp. 573–4.

chiao sacrifice at his accession to the throne. The Ming founder (Chu Yüan-chang, r. 1368–98) had been a humble Buddhist monk in his youth, but as ruler preferred Taoism. He was author of still another commentary on the *Lao-tzu*, and dedicated a temple to the deified philosopher-sage in Nanking, his capital. His successors moved the capital to Peking (Beijing) but continued to patronise Taoism. The situation changed only with the Manchu conquest in 1662.

One might say that the religious support offered to a secular ruler 'anoints' the ruler figuratively as a messiah already come, perhaps even as a return of Lao-tzu, together with the claims of blood descent, such as from Lao-tzu himself.

Taoism appears much more ambivalent than Buddhism *vis-à-vis* the ruler. In fact, the Buddhist religion prided itself on its independence from the state, and Buddhist monks in China – as elsewhere – refused to make ritual obeisance to the rulers. This became a church–state problem that the state referred to an eminent monk, Hui-yüan (334–417), for resolution. Hui-yüan acknowledged that the Buddhist laity should abide by the customary etiquette governing such matters, but argued that the monk does not 'bow down before a king', since he has left the household life, and need not follow the rules of court etiquette.[46]

THE CAKRAVARTIN IN THE BUDDHIST PARADIGM

But there is a Chinese Buddhist messianism as well as a Taoist or Confucian variety. For this, we have to examine its origins in Buddhist political thought.

The Sanskrit term referring to an ideal universal king is *cakravartin*, literally, a monarch whose chariot wheels turn freely. Implied is a sense of the universality of his rule: that it pertains to creatures everywhere. Buddhist literature has spoken of the religion's founder in similar terms, presumably because religious truth transcends regional limitations and applies to all people. While the term refers to an ideal, the most appropriate person to become a universal monarch is presumably someone who is an actual king, who could extend his rule through martial and diplomatic skill. Besides, since Buddhism believes especially in the power of its religious message, it

---

[46] Hui-yüan, 'Sha-men pu-ching wang-che lun' (On monks not making obeisance to kings), is included in the sixth-century work, compiled by Seng-yu, *Hung-ming chi*, SPPY ed., 5:5b–6a.

also maintains that the founder, Śākyamuni, although born in a royal family, chose not to assume political leadership, but rather to guide all people through the power of his teachings and virtues.[47]

The Buddhist concept of kingship developed in part in opposition to the Hindu doctrine of royal divinity issuing laws and decrees. Instead, a Buddhist story speaks of the choice in assembly of the most handsome of those present, as the *Mahāsammata* ('The Great Approved One') to protect the people's rights to life and property in return for a share of their crops and herds, as well as their most beautiful daughters for his harem.[48] One is also left with the impression that the king is regarded as a father figure by his people, who are to respect and obey him.

A most important figure in Buddhist messianism is Śākyamuni's Buddha-successor, Maitreya, or the Buddha of the Future. He is believed to be awaiting rebirth in the Tuṣita heaven, and since Buddhist time is calculated in extremely long aeons, he is usually taken to have to wait for millions of years. When reborn, however, it is believed that he will come also as *cakravartin* or the universal monarch and usher in an era of unlimited peace and prosperity. But while Western scholars sometimes call him a messiah, his mission is not socially or politically oriented.

Does that not make the historical Buddha and even the Buddha of the Future a Confucius-like figure, dominating in the realm of doctrine rather than politics? I would say so. But popular piety has developed other expectations, in the context of a Buddhist understanding of time and eschatology.

Buddhist time is essentially cyclical, much more so than Confucian time, with the universe passing through endless sequence of cosmic periods (*kalpas*) during which it comes to full growth only to begin to disintegrate. It is then destroyed in a cataclysm that spares only the highest heavens and those beings reborn there, who are to be once more reborn on lower levels of existence according to individual karmic destinies.

True, in orthodox Buddhism, there is little room for the development of ideas of political messianism, as in Taoism and even

---

[47] See William K. Mahony, 'Cakravartin', *The Encyclopedia of Religion*, vol. 3, pp. 6–7; Indumati Armelin, *Le Roi détenteur de la roue solaire en révolution, 'cakravartin': selon le brahmanisme et selon le bouddhisme* (Paris: P. Geuthner, 1975).

[48] A. L. Basham, 'Kingship in Hinduism and Buddhism', in A. L. Basham (ed.), *Kingship in Asia and Early America* (Mexico City: El Colegio de Mexico, 1981), pp. 121–2.

Confucianism. But even within the Buddhist belief system, as we have noted, the talk is of a perfect ruler as *cakravartin*, whose reign is characterised by universal peace, longevity, and material well-being. And popular expectations are such that a political messiah figure often has to be reinvented. This eventually happened in China to devotion to Maitreya, which transformed him from a benign teacher into a powerful messiah king. We are now speaking of the development of a new Maitreya-cult with strong messianic overtones, which became influential from the fifth century on, to continue until modern times.

Whereas, in the orthodox Buddhist writings, the Maitreya is expected to come when the world is flourishing, and already ruled by a wide and benevolent king, in some non-canonical Chinese texts he is represented as a militant saviour descending in a time of chaos to cleanse the world of evil and establish a purified community. Already in the seventh and eighth centuries, individuals are known to have led political uprisings in Maitreya's name.[49]

The Bodhisattva as humane king

Already, during the second half of the fifth century, a new Buddhist scripture was circulating in North China. This was the *Prajñāpāramitā* (Perfection of Wisdom) *Sutra for Humane Kings Who Wish to Protect their States*, in short, the 'Scripture for Humane Kings' (*Jen-wang ching*). The title suggests its claim of being a 'perfection of wisdom' sutra bequeathed by the Buddha to humane kings as an antidote to the impending apocalyptic end of the preaching of Dharma, or, put more briefly, the 'last days'. Intended to serve as a charter for Buddhist state cults throughout East Asia, it proclaims many powers, including avoiding illness, bringing about rain, and preventing fires. And interestingly, it addresses itself not to monks and nuns, but to all the kings of states.[50]

---

[49] Joseph M. Kitagawa, 'The Many Faces of Maitreya: A Historian of Religion's Reflections', and Daniel L. Overmyer, 'Messenger, Savior, and Revolutionary: Maitreya in Chinese Popular Religious Literature of the Sixteenth and Seventeenth Centuries', in Alan Sponberg & Helen Hardacre (eds.), *Maitreya, the Future Buddha* (Cambridge University Press, 1988), pp. 16-17; 113-15.

[50] *Jen-wang hu-kuo po-je po-lo-mi-tuo ching* (The Perfection of Wisdom Scripture for Humane Kings), *T* 8.246 (2 ch.). For a discussion of the text, see M. W. De Visser, *Ancient Buddhism in Japan: Sutras and Ceremonies in Use in the Seventh and Eighth Centuries* A.D. *and Their History in Later Times*, 2 vols. (Leiden: E. J. Brill, 1935), vol. 1, pp. 116-42. I wish here to acknowledge the contributions of Charles D. Orzech to this topic, at the Paris conference, June, 1995.

In spite of the claims of its having come from the Buddha himself, the *Scripture for Humane Kings* presumably originated in China, notwithstanding its two versions: a Kumārajīva translation of the fifth century, and an eighth-century version by the monk Amoghavajra, a proponent of Tantric Buddhism who worked under imperial auspices.[51]

The scripture itself configures Buddhist notions of the world, the path, and authority in ways that indicate its dual Chinese-Buddhist parentage, even reinterpeting the *bodhisattva* path in response to specific Chinese circumstances of the time. Responding to the main question of how rulers are to protect their states, the Buddha first describes how the ten stages of bodhisattva-hood are to be protected, especially through the proper contemplation (*kuan / guan*) of reality, a contemplation that transcends all opposites, culminating in the perception of the 'edge of reality'.

The scripture offers a typology of 'seed-natures' or 'lineages', inspired by Yogācāra works. Its fourth chapter presents a discussion of the Two Truths, a topic hotly debated in the fourth and fifth centuries. And its fifth chapter addresses the question of how 'humane kings' protect and cultivate their states, while chapter 6 gives a brief series of miracles or wonders, characteristic of Mahāyāna scriptures. Chapter 7 returns to the Bodhisattva path, with predictions of the troubling End of Dharma, as well as rituals to forestall such. Chapter 8, the last, reiterates the dire prophecies and details the deeds of rulers which lead to calamities, once again admonishing all to keep their obligations and protect the Buddha's teaching.

The very term *humane kings* is a Confucian notion, and the scripture possesses only a small sprinkling of transliterations from Sanskrit to give it a foreign flavour. The language and style point to the fifth century, and we have evidence of its use under Emperor Wu (r. 557–9) of Ch'en and the last ruler of his line, Hou-chu (r. 582–8), in south China. The latter installed the first T'ien-t'ai patriarch, Chih-yi, at the Kuang-wu monastery and ordered him to lecture on this scripture. Several decades later, the second T'ang emperor, T'ai-tsung (r. 626–49), would set aside the twenty-seventh day of the month each time for the recitation of this scripture, in order to

---

[51] Consult *T* 8.245 and *T* 8.246 respectively. A partial English translation is available in Edward Conze, trans., *The Short Prajñāparamitā Texts* (London: Luzac, 1973), pp. 165–83.

secure benefits for the state and its officials. Some time after that, during the aftermath to the An Lu-shan rebellion, the devoutly Buddhist Empeor Tai-tsung (r. 762–79) also invoked the protection and aid of the Buddha in an assembly in which he promised to perform appropriate rites and produce a new translation of the text.

Interestingly, when we look at the scripture, we discover – to no surprise – the lowly positions of kings in a Buddha's assembly, which first lists, in an ascending order, *bhikṣu* / *arhats*, *pratyekabuddhas* and *bodhisattvas*, comprising the three vehicles and their seed-natures. After that, it lists in descending order lay 'worthies' who keep the five precepts, women of pure faith who also keep the precepts, those in the seven 'worthy' stages, the nine *brahmadevas*, various gods and 'sons of heaven' (*t'ien-tzu*) of the realm of desire, the kings of the sixteen states (to whom the scripture is entrusted), and their entourages, and all other beings.

The ambivalent position of these kings obliges them to undertake pious acts as necessary first steps on the *bodhisattva* path, which allegedly will bring them to some kind of sagehood. Besides, the text suggests a basic kinship among all kings, the petty rulers, the great *cakravartins*, and also the advanced *bodhisattvas* and even Buddhas, who are also proclaimed kings. After all, there is a parallel to rulers who nurture and protect their states, and *bodhisattvas* who nurture and protect Buddhism. And what is basically expected of the petty kings is the protection of the *sangha* as Buddhist community, much as do mothers in their wombs which shelter, metaphorically, the *bodhisattvas* as embryos, to be born as Buddhas.

But the same scripture also proclaims that progress on the path of the *bodhisattvas*, which is also the path of kings, will turn back the last days, or the End of Dharma, in the vision of true emptiness and the edge of reality. In this way, the text seeks to reconcile the true nature of Buddhist teachings with what it can offer secular kings within its own doctrinal framework, thus joining kings and *bodhisattvas* in an interesting fraternity of purpose, while preaching humaneness or forbearance (*jen*[b]) as the principal virtue to be practised.

Buddhist monks had earlier challenged the authority of the state with regard to themselves, asserting that they were no longer under secular control. However, some of the most devout Buddhist sovereigns challenged the independence of the Buddhist community or *sangha*.

Such a ruler was the sixth-century Emperor Wu of the short-lived

Liang dynasty, established in the south. A military man, but familiar with the early classics, the new emperor looked back to the sage-kings of antiquity for political inspiration. He organised a bureaucracy roughly along the lines of the Institutes of Chou, together with a certain revival of ancient rites and music. His minister, Shen Yüeh, also formulated a model of historical progress, claiming that history developed and changed in response to the eternal principles of Buddhist Law revealed to a few select sages of Chinese antiquity as the conditions made it 'ripe' for them. Accordingly, Mahāyāna Buddhism was the ultimate revelation of the whole truth, about to be revealed to the Emperor, as the country was also being gradually prepared to embrace a vegetarian diet more suited to Buddhist beliefs of the potential Buddhahood of all sentient beings, as well as universal Buddhist compassion.[52]

We know ordinarily of two kinds of Buddhists: the ordained monks and the laity. With the Mahāyāna Buddhist affirmation of the lay *bodhisattva*, came the opportunity for a secular ruler to declare himself one such, creating thereby a third category, and a special one where the ruler was concerned. In 519, Emperor Wu designed for himself a special ritual and staged a grand ceremony in which he took the *bodhisattva* vows, and was ordained to the role. The ritual entailed a direct ordination, without the usual loud recitation of the precepts to be conferred. Thus the emperor was perceived as someone who had privileged access to universal truth, unlike the other members of the *sangha*, who were to attain it indirectly through observance of their rules and precepts.[53] In fact, the emperor's action placed himself above the *sangha*, uniting the religious and the secular realms in his own rule. In this sense, and using Buddhist doctrines, he became a sage-ruler.

Soon afterwards, the emperor abolished all animal sacrifices, substituting for these offerings of noodles and vegetables, in the imperial ancestral temple as well as at the suburban altars to Heaven and Earth. He also commissioned new ritual music, drawn from the Confucian classics. From time to time, he hosted huge vegetarian feasts called 'great assemblies open to all people', modelled on

---

[52] Shen Yüeh, *Jün-sheng lun*, in Tao-hsüan, *Kuang Hung-ming chi*, SPPY ed., 5:8b–9b. Consult Richard Mather, *The Poet Shen Yüeh (441–513), the Reticent Marquis* (Princeton University Press, 1988), pp. 138–40.

[53] On this topic, I wish to acknowledge the contributions of Andreas Janousch, at the Paris conference of June, 1995.

traditional court banquets, and centred on sutra lectures, renewal of
vows and the like, to enact the vision of a new community, including
both men and women. The numbers of people he hosted were
reported to be up to 500,000. In the presence of all, he renewed his
bodhisattva vows, and promised among other things to take upon
himself the sufferings of the beings in hell, dedicating his own merits
to people living in and out of his empire, and even to all beings in
the metaphysical Three Realms (*triloka*) of desire, form and formless-
ness. And all this, he emphasised, was to achieve oneness with all
sentient beings.[54]

And so, we have the vision of a Chinese *cakravartin*, which made of
a huge vegetarian feast a symbol of a universal assembly including
innumerable Buddhas and *bodhisattvas*, somewhat like one of those to
which the Buddha allegedly preached. Such an event elevated the
ruler's status, as the centre of a concentrically structured universe, in
a spiritual union with all sentient beings. It evoked the Confucian
vision of oneness with all things, while going far beyond it, if only
because, among other things, the Confucian view of life was more
linear and singular, without the ambivalent benefit of rebirth.

Here we should explain the Chinese cultural dilemma regarding a
suitable Buddhist diet. Although the Chinese have usually been
carnivorous, beliefs in rebirth pose an insurmountable obstacle to
their eating habit: the fear that they might be including in their diet
the flesh of their erstwhile ancestors, reborn in some lower form of
life.

The only female ruler in Chinese history, the seventh-century
Empress Wu (r. 684–704), relied on religious legitimation to establish
her power base. For example, she was offered an obviously fabricated white stone from the River Lo bearing these words: 'Sage
Mother [to] come [and rule] humankind; eternally prosperous [the]
empire.' [55] This was a reminder to people of the legendary Book of
Lo, which came to the sage-kings of old. But she made special use of
the *Mahāmegha* or *Great Cloud Sutra* (*Ta-yün-ching*), which asserts that
the Maitreya is to appear in a woman's form, to justify her own rule,

---

[54] Consult Paul Groner, 'The *Fan-wang ching* and Monastic Discipline in Japanese Tendai: A
Study of Annen's *Futsu jubosatsukai koshaku*', in Robert E. Buswell, Jr (ed.), *Chinese Buddhist
Apocrypha* (Honolulu: University of Hawaii Press, 1990), p. 256; Jacques Gernet, *Les Aspects
économiques du bouddhisme dans la société chinoise du Ve au Xe siècle* (Paris: École Française
d'Extrême-Orient, 1956), p. 258.

[55] R. W. L. Guisso, *Wu Tse-t'ien and the Politics of Legitimation in T'ang China* (Bellingham:
Western Washington University, 1978), p. 65.

and her sycophants made use of a commentary to demonstrate that this Maitreya reborn was none other than herself.[56] And she showed herself an eager claimant to be the *cakravartin* or Buddhist universal monarch as well. Indeed, she was a great patroness of the religion, making use of Buddhism for support and legitimation much as the T'ang emperors before her had used Taoism as a legitimation device. Her administrative competence won her sufficient support to govern the country during her own long life, until she finally decided to return the throne to a son, who revived the name of the T'ang dynasty.

In 699, Empress Wu invited the famous Hua-yen monk Fa-tsang to preach at the palace. Pointing to a statue of a golden lion in the palace, Fa-tsang used the metaphor of gold and lion to illustrate his teachings of the interdependence of all things. He reasons, according to Buddhist premises, that the gold and the lion come into being at the same time, each compatible with the other, with either one being the manifest, and the other being the latent. In Hua-yen philosophical terms, the manifest is *shih*[c] (phenomenal), and the latent is *li*[b] (noumenal, the principle), and each is present in the other, and in each and every part of the other.

If one contemplates the lion, then it is only a lion, and there is no gold about it . . . If one contemplates the gold, then there is only gold, and there is no lion about it . . . If one contemplates both, then both are manifest, and both are also hidden . . . The lion's eyes, ears, limbs, joints, and every single pore complete . . . Each and every hair contains unlimited lions.[57]

And so, he declares, just as the gold is in each and every part of the figure of the lion, so does the jewel decorating every loop of Indra's net reflect not only the image of every other jewel, but also all the multiple images reflected in each jewel. That is why 'One is all, and all is one' is the Chinese Buddhist expression for how all things are basically one, in spite of their myriad manifestations.[58] It is an expression that also entered neo-Confucian philosophical language. And while it teaches the transitoriness of all phenomena, it also points to a noumenal level, suggesting that the two actually interpenetrate.

---

[56] See Guisso, *Wu Ts'e-t'ien*, pp. 36–46.
[57] Chin-yüan, *Chin-shih-tzu chang yün-chien lei-chieh* (Explanations on the Golden Lion chapter) in *T* 45.1880, pp. 663a–67a. Eng. trans. in de Bary (ed.), *Sources*, pp. 371–3.
[58] Fung, *History*, vol. 2, p. 353.

And might it also point to the position of the ruler, the self-declared *cakravartin*, once more, at the centre of a concentrically structured universe, in spiritual union with all sentient beings?

To gain access to the spiritual universe, rulers built imitations of the early sacred tower (*ling-t'ai*). In the first century CE, Emperor Wu of the Western Han dynasty constructed a 'tower to communicate with Heaven' (*t'ung-t'ien-t'ai / tongtiantai*), a kind of *axis mundi* with Taoist connotations, where he wished also to receive spirits and immortals.[59]

On assuming imperial power, Empress Wu chose to call her dynasty the Chou, in conscious imitation of that period which became a norm for later times. She also built a grandiose *ming-t'ang*, with a very high *t'ien-t'ang / tiantang* that has been described as a 'sacred tower', a religious and political centre as well as an astronomical observatory.[60] She found it impossible, however, to change the deeply rooted Confucian prejudice favouring a male sovereign.

Buddhist Messianism in China has also propelled a relatively obscure *bodhisattva* into prominence. This is Candraprabhā-kumāra, best known for his role in a short sutra preserved in several Chinese versions of the late third century and later. The story told is that of a virtuous sixteen-year-old son, Yüeh-kuang t'ung-tzu (literally, the Boy Moonlight), who sought in vain to deter his depraved father from plotting to kill the Buddha. But the Buddha, being who he was, escaped death by miracle and converted the father.

Evidently, the motif of the filial son was attractive to the Chinese reader. And prophecies were added that the boy was to be reborn in China as a saintly ruler, Prince Moonlight. His name would be invoked by Emperor Wen, founder of the short-lived Sui dynasty (589–617), who proclaimed Buddhism a state religion, and once again by Empress Wu, who justified her rule by claiming to be the reborn Maitreya and/or the Prince Moonlight. In each of these two cases, it appears that textual evidence was mustered, with interpolations added to a 583-CE translation of the Indian text in which the boy appeared, and to the *Ratnameghasūtra*, where he is predicted to be

---

[59] *Shih-chi*, ch. 28, p. 114; see Antonino Forte, *Mingtang and Buddhist Utopias in the History of the Astronomic Clock: The Tower, Statue and Armillary Sphere Constructed by Empress Wu* (Rome: Istituto Italiano per il Medio e Estremo Oriente / Paris, École Française d'Extrême-Orient, 1988), p. 20.

[60] For the T'ang model, see Forte, ch. 1, especially pp. 19–20, 104–7, 122–3, 238–9.

reborn as a powerful female monarch in a country called Great China (Mahācīna).[61]

Somewhat later, the popular mid-fourteenth-century rebellion that overthrew the Mongol Yüan dynasty was associated in people's minds with the Maitreya figure as well as with the figure of the Iranian prophet Mani as Prince of Light. Very possibly, the two were confused as one by many followers, and the new Ming dynasty that began in 1368 took its name ('Bright') from the Prince of Light, also known sometimes as the Buddha of Light.

Even later, in the middle of the nineteenth century, Hung Hsiu-ch'üan claimed to be God's second son and Jesus' younger brother and led the T'ai-p'ing rebellion against a troubled Ch'ing dynasty. For a few years, he and his followers from southern China appeared ready to overthrow and replace the Manchu rulers. While they invoked a T'ai-p'ing vision with resonances in tradition, their messianism was inspired by Western Christianity, and their movement was ideologically anti-tradition.[62]

CONCLUSION

Each in its own way, Taoism and Buddhism appropriated the sage-king paradigm. Time and again, the figure of a divinised Lao-tzu, identified with some specific historical person, became the focus of messianic dreams and rebellions. On the other hand, as an institutional religion, Taoism played occasionally a legitimating role vis-à-vis the secular state.

The Taoist ideal of a ruler remained that of one who models his government on nature, which flourishes without anyone apparently doing very much, and that means, by governing through non-action, through 'small government'. In religious terms, this meant increasingly honouring the Taoist deities, especially the divinised Lao-tzu. And in return, religious Taoism could also offer assistance to those

---

[61] *Fo-shuo Yüeh-kuang t'ung-tzu ching* (The Scripture of Prince Moonlight), *T* 14.534. Consult Erik Zürcher, 'Prince Moonlight: Messianism and Eschatology in Early Medieval Chinese Buddhism', *T'oung Pao* 68 (1982), 1–14. Consult C. P. Fitzgerald, *The Empress Wu* (Melbourne: F. W. Cheshire, 1955).

[62] Consult Jonathan D. Spence, *God's Chinese Son: the Taiping Heavenly Kingdom of Hong Xiuquan*, (New York: Norton, 1996); Rudolf G. Wagner, *Reenacting the Heavenly Vision: the Role of Religion in the Taiping Rebellion* (Berkeley: Institute of East Asian Studies, University of California, 1982).

rulers who sought longevity, whether from herbal medicine, alchemical elixirs or yoga-like practices.

With Buddhism the picture is somewhat different. Buddhism is mainly interested in religious salvation rather than politics. Buddhist mysticism has a very personal character. Buddhist Maitreya beliefs had to be changed, even corrupted, to become messianic. And as an institutional religion, it had little interest in proclaiming an impending end of the world, since that would be an acknowledgement of its own corruption as well. It is interesting to see how the T'ang dynastic house – and the Sung after them – relied essentially on Taoism to legitimise their mandates.

In many of these legitimation attempts, scriptures had to be fabricated, or interpolations created, or para-normal phenomena reported, to make possible such claims. The legitimation process was more of a theatrical show, or a pubic-relations campaign, directed at a population whose loyalty was uncertain. And usually, even when Buddhism or Taoism was preferred as an ally for the throne, Confucianism continued to be maintained, especially through the study of its classics and the civil-service examinations. In naming her dynasty the Chou, even Empress Wu appealed to Confucian ideals of rulership. In this way, Confucianism worked together with Taoism and Buddhism to serve the state in all its needs. But then, Confucian expectations eventually persuaded the empress to return the throne to her son as the heir of the T'ang lineage.

And so: sage-kings never existed, but the *myth* of their existence in antiquity led to the sage-king ideal type or paradigm, which rulers sought to manipulate for the enhancement of their own positions. In doing so, they called alternately on Confucianism, Taoism and Buddhism for assistance, to invoke for them a higher power, that from which the mandate to rule presumably came. For their own part, Taoist and Buddhist monks, like Confucian scholars, attempted two things. They sought protection from the state while offering it their support. They also appropriated the sage-king ideal for their own use, *privatising* a paradigm that was previously in the public domain. While I do not say that Taoism and Buddhism would not have produced mystics had there not been a sage-king ideal, I think that under the circumstances, much of ethics and teachings on self-cultivation, as well as mystical philosophy, developed in China as a result of this private appropriation of a public legacy.

CHAPTER 8

All under Heaven: political power and the periphery

INTRODUCTION

Just as the government of . . . a household is modelled on the government of one's self . . . on account of similitude, [the Chinese] came to equate the notion of a state to that of a house or family, with the ruler . . . representing the head of the family, thus arguing by virtue of an analogy from a family to a civil society.[1]

The eighteenth-century German philosopher Christian Wolff is correct in his interpretation of Chinese political theory, as the Great Learning also demonstrates. And Wolff's works were read with admiration by Frederick II of Prussia, the European Enlightenment's model despot, a patron, for some time, of France's Voltaire, and like Wolff a friend of Chinese civilisation.

Enlightened despotism appears to have been a theory born of necessity, at a time when kings were all powerful. But there was no way to assure that a despotism, in Europe or China, would be enlightened. For China, the effects were and remain more serious, as the land area is large, and the population huge. We might add to geography and demography the dimension of time: the unusual dynamism of Chinese civilisation, and with it, the rule of the absolute monarchy, through history. Even in our own days, China's political behaviour behind a Bamboo Curtain and also otherwise has led to charges that it still considers itself centre of the world, refusing to accept norms from elsewhere.

If there are parallels, there are also differences with Western European civilisation. We find in China a uniquely coherent and integrated civilisation, ancient yet enduring, which developed more

---

[1] Christian Wolff, 'On the Philosopher King and the Ruling Philosopher,' sect 6. See Ching and Oxtoby, *Moral Enlightenment*, p. 195.

or less independently of other civilisations. With this came the consciousness of uniqueness and even superiority, a consciousness strengthened by the fact that the Chinese civilisation extended its benefits to the whole of East Asia. And, as the centre of its world, China had a low regard for all that is called foreign, also called barbarian. This recalls the custom in ancient Greece to call 'barbarian' what is not Greek. But Chinese culture has enjoyed a more continuous and less interrupted history over a larger continental land mass, and spread over to Japan, Korea and what is now Vietnam. Greek culture, by contrast, served more as an impetus for than as the actual content of what today we call Western civilisation.[2]

We have discussed the sage-king paradigm and its appropriation by philosophy, religion, and even exegesis. Even earlier on, in chapter one, we have assumed, although we have not much discussed, the appropriation of the ideal by political power, especially when we spoke of efforts to legitimise power, before and after acquiring such. In terms of competing philosophies, religions, or ideologies, we have dwelt on Confucianism, and to some extent on Taoism and Buddhism, but we have only touched on Legalism, that distinctively Chinese way of thinking that promotes absolute power.

In the classical age of the philosophers, when the country was still under feudal rule, Taoist thinkers criticised Confucian moralism for making artificial norms and distinctions, claiming that the best solution for human ills was to return to nature, while Confucians retorted that Taoists were escapists. But both Confucianism and Taoism would be regarded as irrelevant to the times by the Legalists, who were quite unconcerned with either nature or culture, while deriving some of their inspirations from both Confucianism and Taoism.

POWER APPROPRIATES THE PARADIGM: THE LEGALISTS

Legalism can hardly be described as a response to the big questions of life, since it does not address these. It is essentially a response to the problem of finding order in a time of social and political chaos, during the disintegration of feudal society. Other schools, whether Confucianism, Mohism, or Taoism, had also offered their answers, both moral and metaphysical. Legalism offers a *political* answer –

---

[2] Consult Ching, *Chinese Religions*, introduction.

that of despotism and power politics. It is utterly devoid of any religious belief, moral sense or sensitivity to nature. Where the Confucians and the Taoists addressed themselves to both rulers and the ruled, Legalists spoke only to the actual or would-be rulers. Having no belief in God and no reverence for nature, they used the term *Tao* in a pseudo-metaphysical manner to refer to the mysterious way of power politics. 'The Way lies in what cannot be seen, its function in what cannot be known. Be empty, still, and idle, and from your place of darkness observe the defects of others . . . Hide your tracks, conceal your sources, so that your subordinates cannot guess what you are about.'[3]

Subordinating all human relations to that between ruler and minister, they divested this of any moral significance, and recommended that the ruler ascertain the loyalty of his subjects by using the 'two handles' of rewards and punishments.[4]

All through the Chou dynasty, the belief in Heaven had witnessed its own vicissitudes. By the fourth and third centuries BCE, the word Heaven had lost much of its religious import, and referred more and more to nature (as with the Taoists) or fate (as with some latter-day Confucians). Even the Mandate of Heaven doctrine could not carry any compelling force, while the loyalties of feudalism and the hold of tradition were disintegrating. For the Legalists, 'Heaven' meant the progression of seasons, and the 'way the universe works', very much in a mechanical manner.[5]

The best-known Legalist thinker is Han Fei Tzu (c. 280–233 BCE), who was of princely origin. He was the intellectual heir of a tradition that counted among its forebears the seventh-century-BCE statesman Kuan Chung (whose ideas are allegedly in the later text *Kuan-tzu*), the fourth-century-BCE statesman Wei Yang, the Lord of Shang, to whom is attributed another text, *Shang-chün shu*, and other figures like his contemporary Shen Pu-hai (d. 337 BCE), who left behind counsels on the art of governing. Han's own treatise, *Han Fei Tzu*, would be a synthesis of Legalist thinking, a handbook of *Realpolitik* addressed to any ruler who was willing to give it a try.

The Legalists' only concern was to help the ruler to survive and prosper in the world of their own times. And it was in this light that

[3] *Han Fei Tzu*, sect. 5; Watson (trans.), pp. 17–18.
[4] *Han Fei Tzu*, sect. 7; Watson (trans.), p. 30.
[5] H. G. Creel, *Shen Pu-hai: A Chinese Political Philosopher of the Fourth Century B.C.* (Chicago: University of Chicago Press, 1974), pp. 62, 168–70.

the text *Kuan-tzu* encouraged the ruler to meditate and achieve clarity of mind and judgement. Their other proposals included strengthening central government, establishing greater control over land and population, replacing the old aristocracy by a new bureaucracy, encouraging agriculture to assure plentiful food supplies, and the military expansion of the state. And all this was to be realised within the state especially through the use of *fa*, an impersonal system of positive laws applied impartially to nobles and commoners.[6]

*The devolution of law (*fa*) into punishment (*hsing / xing*)*

In chapter 3, we discussed how incipient ideas of human equality and popular sovereignty arose very early in Chinese thought. However, as we know, they did not lead to a political structure other than a benevolent despotism. If the belief in human perfectibility, a cornerstone of Confucian philosophy, implied a belief in personal freedom, this was more an interior, spiritual freedom to improve one's own moral character. And the freedom of Taoist philosophers like Chuang-tzu was the freedom to be their natural selves, without that of political participation. The concept of freedom as a *right*, such as the right to freedom of thought and religion, to freedom of speech and assembly, was never clearly articulated until modern times, and then under Western influence. And of course, the concept of law as a protection of individual rights was unknown to pre-modern China.

Fa is the Chinese word for law, a graph with a water radical and what could be a mythical animal, later symbolic of justice, as a semantic component. Its etymology is difficult, but it represents a transcendent order.[7] Allegedly, in an ancient rite or ordeal, a bull was presented to the altar of the god of the soil, over which lustrations were sprinkled. The contestants then read their oaths of innocence, which the guilty party was unable to finish, and was gored to death by the bull.[8]

It is interesting that a mythical animal instilling a sense of fear in

---

[6] Léon Vandermeersch, *La Formation du Légisme: Recherche sur la constitution d'une philosophie politique caracteristique de la Chine ancienne* (Paris: École Française d'Extrême-Orient, 1965), ch. 7.

[7] For *fa*, see Hsü Chin-hsiung, *Chung-kuo ku-tai she-hui wen-tzu yü jen-lei hsüeh te t'ou-shih* (Ancient Chinese society: an examination of writing and anthropology), Rev. ed. (Taipei, Commercial Press, 1995), pp. 542–3.

[8] Joseph Needham (ed.), *Science and Civilisation in China* vol. 2, p. 205, especially note a.

contestants or litigants should serve as a symbol of justice. Justice, it would seem, inspires fear in the unjust, especially in those who seek, without merit, to take advantage of the system. Perhaps, it is not surprising that the Chinese have traditionally and until our own days avoided the law courts in their search for conflict resolution, preferring to avoid conflict, or at least, to find arbitration to overcome conflict.

What the legendary ordeal also reveals is that the contestants are somehow presumed guilty unless proved innocent, which imposes not only the burden of proof, but also the taint of suspicion on those who contest an issue or are detained by the authorities for alleged offences.

In ancient texts, *fa* designates the law of Heaven to which sages look up, whereas another word, *hsing / xing*, with a knife radical, signifies penal law. In antiquity, the 'five penalties' all referred to physical mutilations: branding, cutting off the nose, chopping off the feet, castration and beheading.[9]

The Book of History voices Confucian humane sentiments in explaining that the punishments may be replaced by fines in cases where there is reasonable doubt regarding the alleged crime. Judges are told to 'stand in awe of the dread majesty of Heaven' and the importance of wise, personal judgement is emphasised. Judges should not be men of artful tongue, but 'really good persons'. And the king is made to say:

Oh! Let there be a feeling of reverence [toward Heaven] . . . I think with reverence of the subject of punishment, for the end of it is to promote virtue. Now Heaven, wishing to help the people, has made us its representatives here below. . . The right ordering of the people depends on the impartial hearing of the pleas on both sides.[10]

While the ancient concept of law was interpreted as belonging to the transcendent order, Confucian society regarded itself as being governed more by *li*[a] (literally, ritual, or ritual law), a term rooted in ancient religion, and presuming a distinction between nobility and commoners. *Li*[a] may be described also as customary, uncodified law, internalised by individuals and governing gentlemen in their personal and social lives, in their behaviour toward the spirits as well as

---

[9] The Book of History, *Lü-hsing*, English trans. in Legge, *Chinese Classics*, vol. 3, pp. 605–6; see Vandermeersch, *La Formation du Légisme*, p. 186.

[10] Legge, *Chinese Classics*, vol. 3, pp. 604, 607; the quotation is from pp. 609–10.

the rest of the world. For that reason, and as we have discussed in chapter 3, *li*ᵃ has the extended meaning of propriety or correct behaviour. It was based on justice, righteousness (*yi*), even humaneness (*jen*ᵇ). A classical education was an education in the rites, one that prepared the young nobles for life. *Fa*, on the other hand, referred to ritual customs, selected and codified, which became a penal code, to be applied especially to commoners who had not the privilege of a ritual education.

The evolution of law in China may be described as the *devolution* of ritual (*li*ᵃ) into law (*fa*) and of law into punishment.[11] For this reason, law is regarded as having played a mainly penal role in Chinese society, protecting the rights of the rulers and enjoining passive obedience on the part of the subjects. Until today, the Chinese fear law, because law has been an arbitrary instrument in the hands of the rulers.

In Legalist texts, the two words are actually used interchangeably, confusing transcendent law with penal law. Here, the spirit of Legalism is quite different from that of the Confucians. For the Legalists, law is less an instrument of justice, but more a method for the ruler to keep himself in power. *Han Fei Tzu* frequently uses the language of the jungle to describe the relationship between the ruler and the subjects. The ruler's power is like the tiger's claws, but the subjects, when not well governed, may turn into tigers themselves. 'Let the rulers apply the laws, and the greatest tigers will tremble; let him apply punishments, and the greatest tigers will grow docile. If laws and punishments are justly applied, then tigers will be transformed into human beings again and revert to their true form.'[12]

Very early, the law had become codified and published in the annals of the states. But controversy arose when it was inscribed for the first time on the bronze cauldrons (536 BCE) by Tzu-ch'an in the state of Cheng, a measure that angered the Confucians because it prevented the intervention of personal interpretation on the part of the magistrates. Their fear was that, in becoming objectified, the law was dehumanised.[13] Throughout history, Chinese law served public interest only insofar as it also served the interests of the government.

Until the law was inscribed on the bronze cauldrons, an act that

---

[11] Consult Sa Meng-wu, *Chung-kuo fa-chih ssu-hsiang* (Chinese thinking on government by law) (Taipei: Yenbo Press, 1978).
[12] *Han Fei Tzu* 2:12b–13a; Eng. trans. adapted from Watson, pp. 39–40.
[13] Vandermeersch, *La Formation du Légisme*, pp. 188–9.

resembled the institution of the Tables of the Law by the Romans (4th cent. BCE), the rites had had the force of law for nobles, and so-called punishments were only applied to the common people. This did not mean that the nobility were never punished for their transgressions, but that they were not subject to physical mutilation aside from the pain of death. But the contribution of the Legalists as a group was to objectify the law further, and to subject everyone to it, whether noble or commoner.

The law no more makes exceptions for men of high station than the plumb line bends to accommodate a crooked place in the wood. What the law has decreed the wise cannot dispute nor the brave venture to contest. When faults are to be punished, the highest minister cannot escape; when good is to be rewarded, the lowest peasant must not be passed over.[14]

The force of the sage-king ideal was such that traditional Chinese political thought always assumed that monarchy was the best form of government. Confucianism obviously preferred benevolent monarchs and had no use for tyrants, but Confucian ministers were unable to keep tyrants from the throne. There were changes in the dynastic cycle but the individuals who acquired power were often of the wrong kind, even if they did so in the name of the Mandate of Heaven. In the light of events, this doctrine became understood by many as a kind of historical determinism governing the rise and fall of political dynasties. Except, of course, for the Legalists, who were no fatalists. Instead, they plotted every step of their way to power.

Besides, the sage-king ideal did not bring with it a carefully articulated programme for good government. The Institutes of Chou, presumed to contain a model for good government, offers mainly an idealised bureaucracy. Too much was expected of the personal, ethical qualities of the sage-king, and too little was done to regulate his rule, another reason for the ideal to become nothing other than a generalised endorsement of benevolent despotism.

The enlightened ruler (ming-chu/mingzhu) versus the sage

If the Confucians praised Yao and Shun, the followers of Mo-tzu the great Yü, and the Taoists the Yellow Emperor, Legalists also recognised some ancient sages, especially in those culture heroes who advanced material culture, like the legendary Nest-builder, and

---

[14] *Han Fei Tzu* 2:5b; English trans. adapted from Watson, p. 28.

Fire-maker, whom they claimed were made rulers by the people who needed their leadership in a struggle for existence against the birds, beasts, insects and reptiles: that is, wild and untamed nature.[15]

But *Han Fei Tzu* also made sure that the ancients should not be imitated just because they were ancients, or even because they were sages. The sage of today, he says, does not follow the ways of antiquity, or abide by a fixed standard. He learns from the past, and takes whatever precautions are necessary for the present.[16]

Legalists believed in moving with the times and situations, rather than in fixed norms of benevolence or righteousness. They were the progressives of their times, and they adhered to no principle outside of power and personal advantage. 'Men of high antiquity strove for moral virtue; men of middle times sought out wise schemes; men of today vie to be known for strength.'[17]

And what is this strength? It is compared to brute force. 'The tiger is able to overcome the dog because of his claws and teeth. If he discards his claws and teeth and lets the dog use them, then he will be overpowered by the dog. In the same way the ruler of men uses punishments and favors to control ministers.'[18] With a touch of irony, the Legalist thinker says of Confucius and political power that

Confucius was the great sage of the world . . . [But] those who rejoiced in his benevolence, admired his righteousness, and were willing to be his disciples numbered only seventy . . . Duke Ai of Lu was an inferior ruler, yet when he ascended the throne . . . there was no one within its boundaries who did not acknowledge allegiance to him . . . [Therefore] Confucius remained a subject and Duke Ai continued to be his ruler.[19]

For the Legalists, the ideal ruler is an 'enlightened ruler'. He bestows honours and favours, and inflicts mutilation and death, according to the circumstances. 'The ruler of men must be enlightened enough to comprehend the way of government and strict enough to put it into effect. Though it means going against the will of the people, he will enforce the rule.'[20] Legalist writings seldom touch upon moral and religious subjects. In the *Han Fei Tzu*, there is a story with mythical content about a certain duke, intent upon

[15] *Han Fei Tzu*, sec. 49; Watson (trans.), p. 96.   [16] Ibid.
[17] *Han Fei Tzu*, sect. 49, 19:2b; Eng. trans. adapted from Watson, p. 100.
[18] *Han Fei Tzu*, sect. 7; Eng. trans. adapted from Watson, p. 30.
[19] *Han Fei Tzu*, sect. 49, 19:3a–b; Eng. trans. adapted from Watson, p. 102.
[20] *Han Fei Tzu*, sect. 18; Watson (trans.), p. 94.

hearing ancient music even when the musician warned him of the possible consequences.

In ancient times, the Yellow Emperor called the spirits together on the top of Mount T'ai. Riding in an ivory carriage drawn by six dragons, the god Pi-fang keeping pace with the linchpin, the god Ch'ih-yu stationed before him, the Wind Earl to sweep the way, the Rain Master to sprinkle the road, tigers and wolves in the vanguard, ghosts and spirits behind, writhing serpents on the ground below, phoenixes soaring above him, he called the spirits to a great assembly and created this [ancient] music. But you, my lord, are still deficient in virtue . . . If you were to hear it, I fear some misfortune would come about![21]

On the duke's insistence, this music was played for him, and the following happened:

As he played the first section . . . black clouds began to rise from the northwest. With the second section, a fierce wind came forth, followed by violent rain, that tore the curtains and hangings . . . overturned the cups and bowls, and shook down the tiles from the gallery roof. Those who had been sitting in the company fled . . . while the duke, overcome with terror, cowered in a corner of the gallery. The state of Chin was visited by a great drought . . . for three years, and sores broke out all over Duke P'ing's body.[22]

We note that the duke was told he was deficient in virtue (*te / de*). But that word could also mean power, which matters when one confronts spiritual powers.

Should the reader be struck by Han Fei Tzu's possible superstition, let it be noted that the moral *he* drew from the story is a simple and pragmatic one: 'To give no ear to government affairs but to long ceaselessly for music is the way to ruin yourself.'[23] And that appears also to represent the Legalist's unconcern for culture in general.

In the state of an enlightened ruler there are no books written on bamboo slips, since law supplies the only instruction. There are no sermons on the former kings, since officials serve as the only teachers. There are no fierce feuds of private swordsmen. Cutting off the heads of the enemy is the only deed of valor.[24]

---

[21] *Han Fei Tzu*, sect. 10, 3:3a–b; Eng. trans. adapted from Watson, p. 55.
[22] *Han Fei Tzu*, sect. 10, 3:3b; Watson (trans.), pp. 55–6.
[23] *Han Fei Tzu*, 3:3b; Eng. trans. adapted from Watson, p. 56.
[24] *Han Fei Tzu*, sect. 49; 19:6b. Eng. trans. adapted from Watson, p. 111.

The opposition between humanity and Heaven

The unity of Heaven and humanity has been a philosophical belief for many, although not all, of China's many schools of thought. In fact, its varying interpretations have distinguished Confucianism from Taoism and Chinese Buddhism, while also marking Buddho-Taoist influence on Confucianism, as I have suggested. It has also served as the cornerstone for the overarching harmony in Chinese wisdom, which, as a whole, includes Confucianism, Taoism and Buddhism, and also goes beyond it. The expression itself has seen other forms. Under Buddhist influence, it was articulated as 'the Oneness of All Things', pointing to the continuum of all sentient beings, and indeed, of all that exists, and illustrated as the presence of 'One in all, and all in One', according to the Hua-yen school's understanding of the interconnectedness of all things.

But this belief has some inherent problems. We have discussed its implications for the subject/object tension in an earlier chapter. And without any subject/object distinction, there can be no scientific thinking. Unsurprisingly, Lucien Lévy-Bruhl has called correlative or associative thinking, the kind one finds in China, pre-logical, indeed, symptomatic of 'the primitive mind'.[25]

Joseph Needham has acknowledged that the Chinese think less in causal terms, and more in symbolic correlations. He has in mind especially Tung Chung-shu's correspondences between the natural and human orders. But he asserts that this system is not primitive, and has its own logic.

In coordinative thinking, conceptions are not subsumed under one another, but placed side by side in a *pattern*, and things influence one another not by acts of mechanical causation, but by a kind of 'inductance' . . . The symbolic correlations or correspondences all formed part of prior actions or impulsions of other things . . . They were thus parts in existential dependence upon the whole world-organism.[26]

For myself, and I repeat, I prefer to regard the 'oneness' or correlation of the human and natural orders, a metaphorical and analogical expression giving a mystical view of human participation in an organic universe where things usually proceed in a regular pattern. There remain possibilities of flexibility and adaptation,

[25] L. Lévy-Bruhl, *How Natives Think* (London: Allen & Unwin, 1926), p. 380.
[26] Joseph Needham, *Science and Civilisation in China*, vol. 2, pp. 280–1.

opening the way to scientific thinking without reducing it to a rigid system of mechanical causality. Where a Westerner would oppose subject and object, mind and body, reason and intuition, the Chinese somehow combines them in a holistic manner. This becomes more comprehensible as we discover increasingly the inherent complexities in human knowledge, and speak more in terms of a world of intersubjectivity.

Unsurprisingly, Legalists did not subscribe to the theory of harmony or correspondence between man and nature. Unlike the Confucians, Han Fei Tzu recommended separate investigations of the way of Heaven and the way of human affairs. 'Heaven (Nature) and man have each its great destiny . . . Thus it is said: The Way does not identify itself with the myriad beings; its power does not identify itself with *yin* and *yang*, any more than a scale identifies itself with heaviness or lightness . . . or a ruler with his ministers.'[27]

We may dwell a little on the advice against the ruler's identifying himself with his ministers. This is obviously based on the conflict of interests, and the suspicion that any minister may become a ruler's rival. On the other hand, ministers have been told to 'identify themselves with their superiors', specifically by Mo-tzu, who had authoritarian tendencies. But in an effort to balance the ruler–minister tension, Mo-tzu also counselled the ruler to esteem the worthy, and listen to good advice.[28]

THE TRAVESTIES OF THE PARADIGM

As we know from archaeology, antiquity in China was dominated by men of war, wielding spears and riding in chariots. Unsurprisingly, these preferred the instruments of power, while fearing the influence of the spoken or written words of the scholars as potential threats. As history unrolled, it was usually might that made power, and power usually sought to use scholars to its own ends, choosing those that appeared to offer the best means to these ends.

The benevolent despots

Until the second century BCE, many philosophers who failed to attain high political status during their lifetimes acquired a strong following

---

[27] *Han Fei Tzu*, sect. 8, 2:8a–10b; Watson (trans.), pp. 35–7.   [28] *Mo-tzu*, chs 2–3.

of disciples as well as a posthumous authority, which became inherent in those texts associated with their teachings. Some of them were Confucians, others Taoists or Mohists or followers of lesser schools. These scholars, deceased or living, usually had messages with political meaning. Interestingly, Legalists and Taoists had the rulers' ears before the Confucians took over, and that, only in the second century BCE.

Two of China's best historical rulers were the Han dynastic founder, Kao-tsu (r. 206–195 BCE) and the second T'ang emperor, T'ai-tsung (r. 627–49), who helped his father gain the throne. Each used military means to overthrow an earlier dynasty, although Kao-tsu started as a commoner, while T'ai-tsung came from an important military family. And each ruled over a population content with, and grateful for, the peace and prosperity that ensued.

Emperor Kao-tsu and his immediate successors favoured Taoism, diminishing taxes and corvée to offer respite to a people oppressed under the Ch'in dynasty. Emperor T'ai-tsung venerated Lao-tzu as an imperial ancestor, but offered freely his patronage to Buddhist monks as well as Confucian scholars, initiating the effort that produced the *Correct Meaning of the Five Classics* series. These two men exemplified benevolent despotism, and earned the respect of later generations. But they were no sages. Emperor Kao-tsu harboured such suspicion of his strongest supporters that he eliminated them, one by one. Emperor T'ai-tsung gained the throne only after personally killing his two brothers, one of whom was the designated heir.

The philosopher Chu Hsi argued with his contemporary Ch'en Liang about the merits and demerits of these earlier rulers. A pragmatic thinker, Ch'en admired the institutions of Han and T'ang, left behind by these two emperors, whom he wished to call benevolent monarchs or kings, using the word in its ideal sense. Chu Hsi, however, insisted that there had been no such kings since the legendary Three Dynasties. He criticised Kao-tsu for his cruelty to his supporters, and for continuing certain penal measures inherited from the Ch'in dynasty, and he attacked T'ai-tsung for transgressions of principles governing family relationships.

In the case of Emperor Kao-tsu of Han, the selfish motive might not have been manifest, but you cannot deny their presence. In the case of Emperor T'ai-tsung of T'ang, his actions were certainly motivated by human passion . . . If his righteousness is justified merely on the grounds that he left the world in a long period of peace and order, this would be to define righteousness in terms of success . . . [29]

The tyrants

For Chu Hsi, as for Confucius and Mencius, the morality of ends cannot justify that of the means. And presumably, this kind of political ethics struck fear over a thousand years earlier in the hearts of the rulers of the state of Ch'in, destined to unify the whole of China. In that state, the Legalist chief minister, the Lord Shang Yang (mid-fourth century BCE), counselled the destruction of two classics: the Book of History and the Book of Songs.[30]

China's first unifier: the Ch'in emperor

In making use of Legalist ideas to centralise power, keep the people disciplined and battle-ready, the feudal state of Ch'in, based in western China, with its capital near today's Xi'an, was able to aggrandise itself during the late years of the Chou dynasty. Eventually, it unified the country under its own rule by military might. And the political leader, Yin Cheng, who founded the new Ch'in dynasty, decided to call himself an emperor (*huang-ti / huangdi*), using a title with divine connotations. He also proclaimed himself the first ruler of a new line, with the implication that his dynastic house will last forever.

In so doing, he had been helped by many followers of Legalist thought, especially his chief minister, Li Ssu (d. 208 BCE), a fellow student of Han Fei Tzu's, who was also responsible for Han's death. Li urged the emperor to carry out a series of innovations that radically altered the entire structure of Chinese life and society. The remnants of feudal power were all swept away. The country centralised its administration with prefectures and counties under the direct control of the imperial court; built roads and bridges to enable the speedy transport of troops and supplies, strung together the Great Wall from existing smaller ones for defence against nomadic tribes; standardised measures and weights. This was the rule of a strongman, like that of the much later Napoléon, who made similar contributions in France.

[29] *CWWC*, 36:22b. Consult Julia Ching, 'Neo-Confucian Utopian Theories and Political Ethics', *Monumenta Serica* 30 (1972–3), 1–56.
[30] *Han Fei Tzu*, Sect. 13, in 4:13b.

As Son of Heaven, the Ch'in emperor was the first to offer the Feng and the Shan sacrifices on Mount T'ai, an act of legitimation of his rule, and also a precedent for later rulers to follow. This has great significance, as he was acting as undisputed and unique ruler of the entire empire, having supplanted the various feudal lords not only in secular power, but also as the only High Priest. It mattered little that he was an acknowledged and unabashed tyrant.

Here, it may be useful to recall a conversation regarding Heaven's Mandate in the case of the first emperor's ancestor, a feudal lord of the state of Ch'in (540 BCE):

'How is the ruler of Ch'in?'
The reply: 'He is without principle.'
Chao Meng asked: 'Will the state perish?'
The reply: 'But why? A state will not perish on account of one unprincipled reign. The state is related to Heaven and Earth, and stands with them. Unless there are several rotten reigns, it will not perish.'
Chao Meng asked: 'Will Heaven do something?'
The reply: 'Yes.'
He asked: 'In how much time?'
The reply: 'I have heard, that when [a ruler] is without principle, and yet the yearly harvest is good, Heaven is [still] assisting him. It seldom lasts for less than five years.'[31]

Heaven was very patient, even generous, with the state of Ch'in, permitting it to flourish for several hundred more years, and eventually to conquer the entire country and establish the short-lived Ch'in dynasty.

Following unification under the sword, the notorious edict of 213 BCE ordered the burning of all publicly held copies of those works that represented any opposition to the views and policies of the powers that be. To quote from the memorial submitted by Li Ssu:

[Scholars] seek a reputation by discrediting their sovereign; they appear superior by expressing contrary views, and they lead the lowly multitude in the spreading of slander. If such license is not prohibited, the sovereign power will decline . . .

Your servant suggests that all books in the imperial archives, save the memoirs of Ch'in, be burned. All persons . . . in possession of the Book of Songs, the Book of History, and discourses of the hundred philosophers should take them to the local governors and have them indiscriminately burned. Those who dare to talk to each other about the Book of Songs and the Book of History should be executed . . . Books not to be destroyed will

---

[31] *Tso-chuan*, see Legge, *Chinese Classics*, vol. 5, pp. 572, 579.

be those on medicine and pharmacy, divination by the tortoise and milfoil, and agriculture and arboriculture.[32]

The destruction included five of the classics, with the exception of the Book of Changes. The writings of the philosophers, whether *Hsün-tzu*, *Mo-tzu*, or others, were not as systematically rooted out.[33]

According to the *Historical Annals*, just before the burning of books, over 460 scholars of Hsien-yang, the Ch'in capital, including those involved in esoteric arts such as seeking longevity and interpreting dreams, as well as followers of the Confucian school (*ju*[b]), were buried alive (214 BCE) Such was the immediate consequence of the emperor's anger at criticisms levelled against his government. But it reflects as well as his sense of a threat coming from those 'weaklings' suspected of possessing superior power. These tragic events became known as 'the Burning of Books and Burying of Scholars'.[34]

But the fires of Ch'in could not reduce the classics to ashes, or silence the scholars for ever. The reverse was true historically. The first Ch'in emperor had hoped that his dynasty would remain eternally in power. It lasted less than twenty years (221–207 BCE). On the contrary, the Han dynasty that followed eventually established the Confucian school as state orthodoxy and recovered the lost classical texts. In the struggle between the books and political authority, the books won out, becoming acknowledged by the state as canonical scriptures, and retaining, even today, some of their past authority.

The Ch'in state actually contributed to the spread of literacy: it unified the writing system, selecting one form of script, its own, as the standard. This was in effect a simplified system better suited to the business of central administration, and it would be inherited by the Han dynasty.[35]

China's recent unifier: Chairman Mao Zedong

This land so rich in beauty
Has made countless heroes bow in homage

---

[32] Ssu-ma Ch'ien, *Shih-chi*, K'ai-ming ed., ch. 6, p. 25. Eng. trans. adapted from de Bary (ed.), *Sources*, vol. 1, p. 155.

[33] *Lun-heng* 28:2a.

[34] *Shih-chi*, ch. 6, p. 25. Wang Ch'ung's *Lun-heng* 7:16, gives the figure of the dead as 467. See also Yang Kuan, *Qin Shihuang* (The first Ch'in Emperor) (Shanghai: Renmin, 1956), pp. 98–100.

[35] Consult Hsü Shen's preface, in the *Shuo-wen chieh-tzu Tuan-chu*, 15A:6a–7b.

But alas! The Ch'in emperor and Wu of Han
Were lacking in literary grace,
T'ai-tsung of T'ang and T'ai-tsu of Sung,
Had little poetry in their souls;
And Genghis Khan, proud Son of Heaven for a day,
Knew only shooting eagles, bows outstretched.
For truly great men,
Look to this age alone.[36]

Mao Zedong was praised by his followers as a messiah arisen in the East, like the red sun which comes up on the horizon. He compared himself to China's first unifier, and we can find quickly many similarities. To take first their accomplishments: against great odds, both unified the country by military force, making it a world power of sorts; both standardised measures and weights, Mao's government putting in the metric system and even opting for the Western, solar calendar. To top it off, Mao also sought to change the written script, which he ordered simplified. This last of achievements could also only have been carried out by a despot. And it signified ultimate power, such as wielded by the mythical Ts'ang Chieh, who first invented the Chinese script.

Mao's greatest achievement was the Communist triumph of 1949, which drove the incumbent Nationalists to the island of Taiwan and laid the foundation for the People's Republic of China. That this did happen was not the triumph of good over evil, of clean government over corruption. It was the result of many historical circumstances, including the consequences of the war with Japan (1937–45), which debilitated the Nationalist régime and diverted it from earlier attempts to suppress the Communists. On their part, Mao and his men got from the war the breathing space they needed and the opportunity to organise the countryside. That they won the civil war made them a conquering dynasty, winning the Mandate to rule over all under Heaven – except for the island of Taiwan.

In the West, various authors have represented Chinese Communism as Confucianism in a different dress, on account of the common authoritarian bias in the two ideologies. And they also portrayed Chairman Mao as a Confucian despot, partly on the strength of his penchant to quote from history or literature or write classical poetry. This is a distortion, since not all history or literature represent Confucian ideas. Mao's references have usually been to

---

[36] Mao Zedong, 'Snow' (1936). See Mao Tsetung, *Poems* (Beijing: Xinhua, 1976), pp. 46–7.

myths and legends and popular novels, like the account of the Sung-dynasty outlaws translated as *All Men are Brothers*, or the many stories of historical intrigues in the *Romance of the Three Kingdoms*, or the well-known tale of *Journey to the West*, which gives the Buddhist monk Hsüan-tsang a monkey and a pig as travel companions. These sources give him a wealth of lore, known to many millions in the country. Occasionally, he refers as well to historical episodes, but seldom does he mention Confucius or the classics.

If we search the Communist record during Mao's years of power, we find a strong official antagonism toward Confucianism, manifested in reinterpretations of the sage's teachings and diatribes against them. If Mao's rival Liu Shaoqi showed a personal fondness for the Four Books, and even for the Confucian teachings on self-cultivation, and sought to extend these to other party members, such action only contributed eventually to Liu's peril. The worst came in 1973–4, during the Anti-Confucius campaign, when the ancient philosopher was depicted as a political reactionary, a hypocrite and a murderer.

Another book Mao refers to is Sun Tzu's *Art of War*, often considered a fourth-century-BCE Legalist text. This short treatise insists on the importance of knowing the facts, both about oneself and about the enemy. Naturally, the most important chapter concerns the gathering and use of military intelligence, considered the secret of success on the battlefield. Military strategy favours manipulation and even conspiracy. And Mao showed himself a supreme manipulator, even if he was at times deficient in his knowledge of the facts of the situations.[37]

In many ways, we can discern Legalist influence on Mao Zedong. Lauded during the Cultural Revolution as the 'reddest sun in our hearts', the Chairman was actually capricious and mysterious like the moon. He was adept at manipulating the masses, using them to accomplish his own ends, including that of destroying his political rivals. The casualties of the attack on culture included also books and scholars, on a scale unprecedented, unless we are to return to the days of the First Emperor. Mao had this to say of his own espoused ideology, Marxism–Leninism, with its own classics which substituted for the Confucian texts of the past:

[37] Consult Julia Ching, *Probing China's Soul: Religion, Politics, Protest in the People's Republic* (San Francisco: Harper & Row, 1990), especially chs 3–4.

Our comrades must understand that we do not study Marxism–Leninism because it is pleasing to the eye, or because it has some mysterious value, like the doctrines of the Taoist priests who ascended Mao Shan to learn how to subdue devils and evil spirits. Marxism–Leninism has no beauty, nor has it any mystical value. It is only extremely useful.[38]

On another occasion, when Mao was answering questions about the withering of the state, which is part and parcel of Marxist philosophy, he responded that the moment had not yet come. And then, referring specifically to the Confucian form of 'humane' or benevolent government, he said quite bluntly: 'The state apparatus, including the army, the police and the courts, is the instrument by which one class oppresses another. It . . . is violence and not "benevolence". "You are not benevolent." Quite so. We definitely do not apply a policy of benevolence to the reactionaries.'[39]

It is interesting that the courts should be mentioned together with the army and the police as the instrument of class oppression. There is, of course, no independent judiciary in China. And since benevolent government is a hallmark of Confucian politics, it is difficult to regard Mao Zedong as a Confucian statesman. He stood, rather, in the tradition of Chinese despotism.

And finally, Mao and the Chinese Communists rejected the traditional belief in the oneness between Heaven and humanity. For them, nature is what the human being must conquer and harness, and their attitude toward it has been irrational and ruthless, leaving behind a whirlwind legacy of environmental devastation. Here, Mao unabashedly compared himself to the mythical villain Kung-kung (Gonggong), whose struggle for power led him, in a fit of rage, to break the pillars that supported heaven as a vault over earth. As a consequence, the sky tilted in the northwest, and the earth sank in the southwest.[40]

Commenting on the story, Mao said, 'Did Kung-kung perish in the attempt? The *Huai-nan-tzu* is silent on this question. We may take it that he did not, but came out victorious.'[41]

---

[38] Mao Zedong, 'Reform in learning, the Party and Literature' (1942), in Stuart R. Schram, *The Political Thought of Mao Tse-tung* (New York: Praeger, 1963), p. 179.

[39] Mao Zedong, 'On the People's Democratic Dictatorship', in Schram, *Poliltical Thought*, p. 300.

[40] That is, until the goddess Nü-wa repaired the broken universe with turtles' legs. The story referred to is from *Huai-nan-tzu* 3:1a–b. For Nü-wa, see 6:7a; see also chapter 1.

[41] See Mao, *Poems*, p. 22.

THE LIMITS OF ABSOLUTE POWER

Even in a political despotism, power is absolute only in theory. In practice, its exercise is inherently limited by many factors. These include the merits of the office-holder, his inner and outer courts, as well as the voices of restraint coming from various sources, including not only the population at large, but also the superhuman powers.

Absolute power invited challenges on account of its temptations, both to the office-holder and to those who were his potential rivals. The ruler's own strength of character was always a basic indicator of the amount of power he could exercise. But in its very exercise, he depended on both the inner court, which assured his comforts and pleasures, and the outer court, which assisted him in his governing mandate. In the former case, there were his immediate family, including his numerous wives and sons, and their other relatives, as well as the guards and eunuchs who attended them, each of whom had particular interests to pursue, if only to prevent his displeasure. In the latter case, there were the civil and military officials in charge of the bureaucracies and the armies, who had their own vested interests. Indeed, as the ruler's deputy, each of his ministers or servants participated in a power that could be total. More frequently, dynasties were toppled by the rulers' intimates, or by others close to the source of power at court, than by popular rebellions. And over and again, reforms were obstructed by rival ministers, or abuses were perpetrated by eunuchs and imperial relatives.

The tolerance of the subject population also had its limits. Being far removed from the masses, however, the historical ruler relied on his outer court for information about his subjects. He also relied on so-called supernatural signs and wonders, to measure his own acceptance by higher powers. The common belief in the oneness of Heaven and humanity was such that Heaven's displeasure could spell the end of a mandate, and even if the ruler did not believe in this personally, he had to deal with those of his subjects who were believers. So astronomical phenomena served as signs of Heaven's attitudes regarding the quality of government and the degree of popular consent. Here, those ministers with special skills to predict eclipses of the sun or moon or other unusual movements in the celestial sphere were assisted by others who interpreted these phenomena in the context of social approval or disapproval of the

ruler's actions. Indeed, for its own better survival, the state instituted critiques of public policy, by obliging its own censorate to
offer timely criticism, even if such was offered at the individuals'
peril.

Critiques of absolute power

Many were the critics of power abuses in traditional China,
including those in the inner circles of power itself. The Ch'in
emperor's elder son and heir articulated disapproval of his father's
ruthlessness, and was demoted and exiled. His less competent
younger brother eventually succeeded to the throne, but was unable
to keep it.

Chairman Mao also had his critics in his inner circles: the best
known was Peng Dehuai, the defence minister who criticised the
Great Leap Forward policies (1957–8), intended to increase produc-
tivity, transform social consciousness and even social organisation.
But workers had to work longer hours, often for lower wages, to
meet higher and unrealistic production quotas. Peasants first saw
their private plots reduced, and then transformed into 'people's
communes', as all property became communal. Peng was purged for
his boldness, while Mao's inability to listen to criticism basically
sealed the country's fate.

As Lord Acton puts it: 'Power corrupts; absolute power corrupts
absolutely.' In the two cases of the Ch'in emperor and of Chairman
Mao, it is difficult not to consider megalomania as a factor in the
eventual demise of the empire, or of Mao's original vision for the
country.

Among the critics of despotism, the younger could be expected to
act more impulsively. Student protests were known nearly two
thousand years ago, in the second century CE, when a greatly
expanded Han-dynasty imperial academy had an enrolment of
thirty thousand students, who, understandably concerned about
their future career possibilities at an uncertain period of history,
were given to mass protests and demonstrations. Another large-
scale protest took place about one thousand years later during the
Sung dynasty, which also favoured having a large imperial college at
the capital. In February 1126, a group of several hundred students
under their leader Ch'en Tung knelt before the palace gate in
Hangzhou to petition for the restoration to office of Li Kang, a

much loved general. They were joined by a crowd, possibly tens of thousands of sympathisers, who rioted on the sight of soldiers and caused the death of a dozen or more eunuchs. The government proceeded to reinstate the general and debated the question of punishing the students for causing the riot, but decided in favour of a pardon.

There were also other voices, of more mature 'dissidents', intellectual leaders. Long after the time of Mencius, critiques of power were increasingly made obliquely or in secret. A seventeenth-century thinker, Huang Tsung-hsi, well known as a philosopher and intellectual historian, condemned the rulers for regarding their domains as their private property, and their subjects as their servants and slaves. He proposed that law (*fa*) be established for the interest of all rather than of the few, and that government be by laws rather than human beings. And he denounced those laws that enslave people.[42]

Unfortunately for China, Huang's ideas did not get the same reception as for example, John Locke's in seventeenth-century England and beyond. With time, political power became more despotic in pre-modern and modern China, as the voices of criticism and protest were increasingly stifled. This process continued under Communist rule, as a Western imported ideology – Marxism–Leninism – was used for the theory and practice of power. True, certain trappings surrounding court ritual, as well as institutional abuses inherited by the absolute monarchy, were discontinued. But decisions affecting the lives of the entire population continued to be made by the few, or rather, by the 'one man', be this Mao Zedong or Deng Xiaoping, and without the benefit of traditional institutional balances. Besides, the question of succession to power became pivotal.[43]

The question of civil society[44]

In 1990, as the countries in eastern Europe hastened, one after another, to overthrow their respective Communist régimes, there was talk in the West of a 'civil society' comprising churches and other so-called voluntary groups that spurred the revolutionary

---

[42] See *Ming-yi tai-fang-lu*, chs 1–3. Eng. trans. by de Bary, *Waiting for the Dawn*, pp. 91–9.
[43] Ching, *Probing*, pp. 105–7.
[44] For an elaboration of this idea, consult Léon Vandermeersch (ed.), *La Société civile face à l'état* (Paris: École Française d'Extrême-Orient, 1994).

changes. Since then, more realistic information has led to increasing doubt regarding the strength of such groups, as the events that unfolded are seen more as the consequences of a Soviet indifference under Gorbachev regarding an extended Communist 'empire'.

All the same, developments in eastern Europe led also to recent discussions about civil society in pre-modern China. In this case, tradition knew only a one-career society for the educated, who depended on the state's support for promotions to positions in the civil service. Private academies and a few voluntary groups, however, promoted this very scarce space for free discussions without state supervision, even if some of the academies and groups were managed by local officials.

Nevertheless, civil society was usually permitted by default rather than by design. Many were the educated and literary men who resorted to earning a living by teaching, even by teaching as private tutors to families who could afford to support them, because they could not pass the examinations. Sometimes, these people lacked the merit; other times, the examinations were defective in the selection of real talent. These men might be described as living in semi-retirement, while others like them formed artists' circles, or poetry clubs, or joined the ranks of Buddhist monks and Taoist priests. But this is really saying that such 'civil space' was hard to find, which it was.

An interesting civil space was actually the schools, especially the privately run academies, which maintained their independence *vis-à-vis* the imperial court. It is not surprising that besides educating the young, the schools, and in our own days, the universities, should prove to be fertile ground for free discussion and political protest.[45]

But there is another way of looking at civil society in pre-modern China: to regard the same people, in and out of office, as belonging at times to government service, and at other times to so-called civil society. This happened rather frequently, not only because of the many difficulties associated with public service, but also because the demands of Confucian society obliged men to retire to their native places to mourn the deaths of their parents for nearly three years each time. We notice this in the lives of many high officials, and a man like the sixteenth-century grand secretary Chang Chü-cheng

---

[45] See de Bary, *Waiting for the Dawn*, Introduction, 30–2.

was very much criticised by his contemporaries as well as by later generations for breaking precedent.

Actually, there were sinecure-holders who basically led private lives, and were therefore available for participation in civil society. Chu Hsi was one such. For much of his life, he was in charge of Taoist temples, deriving a small official income to continue with his research and teaching activities, while he continued to offer unsolicited advice and admonition to the throne.

In China, state and civil society were each the focus of one dimension of a person's life, rather than being two separate realms involving different people. One is, after all, subject to the ruler, but also son to a father, and brother and friend to other people. To the extent that the kinship group remained important in society, the state's long arms were unable to control everyone at all times.

THE PEOPLE AS KING: A GRAND DECEPTION

On looking back into recent and even remote history, I get the impression that the theory of the Mandate of Heaven, most probably devised by the Chou rulers to justify their conquest of the Shang house, has served also as a grand deception: that somehow, the people could choose their own kings, or even become their own kings.

Frequently cited as a reason why rebellions against tyranny are justifiable, this theory has spawned many dynastic turnovers and even more numerous attempts at such. But even if many dynastic founders were able to remedy the political oppression that occasioned the fall of their predecessors, none of them sought a thoroughgoing change of the dynastic system itself. It has therefore been said that prior to modern times, China knew only rebellions but not a revolution, as the new governments ushered in resembled too much the ones that they replaced.

Rebellions and revolutions

One person who articulated such an opinion was Karl Marx. Like Hegel before him, Marx thought the Oriental peoples were too passive and 'submissive', even 'slave-like' in their attitude to institutional authority, and that Oriental empires demonstrate a historical immobility. He acknowledges the recurrence of change on the leadership level, that is, where the political superstructure is con-

cerned, which involved palace coups and power struggles. But he
sees no real change where the social infrastructure is concerned.
Besides, according to his economic interpretation of history, Marx
observes that the 'Asiatic mode of production' is dependent on the
combination of 'small agriculture and domestic industry' with its
lack of impetus for social change. Against this perspective, he
regarded favourably the changes set in motion by the British in India
as 'the only *social* revolution ever heard of in Asia', that is, one
started by the forces of colonialism or imperialism.

Karl A. Wittfogel, who spent many years studying Chinese
history, asserts that Karl Marx was ignorant of the peasant movements seeking economic and political change. Wittfogel considers
that these *were* revolutionary mass movements, even if they involved
little class struggle as Marx understood that. And Chinese Communists had always looked back to peasant uprisings as historical role
models.[46]

Notes on peasant rebellions

There is much that is true in Marx's way of looking at Chinese
history and the many rebellions that occurred in premodern times.
Successful people's uprisings, especially in peasant revolts, began
especially with the overthrow of the Ch'in by the Han dynasty, led
by a commoner called Liu Pang, who became Emperor Kao-tsu, the
dynastic founder of a great empire whose rule lasted about six
hundred years. Another famous peasant rebel turned dynastic
founder was Chu Yüan-chang, the first Ming emperor, who was
driven by famine about six hundred years ago to join the Buddhist-
and Manichaean-inspired rebels of the day.

There were also other, less successful peasant revolts. In an earlier
chapter, we talked about the Taoist-inspired Yellow Turbans of the
second century, who met with eventual failure. Later ones included
those occurring in the mid-seventeenth century, hastening the
demise of the Ming dynasty, as well as the Christian-inspired mid-
nineteenth-century T'ai-p'ing rebellion, which set up a temporary
Heavenly Kingdom of the Great Peace, with a capital in Nanking.
Several of these had real potential for bringing in revolutionary
change, the T'ai-p'ing rebels initiating a new civil service examina-

---

[46] Karl A. Wittfogel, 'Social Revolution in China', in Eugene Kamenka (ed.), *A World in
Revolution?* (Canberra: Australian National University, 1970), 42–9.

tion system based on a Christian curriculum and admitting both women and men as examination candidates. Unfortunately, once in power, the T'ai-p'ing leaders sought solace in old-styled harems, and dissipated their energies by factional struggles while also fighting the Manchus and their allies, until defeat became certain. All this predated the so-called bourgeois Nationalist Republican revolution of 1911 and the Communist revolution of 1949, both of which bore the mark of foreign influences.

If we compare Liu Pang's rebellion and Chu Yüan-chang's, we shall find that in each case, the rebellion mainly replaced with a new dynastic rule a moribund political leadership. If Liu's and Chu's rebellions each succeeded in establishing several hundred years of peaceful government, they did not alter greatly the infrastructure in state or society, after first removing the worst instances of abuse of state power that had led to rebellions. In each case, the victors took the spoils of power for themselves and their own families, and conceded what was necessary to their followers and the populace in order to govern with a semblance of consent. In both cases, the commoners turned emperors demonstrated great suspicion toward those who most assisted them, relentlessly persecuting and even devouring these potential rivals to consolidate their own dynastic gains. With the help of a strong secret police supervised by eunuchs, the power of the Ming state grew by leaps and bounds, an important link in the chain of increasing centralisation of power in the hands of the few in China's history. And this should perhaps be pointed out as the most visible evolutionary change throughout the past four thousand years of known history, with the greatest concentration of power occurring under today's Communists.

No pre-modern political movement revolutionised Chinese society during the time that followed the Han dynasty, even though tremendous social and cultural changes occurred. A religious movement succeeded in bringing in major social changes: Buddhism, a religion introduced from India and Central Asia. Although Buddhism learnt to adapt itself to Chinese culture, some of its teachings served as real challenges to cherished beliefs, and their implementation resulted in new religious and social institutions. I think especially of the belief in *karma* and rebirth, calling into question the custom of ancestral veneration. It basically made ontological equals of descendants and their ancestors and opened the way to toleration of Buddhist monasticism.

The Communist revolution

Our point of departure is to serve the people whole-heartedly and never for a moment divorce ourselves from the masses, to proceed in all cases from the interests of the people and not from one's own self-interest or from the interests of a small group.　　　　　　　　　　　　Mao Zedong[47]

During the years when Communist China had its doors closed, the rest of the world often looked to it as a functioning political utopia, where the beloved Chairman served the interests of his people, and they, in turn, served one another. Such was not unlike the situation during the European Enlightenment, when Western thinkers drew from missionary sources favourable to China to flatter a distant civilisation and society in their zeal to correct abuses in their own world. But, as the outside world of our own times was to find out, the actual facts were quite different.

There is little doubt that Mao Zedong and others of China's leaders rose to power by addressing themselves to the immediate felt needs of the peasant masses. But they did not thereby become the embodiment of the people's aspirations, even if such is party propaganda: a myth designed to sanction all their activities, including those of the repression of all potential rivals.

And the Party in China did assimilate a basic faith underlying Marxism–Leninism: its Hegelian and Marxist faith in the redemptive character of the historical process, and its Leninist faith in the Party as the sole agent of such redemption. Despite the doubt regarding the party's credentials as a party representing the proletariat, its leaders – both Mao and Deng – saw themselves as instruments of history, destined to lead China on the road to modernisation and socialism.[48]

On balance, Mao showed himself a better guerrilla leader than an administrator. He represented a curious combination of visionary and crafty politician. As a visionary, he had the contradictory desires: to modernise the country, and to keep the revolution going on. He shifted from one to another, first trying to modernise – in a naïve way – and then, on failing to achieve that goal, trying to perpetuate the revolution and manipulate it against his own political foes.

---

[47] 'On Coalition Government' (1945), from *Selected Works of Mao Tse-tung* (Beijing: Foreign Languages Press, 4 vols. 1967–9), vol. 3, p. 315.

[48] Benjamin I. Schwartz, *Chinese Communism and the Rise of Mao* (Cambridge, Mass.: Harvard University Press, 1951), 192–99.

In a totalitarian régime like that of China, political criticisms are usually veiled. Under the Communist rule, the use of historical parables became a standard practice, as Mao was recognised as a parallel to the notorious third-century-BCE emperor. Indeed, the first act of Mao's Cultural Revolution was the attack on a historical play written by the scholar Wu Han, which satirised Mao's earlier dismissal of Peng Dehuai.

Still suspicious of the bureaucracy which his own government had created, Mao unleashed the energies of the masses against his own political rivals as well as the party apparatus they controlled. 'Bombard the Headquarters!' he wrote on 5 August 1966, on a 'big-character poster' of his own. He had the help of Lin Biao and the Army. Lin proceeded to build up an exaggerated 'cult' of the Great Helmsman, especially making a fetish of the 'Little Red Book' of quotations from Mao Zedong.

It should be remembered that Mao was already seventy-two years old in 1966, and very worried that the revolution, his life work, was to be destroyed by his comrades who were also the party bureaucrats, bent more on normalising the country than on continuing change. Power struggle was at the core of this man's dreams, and in the course of this struggle, Mao turned the country upside down but emerged personally victorious, as the paramount leader and saviour of the Chinese people, the ultimate 'wise man' of the Communist world, with the status close to deification. In a 1965 poem, which used a mythological context, Mao revealed his ambitions as well as his megalomania:

> I have long aspired to reaching the clouds . . .
> We can clasp the moon in the North Heaven,
> And seize turtles deep down in the Five Seas.
> We'll return amid triumphant song and laughter.
> Nothing is hard in this world,
> If you dare to scale the heights.[49]

For a while, the new China provoked much interest and admiration, to the extent of arousing discussions outside regarding its concerned efforts at remaking humanity, at creating a 'New Man' according to the Marxist–Maoist model. But, when the Bamboo Curtain was finally lifted, those who looked in found a nation impoverished, and reduced, in external appearance, to 'blue ants',

---

[49] Mao, *Poems*, 'Reascending Chingkangshan', pp. 99–100.

who only knew how to sing the praises of the great Chairman, bigger than life in his numerous statues around the country.[50] And the outside world sometimes wondered: was this the sage-king promised by Confucian messianic teachings? When the light finally came regarding Mao's callousness and cruelty, and the tens of millions of people sacrificed in man-made famines and other disasters, this question sounded ridiculous.

But where lies the sage-king paradigm in all this?

The Mao cult, at its peak during the decade-long Cultural Revolution, had claimed for Mao Zedong all power and wisdom. Given Mao's opposition to China's known sages, we might regard him more as the Legalists' ideal ruler, and he certainly behaved as such, frequently hiding from public view and never trusting anyone, even his closest associates. Ironically, Mao was the great rebel against tradition, an individualist at the helm of a socialist régime, restless in the fomenting of permanent revolution. The state he founded revered him enough to add Mao Zedong Thought to the principles of Marxism–Leninism as its official ideology, declaring him in this way to be the sage-ruler, not only during his life, but also after – even if it overturned his policies posthumously.

Has the sage-king paradigm led to the institutions of so-called 'Oriental despotism', which continue to thrive after the Communist Revolution, possibly substituting totalitarian rule for the authoritarian?

True, the sage-king ideal was basically that of a 'benevolent despot', with a government by decree, and an order of succession, whether hereditary or otherwise, also from on high. Even if the ruler is supposed to heed the advice of wise ministers, there is no enforcement possible of benevolent government since a supreme solitary will is what made the ultimate choices. Even if the ruler emptied his mind in meditation or practised *ch'i-kung*, there is no telling that his sharpened wits might not be swayed by other directions than the people's welfare.

I am not thereby saying that the sage-king ideal has been directly responsible for a history of despotism. Not only did the worst despots reject the ideal, but wise ministers frequently invoked it to moderate their rulers' excesses. I am saying that as ideal, and without

---

[50] Consult Lucian W. Pye, *The Mandarin and the Cadre: China's Political Cultures* (Ann Arbor: Center for Chinese Studies, the University of Michigan, 1988), ch. 5, on 'The Mystique of Leadership.'

institutional support, it lacked the power of making its promises come true. I am also saying that the intellectual leaders had persevered too long in their attachment to this powerless ideal, which had shown itself wanting, time and again.

It has been asserted that the intellectuals were, and are, weak-kneed, that they usually preferred collaboration – to the point of enslavement – to criticism or protest, and that they should accept responsibility for the system's shortcomings.

Yet the historical record shows that many intellectuals risked their lives and careers in efforts to criticise or protest, but lacked the military force which made or unmade dynasties. Might made right, and rulers summoned to their assistance those intellectuals ready to put their programme into action. And somehow, might was able to draw upon charisma as well to defend its interests, even though the state continued to secularise itself.

This is not necessarily an indictment of intellectuals. Rather, it is a reflection on the powerlessness of the intellectuals, as a group, who depended for their own political participation on a despotic system, a system which instituted laws for its own consolidation and perpetuation rather than for the welfare of the people. It is also a reflection on the extraordinary resilience of Chinese civilisation, which has resisted correction in its fundamental political outlook. And when certain intellectuals relied upon the spiritual resources of tradition, including meditation and mysticism, for their inner strength, they were not usually able to cloak themselves with that special destiny and charisma, the destiny to rule.

And today (1996), we find that education is at its lowest ebb, with high tuitions introduced especially in universities. The government has shown little sensitivity to the country's millions of illiterates, while permitting the pursuit of instant wealth at any cost. The gap between the rich and the poor, the educated and the others continues to increase, and the impact on the coming generations will be enormous. Before these problems are resolved, it is difficult to speak of China as a modernised country.

THE FUTURE?

Compared to developments in feudal Europe, China's unification took place very early, in 221 BCE. Before that, we knew of the peripatetic philosophers, moving from state to state, looking for a feudal ruler's ears. Since that time, its course has more often been unification than regional division, even when compared to the Indian subcontinent, while its culture had remained relatively homogeneous. For Marxist–Leninists, the implications of when feudalism ended are serious, as is the periodisation of Chinese history, which resists facile categories.

However, in today's Chinese, *feng-chien* or 'feudal' refers to traditional forms of political, social, economic and ideological control and indicates basically the continuance of 'Oriental despotism'. In this perspective, we may better understand those intellectuals who assert that the government no longer represents Communism as an ideology, but is rather the reincarnation of the forces of 'feudalism', subjecting the modernisation drive and everything else to a political dictatorship to be passed on to a new collective élite, composed of the 'princelings' – children of the old cadres.

Oriental Despotism is of course the title of a book by Karl Wittfogel, in which he outlines his theory of hydraulic society. Put simply, it alleges that the control of water for agricultural purposes in ancient societies contributed to the accumulation of total power in the state. For him, China is an example of an ancient hydraulic society.[51] At present, the government in China is set on a huge hydroelectric project near the scenic Three Gorges on the Yang-tze River, despite opposition voiced on the part of those who fear side-effects on the environment as well as the risks of population removal. The difference today is the goal: to enhance industry rather than agriculture.

And as we gaze into an imaginary crystal ball, what can see say about the future of China, and its long-assaulted age-old wisdom?

In Communist countries, where the régime undertakes the political education of the masses, it often awakens political consciousness as well as economic expectations without being able to satisfy such. The constitutional pledges to safeguard democratic rights have actually aroused a hunger and thirst that the powers that be are unable to satisfy. Instead, we see a régime creating an active volcano for itself, and then sitting upon it.

As of this writing, the faction in power has suppressed the voices of reform and even eroded the middle ground itself. The dilemma

[51] Karl A. Wittfogel, *Oriental Despotism: A Comparative Study of Total Power* (New Haven: Yale University Press, 1957), ch. 1.

facing the government is between continuing with a hard-line dictatorship on the one hand, and alternatively permitting a complete overhaul of its own structure through a gradual democratisation. The latter road was that followed successfully by Taiwan and south Korea.

Perhaps, what one might look forward to in China is a kind of compromise: to introduce such structural changes as would enable the separation of powers, to prevent abuses of bureaucratic corruption, and to assure a proper political succession. This will be, in effect, a 'mixing' of two models, of despotism and democracy.[52]

And as a generation of the strong men, the charismatic leaders, passes away, their successors would do well to pay heed to these words of Jean-Jacques Rousseau:

The strongest is never strong enough to be always the master, unless he transforms strength into right, and obedience into duty. . . .

It will always be equally foolish for a man to say to a man or to a people: 'I make with you a convention wholly at your expense and wholly to my advantage; I shall keep it as long as I like, and you will keep it as long as I like.'[53]

CONCLUDING REMARKS

In the earlier chapters, I have attempted to demonstrate the special character of Chinese civilisation: that of the harmony of the parts within the whole, as well as that of theory existing for the sake of practice. Joseph Needham has described the unity of Chinese civilisation as *organismic*, with the various parts functioning like those of a living organism. We think of Confucianism, Taoism and Buddhism, and even of popular religion. These are separate traditions; they are also parts of a greater whole. That is why the term 'Chinese tradition' may be used both in the singular and in the plural. That is why many Chinese still claim to be at the same time, Confucian, Taoist and Buddhist. And that is why Western students of Chinese civilisation encounter such difficulty in seeking to find 'a handle' on China, in looking for a key to resolve the puzzle of China.[54]

---

[52] For related questions, consult Francis Fukuyama, 'Confucianism and democracy', *Journal of Democracy* 6 (April, 1995), pp. 20–33.

[53] Jean-Jacques Rousseau, *The Social Contract and Discourses* (1762) (London: J. M. Dent, 1982), 165, 168.

[54] For Needham, consult *Science and Civilisation*, vol. 2.

There is, I think, a problem with theory existing for the sake of practice. True, it keeps our theorists relevant, so that Chinese philosophies have always been philosophies of life. And as life comprises many levels of experience, including the deepest or mystical, these philosophies have not been merely superficially practical. But our examination of the tradition of Chinese wisdom as a whole, which includes many philosophies, shows that the practical orientation has tended to subject them to state control and manipulation. The country, it appears, always needed an ideology, which can be spelled out in imperial decrees or examination essays, to which truth, so much more elusive, and seemingly always beyond one's immediate grasp, is often made subordinate. The reaction to such a situation has been eremitism and monasticism, as represented especially by Taoists and Buddhists, and occasionally by Confucians living in retirement.

Ancient culture as known to us appears to have been much more that of the nobility than that of the peasants. And where the nobility is concerned, there remains disagreement regarding the identity of the ancient sage-kings, and the manner of their royal succession. The disappearance of political feudalism paved the way, among other things, for greater participation on the part of some commoners in an élitist ritual and moral tradition. On the other hand, the position of women generally deteriorated in pre-modern Chinese history, as a so-called rationalist patriarchal system set in early in the Chou dynasty. Women generally fared better in those ages when Taoism and Buddhism, rather than Confucianism, was dominant, since Confucianism supported a merit system – for males only. Hence the times of Confucian dominance were times when there was less class stratification, but more gender inequality. And this was accompanied by the centralisation of political power which kept all but the actual ruler under near-bondage.

In ancient Greece, in a work entitled the *Republic*, the philosopher Plato wrote about an ideal state governed by a class of Guardians, male and female, who first received rigorous training in philosophy, and whose rule was to be perpetuated by heredity with the help of eugenics. Much like the Chinese government by sage-kings, it was an unrealisable dream.

The Chinese philosophers also came to the conclusion that sagehood was not the preserve of an elect few, say those of royal blood, but accessible to all. They articulated the doctrine of human perfectibility, articulated especially by Mencius. An implicit corollary was the natural equality of all human beings, and the potential for every man to become a king as well. This offered a solid basis for future political transformation, including the flowering of democracy, even if this never quite occurred. However, the sage-king ideal maintained such a strong hold over popular imagination that the country never expected more than a benevolent monarchy, or, perhaps we should say, a benevolent despotism. True, the meaning of this ideal became transformed during the millennia that transpired, until tacit admission was made that the sage need not be a king and the king was usually not a sage. But the drastic demarcation of lines between sagehood and kingship was never drawn, perhaps because such ambiguity suited both the interpreters of the tradition and the power-brokers.

Taoist philosophers yearned for freedom, but it was the freedom of being themselves, as individuals, in contemplation of nature. In many ways, theirs is an escapist philosophy, a source of spiritual consolation for those without power, and as such, it has served rather well even in recent decades. Confucianism has not articulated a theory of human freedom as such. Yet the theme of freedom runs through the entire spectrum of its thought. Without freedom, there can be no self-determination, no self-transcendence, not only in the ethical and spiritual sphere, but also in the social and political spheres. The Sage, the True Man, the Perfect Man, is he who also deserves to rule. The people, on other hand, have always preserved their right to rebel against tyrants.

This is not to deny that proper criticisms can be levelled against certain aspects of Confucianism. In the Confucian social order, human relationships were hierarchically fixed and rigid – with the superior partners, the fathers, husbands, rulers, exercising more right and privilege and the inferior partners performing more duty and submission. Speaking historically, however, this was less the product of Confucianism, and more the combined product of Confucian philosophy developed under the influence of Legalism and its theory of power, and Yin–Yang philosophy with its arbitrary correlation of cosmic forces and human relationships. In the later ages, with the development of neo-Confucianism and its emphasis on spiritual cultivation, Confucian philosophy also took on some of the functions of an escapist consolation for scholars in retirement.

In the post-Christian West, liberal humanism, beginning as a revolt against theism, and eventually influencing many believers in God, has offered a climate of openness for the assertion and discussion of universal moral values. In China, where a Western ideology, Marxism–Leninism, nominally reigns as absolute dogma, the population remembers a native humanist tradition going back more than two millennia to Confucius and even earlier. While ideas of human equality and government by consent arose early, they never led to a political structure that protects human rights. Even the twentieth century has not seen the proper development of institutions of participatory democracy which could assure these rights in China.

Recently, the American political scientist Samuel P. Huntington proposed the possibility of a civilisational clash between Western civilisation and an alliance between what he terms the Confucian civilisation of today's China and the Islamic civilisation of the Middle East.[55] I wish to comment briefly, by pointing out first the incongruity of calling Communist China, which spent many years fighting Confucian values, a Confucian civilisation, and second, the inherently peaceful and harmonious thrust of Confucian culture throughout history. I do not discard the possibility of alliances between *states*, such as between Communist China and any of the Islamic states. But a civilisational alliance, based on common opposition to Western values, is much less likely. Moreover, we have discussed what may be termed the dialectical unity of the secular and the sacred in Chinese wisdom, including Confucianism and Taoism. Ideologically, this has contributed to China's openness to Western, often post-Christian, values, especially those associated with the free market, even if the Communist state still feels itself threatened by the same.[56]

I touch here on the question of whether Chinese civilisation, in particular the Confucian tradition which originated in China and spread to Korea, Japan and Vietnam, promotes or impedes modernisation, including what Max Weber has called the spirit of capitalism. I must be brief. Historical evidence appears to suggest that it

---

[55] Consult Samuel P. Huntington, 'The Clash of Civilizations?' *Foreign Affairs* 72 (summer, 1993), 22–49, and the responses that appeared in the September/October issue that same year.
[56] Consult Liu Binyan, 'Civilization Grafting: No Culture is an Island', *Foreign Affairs*, 72 (Sept./Oct., 1993), 19–21.

opposed modernisation in the beginning of the East–West encounter, but this is now embracing it in those areas where its diffused
values still exercise an influence. More so than Puritan Christianity,
it represents an ethic focused on this world that is possibly reinforced
by its mysticism of cosmic harmony. If initially, an absence of
creative tension between man and nature impeded the development
of science and technology, the tradition is well prepared to respond
positively to the challenge of the West combined with a desire for
improving this life. The problem remains whether modernisation
may render this tradition less relevant, as new problems associated
with high technology ruling over human life demand answers that
are not always so readily found in tradition – a problem that is
confronting Western religious and spiritual civilisation itself.

Indeed, has the wisdom of China yet something to offer us today –
to China, and to the larger world?

My own answer is a cautious Yes, where China is concerned, with
the understanding also that there is as yet little other cultural option
available. In the recent past, Chinese humanism has been tested by
the invasion of Western values, purified by the fires of revolution,
and challenged by the ideology of Marxism–Leninism. No longer
orthodox or established, Confucianism has once more become a
diffused teaching rather than a state system. With self-examination
and self-criticism, it may yet find new life, with which to reinvigorate
a tottering civilisation. And it will do so only in a pluralistic society,
as one school among many others, the way it was when Confucius
himself was alive and teaching.[57]

Where the rest of the world is concerned – especially where the
West, which has so changed China's destiny, is concerned – Chinese
humanism has perhaps also a few things to offer: what some people
call family values and work ethic, but what may more simply be

---

[57] There are many books in Chinese on the subject of contemporary Confucianism and its
problems. Consult Chin Yao-chi, *Chung-kuo she-hui yü wen-hua* (Chinese Society and Culture)
(Hong Kong: Oxford University Press, 1992); Li Ming-hui, *Tang-tai ju-hsüeh te tzu-wo chuan-
hua* (The transformation of contemporary Confucianism) (Nankang, Taiwan: Academia
Sinica, Institute of Philosophy and Literature, 1994), especially ch. 1; Liu Shu-hsien (ed),
Tang-tai ju-hsüeh lun-chi: ch'uan-t'ung yü ch'uang-hsin (On contemporary Confucianism:
tradition and innovation) (Taipei, Academia Sinica, 1995), and *Tang-tai ju-hsüeh lun-chi: t'iao-
chan yü hui-ying* (On Contemporary Confucianism: challenge and response) (Nankang,
Taiwan: Academia Sinica, 1995); Tu Wei-ming, *Ju-chia ti-san-ch'i fa-chuan te ch'ien-ching wen-t'i*
(On the development of a third phase in Confucianism) (Taipei: Linking, 1989); Yü Ying-
shih, *Chung-kuo wen-hua yü hsien-tai pien-ch'ien* (Chinese culture and modern changes) (Taipei:
Sanmin, 1992).

described as discipline and tolerance and a new harmony. Chinese observers of the West have also pointed out what the West could learn from the East. For example, they find excessive individualism, a litigious spirit promoting conflict rather than harmony, and especially in the United States, an unacceptably high crime rate. There is also an increasing gap between the rich and the poor in capitalist societies, a monopoly of political election campaigns by those who can afford them, and the social deprivation of various minorities.[58] Within China, and with official tolerance, religions and spiritualities have been enjoying a mini-revival of sorts during the recent decades. And the ancient art of *qigong* or Chinese yoga, promoting the unity of body and spirit, has been recognised increasingly as a healing resource. The peaceful, disciplined and thriving societies in East Asian countries outside of China with very dense populations demonstrate the people's sense of social harmony. East Asians value what they call humaneness, or human warmth, which they find lacking in a system where human relationships have lost a personal touch. East Asians are also beginning to learn to avoid pollution of their natural environment through unbridled economic development.

To go even deeper, we may find a source for universal harmony and global ethics in the original, mystical, insight that made of kingship in China, a paradigm of wisdom and sageliness. I am speaking of the unity between the human and the heavenly, be that called divinity, nature, or the Tao. I am speaking of the oneness of all things, that unity in which the whole universe finds itself, in which all human beings are related and interrelated, as children of heaven and earth, as stewards of nature and of one another, without being separated from nature itself. As Chang Tsai puts it, and I repeat:

Heaven is my father, earth is my mother,
And even a small creature as I finds an intimate place in their midst.
. . .
All people are my brothers and sisters, and all things are my companions.[59]

Today we may not subscribe with equal zeal to the next line, that 'The great ruler (emperor) is the eldest son of my parents', but we may adjust the line following to say that 'the great ministers [namely,

---

[58] Consult Kishore Mahbubani, 'The Dangers of Decadence: What the Rest Can Teach the West', *Foreign Affairs* 72 (Sept./Oct., 1993), pp. 10–14.
[59] From 'The Western Inscription', see chapter 4.

the world's leaders] are also its stewards'. Yes, they are the stewards of the world's resources: servants, not masters.

And then I might also say with some confidence that East and West have yet something to learn from each other.

A glossary of Sino-Japanese names and terms

Akihito 明仁
Amaterasu Ōmikami 天照大神
An Lu-shan 安祿山
Archer Yi 羿
ch'an / chan 識
Ch'an / Chan (Japanese: *Zen*) 禪
chan-jen / zhanren 占人
Chang Chü-cheng / Zhang
    Juzheng 張居正
Chang Heng / Zhang Heng 張衡
Chang Lu / Zhang Lu 張魯
Chang Tao-ling / Zhang Daoling
    (or Chang Ling / Zhang Ling)
    張道陵 (張陵)
Chang Tsai / Zhang Zai 張載
chao / zhao 詔
Chao Meng / Zhao Meng 趙孟
Chao-chou / Zhaozhou 趙州
Ch'en Liang / Chen Liang 陳亮
Ch'en Meng-chia / Chen Mengjia
    陳夢家
Ch'en Tung / Chen Dong 陳東
Ch'en-hao / Chenhao 宸濠
chen-hsin / zhenxin 眞心
chen-jen / zhenren 眞人
Chen-tsung / Zhenzong 眞宗
Ch'eng Hao / Cheng Hao 程顥
Cheng Hsüan / Zheng Xuan
    鄭玄
Ch'eng Yi / Cheng Yi 程頤
cheng-ming / zhengming 正名
Cheng-tsung / Zhengzong 正宗

chi / ji 祭
ch'i[a] */ qi* 氣
ch'i[b] */ qi* 器
Chi / Ji 稷
Ch'i / Qi 啓
Chi Hsien / Ji Xian 季咸
ch'i-kung / qigong 氣功
ch'i-lin / qilin 麒麟
chi-wei / jiwei 即位
chia-tzu / jiazi 甲子
chiao / jiao 郊
Chieh / Jie 桀
Ch'ien / Qian 乾
Ch'ien Hsüan-tung / Qian
    Xuantong 錢玄同
Ch'ien T'ang 錢唐
chien-ai / jian'ai 兼愛
chih / zhi 知
Chih-yi 智顗
Ch'ih-yu / Chiyou 蚩尤
Ch'in / Qin 秦
ching[a] */ jing* 靜
ching[b] */ jing* 敬
ching[c] */ jing* 經
Ch'iu Ch'u-chi / Qiu Chuji 丘處機
chiu-chou / jiuzhou 九州
chiu-ting / jiuding 九鼎
chou / zhou 咒
Chou / Zhou 周
Chou Tun-yi / Zhou Dunyi 周敦頤
Chou Yü-t'ung / Zhou Yutong
    周予同

Chou-kuan hsin-yi / *Zhouguan xinyi*
周官新義
Chou-li / *Zhouli* 周禮
chu / *zhu* 祝
Chu Hsi / Zhu Xi 朱熹
Ch'ü Yüan / Qu Yuan 屈原
Chu Yüan-chang / Zhu Yuanzhang
朱元璋
Ch'u-tz'u 楚辭
chuan / *zhuan* 傳
chüan / *juan* 卷
ch'uan-kuo hsi / *chuanguo xi* 傳國璽
Chuang-tzu / Zhuangzi 莊子
Ch'un-ch'iu / *Chunqiu* 春秋
Chün-sheng lun 均聖論
chün-tzu / *junzi* 君子
chung[a] / *zhong* 忠
chung[b] / *zhong* 中
Chung-kuo / Zhongguo 中國
chung-min / *zhongmin* 種民
chung-tsai / *zhongzai* 冢宰
chung-wang / *zhongwang* 中王
Daijôsai 大嘗祭
Deng Xiaoping (Teng Hsiao-p'ing)
鄧小平
Duke Ai of Lu 魯哀公
Duke Huan 桓公
Duke Hui of Ch'in / Qin 秦惠公
Duke Ling of Wei 魏靈公
Duke of Chou / Zhou 周公
Duke P'ing 平公
Emperor Wen 文帝
Emperor Wu of Han 漢武帝
Emperor Wu of Liang 梁武帝
Empress Wu 武后
Erh-ya / Erya 爾雅
Fa-tsang / Fazang 法藏
fa 法
fang 方
fang-shih / *fangshi* 方士
Fei Lien / Fei Lian 蜚廉
Feng 封

feng-chien / *fengjian* 封建
Feng-su t'ung-yi 風俗通義
Fo-shuo / *Fo shuo* 佛說
Fo-t'u-ch'eng / Fotucheng 佛圖澄
fu 符
Fu-hsi / Fuxi (or Pao-hsi / Baoxi)
伏羲(包羲)
Fu-sheng / Fusheng 伏勝
fu-tzu / *fuzi* 夫子
Fung Yu-lan / Feng Youlan 馮友蘭
Han 漢
Han-shan Te-ch'ing / Hanshan
Deqing 憨山德清
Hirohito 裕仁
Ho Hsiu / Ho Xiu 何休
Ho-t'u / *Hetu* 河圖
Hou-chu / Houzhu 後主
hsi / *xi* 覡
Hsi K'ang / Xi Kang 嵇康
Hsi-men Pao / Ximen Bao 西門豹
Hsi-wang-mu / Xi Wangmu
西王母
Hsia / Xia 夏
Hsiang Hsiu / Xiang Xiu 向秀
hsiao-jen / *xiaoren* 小人
hsiao-k'ang / *xiaokang* 小康
Hsiao-tsung / Xiaozong 孝宗
Hsiao-yao yu / *Xiaoyao you* 消遙遊
Hsieh / Xie 契
Hsien-pei / Xianbei 鮮卑
hsin / *xin* 心
hsin-chai / *xinzhai* 心齋
hsing / *xing* 性
Hsü Shen / Xu Shen 許慎
hsüan-hsüeh / *xuanxue* 玄學
Hsüan-tsung / Xuanzong 玄宗
hsün-ku / *xungu* 訓詁
Hsün-tzu / Xunzi 荀子
hu 胡
Hu Shih / Hu Shi 胡適
hua-t'ou / *huatou* 話頭
Hua-yen / Huayan 華嚴

Huang Tsung-hsi / Huang Zongxi
  黃宗羲
huang-chi / huangji 皇極
Huang-Lao Chün 黃老君
huang-ti / huangdi 皇帝
Huang-t'ing ching 黃庭經
Huang-t'ing nei-ching 黃庭內經
Hui-neng / Huineng 惠能
Hui-tsung / Huizong 徽宗
Hui-yüan / Huiyuan 慧遠
hun 魂
Hung Hsiu-ch'üan / Hong
  Xiuquan 洪秀全
jen[a] / *ren* 人
jen[b] / *ren* 仁
jen-hsin / renxin 人心
Jen-tsung / Renzong of Sung /
  Song 宋仁宗
Jen-wang ching 仁王經
jiriki 自力
jou / rou 柔
ju[a] / *ru* 如
ju[b] / *ru* 儒
Juan Chi / Ruan Ji 阮籍
jui / rui 睿
jung / rung 戎
Kaizuka Shigeki 貝塚茂樹
kami 神
kamikaze 神風
k'an / kan 看
K'ang Yu-wei / Kang Youwei
  康有爲
*K'ang-wang chih kao / Kangwang
  zhigao* 康王之誥
Kao P'an-lung / Gao Panlong
  高攀龍
k'ao-chü / kaoju 考據
Kao-tsu / Gaozu 高祖
Kao-tsung / Gaozong 高宗
Katô Jôken 加藤常賢
King Chao / Zhao of Ch'in / Qin
  秦昭王

King Ch'eng 成王
King Mu of Chou / Zhou 周穆王
King T'ang / Tang 湯王
King Wen 文王
King Wu 武王
King Yao 堯王
King Yü 禹王
Ko Hung / Ge Hong 葛洪
ko-ming / geming 革命
ko-wu / gewu 格物
K'ou Ch'ien-chih / Kou Qianzhi
  寇謙之
ku / gu 孤
Ku Chieh-kang / Gu Jiegang
  顧頡剛
Ku Yen-wu / Gu Yanwu 顧炎武
Ku-liang / Guliang 穀梁
Ku-ming / Guming 顧命
kua-jen / Guaren 寡人
kuan / guan 官
Kuan Chung / Guan Zhong 管仲
K'uei / Kui 夔
kuei-shen / guishen 鬼神
K'un / Kun 坤
Kun / Gun 鯀
K'ung An-kuo / Kong Anguo
  孔安國
K'ung Ch'iu / Kong Qiu 孔丘
K'ung Chung-ni / Kong Zhongni
  孔仲尼
K'ung Ts'ung-tzu / Kong Congzi
  孔叢子
K'ung Ying-ta / Kong Yingda
  孔穎達
kung-an / gong'an (Japanese: *Koan*)
  公案
Kung-kung / Gonggong 共公
K'ung-tzu chia-yü / Kongzi jiayu
  孔子家語
Kung-yang / Gongyang 公羊
Kuo Hsiang / Guo Xiang 郭象
Lao Tan / Lao Dan 老聃

Lao-tzu / Laozi 老子
Lao-tzu pien-hua ching 老子變化經
lei 類
*li*ᵃ 禮
*li*ᵇ 理
Li Ch'üan / Li Quan 李筌
Li Hung / Li Hong 李洪
Li Kang / Li Gang 李剛
Li Kung / Li Gong 李塨
Li Ssu / Li Si 李斯
Li-chi / Liji 禮記
li-hsüeh / lixue 理學
li-jang / lirang 禮讓
Li-sao / Lisao 離騷
Li-yün / Liyun 禮運
Liang Ch'i-ch'ao / Liang Qichao
　梁啓超
Lin Biao (Lin Piao) 林彪
Lin-chi / Linji 臨濟
ling-t'ai / lingtai 靈台
Liu Hsin / Liu Xin 劉歆
Liu Pang / Liu Bang 劉邦
Liu Shaoqi (Liu Shao-ch'i) 劉少奇
liu-sha / liusha 流沙
Liu-yi / Liuyi 六藝
Lo-shu / Loshu 洛書
*lu*ᵃ 錄
*lu*ᵇ 籙
Lu Chiu-yüan / Lu Jiuyuan 陸九淵
Lu Hsiu-ching / Lu Xiujing 陸修靜
Lü-shih ch'un-ch'iu 呂氏春秋
Lu-t'u / Lutu 魯圖
man 蠻
Mao Heng 毛亨
Mao Zedong (Mao Tse-tung)
　毛澤東
Mao-shan / Maoshan 茅山
Mawangdui (Ma-wang-tui) 馬王堆
Meng-tzu tzu-yi shu-cheng
　孟子字義疏證
miao-wu / miaowu 妙物
ming 名

Ming 明
ming-chu / mingzhu 明主
ming-t'ang / mingtang 明堂
Mo-tzu / Mozi 墨子
Mou Tsung-san / Mou Zongsan
　牟宗三
Nan-tzu / Nanzi 南子
Nei-ching t'u / Neijing tu 內經圖
nei-sheng wai-wang / neisheng
　waiwang 內聖外王
Nü-wa / Nuwa 女媧
nuo 儺
pa-tao / badao 霸道
Pan Chao / Ban Zhao 班昭
*pao*ᵃ */ bao* 胞
*pao*ᵇ */ bao* 寶
Peng Dehuai (P'eng Te-huai)
　彭德懷
P'eng Meng / Peng Meng 彭蒙
P'i Hsi-jui / Pi Xirui 皮錫瑞
Pi-fang / Bifang 畢方
Pien / Pian 扁
pin / bin 賓
p'in-yin / pinyin 拼音
p'o / po 魄
Po-ch'in / Boqin 伯禽
pu / bu 卜
samurai 侍
Seng-chao / Sengzhao 僧肇
Seng-fa / Sengfa 僧法
Sha-men pu-ching wang-che lun
　沙門不敬王者論
shan 禪
shan-jen / shanren 善人
Shang 商
Shang Yang (also Wei Yang)
　商鞅 (衛鞅)
Shang-ch'ing / Shangqing 上清
Shang-ti / Shangdi 上帝
she-shen / sheshen 社神
shen 神
Shen Pu-hai / Shen Buhai 申不害

Shen Yüeh / Shen Yue 沈約

Shen-chou / shenzhou 神州

Shen-hsiu / Shenxiu 神秀

shen-ming / shenming 神明

Shen-nung / shennong 神農

shen-wu / shenwu 神巫

sheng 聖

sheng-jen / shengren 聖人

sheng-shang 聖上

shih[a] / *shi* 尸

shih[b] / *shi* 士

shih[c] / *shi* 事

Shih-ching / Shijing 詩經

Shih-huang-ti / Shihuangdi 始皇帝

Shôwa 昭和

shu 恕

Shu-ching / Shujing 書經

Shun 舜

ssu-ling / siling 四靈

Ssu-ma Ch'ien / Sima Qian
  司馬遷

su-wang / suwang 素王

Sui 隋

Sui-jen / Suiren 燧人

Sun Tzu / Sunzi 孫子

Sung / Song 宋

*ta-ch'eng chih-sheng wen-hsüan-wang
  / dacheng zhisheng wenxuanwang*
    大成至聖文宣王

Ta-chu / Dazhu 大祝

ta-fu / dafu 大夫

Ta-hui Tsung-kao / Dahui
  Zonggao 大慧宗杲

ta-ju / daru 大儒

ta-t'ung / datong 大同

Ta-t'ung shu / Datong shu 大同書

Ta-yün ching 大雲經

Tai Chen / Dai Zhen 戴震

t'ai-chi / taiji 太極

T'ai-p'ing / Taiping 太平

T'ai-p'ing ching 太平經

T'ai-p'ing ch'ing-ling shu 太平清領書

T'ai-p'ing Tao / Taiping Dao 太平道

T'ai-shang Lao-chün / Taishang
  Laojun 太上老君

T'ai-shang Tao-chün / Taishang
  Daojun 太上道君

t'ai-shih / taishi 太史

T'ai-tsu / Taizu 太祖

T'ai-tsung / Taizong 太宗

T'ai-wu / Taiwu 太武

T'ai-yi / Taiyi 太一

T'an Ssu-t'ung / Tan Sitong
  譚嗣同

T'ang / Tang 唐

T'ang Chün-i / Tang Junyi 唐君毅

Tao / Dao 道

Tao-hsin / Daoxin 道心

tao-shih / daoshi 道士

Tao-tsang / Daozang 道藏

Tao-t'ung / Daotong 道統

tao wen-hsüeh / dao wenxue 道問學

te / de 德

teng-chi / deng-ji 登極

Ti[a] / *Di* 狄

ti[b] / *di* 禘

ti[c] / *di* 帝

ti-chih / dizhi 地支

Ti-chün / Dijun 帝俊

tien / dian 顛

t'ien / tian 天

T'ien-hsia / Tianxia 天下

t'ien-jen / tianren 天人

T'ien-jen ho-yi / Tianren heyi
    天人合一

t'ien-kan / tiangan 天干

T'ien-ming / Tianming 天命

T'ien-t'ai / Tiantai 天台

t'ien-t'ang / tiantang 天堂

T'ien-tzu / Tianzi 天子

t'ien-wang / tianwang 天王

ting[a] / *ding* 鼎

ting[b] / *ding* 定

T'o / Tuo 鮀

T'o-pa Wei / Tuo ba Wei 拓跋魏

Tsai-wo / Zaiwo 宰我

Ts'ang Chieh / Cang Jie 蒼頡

ts'e-ming / *ceming* 冊命

ts'e-tu / *cedu* 冊度

Tseng Tien / Zeng Dian 曾點

Tseng-tzu / Zengzi 曾子

Tso / Zuo 左

tso-wang / *zuowang* 坐忘

tsun te-hsing / *zun dexing* 尊德性

tsung-fa / *zongfa* 宗法

tsung-mu / *zongmu* 縱目

Tung Chung-shu / Dong Zhongshu 董仲舒

t'ung-t'ien / *tongtian* 通天

t'ung-t'ien-t'ai / *tongtian tai* 通天台

Tzu-ch'an / Zichan 子產

Tzu-chang / Zizhang 子張

Tzu-hsia / Zixia 子夏

Tzu-kung / Zigong 子貢

Tzu-lu / Zilu 子路

Tzu-yüeh / *Zi yue* 子曰

Wan-wu yi-t'i / *wanwu yiti* 萬物一體

wang[a] 望

wang[b] 王

Wang An-shih / Wang Anshi 王安石

Wang Ch'ung / Wang Chong 王充

Wang Mang 王莽

Wang Pi / Wang Bi 王弼

Wang Su 王肅

Wang Yang-ming / Wang Yangming 王陽明

wang-hsin / *wangxin* 妄心

wang-tao / *wangdao* 王道

wei 緯

Wen-hsüan / Wenxuan 文宣

wu[a] 巫

wu[b] (Japanese: *satori*) 悟

wu[c] 無

Wu Han 吳晗

Wu Hsien / Wu Xian 巫咸

Wu-chi / *Wuji* 無極

wu-chu / *wuzhu* 巫祝

wu-hsin / *wuxin* 無心

Wu-ti / Wudi 武帝

Wu-tsung / Wuzong 武宗

wu-wei / *wuwei* 無爲

wu-yü / *wuyu* 無欲

yang 陽

Yang Hsi / Yang Xi 楊羲

Yang Hsiang-k'uei / Yang Xiangkui 楊向奎

Yen Hui / Yan Hui 顏回

Yen Jo-ch'ü / Yan Roqu 閻若璩

Yen Yüan / Yan Yuan 顏淵

Yi 夷

Yi-ching 易經

Yi-yin 伊尹

Yi-li / *Yili* 儀禮

yi-nien san-ch'ien / *yinian sanqian* 一念三千

yin 陰

Yin Cheng / Yin Zheng 贏政

Yü 禹

Yü Chi / Yu Ji (also Kan Chi / Gan Ji) 于吉 (干吉)

Yü Ying-shih / Yu Yingshi 余英時

yü-lu / *yulu* 語錄

Yü-wen / Yuwen 宇文

Yüan 元

Yüan-shih T'ien-tsun / Yuanshi Tianzun 元始天尊

Yüeh-kuang t'ung-tzu 月光童子

yung[a] / *yong* 俑

yung[b] / *yong* 勇

Bibliography

I. CHINESE AND JAPANESE WORKS

Akatsuka Kiyoshi 赤塚忠. *Chûgoku kodai no shûkyô to bunka* 中國古代の宗教と文化. Tokyo: Kadokawa, 1977.

Araki Kengo 荒木見悟. *Shinpan Bukkyô to Jukyô* 新版佛教と儒教. Tokyo: Kenbun shuppan, 1993.

Chang T'ing-yü 張廷玉 *et al.. Ming-shih* 明史. K'ai-ming ed.

Chang Tsai 張載. *Chang-tzu ch'üan-shu* 張子全書. SPPY ed.

Ch'en Chien 陳建. *Hsüeh-pu t'ung-pien* 學部通辨. Supplement, Cheng Yi-t'ang ch'üan-shu edition.

Chen Guofu (Ch'en Kuo-fu) 陳國符. *Daozang yuanliu kao* 道藏源流考. Beijing: Zhonghua, 1963.

Chen Lai 陳來. *Gudai zongjiao yu lunli: Rujia sixiang de genyuan* 古代宗教與倫理: 儒教思想的根源. Beijing: Joint Publishing, 1996.

Ch'en Meng-chia 陳夢家. *Yin-hsü pu-tz'u tsung-shu* 殷墟卜辭綜述. Peking: Institute of Archaeology, Chinese Academy of Science, 1956.

Ch'en Shou 陳壽. *San-kuo chih* 三國志. K'ai-ming ed.

Ch'eng Hao & Ch'eng Yi 程顥, 程頤. *Erh-Ch'eng ch'üan-shu* 二程全書. SPPY ed.

Chi Yün 紀昀 (ed.). *Ssu-ku ch'üan-shu tsung-mu t'i-yao* 四庫全書總目題要. Shanghai: Commercial Press, 1900.

Ch'ien Mu 錢穆. *Chung-kuo hsüeh-shu-shih lun-ts'ung* 中國學術史論叢. Taipei: Tung-ta, 1976.

Chin Yao-chi 金耀基. *Chung-kuo she-hui yü wen-hua* 中國社會與文化. Hong Kong: Oxford University Press, 1992.

Chin-yüan 淨源. *Chin-shih-tzu chang yün-chien lei-chieh* 金師子章雲間類解. *Taishô Shinshû Daizôkyô* 大正新修大藏經 no. 1880.

Chou-li Cheng-chu 周禮鄭注. SPPY ed.

Chou-li cheng-yi 周禮正義. SPPY ed.

Chou Tun-yi 周敦頤. *Chou Tzu T'ung-shu* 周子通書. SPPY ed.

Chou-yi cheng-yi 周易正義. SPPY ed.

278

Chu Hsi 朱熹. *Shih-ching chi-chuan* 詩經集傳. Taipei reprint: Ch'u-ming, [1952].

   Chou-yi pen-yi 周易本義. *Chu-tzu yi-shu* 朱子遺書 series. Taipei reprint: Yi-wen, 1969.

   Yi-li ching-chuan chi-chieh 儀禮經傳集解. The Four Libraries Rare Book series, 1980 reprint, 10th series.

   Chu Wen-kung wen-chi 朱文公文集. SPPY ed.

Chu-tzu Yin-fu ching k'ao-yi 朱子陰符經考義. *Chu-tzu yi-shu* series. Taipei reprint: Yi-wen, 1969.

Chu-tzu yü-lei 朱子語類, 1473 ed. Taipei reprint: Cheng-chung, 1973.

Chu Wei-mo-chieh ching 注維摩詰經. *Taishô Shinshû Daizôkyô* no. 1775.

Chuang-tzu 莊子. SPPY ed.

Chung Tsai-chün 鍾彩鈞 *et al.* (eds.). *Kuo-chi Chu-tzu hsüeh hui-yi lun-wen chi* 國際朱子學會議論文集. Nankang, Taiwan: Academia Sinica, 1993.

Fan Yeh 范曄. *Hou Han-shu* 後漢書. K'ai-ming ed.

Fo-shuo Yüeh-kuang t'ung-tzu ching 佛說月光童子經. *Taishô Shinshû Daizôkyô* no. 534.

Fukui Kôjun 福井康順 (ed.). *Dôkyô no kisoteki kenkyû* 道教の基礎的研究. Tokyo: Shoseki bunbutsu ryûtsûkai, 1965.

Fukui Kôjun *et al.* (eds.). *Dôkyô* 道教, 3 vols Tokyo: Hirakawa, 1983.

Han Fei Tzu 韓非子. SPPY ed.

Hsü Chin-hsiung 許進雄. *Chung-kuo ku-tai she-hui: wen-tzu yü jen-lei hsüeh te t'ou-shih* 中國古代社會：文字與人類學的透視, revised edition. Taipei: Commercial Press, 1995.

   Ku-wen hsieh-sheng tzu-ken 古文諧聲字根. Taipei: Commercial, 1995.

Hsü Cho-yün 許綽雲. *Hsi Chou shih* 西周史. Taipei: Linking, 1984.

Hsü Shen 許慎. *Shuo-wen chieh-tzu Tuan-chu* 說文解字段注. SPPY ed.

Hsün-tzu 荀子. SPPY ed.

Hu Shih 胡適. *Tai Tung-yüan te che-hsüeh* 戴東原的哲學. Shanghai: Commercial Press, 1928.

Huai-nan-tzu 淮南子. SPPY ed.

Huang Tsung-hsi 黃宗羲. *Ming-yi tai-fang-lu* 明夷待訪錄. SPPY ed.

Huang Tsung-hsi (comp.). *Ming-ju hsüeh-an* 明儒學案. SPPY ed.

Huang Tsung-hsi & Ch'üan Tsu-wang 全祖望 (comp.). *Sung-Yüan hsüeh-an* 宋元學案. SPPY ed.

Hui-chiao 慧皎. *Kao-seng chuan* 高僧傳. *Taishô Shinshû Daizôkyô* no. 2059.

Hung Chin-shan 洪金山. *Han-Wei nan-pei-ch'ao pei-hsüeh chih yen-chiu* 漢魏南北朝碑學之研究. N.P., 1974.

Ikeda Suetoshi 池田末利. *Chûgoku kodai shûkyô shi kenkyû* 中國古代宗教史研究. Tokyo: Tôkai University Press, 1981.

Itô Michiharu 伊藤道治. *Chûgoku kodai ôchô no keisei* 中國古代王朝の形成. Tokyo: Sôbunsha, 1975.

Jao Tsung-i 饒宗頤. *Yin-tai chen-pu jen-wu t'ung-k'ao* 殷代貞卜人物通考. Hong Kong University Press, 1959.

"Ssu-fang feng hsin-i 四方風新義" in *Chung-shan ta-hsüeh hsüeh-pao* 中山大學學報, 4 (1988) 68-69.

Jen-wang hu-kuo po-je po-lo-mi tuo ching 仁王護國般若波羅蜜多經. *Taishô Shinshû Daizôkyô* no. 246.

Jung Chao-tsu 容肇祖. *Wei-Chin te tzu-jan chu-yi* 魏晉的自然主義. Taipei: Commercial Press, 1970.

Jung Keng 容庚 *et al.. Yin Chou ch'ing-t'ung-ch'i t'ung-lun* 殷周青銅器通論. Beijing: Institute of Archaeology, Chinese Academy of Science, 1958.

Kageyama Seiichi 影山誠一. *Chûgoku keigakushikô* 中國經學史綱. Tokyo: Daitô Bunka University, 1970.

Kaizuka Shigeki 貝塚茂樹. *Chûgoku no shinwa: Kamigami no tanjô* 中國の神話: 神がみの誕生. Tokyo: Iwanami, 1963.

Kanaya Osamu 金谷治. *Kanshi no kenkyû: Chûgoku kodai shisôshi no ichimen* 管子の研究 - 中國古代思想史の一面. Tokyo: Iwanami, 1987.

K'ang Yu-wei 康有爲. *Ta-t'ung shu* 大同書. Shanghai: Chung-hua, 1936.

Hsin-hsüeh wei-ching k'ao 新學僞經考. Taipei: World Bookstore, 1962.

K'ung-tzu kai-chih k'ao 孔子改制考. 1920 ed. Taipei: Commercial Press, 1968 reprint.

Kanô Naoki 狩野直喜. *Ryôkan gakujutsu kô* 兩漢學術考. Tokyo, Chikuma Shobô, 1964.

Katô Jôken 加藤常賢. *Chûgoku kodai bunka no kenkyû* 中國古代文化の研究. Tokyo : Nishô Gakusha Daigaku Shuppanbu, 1980.

Ku Yen-wu 顧炎武. *T'ing-lin shih-wen-chi* 亭林詩文集. Ssu-pu ts'ung-k'an first series.

Kuan-hsin lun 觀心論. *Taishô Shinshû Daizôkyô* no. 2833.

Kuan-tzu 管子. SPPY ed.

Kuo-yü 國語. SPPY ed.

Lao-tzu 老子. *Ma-wang-tui Han-mu po-shu: Lao-tzu*. Peking: Wen-wu, 1976.

Li-chi Cheng-chu 禮記鄭注. SPPY ed.

Li Chih 李贄. *Feng-shu* 焚書. Beijing: Zhonghua, 1974.

Li Hsiao-ting 李孝定 (ed.). *Chia-ku wen-tzu chi-shih* 甲骨文字集釋. Nankang, Taiwan: Institute for History and Philology, Academia Sinica, 1982.

Han-tzu te ch'i-yüan yü yen-pien lun-ts'ung 漢字的起源與演變論叢. Taipei: Linking, 1986.

Li Kung 李塨. *Ta-hsüeh pien-yeh* 大學辨業, in *Yen-Li ts'ung-shu* 顏李叢書. N.P.: Ssu-ts'un hsüeh-hui, 1923.

Li Ming-hui 李明輝. *Tang-tai ju-hsüeh te tzu-wo chuan-hua* 當代儒學的自我轉化. Nankang, Taiwan: Institute of Philosophy and Literature, Academia Sinica, 1994.

Li Yen-shou 李延壽. *Pei-shih* 北史. K'ai-ming ed.

Liang Ch'i-ch'ao (Liang Qichao) 梁啓超. *Qingdai xueshu gailun* 清代學術概論, in Zhu Weizheng 朱維錚 (ed.), *Liang Qichao lun Qing xueshu liangzhong* 梁啓超論清學術兩種. Shanghai: Fudan University Press, 1983.

"Fo-tien chih fan-yi 佛典之翻譯," in *Fo-hsüeh yen-chiu shih-pa p'ien* 佛學研究十八篇, 1936 ed. Reprinted Taipei: Chung-hua, 1971.

Lieh-tzu 列子. SPPY ed.

Liu Hsü 劉昫. *Chiu T'ang-shu* 舊唐書. K'ai-ming ed.

Liu Shih-p'ei 劉師培. *Han Sung hsüeh-shu yi-t'ung lun* 漢宋學術異同論, in *Liu Sheng-shu hsien-sheng yi-shu* 劉申叔先生遺書 (n.p., 1936), vol. 15.

Liu Shu-hsien 劉述先 (ed.). *Tang-tai ju-hsüeh lun-chi: ch'uan-t'ung yü ch'uang-hsin* 當代儒學論集: 傳統與創新. Nankang, Taiwan: Academia Sinica, 1995.

Tang-tai ju-hsüeh lun-chi: t'iao-chan yü hui-ying 當代儒學論集:挑戰與回應. Nankang, Taiwan: Academia Sinica, 1995.

Liu Xiang 劉翔. *Chung-kuo ch'uan-t'ung chia-chih kuan-nien ch'uan-shih hsüeh* 中國傳統價值觀念詮釋學. Taipei: Kui-kuan Publishing, 1993.

Lo Meng-ch'e 羅夢冊. *K'ung-tzu wei-wang erh wang lun* 孔子未王而王論. Taipei: Hsüeh-sheng, 1982.

Lu Chiu-yüan 陸九淵. *Hsiang-shan ch'üan-chi* 象山全集. SPPY ed.

Lü-shih ch'un-ch'iu 呂氏春秋. SPPY ed.

Lü Ssu-mien 呂思勉 *et al. Ku-shih pien* 古史辨, 1941 ed. Reprinted Hong Kong: T'ai-p'ing, 1963.

Lun-yü cheng-yi 論語正義. SPPY ed.

Ma-wang-tui Han-mu po-shu: Lao-tzu 馬王堆漢墓帛書: 老子. Beijing: Wen-wu, 1976.

Mao-shih cheng-yi 毛詩正義. SPPY ed.

Meng-tzu chu-shu 孟子注疏. SPPY ed.

Mo-tzu 墨子. SPPY ed.

Morohashi Tetsuji 諸橋轍次. *Keigaku kenkyū josetsu* 經學研究序說. Tokyo: Meguro shoten, 1941.

Mou Tsung-san 牟宗三. *Ts'ai-hsing yü hsüan-li* 才性與玄理. Taipei: Student Bookstore, 1983.

Nemoto Makoto 根本誠. *Chūgoku koten shisō no kenkyū* 中國古典思想の研究. Tokyo: Gendai Ajia shuppankai, 1971.

Pan Ku 班固. *Han-shu* 漢書. K'ai-ming ed.

Po-hu t'ung shu-cheng 白虎通疏證, 1875 ed. Taipei reprint, Chung-kuo tzu-hsüeh ming-chu chi-ch'eng, Rare Books Collection.

Pao-p'u-tzu 抱朴子. SPPY ed.

Pi Xirui (P'i Hsi-jui) 皮錫瑞. *Jingxue tonglun* 經學通論. Beijing: Zhonghua, 1954.

Jingxue lishi 經學歷史, 1928 ed. Beijing: Zhonghua, 1959.

Sa Meng-wu 薩孟武. *Chung-kuo fa-chih ssu-hsiang* 中國法治思想. Taipei: Yen-po Press, 1978.

Sakade Yoshinobu 坂出祥伸. *Dôkyô to yôjô shisô* 道教と養生思想. Tokyo: Perikansha, 1992.

'*Ki' to yôjô: Dôkyô no yôjôjutsu to jujutsu* 氣と養生 - 道教の養生術と呪術. Kyoto: Jinbun shoin, 1993.

Satô Hitoshi 佐藤仁. *Shushi: oi yasuku gaku narigatashi* 朱子: 老い易く學成り難し. Tokyo: Shûeisha, 1985.

Seng-chao 僧肇. *Chao-lun* 肇論. *Taishô Shinshû Daizôkyô* no. 1858.

Seng-yu 僧祐. *Hung-ming chi* 弘明集. SPPY ed.

Shang-shu K'ung-chuan 尚書孔傳. SPPY ed.

Shen Yüeh 沈約. *Chün-sheng lun* 均聖論, in Tao-hsüan 道宣 (ed.), *Kuang Hung-ming chi* 廣弘明集. SPPY ed.

Shima Kunio 島邦男. *Inkyo bokuji kenkyû* 殷墟卜辭研究. Hirosaki, 1958.

Shirakawa Shizuka 白川靜. *Chung-kuo ku-tai wen-hua* 中國古代文化. Taipei: Wen-ching, 1983.

Ssu-ma Ch'ien 司馬遷. *Shih-chi* 史記. K'ai-ming ed.

Su-ling ching 素靈經. Tao-tsang 道藏 no. 1026.

Sung Shou 宋綬 *et al.*. *T'ang Ta-chao-ling chi* 唐大詔令集, Ming edition. Taipei: Ting-wen, [1972]

Ta-ch'eng wu-sheng fang-pien men 大乘無生方便門. *Taishô Shinshû Daizôkyô* no. 2834.

Tai Chen 戴震. *Tai-chen wen-chi* 戴震文集. Beijing: Zhonghua, 1980.

T'ai-shang chu-kuo chiu-min tsung-chen pi-yao 太上助國救民總眞秘要. *Tao-tsang*, no. 987.

T'an Ssu-t'ung 譚嗣同. *Jen-hsüeh* 仁學. Shanghai: Zhonghua edition, 1962.

T'ang Hua 唐華. *K'ung-tzu che-hsüeh ssu-hsiang yen-chiu* 孔子哲學思想研究. Taipei: Cheng-chung, 1977.

Tao-hsüan 道宣 (ed.). *Kuang Hung-ming chi* 廣弘明集. SPPY ed.

Te-ch'ing 德清. *Chao-lun lüeh-chu* 肇論略注. *Hsü Tsang-ching* 續藏經, vol. 96.

Tso-chuan 左傳. SPPY ed.

Tsuda Sôkichi 津田左右吉. *Rongo to Kôshi no shisô* 論語と孔子の思想, in *Tsuda Sôkichi zenshû* 津田左右吉全集. Tokyo: Iwanami, 1964.

Tu Wei-ming 杜維明. *Ju-chia ti-san-ch'i fa-chan ti ch'ien-ching wen-t'i* 儒家第三期發展的前景問題. Taipei: Linking, 1989.

Tung Chung-shu 董仲舒. *Ch'un-ch'iu fan-lu* 春秋繁露. SPPY ed.

Uchino Kumaichirô 內野熊一郎. *Shindai ni okeru keisho keisetsu no kenkyû* 秦代に於ける經書經說の研究. Tokyo: Tôhôbunka Gakuin, 1939.

Wang An-shih 王安石. *Chou-kuan hsin-yi* 周官新義. Four Libraries Rare Books ed. Special Collection.

Wang Ch'ung 王充. *Lun-heng* 論衡. SPPY ed.

Wang Yang-ming 王陽明. *Yang-ming ch'üan-shu* 陽明全書. SPPY ed.

Wei Cheng 魏徵. *Sui-shu* 隋書. K'ai-ming ed.

Wei Cheng-t'ung 韋政通. *Ju-chia yü hsien-tai Chung-kuo* 儒家與現代中國. Taipei: Tung-ta, 1984.

Wei Shou 魏收. *Wei-shu* 魏書. K'ai-ming ed.

Wen T'ien-hsiang 文天祥. *Wen-shan hsien-sheng chi* 文山先生集. Ssu-pu ts'ung-k'an 1st series.

Yang Kuan (Yang K'uan) 楊寬. *Qin Shihuang* 秦始皇. Shanghai: Renmin, 1956.

Zhanguo shi 戰國史, 2nd edition. Shanghai: Renmin, 1983.

Yen Jo-chü 閻若璩. *Ku-wen Shang-shu shu-cheng* 古文尚書疏證 in Wang Hsien-ch'ien 王先謙 (comp.), *Huang Ch'ing ching-chieh hsü-pien* 皇清經解 續編. (Preface, 1889).

Yen T'ieh lun 鹽鐵論. SPPY ed.

Yen Yüan 顏元. *Ts'un-hsüeh p'ien* 存學篇. SPPY ed.

Yi-li Cheng-chu 儀禮鄭注. SPPY ed.

Yü Ying-shih 余英時. *Chung-kuo chih-shih chieh-ts'eng shih-lun (Ku-tai p'ien)*. 中國 知識階層史論(古代篇). Taipei: Linking, 1980.

Chung-kuo wen-hua yü hsien-tai pien-ch'ien 中國文化與現代變遷. Taipei: Sanmin, 1992.

Yuan Ke (Yüan K'o) 袁珂 (ed.). *Shan-hai-ching chiao-chu* 山海經校注. Taipei reprint, 1978.

Zhu Weizheng 朱維錚 (ed.). *Zhou Yutong jingxueshi lunzhu xuanji* 周予同經學史 論著選集. Shanghai: Renmin, 1983.

2. WORKS IN WESTERN LANGUAGES

Allan, Sarah, *The Heir and the Sage: Dynastic Legend in Early China*, San Francisco: Chinese Materials Center, 1981.

The Shape of the Turtle: Myth, Art and Cosmos in Early China, Albany: State University of New York Press, 1991.

Allan, Sarah (ed.), *Legend, Lore and Religion in China*, Los Angeles: Chinese Materials Center, 1979.

Armelin, Indumati, *Le Roi détenteur de la roue solaire en révolution, 'cakravartin': selon le brahmanisme et selon le bouddhisme*, Paris: P. Geuthner, 1975.

Basham, A. L. (ed.), *Kingship in Asia and Early America*, Mexico City: El Colegio de Mexico, 1981.

Bell, Catherine, 'Ritualization of Texts and Textualization of Ritual in the Codification of Taoist Liturgy', *History of Religions* 27 (1988), 366–92.

Bendix, Reinhard, *Max Weber: An Intellectual Portrait*, New York: Doubleday, 1962.

Biot, Édouard (trans.), *Le Tcheou li ou rites de Tcheou*, 2 vols, Paris: L'Imprimérie Nationale, 1851.

Blacker, Carmen, 'The *Shinza* in the *Daijōsai*: Throne, Bed or Incubation Couch?' *Japanese Journal of Religious Studies* 17 (1990), 179–90.

Blakney, Raymond B. (trans.), *Meister Eckhart: A Modern Translation*, New York: Harper, 1941.

Bleicher, Josef. (ed.), *Contemporary Hermeneutics*, London: Routledge and Kegan Paul, 1980.

Bochenski, J. M., *Soviet Russian Dialectical Materialism (DIAMAT)*, Dordrecht: Reidel, 1963.

Bodde, Derk, 'Myths of Ancient China', in S. N. Kramer (ed.), *Mythologies of the Ancient World*, Garden City: Doubleday, 1961, pp. 369–408.

Bol, Peter Kees, *'This Culture of Ours': Intellectual Transitions in T'ang and Sung China*, Stanford University Press, 1992.

Bruce, F. F.; and E. G. Rupp (eds), *Holy Book and Holy Tradition*, Manchester University Press, 1968.

Buswell, Robert E., Jr (ed.), *Chinese Buddhist Apocrypha*, Honolulu: University of Hawaii Press, 1990.

Carter, Thomas F., *The Invention of Printing in China and its Spread Westward*, revised by L. Carrington Goodrich, 2nd ed., New York: Ronald Press, 1955.

Chaffee, John W., *The Thorny Gates of Learning in Sung China: A Social History of the Examinations*, Cambridge University Press, 1985.

Chan, Wing-tsit, *Chu Hsi: New Studies*, Honolulu: University of Hawaii Press, 1989.

'The Evolution of the Confucian Concept *Jen*', *Philosophy East and West* 4 (1955), 295–319.

A Source Book in Chinese Philosophy, Princeton University Press, 1964.

Chan, Wing-tsit (ed.), *Chu Hsi and Neo-Confucianism*, Honolulu: University of Hawaii Press, 1986.

Chang Chung-yuan (ed. and trans.), *Original Teachings of Ch'an Buddhism: Selected from the Transmission of the Lamp*, New York: Grove Press, 1969.

Chang, Kwang-chih, *The Archaeology of Ancient China*, 4th ed., revised, New Haven: Yale University Press, 1986.

Art, Myth and Ritual: The Path to Political Authority in Ancient China, Cambridge, Mass.: Harvard University Press, 1983.

Shang Civilization, New Haven: Yale University Press, 1980.

Chang Tsung-tung, *Der Kult der Shang-Dynastie im Spiegel der Orakelinschriften*, Wiesbaden: Otto Harrassowitz, 1970.

Chappell, David W. (ed.), *Buddhist and Taoist Practice in Medieval Chinese Society*, Honolulu: University of Hawaii Press, 1987.

Buddhist and Taoist Studies, Honolulu: University of Hawaii Press, 1987.

Chavannes, Édouard, *Le T'ai chan: essai de monographie d'un culte chinois*, 1910 ed., Taipei, 1970 reprint.

Ch'en, Kenneth, *Buddhism in China: A Historical Survey*, Princeton University Press, 1964.

Cheng Chung-ying, *New Dimensions in Confucian and Neo-Confucian Philosophy*, Albany: State University of New York Press, 1991.

Chevreau, Guy, *Catch the Fire: The Toronto Blessing, An Experience of Renewal and Revival*, Toronto: HarperCollins, 1995.

Ching, Julia, *Chinese Religions*, London: Macmillan/New York, Orbis, 1993.
Confucianism and Christianity: A Comparative Study, Tokyo: Kodansha International, 1977.
'Neo-Confucian Utopian Theories and Political Ethics', *Monumenta Serica* 30 (1972–3), 1–56.
Probing China's Soul: Religion, Politics, Protest in the People's Republic, San Francisco: Harper & Row, 1990.
To Acquire Wisdom: The Way of Wang Yang-ming, New York: Columbia University Press, 1976.
Ching, Julia; and Chao-ying Fang (eds), *The Records of Ming Scholars by Huang Tsung-hsi: A Selected Translation*, Honolulu: University of Hawaii Press, 1987.
Ching, Julia; and R. W. L. Guisso (eds), *Sages and Filial Sons*, Hong Kong: Chinese University Press, 1991.
Ching, Julia; and Willard G. Oxtoby (eds), *Moral Enlightenment: Leibniz and Wolff on China*, Nettetal: Steyler Verlag, 1992.
Chow, Kai-wing, *The Rise of Confucian Ritualism in Late Imperial China: Ethics, Classics, and Lineage Discourse*, Stanford University Press, 1994.
Chung Tsai-chun, *The Development of the Concepts of Heaven and of Man in the Philosophy of Chu Hsi*, Nankang, Taiwan: Institute of Literature and Philosophy, Academia Sinica, 1993.
Conze, Edward (trans.), *The Short Prajñāpāramitā Texts*, London: Luzac, 1973.
Creel, Herrlee G., *The Birth of China*, New York: Frederick Ungar, 1937.
Confucius: The Man and the Myth, New York: J. Day, 1949.
The Origins of Statecraft in China, University of Chicago Press, 1970.
Shen Pu-hai: A Chinese Political Philosopher of the Fourth Century B.C. University of Chicago Press, 1974.
Creel, Herrlee G. (ed.), *What is Taoism and Other Studies in Chinese Cultural History*, University of Chicago Press, 1970.
Davies, Stevan L., *Jesus the Healer: Possession, Trance and the Origins of Christianity*, New York: Continuum, 1995.
Davis, Michael C. (ed.), *Human Rights and Chinese Values: Legal, Philosophical and Poltical Perspectives*, Hong Kong: Oxford University Press, 1995.
de Bary, Wm. Theodore, *The Message of the Mind in Neo-Confucianism*, New York: Columbia University Press, 1989.
de Bary, Wm. Theodore (ed.), *Sources of Chinese Tradition*, New York: Columbia University Press, 1960.
(ed.), *The Unfolding of Neo-Confucianism*, New York: Columbia University Press, 1975.
de Bary, Wm. Theodore (trans.), *Waiting for the Dawn: A Plan for the Prince*, New York: Columbia University Press, 1993.
De Jong, J. W., *Buddha's Word in China*, Canberra: Australian National University, 1968.
De Visser, M. W., *Ancient Buddhism in Japan: Sutras and Ceremonies in Use in the Seventh and Eighth Centuries A.D. and Their History in Later Times*, 2 vols, Leiden: E. J. Brill, 1935.

Dean, Stanley R. (ed.), *Psychiatry and Mysticism*, Chicago: Nelson-Hall, 1975.
Denny, Frederick M.; and Rodney L. Taylor (eds), *The Holy Book in Comparative Perspective*, Columbia: University of South Carolina Press, 1985.
Dumoulin, Heinrich, *Zen Buddhism: A History*, trans. by James W. Heisig and Paul Knitter, 2 vols, New York: Macmillan; London: Collier Macmillan, 1988–90.
Eber, Irene (ed.), *Confucianism: The Dynamics of Tradition*, New York: Macmillan, 1986.
Eichhorn, Werner, *Beitrag zur rechtlichen Stellung des Buddhismus und Taoismus im Sung-Staat*, Leiden: E. J. Brill, 1968.
Die Religionen Chinas, Stuttgart: Kohlhammer, 1973.
Eliade, Mircea, *Cosmos and History: The Myth of the Eternal Return*, New York: Pantheon, 1954.
Shamanism: Archaic Techniques of Ecstasy, Princeton University Press, 1964.
Eliade, Mircea (ed.), *The Encyclopedia of Religion*, 16 vols, New York: Macmillan, 1987.
Ellwood, Robert S., *The Feast of Kingship: Accession Ceremonies in Ancient Japan*, A *Monumenta Nipponica* Monograph, Tokyo: Sophia University, 1973.
Elman, Benjamin A., *Classicism, Politics and Kinship: The Ch'ang-chou School of New Text Confucianism in Late Imperial China*, Berkeley: University of California Press, 1990.
From Philosophy to Philology, Cambridge, Mass.: Harvard University Press, 1984.
Eno, Robert, *The Confucian Creation of Heaven: Philosophy and the Defense of Ritual Mastery*, Albany: State University of New York Press, 1990.
Feuchtwang, Stephan, *The Imperial Metaphor: Popular Religion in China*, London & New York: Routledge, 1992.
Fingarette, Herbert, *Confucius: the Secular as Sacred*, New York: Harper & Row, 1972.
Firth, Raymond, *Tikopia Ritual and Belief*, London: Allen & Unwin, 1967.
Fitzgerald, C. P., *The Empress Wu*, Melbourne: F. W. Cheshire, 1955.
Forte, Antonino, *Mingtang and Buddhist Utopias in the History of the Astronomic Clock: The Tower, Statue and Armillary Sphere Constructed by Empress Wu*, Rome: Istituto Italiano per il Medio e Estremo Oriente / Paris: École Française d'Extrême-Orient, 1988.
Frankfort, Henri, *Kingship and the Gods*, University of Chicago Press, 1948.
Fukuyama, Francis, 'Confucianism and democracy', *Journal of Democracy* 6 (April, 1995), 20–33.
Trust: The Social Virtues and the Creation of Prosperity, New York: Free Press, 1995.
Fung Yu-lan, *A History of Chinese Philosophy*, trans. by Derk Bodde, 2 vols, Princeton University Press, 1953.
Gadamer, Hans-Georg, *Truth and Method*, New York: Continuum, 1975.

Gernet, Jacques, *Les Aspects économiques du bouddhisme dans la société chinoise du Ve au Xe siècle*, Paris: École Française d'Extrême-Orient, 1956.

Girardot, N. J., *Myth and Meaning in Early Taoism*, Berkeley: University of California Press, 1983.

Graham, A. C., *Disputers of the Tao: Philosophical Argument in Ancient China*, La Salle, Ill.: Open Court, 1989.

Studies in Chinese Philosophy and Philosophical Literature, Albany: State University of New York Press, 1990.

Graham, A. C. (trans.), *The Book of Lieh-tzu*, London: John Murray, 1960.

(trans.), *Chuang Tzu: The Inner Chapters*, London: Allen & Unwin, 1981.

Granet, Marcel, *Festivals and Songs of Ancient China*, New York: Dutton, 1932.

The Religion of the Chinese People, Oxford: Blackwell, 1975.

Gregory, Peter N. (ed.), *Sudden and Gradual Approaches to Enlightenment in Chinese Thought*, Honolulu: University of Hawaii Press, 1987.

(ed.), *Traditions of Meditation in Chinese Buddhism*, Honolulu: University of Hawaii Press, 1986.

Griffith, Samuel B. (trans.), *Sun Tzu pin-fa* (Sun Tzu's Art of War), London: Oxford University Press, 1963.

Grim, John A., *The Shaman: Patterns of Siberian and Ojibway Healing*, Norman: University of Oklahoma Press, 1983.

Guisso, R. W. L., *Wu Tse-t'ien and the Politics of Legitimation in T'ang China*, Bellingham: Western Washington University, 1978.

Hall, David H.; and Roger T. Ames, *Thinking Through Confucius*, Albany: State University of New York Press, 1987.

Harvey, Peter, *An Introduction to Buddhism: Teachings, History, Practices*, Cambridge University Press, 1990.

Hawkes, David (trans.), *Ch'u Tz'u: The Songs of the South*, London: Oxford University Press, 1959.

Henderson, John B., *Scripture, Canon and Commentary: A Comparison of Confucian and Western Exegesis*, Princeton University Press, 1991.

Hendricks, Robert G. (trans.), *Lao-tzu Te-tao ching: A New Translation Based on the Recently Discovered Ma-wang-tui Texts*, New York: Ballantine Books, 1989.

Hershock, Peter D., 'Person as Narration: The Dissolution of "Self" and "Other" in Ch'an Buddhism', *Philosophy East and West* 44 (1994), 685–710.

Hocart, A. M., *Kingship*, London: Watts, 1941.

Holzman, Donald, *Poetry and Politics: The Life And Works of Juan Chi*, A.D. 210–263, Cambridge University Press, 1976.

Hsiao Kung-ch'üan, *A History of Chinese Political Thought*, trans. by Frederick Mote, Princeton University Press, 1979.

Hsü, Sung-peng, *A Buddhist Leader in Ming China: The Life and Thought of Han-shan Te-ch'ing*, University Park: Pennsylvania State University Press, 1978.

Hu Shih, 'Confucianism', *Encyclopaedia of Social Sciences* (New York: Macmillan, 1930–5), vol. 4, pp. 198–201.
Huntington, Samuel P., 'The Clash of Civilizations?' *Foreign Affairs* 72 (summer, 1993), 22–49.
The Third Wave: Democratization in the Late Twentieth Century, Norman: University of Oklahoma Press, 1991.
Huntington, Samuel P.; and H. Moore, *Authoritarian Politics in Modern Society: The Dynamics of Established One-Party Systems*, New York: Basic Books, 1970.
Hurtado, Larry (ed.), *Goddesses in Religion and Modern Debate*, Atlanta: Scholars Press, 1990.
Kaltenmark, Max, '*Ling-pao*: note sur un terme du taoïsme religieux', in *Mélanges publiés par l'Institut des Hautes Études Chinoises*, vol. 2 (Paris: Presses Universitaires de France, 1960), pp. 573–4.
Kamenka, Eugene (ed.), *A World in Revolution?* Canberra: Australian National University, 1970.
Keightley, David N., 'Shang divination and metaphysics', *Philosophy East and West* 38 (1988), 367–97.
Kelber, Werner H., *The Oral and the Written Gospel*, Philadelphia: Fortress Press, 1983.
Kohn, Livia, *Early Chinese Mysticism: Philosophy and Soteriology in the Chinese Tradition*, Princeton University Press, 1992.
(ed.), *The Taoist Experience: An Anthology*, Albany: State University of New York Press, 1993.
Kohn, Livia (ed.), *Taoist Meditation and Longevity Techniques*, Ann Arbor: Center for Chinese Studies, University of Michigan, 1989.
Küng, Hans; and Julia Ching, *Christianity and Chinese Religions*, New York: Doubleday, 1988.
Lai, Whalen, '*Yung* and the Tradition of the *Shih*: The Confucian Restructuring of Heroic Courage', *Religious Studies* 21 (1985), 181–203.
Lamotte, Étienne, 'La Critique d'authenticité dans le Bouddhisme', *India Antiqua* (Leiden: E. J. Brill, 1947), 220–1.
Lau, D. C. (trans.), *The Analects*, Harmondsworth: Penguin, 1979.
(trans.), *Lao Tzu: Tao Te Ching*, Harmondsworth: Penguin, 1963.
(trans.), *Mencius*, Harmondsworth: Penguin Books, 1970.
Le Blanc, Charles; and Dorothy Borei (eds), *Essays on Chinese Civilization*, Princeton University Press, 1981.
Le Blanc, Charles; and Rémi Mattieu (eds), *Mythe et philosophie à l'aube de la Chine impériale*, Les Presses de l'Université de Montréal; Paris: de Boccard, 1992.
Leach, Edmund, 'Ritual', *International Encyclopedia of the Social Sciences* (New York: Macmillan & Free Press, 1968), vol. 13, pp. 520–6.
Van der Leeuw, Gerardus, *Religion in Essence and Manifestation*, trans. by J. E. Turner, London: Allen & Unwin, 1938.
Legge, James (trans.), *The Chinese Classics*, 4 vols, Oxford: Clarendon, 1893–5.

(trans.), *Yi King*, in F. Max Müller (ed.), *Sacred Books of the East*, vol. 16, Oxford: Clarendon, 1885.

(trans.), *Li Ki*, in F. Max Müller (ed.), *Sacred Books of the East*, vol. 27, Oxford: Clarendon, 1885.

Levenson, Joseph R., *Confucian China and Its Modern Fate: A Trilogy*, vol. 2, *The Problem of Monarchical Decay*, Berkeley: University of California Press, 1968.

Levering, Miriam (ed.), *Rethinking Scripture: Essays from a Comparative Perspective*, Albany: State University of New York Press, 1989.

Lévy-Bruhl, L., *How Natives Think*, London: Allen & Unwin, 1926.

Lewis, I. M., *Ecstatic Religion: An Anthropological Study of Spirit Possession and Shamanism*, Harmondsworth: Penguin Books, 1971.

Liang Chi'i-ch'ao, *Intellectual Trends in the Ch'ing Period*, trans. by Immanuel C. Y. Hsü, Cambridge, Mass.: Harvard University Press, 1959.

Liebenthal, Walter (trans.), *The Book of Chao*, 2nd rev. ed., Hong Kong University Press, 1968.

Liu Binyan, 'Civilization Grafting: No Culture is an Island', *Foreign Affairs*, 72 (Sept.–Oct., 1993), pp. 19–21.

Loewe, Michael, *Chinese Ideas of Life and Death: Faith, Myth and Reason in the Han Period* (202 BCE–220 CE), London: Allen & Unwin, 1982.

Ways to Paradise: the Chinese Quest for Immortality, London: Allen & Unwin, 1979.

Loy, David, *Nonduality*, New Haven: Yale University Press, 1988.

Lynn, Richard J., *The Classic of Changes: A New Translation of the I Ching*, New York: Columbia University Press, 1994.

MacQueen, Graeme, 'Inspired Speech in Early Mahayana Buddhism I', *Religion* 11 (1981), 303–19.

Mahbubani, Kishore, 'The Dangers of Decadence: What the Rest Can Teach the West', *Foreign Affairs* 72 (Sept.–Oct., 1993), pp. 10–14.

Mahony, William K., 'Cakravartin', in *The Encyclopedia of Religion* (New York: Macmillan, 1987), vol. 3, pp. 6–7.

Mao Tse-tung (Mao Zedong), *Poems*, Beijing: Xinhua, 1976.

Selected Works of Mao Tse-tung, 4 vols. Beijing: Foreign Languages Press, 1967–9.

Maspéro, Henri, *China in Antiquity*, trans. by Frank A. Kierman, Jr, Amherst: University of Massachusetts Press, 1978.

Taoism and Chinese Religion, Amherst: University of Massachusetts Press, 1981.

Mather, Richard, *The Poet Shen Yüeh (441–513), The Reticent Marquis*, Princeton University Press, 1988.

Maverick, Lewis A., *China, A Model for Europe*, translation [with introduction] from the physiocrat Francois Quesnay's 1767 book *Le Despotisme de la Chine*, San Antonio: Paul Anderson, 1946.

McDermott, James P., 'Scripture as the Word of the Buddha', *Numen* 31 (1984), 22–39.

Mei, Y. P., *The Ethical and Political Works of Motse*, London: Probsthain, 1929.

Miyazaki, Ichisada, *China's Examination Hell: The Civil Service Examinations of Imperial China*, trans. by Conrad Shirokauer, New York: Weatherhill, 1976.

Mizuno, Kogen, *Buddhist Sutras: Origin, Development, Transmission*, Tokyo: Kosei, 1982.

Munke, Wolfgang, *Die klassische chinesische Mythologie*, Stuttgart: Ernst Klett Verlag, 1976.

Munro, Donald, *The Concept of Man in Ancient China*, Stanford University Press, 1969.

Naundorf, Gert, *et al.* (eds), *Religion und Philosophie in Ostasien: Festschrift für Hans Steininger zum 65. Geburtstag*, Würzburg: Koenigshausen & Neumann, 1985.

Needham, Joseph, *Science and Civilisation in China*, vol. 2, Cambridge University Press, 1956.

Science and Civilisation in China, vol. 3, Cambridge University Press, 1959.

Science and Civilisation in China, vol. 5, pt 5. Cambridge University Press, 1983.

Time and Eastern Man, [London]: The Royal Anthropological Institute of Great Britain and Ireland, 1965.

Ong, Walter J., *Orality and Literacy: The Technologizing of the Word*, London: Methuen, 1982.

Palmer, Richard E., *Hermeneutics: Interpretation Theory in Schleiermacher, Dilthey, Heidegger, and Gadamer*, Evanston: Northwestern University Press, 1969.

Peerenboom, R. P., 'Nonduality and Daoism', *International Philosophical Quarterly* 32 (1992) 35–53.

Pye, Lucian W., *The Mandarin and the Cadre: China's Political Cultures*, Ann Arbor: Center for Chinese Studies, The University of Michigan, 1988.

Pye, Lucian W.; and Mary W. Pye, *Asian Power and Politics: The Cultural Dimensions of Authority*, Cambridge, Mass.: Harvard University Press, 1985.

Raphal, Lisa, *Knowing Words: Wisdom and Cunning in the Classical Traditions of China and Greece*, Ithaca: Cornell University Press, 1992.

Rickett, W. Allyn (trans.), *Kuan Tzu*, 2 vols, Hong Kong University Press, 1965.

Les Commentaires du Tao To King jusqu'au VIIe siècle, Paris: Collège de France, Institut des Hautes Études chinoises, 1981.

'The Place and Meaning of the Notion of Taiji in Taoist Sources Prior to the Ming Dynasty', *History of Religions* 29 (1990), 373–411.

Taoist Meditation: The Mao-shan Tradition of Great Purity, Albany: State University of New York Press, 1979.

Roetz, Heiner, *Confucian Ethics of the Axial Age*, Albany: State University of New York Press, 1993.

Mensch und Natur im alten China, Frankfurt: Peter Lang, 1984.

Roth, Harold D., 'Psychology and Self-cultivation in Early Taoist Thought', *Harvard Journal of Asiatic Studies* 37 (1977), 612–22.

Rousseau, Jean-Jacques, *The Social Contract and Discourses* (1762), London: J. M. Dent, 1982.

Rowley, H. H., *Prophecy and Religion in Ancient China and Israel*, University of London, Athlone Press, 1956.

Sabourin, Léopold, *Priesthood: A Comparative Study*, Leiden: E. J. Brill, 1973.

Samarin, William J, *Tongues of Men and Angels: The Religious Language of Pentecostalism*, New York: Macmillan, 1972.

Saso, Michael, 'What is the *Ho-t'u*?' *History of Religions* 17 (1978), 399–403.

Schipper, Kristofer M., 'Millénarismes et messianismes dans la Chine ancienne', in *Proceedings of the XXVIth Conference of Chinese Studies*, Supplement, no. 2, 'Cina' Rome: Istituto Italiano per il Medio e Estremo Oriente, 1979, pp. 31–49.

The Taoist Body, Berkeley: University of California Press, 1993.

Schram, Stuart R., *The Political Thought of Mao Tse-tung*, New York: Praeger, 1963.

Schwartz, Benjamin I., *Chinese Communism and the Rise of Mao*, Cambridge, Mass.: Harvard University Press, 1951.

The World of Thought in Ancient China, Cambridge, Mass.: Harvard University Press, 1985.

Seidel, Anna K., *La Divinisation de Lao-tseu dans le Taoïsme de Han*, Paris: École Française d'Extrême-Orient, 1969.

'The Image of the Perfect Ruler in Early Taoist Messianism: Lao Tzu and Li Hung', *History of Religions* 9 (1969–70) pp. 216-47.

Sharma, Arvind (ed.), *Women in World Religions*, Albany: State University of New York Press, 1987.

Shih, C. C., 'A Study of Ancestor Worship in Ancient China', in W. S. McCullough (ed.), *The Seed of Wisdom: Essays in Honour of T. J. Meek* (University of Toronto Press, 1964), pp. 186–8.

Shryock, John K., *The Origin and Development of the State Cult of Confucius: An Introductory Study*, New York: The Century Co., 1932.

Smith, D. H., 'Divine Kingship in Ancient China', *Numen* 4 (1957) 171–203.

Smith, Wilfred Cantwell, *What Is Scripture? A Comparative Approach*, Minneapolis: Fortress Press, 1993.

Spence, Jonathan D., *God's Chinese Son: the Taiping Heavenly Kingdom of Hong Xiuquan*, New York: Norton, 1996.

The Search for Modern China, New York: Norton, 1990.

Sponberg, Alan; and Helen Hardacre, (ed.), *Maitreya, the Future Buddha* Cambridge University Press, 1988.

Stace, W. T., *Mysticism and Philosophy*, London: Macmillan, 1961.

Takasaki Jikido, *An Introduction to Buddhism*, trans. by Rolf W. Giebel, Tokyo: Tōhō Gakkai, 1987.

Taylor, Rodney, *The Religious Dimensions of Confucianism*, Albany: State University of New York Press, 1990.

Tsukamoto Zenryu, *A History of Early Chinese Buddhism: From Its Introduction to the Death of Hui-yüan*, Eng. trans. by Leon Hurvitz, 2 vols, Tokyo: Kodansha International, 1979.

Tu Wei-ming, *Humanity and Self-Cultivation: Essays in Confucian Thought*, Berkeley: Asian Humanities Press, 1979.

Way, Learning and Politics: Essays on the Confucian Intellectual, Albany: State University of New York Press, 1993.

Tu Wei-ming (ed.), *Confucian Traditions in East Asian Modernity: Moral Education and Economic Culture in Japan and the Four Mini-Dragons*, Cambridge, Mass.: Harvard University Press, 1996.

Tu Wei-ming; Milan Hejtmanek, Alan Wachman (eds), *The Confucian World Observed: A Contemporary Discussion of Confucian Humanism in East Asia*, Honolulu: University of Hawaii Press, 1992.

Ueda Hizuteru, 'Silence and Words in Zen Buddhism', *Diogenes* 170 (1995), 1–21.

Vandermeersch, Léon, *Études sinologiques*, Paris: Presses Universitaires de France, 1994.

La Formation du Légisme: recherche sur la constitution d'une philosophie politique caractéristique de la Chine ancienne, Paris: École Française d'Extrême-Orient, 1965.

Wangdao ou la Voie Royale: recherches sur l'esprit des institutions de la Chine archaïque, 2 vols, Paris: École Française de l'Extrême-Orient, 1977.

Vandermeersch, Léon (ed.), *La Société civile face à l'état*, Paris: École Française d'Extrême-Orient, 1994.

Wagner, Rudolf G., *Reenacting the Heavenly Vision: The Role of Religion in the Taiping Rebellion*, Berkeley: Institute of East Asian Studies, University of California, 1982.

Waley, Arthur (trans.), *The Analects of Confucius*, London: Allen & Unwin, 1938.

The Nine Songs, London: Allen & Unwin, 1955.

The Way and Its Power, New York: Grove Press, 1958.

The Book of Songs, New York, Grove Press, 1960.

Walraven, Boudewijn, *Songs of the Shaman: The Ritual Chants of the Korean Mudang*, London: Kegan Paul International, 1994.

Wang, David Teh Yu, '*Nei Jing Tu*, a Daoist Diagram of the Internal Circulation of Man', *The Journal of the Walters Art Gallery* 49–50 (1991/2), 140-58.

Ware, James (trans.), *Alchemy, Medicine, Religion in the China of* A.D. *320: The nei-p'ien of Ko Hung*, Cambridge, Mass.: M.I.T. Press, 1966.

Watson, Burton (trans.), *The Complete Works of Chuang Tzu*, New York: Columbia University Press, 1968.

(trans.), *Han Fei Tzu: Basic Writings*, New York: Columbia University Press, 1964.

(trans.), *Hsün Tzu: Basic Writings*, New York: Columbia University Press, 1963.

(trans.), *Mo Tzu: Basic Writings*, New York: Columbia University Press, 1963.

(trans.), *Records of the Grand Historian of China*, New York: Columbia University Press, 1961.

(trans.), *The Tso Chuan: Selections from China's Oldest Narrative History*, New York: Columbia University Press, 1989.

Weber, Max, *The Religion of China: Confucianism and Taoism*, trans. and ed. by Hans H. Gerth, Glencoe, Ill.: Free Press, 1951.

Weber-Schäfer, Peter, *Oikumene und Imperium: Studien zur Ziviltheologie des chinesischen Kaiserreichs*, München: Paul List Verlag, 1968.

Wechsler, Howard J., *Offerings of Jade and Silk*, New Haven: Yale University Press, 1985.

Welch, Holmes, *The Practice of Chinese Buddhism, 1900–1950*, Cambridge, Mass.: Harvard University Press, 1967.

Welch, Holmes; and Anna Seidel (eds), *Facets of Taoism: Essays in Chinese Religion*, New Haven: Yale University Press, 1979.

Wheatley, Paul, *The Pivot of the Four Quarters: A Preliminary Enquiry into the Origins and Character of the Ancient Chinese City*, University of Chicago Press, 1971.

Wilhelm, Richard; and Cary F. Baynes (trans.), *The I Ching or Book of Changes*, Princeton University Press, 1967.

Williams, C. A. S., *Outlines of Chinese Symbolism and Art Motives*, 3rd rev. ed., Tokyo: Tuttle, 1974.

Wittfogel, Karl A., *Oriental Despotism: A Comparative Study of Total Power*, New Haven: Yale University Press, 1957.

Wright, Arthur F.; and Denis Twitchett (eds), *Confucian Personalities*, Stanford University Press, 1962.

Wu, Kuang-ming, *The Butterfly as Companion: Meditations on the First Three Chapters of the Chuang Tzu*, Albany: State University of New York Press, 1990.

Chuang Tzu: World Philosopher at Play, New York: Crossroad, 1982.

Yuasa, Yasuo, *The Body, Self-cultivation, and ki-energy*, trans. by Shinegori Nagatomo and Monte S. Hull, Albany: State University of New York Press, 1993.

Young, Stephen B.; and Nguyen Ngoc Huy, *The Tradition of Human Rights in China and Vietnam*, New Haven: Yale Center for International and Area Studies, 1990.

Zürcher, Erik, *The Buddhist Conquest of China*, 2 vols, Leiden: E. J. Brill, 1959.

'Prince Moonlight: Messianism and Eschatology in Early Medieval Chinese Buddhism', *T'oung Pao* 68 (1982), 1–75.

Index